THE AUTHORS

ULRICH STEINHILPER was born in Stuttgart during a First World War air raid. His father was away serving on the Western Front and was to return after the war to assume a position as a teacher in Ochesenwang, a small mountain village in the Schwäbische Alb. Ulrich grew up there and in the larger town of Creglingen, later finishing his education in Stuttgart. He was accepted into the Luftwaffe in 1936, attending military school with such notables as Franz von Werra and Helmut Wick. Ulrich flew through-out the Battle of Britain and was finally shot down on 27th October 1940. There followed an eventful six years as a prisoner of war before he was repatriated to Germany where he built a successful career with IBM, being later credited as the man who had the initial concept of Word Processing.

PETER OSBORNE was born in 1949, in London, and was educated at Woolwich Polytechnic. He served in the London Fire Brigade for 22 years before injuries received during his career forced an early retirement. With a lifetime interest in aviation and writing it was natural that he should turn to a combination of both as a second career. For this book, and its sequels, he has joined forces with Ulrich Steinhilper to tell the story of the Battle of Britain, as seen from the other side.

This book is dedicated to the airmen and service personnel of all sides who gave their lives in the belief that their cause was right...

SPITFIRE
ON MY TAIL

A VIEW FROM THE OTHER SIDE

Ulrich Steinhilper & Peter Osborne

Spitfire On My Tail

by Ulich Steinhilper & Peter Osborne

First publication in Great Britain 1989
Reprinted 1991, 1995, 1998, 2001, 2006 & 2009

Independent Books
3 Leaves Green Crescent
Keston
Bromley
BR2 6DN
United Kingdom

Tel: 01959 573360   Fax: 01959 541129

e-mail: mail@indbooks.co.uk

web site: indbooks.co.uk

Edited by Carol Osborne

Jacket illustrations by Richard Geiger

Jacket design and page layout by Peter Osborne

Printed and bound in Great Britain by CPI Antony Rowe

ISBN: 978-1-8728-3679-9   PB
ISBN: 978-1-8728-3600-3   HB

CONTENTS

PHOTOGRAPHS AND ILLUSTRATION

Foreword by Stephen Bungay
Author of 'The Most Dangerous Enemy'

FOREWORD

The twentieth century was the most destructive in history. It saw more armed conflict on a greater scale than ever before. During its course, entire nations put all their resources into the conduct of war, several of them more than once. For the first time in history, they called upon the majority of their young male populations to fight. For the first time, the bulk of those young men were literate and educated. As a result, many of them have written about their experiences. For most of history, most warriors have been mute. In the twentieth century, they found a voice.

One reason for the destructiveness of twentieth century warfare was that for the first time it was waged in three dimensions. The aeroplane transformed warfare on land and sea, and created a new form of combat all its own in the air. Though it emerged during the First World War, it was not until the second great global conflict of the century that airpower became significant in its own right. In 1940, when that conflict was less than a year old, the world experienced the first major campaign to be fought solely in the air, known, in a phrase coined by Churchill, as the Battle of Britain.

Of those who took part in air warfare it is the fighter pilots who have most captured the public imagination. Many have written autobiographies. Others, including some who did not survive, have had biographers.

In Britain, fighter pilots began publishing autobiographies in the early years of the Second World War, and new ones have continued to appear right into the last decade. In the 1950's, famous fighter aces like Douglas

Bader and Bob Stanford Tuck were the subject of best-selling biographies, and a few, like Johnny Johnson, told their stories themselves. Since then the less well-known have joined their ranks, many of them veterans of the Battle of Britain. Ever since John Keegan's groundbreaking study *The Face of Battle* was published in 1976, historians have recognised that a proper understanding of military history involves trying to comprehend the experience of the ordinary soldier at the sharp end of combat. The substantial body of literature provided by British pilots who flew in the Battle of Britain is important in helping us to understand the events of the summer of 1940, for the battle was not fought just by a few celebrities but by many who are less well known.

In Germany, things have been different.

As in Britain, the most famous aces have had their stories placed before the public, but biographies of non-celebrity fighter pilots remain a rarity. Of those that have appeared, most, like those of Günther Blömertz, Heinz Knoke or Robert Jung, cover only the later war years. As far as the Battle of Britain is concerned, the only personal view we have had through the cockpit of a Bf 109 has been that of the celebrity Adolf Galland, whose *The First and the Last* appeared in English in 1954. Galland's rivals Wick and Mölders have found biographers, but their own voices are absent from the texts for the simple reason that they were killed during the war. The only other autobiography by a German fighter pilot covering 1940 is Theo Osterkamp's romantically entitled *Durch Höhen und Tiefen jagt ein Herz*, which despite its historical importance has remained untranslated. Osterkamp's view is important but not typical. A veteran of the First World War, he commanded the fighter forces of Airfleet 2 during the Battle of Britain, and only flew operationally at the beginning of the campaign. We did not hear from a 'typical' German fighter pilot who flew in 1940 until the appearance of this book. It is unique, and revealing.

The main reasons for the one-sidedness of the biographical literature are basic and brutal. More than half of the RAF veterans of the Battle of Britain survived the war, and they have been feted as heroes ever since. The incentive to write about their experiences has been strong and there were some 1,500 of them. We do not know for sure how many Luftwaffe Battle of Britain pilots survived the war, but the figure is probably no more than 10%. War memoirs are not popular in Germany, and in the immediate postwar years writing one was more a matter of coming to terms with painful memories than celebrating a finest hour. The result is a gap in our knowledge which has led to a distorted view. This book provides an important correction.

Ulrich Steinhilper flew with JG 52 in 1940, and will now probably remain the only German fighter pilot apart from Galland and Osterkamp to produce a full-length work covering his experiences of the Battle. We must be grateful to Peter Osborne for helping him to do so, for the book is full of insights. It provides some balance to the celebrity view, which is particularly significant as the main purveyor of that view has been Adolf Galland. He was Ulrich's first squadron commander.

There is nothing tendentious in the pages which follow, the authors have no axe to grind. It is a straightforward tale, honestly told. Born in 1918, Ulrich Steinhilper grew up the rural southwest of Germany, the son of a village schoolteacher. His upbringing was simple, honest and proper. We would regard it as somewhat Victorian. By our standards it was strict and spartan. There are some telling details. When Ulrich was a boy, he would join other children in his village to search the fields after harvest time, gleaning individual ears of corn to take home to grind into flour and bake bread. But only, of course, after asking the farmer for permission.

As a boy, Ulrich exhibited curiosity, a critical independent mind and high intelligence. He loved everything mechanical. He tried to understand how things worked and also sought the thrills mechanical devices could offer, even if it was only riding a bicycle fast downhill. He also learned early on how human beings can harbour jealousy and resentment.

Partly as a way of countering the jealousies of his nominal social superiors, and partly out of indignation at the terms of the Versailles Treaty, Ulrich's father joined 'the Party' a few years before, as a civil servant, he would have been forced to do so anyway. Ulrich's teenage years were hijacked by the Hitler Youth, which he resisted joining as long as he had a choice simply because he did not like the bully-boy types who ran it. Partly to get out of a Party organisation and partly because of his love of machines, in 1936 Ulrich managed to be accepted for training by the Luftwaffe. It seemed an awesome leap for a village lad just turned 18.

His account of the military bull and chickenshit imposed by NCO's resonates with accounts from any country. His experiences during flying training differed little from those of his counterparts in the RAF, including the sobering accident rate – 10 out of 120 of his contemporaries were killed in accidents. He suffered the early trauma of seeing close up the effects of a fatal accident. He was to witness several more and have several terrifying close calls himself, including a mid-air collision. A horror of violent death stayed with him for the rest of his life.

Ulrich was part of a Luftwaffe contingent sent to the Nuremberg Rally of 1937. In the evening after a marching display, he and his comrades clashed with a group of SS recruits in a beer hall. The tension was the natural reaction of any group of young men confronted with another that is too big for their boots. The SS youths appeared to be more silly than sinister, despite their black collar patches. Where that arrogance would lead was still in the future.

The Luftwaffe itself was full of youthful exuberance and silly male machismo. One of his fellow ensigns nearly died of alcohol poisoning after a drinking game. Things got a bit more serious when they talked to some veterans of the Luftwaffe's venture in Spanish Civil War. They realised that they too could be called upon to fight, to kill – and to die.

In 1938, as tensions rose over Czechoslovakia, it looked for the first time as if they might have to. They were grateful the crisis passed. It has often been suggested that Britain was fortunate not to go to war in 1938 as it was woefully unprepared in the air, with only a few squadrons equipped with the Hurricane and the first Spitfires not reaching a front line squadron till August. It is easy to forget that things were no different on the other side. Ulrich's squadron was flying the Arado 68, a single seater biplane. Only a few had guns and they had no armourers to load and maintain them anyway. He was paired with a bomber unit equipped with the Do 23, which with its open cockpit and fixed undercarriage was known as 'the flying coffin'.

But most of the pilots' concerns were more parochial. When the order came through to promote the cadets in Ulrich's group, just three were excluded. Ulrich was one, because, as he later discovered, one officer had filed a negative report about him. One of the other two was Helmuth Wick. Their common rejection led to a friendship. Wick had been left out because he was engaged to a divorcee. He was determined not to give up the woman he loved, and vowed to Ulrich that he would show up the whole lot of them by becoming a real ace, and stop them from treating him like that. On November 28th 1940, Helmuth Wick, having lately been made Commander of the fabled Richthofen Geschwader, insisted on making a sortie out to the Isle of Wight in failing light, where he shot down his 56th victim, making him the highest scoring ace in the Luftwaffe before, moments later, his own aircraft was hit. He baled out into the Channel and was never seen again.

What prompted Wick to make his fatal sortie was the news that Galland had just raised his score to 55. Ulrich's memories of Galland and of the cult of the celebrity ace are among the most fascinating in the book. They show us that although the young men who joined the RAF and the Luftwaffe in the 1930's were very similar to each other, the organisations they joined had very different cultures. His account gives us a unique perspective on the Luftwaffe's culture and its consequences.

In January 1939, Ulrich was posted to the first squadron of JG 433, which was to become JG 52. His squadron leader was Adolf Galland, one

of the powerful old-boy network of Spanish Civil War veterans. They had
accumulated valuable experience in fighter tactics, but also formed a clique
who thought they knew all there was to know. When Ulrich was made
group communications officer he was put on a collision course with his
boss. Whilst in the RAF's Fighter Command, Dowding and his team of
senior officers were working hard on air to air and ground to air communications, in the Luftwaffe there was a lack of strong leadership from the top,
and Ulrich's attempts to introduce his unit to radios was stubbornly resisted by Spanish veterans like Galland who did not see the need for them. In
Spain, they had communicated in the air by waggling their wings, as people had in the First World War. A radio would just add weight – and above
all, no fighter pilot wanted some lowly controller on the ground telling him
what to do. Ulrich quotes with irony Galland's post-war complaints about
the lack of radio communications between fighter and bombers during the
Battle of Britain, a situation he had helped to bring about.

That this group of men should have had such influence does not only
indicate a leadership vacuum at the highest level, but a peculiar cult of the
individual. This stemmed most immediately from the powerful hold that
aces like Richthofen had over the minds of pilots, and also on senior commanders like his successor Göring and Ernst Udet. Udet was the runner up
to the 'Red Baron' in the race to be top ace during World War One. A brilliant pilot, in the 1930's he became Director of Technology in the
Luftwaffe, a job he was uniquely incapable of performing. It was like a
bank appointing its most successful bond dealer as IT Director.

The Luftwaffe's value system was given further impetus by the Nazi
cult of the warrior hero. Whilst their opponents were putting maximum
effort into solving problems of technology, production and logistics, and
emphasising teamwork, the Luftwaffe was preparing for the most techno-
logically sophisticated form of warfare ever known with a mindset more
reminiscent of the Homeric epics. They seemed to believe that what really
counted was the spirit of Achilles and Ajax, and once they had discovered
their modern equivalents, they let them run the whole show. The competition to be a hero was intense, giving rise to the expression 'Halsweh' – a
sore throat – to designate the pain felt by any pilot not having a Knights
Cross dangling round his neck, awarded for shooting down 20 enemy aircraft. There was no equivalent expression in Fighter Command.

Once they had cured their sore throats, the warrior heroes of the
Luftwaffe's fighter arm engaged even more intensively in the fight that
really counted: to become Achilles, the greatest of them all, the new
Richthofen. It was what led Wick to his death. The personality traits
brought out in this tussle are not very attractive. Ulrich's portrait of Galland

is of an arrogant and egotistical prima donna with little sympathy for any 'bed wetter' less gifted than he. The organisational culture seems to have been similar to that which prevailed in the dealing rooms of investment banks in the first decade of this century. The result was a hubris which contributed to calamity in a similar way.

Once war broke out Ulrich did not see action until his unit was transferred to the Channel coast on an improvised airfield at Coquelles, just outside where the Eurotunnel now emerges. On 11th August 1940 he took part in shooting down a Blenheim over the Channel and flew his first mission over England on the 12th. Although the Luftwaffe as a whole had seen a lot of action, many individual pilots like him started the Battle of Britain like many of their opponents with little or no combat experience. This first experience was a shock, particularly as the Blenheim had itself been attacking an unarmed He 59 rescue plane, marked with the Red Cross. Like many other German pilots Ulrich was indignant at the ruthless British policy of shooting down these machines. On the 19th in a strafing attack on Manston he saw his bullets hit someone. Fighter pilots usually just shoot at machines. This was the only time he saw the effect of his actions, and realised that he had killed a man. Ever since he has found it hard to take. The war had become serious and it was a nasty business.

As the Battle intensified, Ulrich and his colleagues began to question its purpose. The opportunistic low level attack on Manston had been effective – the airfield was eventually abandoned – but most of their sorties involved high level sweeps which enabled the aces to build up their personal scores without achieving any military effects. So what were they really trying to do? The price of the leading aces' high personal scores was paid by their wingmen whose job was to protect them while they concentrated on making kills. These wingmen were known as *Katschmareks*, a Polish surname which in Germany came to be used as a derogatory term for an inarticulate peasant labourer who does what he is told without thinking too much. Some German pilots made up a rhyme about them, which might be rendered as 'The one in front shoots Tommies in the back - The one behind takes all the crap – So, folks, here's to your *Katschmarek*!'

Galland picked some of his best pilots to be his *Katschmarek*. He regarded it as an honoured role. Until 22nd August, his tail was guarded by Joachim Müncheberg, an outstanding pilot who nevertheless only made four claims until Galland yielded to pressure and gave him command of a squadron, whereupon his score quickly rose to twenty. By the time of his death in 1943 Müncheberg's total stood at 135. He was replaced by Oberleutnant Horten who despite flying 45 missions with Galland and witnessing 25 of his kills, only filed seven claims himself. As the Group's

Technical Officer, Horten was grounded in mid-September. He later went on to join his brother in designing radical and influential flying wing aircraft. Galland replaced Horten with a new pilot, Walter Kienzle, whom he was evaluating as a potential wing leader, but Kienzle was shot down on the last day of September without having made any claims. One might question whether this was the best way to use talented pilots.

Ulrich describes the negative effect on morale. The wingmen had the most dangerous and unrewarding job and got no recognition. They were effectively out of the medals, and getting medals was the equivalent of getting million dollar bonuses in a bank. It determined status and drove ambition. This system created a fissure in the bond of trust between leaders and led which opened ever wider. When Ulrich's wing leader returned from headquarters sporting an Iron Cross and announced he was leaving for Germany to have his appendix out, there was almost uproar. It looked as if the more senior officers were using their position to get out of the Battle, which had become a matter of grinding attrition.

Others found excuses of their own. Frequent outbreaks of appendicitis were accompanied by an epidemic of what was called *Kanalkrankheit* or 'Channel sickness'. It was a combination of stress and fatigue that found its focus in the symbol of the Channel and the reality of its cold, hostile waters, which claimed many fighter pilots running short of fuel on the way home. Ulrich mentions a secret memo he saw which reported 19 pilots drowned on a single sortie when they ditched in the Channel. They had run out of fuel as a result of a navigational error. *Kanalkrankheit* seemed to affect the 109s themselves as more and more sorties were aborted with pilots claiming low oil pressure, faulty instruments and so on, faults the mechanics were subsequently unable to find.

As losses mounted, so the burden on the survivors grew. Ulrich flew 150 sorties across the Channel, often three or four in one day and up to as many as seven. His wing had begun the campaign with 36 pilots, none with less than three years flying experience. By the beginning of October, Ulrich was able to list almost half of them who were prisoners or 'missing'. Replacements were sent to the front straight out of flying school. Much has been made of the RAF's deployment of barely competent pilots to keep up numbers. The Luftwaffe replacements were just as raw. Ulrich had to look after one of them who had never used oxygen and did not know how to use his radio. He could not keep up with the others because he had not mastered pitch control. When told to turn for home he flew towards Dover and Ulrich had to escort him back. Replacements like this increased the strain on the old hands.

On 27th October, Ulrich found himself leading his wing on an escort mission. He was the most senior pilot available. The wing mustered eight aircraft out of what should have been thirty six. Unlike the RAF, the Luftwaffe's answer to the problem of inexperienced replacements was to allow the ranks to thin.

Ulrich soon experienced problems adjusting pitch. Just as they were due to turn for home, they spotted British fighters above them. As Ulrich turned he heard a bang, and the control column shook. He thought his supercharger had exploded because of the high rev setting he had been forced to use. He was losing oil. Then he saw the temperature gauge rising and realised he had in fact been hit, probably in the radiator. He decided to bale out. It was not the first time he had taken to his parachute, but it was the first time he had done so over England. He landed with an injured leg in a field outside a village in Kent. Being shot down that day probably saved his life. It also began a new episode, as a prisoner of war and an inveterate escaper. But that is another story.

© Stephen Bungay, January 2009

Author of 'The Most Dangerous Enemy' - see page 366

*'There is no doubt in my mind that the RAF broke the back
and the spirit of the Luftwaffe during the Battle of Britain.
The losses of aircraft could be made up but the experienced men
who had formed the cadre of the Luftwaffe could not be replaced.'*

Ulrich Steinhilper

SPITFIRE ON MY TAIL

CHAPTER 1

Time Runs Out

There were just eight of us, the total defence for the bomber force. All that could be mustered out of what should have been three full squadrons; the survivors. For us the odds were high, time was running out. The Battle of Britain had cost us dearly.

Flying 10,000 metres (32,000 ft), we were above the bomb carrying '109s which we had been briefed to escort. But even higher than us, at about 11,000 metres (35,000 ft) were the British Fighters; Spitfires with the new Merlin engine, some of them probably fitted with the hard hitting 20 mm cannon. They flew a straight course, their con-trails just silver parallel lines, boiling out after a while into a fine mist. But there was no time now for aesthetic reverie, they were the hunters and we their intended prey.

We knew their tactics now as well as they knew ours, it was now routine. We would assemble and set course for London. The British Radar would pick us up as we assembled over France and set course. As we began our flight, so the British pilots would still be taking tea, waiting for the word. As we crossed the Channel they would scramble and climb to their service ceiling, ready to pick us up as we approached London. They would follow us, waiting with the advantage of height and speed, then, as we began our turn for home, both at the tactically weakest spot and at the extreme of our range, they would peel off and hell would break loose again.

We were naturally tense in the combat zone, but today it was worse for me. My '109 'Yellow Two' had mechanical trouble and I was finding it hard to keep up with the wing. Every few seconds I would glance up and see those white lines being carved across the sky, hoping that I would survive the attack when it came. *'Achtung Sie Kommen! Sie Kommen!'* The stark warning crackled over the radio and I felt my pulse quicken. I looked up and to the left to where the British Fighters had been. Now there were only con-trails, boiling out as they curved over my head. 'Out of the sun! Out of the sun!' The warning broke through the babble of voices and static on my headphones. I looked back over my shoulder and saw my faithful wingman, *Feldwebel* Schieverhöfer, flying exactly where the sun was brightest. He had heard the warning and stayed flexible, diving below me and coming up on my left side. I made a steep turn, full throttle, rudder bar hard round and the stick against my leg, the engine turning at 2800 rpm - 400 too many! We had to make as much speed as possible - the British fighters were diving towards us.

Feldwebel Lothar Schieverhöfer- always laughing

Now we had our noses pointing towards home and that lifted our morale. Schieverhöfer and I took up our positions in the classic *Rotte*, ready to protect each other's tail when necessary. We'd got some way behind the formation and unless we could make up the distance we'd hang like ripe plums in the sky. Then the curt warning came again! 'Out of the sun! Out of the sun!' Four or five of the Spitfires dived towards Schieverhöfer. My little finger found the radio button on the stick and I pressed it as I shouted the warning, 'Lothar! Watch it!' I made to turn to protect his tail, only to see him turn protectively towards me. Instead of diving away he was turning to shoot behind my tail. I glanced back into the glaring light and there, behind me, was a staircase to the sun, a staircase of Spitfires queuing for the attack, the first one already had red flames dancing along the leading edge of his wings as his guns fired.

Enough is enough! We were fighting for our lives now and both of us would have to act alone. I dived away and saw that the engine was now turning at 3300 rpm, the throttle fully open. I couldn't risk the engine blowing up, so at 7000 metres (22,000 ft) I levelled out. Up until then, I hadn't been hit or so I hoped. Further down there was a layer of cloud which would hide me on the next dive. I made for the sanctuary. How different things were now that we were fighting for our lives.

* * *

Just a few hours earlier, before dawn, I had been awakened in my warm bed. At just 22 years of age, getting up on a cold Sunday in October was well down my list of things I wanted to do. Still, I stumbled about in the cold tent, gradually dragging my flying clothing on over my warm flannel pyjamas.

We were on Early Alarm and that meant being at the air field for dawn. It was cold, and a freezing fog lay heavily over the potato and stubble fields which were our runways. Wafts of steam and wisps of smoke hung around our little canvas village as coffee pots were boiled and some food was cooked. The ground crews stamped around and rubbed their hands in an effort to keep warm as we waited. Pilots chatted in animated bursts of conversation, laughing too easily but with no humour in their eyes, all trying to keep their minds from the mission. Some smoked cigarette after cigarette, their hands shaking as they lit each one from the butt of its predecessor. Few could eat.

We waited for Helmut Kühle, the squadron leader, who was at the Squadron HQ in the Monastery for the morning briefing. We'd been waiting for what seemed to be ages when Kühle suddenly arrived in his car.

Now all was urgency - a scramble. This was nothing new - nor were the orders: 'Protect the fighter/bombers - Target - London. Take off 09:05 hrs.'

We were going to be the second wave, our *Gruppe* being drawn from three squadrons. This should have totalled some 36 aircraft but, due to losses and '*Kanalkrankheit*'[2], we could only muster eight experienced pilots. Ours would be the most vulnerable position - on top of the Wing. Today I was not to fly my new fighter, Yellow 4, which had the automatic variable pitch propeller. This machine was being kept in for its first major service. We had more aircraft than pilots and so I was reunited with my old aircraft, Yellow 2. I wasn't too sad; after all, I had earned five 'stripes' on the tail of this old 'Emil'[3].

My mechanic, Erwin Frei, was happy too. He had a soft spot for this battle worn '109, and was pleased that his special darling was to fly again. 'Maybe, *Herr Oberleutnant*,' he said to me, 'with this one you are more fortunate - with the new one you don't seem to be so lucky.' With that, he firmly closed the canopy. I locked the hood and checked my instruments and controls. As usual, my stomach began to churn and I felt a cold sweat begin to break out down my spine. My hands felt clammy inside my flying gloves, I couldn't wait to get airborne, then the sickness and anxiety would go.

My mechanic's view was optimistic, but my thoughts were different from his. I didn't agree with our present flying tactics, being tied to the bombers as escorts. The role of the fighter is best in the free-hunt, not shackled inflexibly to the bombers. Here we were sitting ducks and couldn't work nearly so successfully. But now, all was routine. It was really stupid to fly in these waves, as they were called. Every twenty minutes a wave would be assembled and set course for London. They were so regular that the British fighters would climb and wait for us, as if we were a train that was running on time.

There above us the British fighters would hold position until we were at our weakest tactical position - in the turn, then down they would come. This day had been exactly like that. We had assembled over France and then set out for London. The weather forecast had been right: clouds above Kent - London clear. As we approached London, all eyes were on the sky, but there was nothing to see as yet. Seeing nothing of the enemy was worse than being able to keep him in sight. The silence on the headphones did nothing to help, only adding to the tension.

Everyone searched the sky in all directions but with special attention being paid to the rear. Still nothing. Then suddenly my radio crackled into life: 'Raven calling! Raven calling! Eleven o'clock high! Eleven o'clock high! Condensation trails, same course.' Yes! There they were, the British fighters. To the left and above, about 1,000 metres (3,000 ft) higher than us. In my position, on top of the Wing, I could see them clearly. It really looked quite pretty. Quiet and peaceful, with those straight silver condensation trails in contrast against the vivid blue of the sky. At first they were mathematically parallel, then they began to boil out into thin hazy mist. It was a beautiful scene, but those beautiful birds were just waiting for their time to attack. We had to stay alert if we were to survive that day. What a day this looked like being, too. Things had started to go wrong as we reached our operational height for the mission. When we flew at that height, the engine only just gave enough pull and we constantly changed propeller pitch and RPM to improve performance. With a flat pitch we could increase the RPM of the engine and get more pressure from the supercharger. Then, by changing the pitch to a coarser setting, we could make up some speed. Speed was crucial to us if we were to keep up with the Wing. They flew a fairly flat course but we, as fighter cover, were constantly in movement for better observation and for our own protection.

Soon I found that I couldn't change pitch very well - something was wrong. The probability was that whilst my aircraft had been standing unused on the cold October nights, condensation had begun to gather in the grease of the pitch gear. Now, with the freezing temperature of altitude, the moisture was turning to ice and this was rendering the pitch gears inoperative. I had thought about turning back but ruled that out. Too many of us were returning to base with mechanical faults which seemed to clear as the wheels touched home-base. No, I would have to stick with it. I decided to set the pitch at its flattest, this way I would be able to run the motor at high revs and gain the benefit from the super-charger. It would mean that the motor would have to be running well above the maximum recommended RPM, but this had happened before in combat, without total disaster.

Nevertheless, it was with some trepidation that I waited for the order to turn for home. We knew that the British fighters would choose that moment to attack. The Wing Leader had told us over the R.T. that we would be making a turn to the right and that suited me and my *Rottenhund*[1] just fine. It meant that we would be on the inside of the curve and would have to travel the shortest distance. It was always those at the end, the poorest rabbits, who were caught by the hunters.

Now we were at the aiming point for the fighter-bombers and they nosed down into a shallow dive for the attack. All was noise and confusion on the radio, so many transmissions that the reception just became a crazy whistling. In moments it was over and the Wing began the turn, but I couldn't believe my eyes. They were turning to the left! There was no time to speculate about what had happened, the British fighters were moving into the attack.

As the wing had turned, we had been left out in the cold - tempting targets for the diving Spitfires. Under the pressure of the attack we had had to abandon the comparative security of the *Rotte* and act independently. I didn't know if Lothar Schieverhöfer had got away, but it seemed that I had been able to shake the pursuing fighters off.

The propeller pitch control gears of a Me 109 where ice formed
to prevent it operating , correctly. Exhibit can be seen at
Kent Battle of Britain Museum

I was taking stock of my position when, bang! There was an explosion at the left side of my fighter, near to the front. The control column shook as something hit the elevators in the tail. For a moment I thought that I had been hit, but a search of the sky revealed no enemy aircraft. 'It must be the super-charger,' I thought. It turns at about ten times the speed of the engine and I had badly over-revved it in my attempt to escape the attack by the British fighters. The super-charger had probably exploded owing to the over-revving, with pieces of it hitting the control surfaces as they passed to the rear. It didn't look as if it was going to be my day.

I checked the instruments and controls to see if there was any obvious damage. All seemed to be working, but I was losing oil from the damaged super-charger. The loss of the super-charger also meant that I would have to fly lower to get power from the engine. My airspeed was about 700 kph (400 mph) in the dive and I was still weaving from left to right, both for protection and for better observation. I put the nose down and glided towards the cloud layer below at about 2,000 metres (6,000 ft). Once inside the milky soup of the cloud I relaxed a little and the control column eased back. In moments I was out in the blinding brightness of the sun; it pained my eyes but at least I was able to check my course. With constant side stepping and weaving, my compass was running wild and I needed the sun for a definite fix. My experience of this route told me that the sun should be ahead and slightly to the right, and I was reassured to see that my course was about right. I therefore let the aircraft slide back into the anonymity of the clouds.

I began to check the instruments to get a firm idea of how things were going, and gradually I slid through the cloud. Suddenly I was below it and I could make out the Thames Estuary. I was surprised that I hadn't made more distance, considering the speed at which I had been flying to escape. Then my heart jumped as I realised that I was flying just above and behind a loose group of Hurricanes, flying in the same direction. Now I had to react quickly - he who aims and shoots first would be the winner. The best defence is attack. I checked the lights which showed if the guns were armed and ready, OK, four green lights. Then I switched on the Revi gunsight but it was no use. The windscreen had collected ice in the clouds. What to do? I would soon be seen. I would have to use the metal emergency sight and I slid the oxygen mask off for freedom of movement. But now my stomach knotted with real fear, the inside of the cockpit smelled like a steam loco-motive - the engine was boiling! My grip tightened on the control column as I gently eased it back and felt the aircraft begin to lift. My eyes were fixed upon the Hurricanes - if I was seen I would be attacked, with little or no chance of escape. Slowly, oh so slowly, I climbed back towards the sanctuary of the clouds.

Now I had real trouble. I looked at the temperature gauge with horror, it was just passing 130° C. Why? I knew that the engine was probably los-ing oil from the damage to the super-charger, but that wouldn't account for the abnormal temperature of the coolant. There was only one conclusion - I had been hit during the attack - probably in the radiator. I was now back in the clouds, using the blind-flying instruments. It was time to try for some help. 'This is *Eule* 2a (Owl), have been hit in the radiator, will try to reach the Channel. Taking course from Thames to Manston. Please confirm.' The only confirmation was the hiss of static on the radio.

Slowly I had reached 2,000 metres again, still within the cloud base. My speed was well down and so I decided to give the aircraft a rest, I even talked to it, 'Now my Yellow 2, see how carefully I will treat you, I will even turn your ignition off, so you don't burn your insides out.' We were gliding and blind-flying which isn't easy under such conditions. Never before had I tried so hard to keep the pointer straight and the mercury ball in the middle of the circle - not even when I had the most discerning instructor beside me. And it worked. At 1,200 metres (4,000 ft) I could see the ground again but I still went further, I wanted the oil to get as much cooling as possible.

Now that I could see the ground again I didn't have to concentrate on the instruments so much. I decided to try another radio call, maybe the clouds had affected the quality of the transmission before. 'From *Eule* 2a. Have been shot in the radiator - will probably make it to the Channel. Confirm.' This time the ground station in France replied. 'Understood *Eula* 2a. Air-Sea rescue will be notified. Only go into the water when absolutely necessary. Think about Geller!' I recognised the voice of good old *Hauptmann* Förster from the ground station in Calais. He was reminding me that our Adjutant, *Leutnant* Geller, had made an emergency landing in the Channel some months before (30.8.40) and, unfortunately, drowned.

I wasn't worried about drowning, I would be happy to make it to the water, 'Just the day for a swim,' I thought. Things began to get better and my spirits lifted. I recognised the voice of my Squadron Leader on the radio, he must have heard my message to Calais. 'From *Eule*, message intercepted and understood. Have some fuel left, will start to search the Channel immediately. Rest of group will be back, refuel and return to search.' That couldn't be better. They could find me and protect me in the water whilst giving air-sea rescue my position. Earlier I had participated in similar missions.

Then I was down to 500 metres (1,600 ft) and began to attract some light anti-aircraft fire. I could see a small town but did not recognise it. Now: ignition on. The propeller was being constantly turned by the airflow and so there was no problem in restarting the engine. Soon I was gaining height and the oil temperature stayed within limits. Just before I entered the clouds I transmitted a better fix for the ground station, telling them that I would fly a fixed course of 100 degrees magnetic. It would all help them to find me in the water. So far so good, the engine was running very well, no special noises and adequate power. But the oil temperature began to rise as I watched it. As I reached cloud base I noticed 100° C and rising. There was only one sensible thing to do, cut the engine and glide again. As I glided down I could see what I thought was The Bay of Manston (Pegwell Bay) and I gave this as my new position. My Chief (Kühle) was talking to the ground station, and they confirmed that the air-sea rescue was on their way.

Communications really were excellent now that I was constantly below the cloud base. All too soon I was at 250 metres (800 ft) and had to act quickly - ignition on and throttle gently forward.

The engine fired quickly but after a few moments it started to run very rough. I eased the throttle back as much as possible but with so little power I could barely maintain height. My heart thumped against my ribs and I sweated in spite of the freezing October temperatures. Even with a minimum throttle setting, the engine cried out in pain - it was now metal on metal, how long could this last? A last hope. Full throttle - would it help? It certainly did - the engine seized!

There was no 'bang' or disintegration of the engine parts, just a soft silence. I had never known this before in a '109 - just the whistling of the wind as it passed at about 220 kph (140 mph). There was only one choice now - jump! A last desperate radio message – 'From *Eule* 2a - engine seized - bailing out.' The message sounded ridiculously loud in the quiet of the cockpit. It was fantastic how many thoughts went through my mind in a few seconds: 'Should I try to land? No! I must destroy my aircraft. It must not fall into enemy hands.' I ran through the emergency procedures in my head. Oxygen equipment off. Throat microphone off. Remove flying helmet with headphones. 'Poor Yellow 2,' I thought, 'This is your last moment.' I pulled the lever to jettison the canopy. All that happened was that the plomb came off in my hand and the release lever wouldn't move any more. I glanced at the altimeter - only 250 metres (800 ft) now - I must hurry. There was only one choice, open the canopy as normal. This would allow me to get out, but the rear section would stay in place. I pulled the lever and pushed up on the perspex. There was a sudden explosion of wind noise as loose items were sucked out of the cockpit by the slipstream. I gasped as freezing air poured into the aircraft. The canopy was wrenched from my hand by the air pressure and torn off of the hinges. I heard it rumble down the side of the fuselage before it fell into the void below.

Now it was my turn. Release seat belts and push up into the gale which was buffeting my body. Suddenly, disaster. The slipstream had forced my body backwards, wedging my parachute under the rear section of the canopy. My legs were jammed under the instrument panel and I was being bent backwards. I tried to claw my hands down towards the control column to bring her up into a stall but I could not reach. To my horror I saw the aircraft begin her last dive. Slowly she rolled to the right and the nose began to drop into a critical dive. There was only one option for me now. I had to risk tearing my parachute pack. I leaned out to the right and with great effort I pulled my legs up towards my body.

Suddenly I was out and rolling along the side of the aircraft - even at only 200 kph (125 mph) you are the victim of a powerstorm. I somersaulted, head over heels and hoped that with luck I would pass the tail without injury. After a second I was clear but still rolling over and over as I fell towards the ground. Now to pull the release for the parachute. My hand reached up to my left shoulder and I took a firm hold of the handle and pulled. Then I waited - nothing. It was only a split second but it seemed too long. My hands groped behind me to try to assist the pack opening. But already a mass of silk and shroud lines was boiling up between my legs and the drogue 'chute, with unbelievable skill, had wound itself around my left leg. As the main parachute deployed I began a series of gyrations which would have done credit to a circus performer. As the canopy opened fully I shouted out in pain - it felt as though my left leg was being torn off.

The circus act was over as suddenly as it began, but I found that I was hanging by my leg, spinning in a perfect inverted axle. Then I dropped with a jolt as I became upright once more. I checked that my canopy was fully open and then looked down to my left leg. I was sure that it would be missing, but there it was, hanging limply below me. I tried to move it but the pain was excruciating. Just at that moment, I saw my brave 'Yellow 2' diving towards some soft ground in the middle of a herd of cows. They scattered in all directions, running with their tails up. Then there was a soft thump as she entered the ground, the ammunition starting to go off immediately, a kind of ridiculous last salute.

Now I was close to the ground and I must prepare for landing. I was swinging gently like the pendulum of a clock. With luck I landed on the right leg and, as I had estimated, the ground was soft. Things couldn't have been better for my injured leg. Before landing I had turned the parachute harness buckle to unlock it ready for landing. Now that I was down I thumped the knob and the webbing harness fell to the ground. In great silken billows the parachute dropped on to the green grass, no more than 5 metres away. From here I couldn't see the crash site of 'Yellow 2' but, I could still hear the ammunition exploding.

I had landed beside the embankment of a canal and this obscured my view in one direction. I looked around at the countryside to see if anyone was approaching. Nothing. Only the grey wet drizzle, blown by the wind. I couldn't believe that just moments before I had been flying in the bright sunshine. Above the clouds I could hear the throb of engines as my comrades made their way back to base. How far away from them I was now. I felt so alone, so hopeless, my throat tightened and I thought that I was about to cry. Then the moment passed. It was time to consider my new position.

I began to drop my equipment which was still with me, rubber dinghy, sea water dye container, flare pistol . . . Bang! - there was a shot. My infantry training took over and I was down on the ground, raising my eyes to see who was shooting. After all I had survived in the past few minutes was I to be shot dead in a cow field?

I lay there for a while, my face pressed against the damp grass. Gradually, I raised my head and peered across the dyke towards the place from where the sound of the shot had come. I saw a man in civilian clothes, holding what seemed to be a shot gun. He had an arm-band tied around the left sleeve of his jacket. 'Get up!' he shouted. My mind went back to the school room and I tried to string my English words together. 'I can't,' I shouted across the water, 'My leg is hurt!' I don't think he imagined that I was unarmed.[4] I tried to walk up the bank of the dyke but I collapsed in pain. 'I'll come around to you,' he shouted to me. I sat there on the cold coarse marsh grass and felt the dampness of the ground through my flying clothes. I was really depressed now. I couldn't get away, my leg was too badly hurt, so I had to sit and wait whilst my would-be captor made his way around the dyke. While I waited, I began to think about the events in my life that had brought me to this bleak and inhospitable place. My schooling, *Hitler Jugend*, Labour Service, early flying training and then my years and tribulations in the *Luftwaffe*. A long, long journey for one who was still so young...

****

Note: Throughout this book there will explanations of technical and foreign terminology at the end of each chapter.

Notes on Chapter 1

1. *Rotte* - The basic element in German fighter tactics. Two aircraft which fly in a loose pair, each able to protect the other's tail. Two *Rotte* made up a *Schwarm* and the whole *Staffel* (squadron of twelve aircraft) would be made up of three *Schwäme* (Swarms). One *Swarm* flying high, one medium height and one low in the formation. Developed by Werner Mölders in the Spanish Civil War and later adopted by the Allies as 'Finger Four'. Also - *Rottenhund* or *Rottenflieger* - Wingman in the *Rotte*.

2. *Kanalkrankheit* - Literally Channel sickness. This is what would now be described as battle fatigue. Signs and symptoms of accumulated stress.

3. Five stripes on the tail - Five confirmed victories.

4. Being unarmed - In September it became forbidden for *Luftwaffe* aircrew to fly with any type of pistol. This was because many bodies of pilots had been recovered from the Channel or washed up shot in the head. This had been a last desperate act when all hope of rescue seemed lost. Cold with a stomach full of sea-water and possibly wounded, many of our air-crew had taken what High Command thought was the 'easy' way out. Side-arms were therefore banned to remove this temptation.

Authors' note:

NCOs - In the *Luftwaffe* NCOs (Non Commissioned Officers) held the rank of *Unteroffizier* and upwards (*Feldwebel* and *Oberfeldwebel*). These made up about 25% of the non-officer aircrew. *Gefreiters* and *Fliegers* (Private First Class) made up the other 75%.

Jabos (abbreviation of *Jagdbomber*) - Me 109s with underslung 250 kg. bombs.

CHAPTER 2

Early Days

At the time I was born, near to the end of the First World War, my mother was living with my grandparents. They lived in Stuttgart and I came into this world kicking and screaming like most babies, but in the middle of an air-raid.

My father, Wilhelm, was away serving in the Army at the time of my birth. He, along with his two brothers, had quite a hard upbringing, being born into a poor farming family. His father died when he was young and later, when his mother remarried, Father's half-brother was born. Father was very good at school and was sent to Stuttgart, to a kind of orphanage school, where he worked well under the strict discipline. Later he qualified as a teacher and, prior to the First World War, he taught at several small schools in outlying villages around Stuttgart. Somewhere during his teaching he met my mother and they married.

At the beginning of the First War he was conscripted into the Imperial Army and served as a *Leutnant* in an Infantry Regiment. He served on the French, Italian, and Rumanian fronts and whilst in Italy his Company Commander was Erwin Rommel. I distinctly remember this because during my time at the *Luftkriegschule* (Air Force Military School), Rommel was teaching tactics at the neighbouring army officers' school at Potsdam. My father and I talked about him a lot, Father was obviously impressed by the ingenuity of Rommel in the First World War.

After the War we moved our family home to Ochsenwang, a small village nestling on the shoulder of the *Schwäbische Alb* (a range of old volcanic hills near Stuttgart), about 40 kilometres from Stuttgart and 800 metres (2600 ft) above sea level. We lived there from 1919 to 1925, and at that time there was no electricity and no piped water. My father was the teacher at the school and part of the remuneration for this post was that we had accommodation provided. The family occupied the top floor of a house which had the distinction of having once been the home of the German poet, Eduard Mörike. The small church where he had been vicar for the year 1832-1833 was opposite the house.

*Ochsenwang - This is the building where we
lived on the first floor from 1919 to 1925*

*The sign reads: To the memo-
ry of the poet Eduard Mörike
who lived in this house from
1832 to 1933 as Vicar.*

*The small church opposite the house.
Today it looks just as it did in 1920*

Our family was quite poor at this time, but despite this I remember that I had a very good time as a young boy. To give some idea of the meagreness of our resources, it was some two or three years before my parents could afford a bicycle. This lack of transport produced some problems because there was only one small shop in Ochsenwang which stocked a few items such as sugar. Any other shopping was done by my father in Kirchheim-unter-Teck involving a 12 kilometre (7.5 miles) walk in each direction; or sometimes at Weilheim which was only 9 kilometres (5.5 miles).

It is strange how the memory selectively retains some things, but rejects so many others. I imagine that it is, perhaps, proportional to the emotion or the trauma which was involved with the event. I know that one of my strongest early memories surrounded a Christmas which was not to be one of my happiest. Father had set off to Weilheim to make the final purchase for Christmas. As was the habit, I was allowed to walk down through a narrow valley called the Zipfelbachtal and wait for him at Hepsisau. After what seemed to be an age he was back and we began to climb back up to our home. As we negotiated a steep hill beside a frozen stream, Father slipped on some ice and fell into the steep valley, his fall only being arrested by some small pine trees. He wasn't badly hurt and no bones were broken, but inside his rucksack could be heard the sound of broken glass. He had made a special purchase of two new glass cylinders for our oil lamp at home. We only had one lamp but he had thought to buy a spare, just in case of an accident. Now both were broken beyond repair. The result was that nobody could read after darkness had come, and the cheerful music of my mother's piano playing and the joy of Christmas Carols in the evening was replaced by the exchange of none too amiable words.

Although this is a personal family story there is, I feel, some social comment in it. At the age of four I was allowed to roam far and wide without fear of molestation. When my father went to Kirchheim-unter-Teck, which was on the other side of the hills to Weilheim, I would walk about 4 kilometres (2.5 miles) to wait for him by an old lime tree. Sometimes I would sit patiently for two or three hours before I could make out his figure in the distance. What caring parent could allow a child of any age to range so freely these days? The world has become a very hostile environment for these innocents.

It is difficult now, I think, for people, particularly young people, to imagine with any degree of accuracy how comparatively primitive the conditions were in those days. Take for example a simple food item like bread, now available in any food shop and with many varieties being stocked in the larger stores. Firstly, in my childhood days, milled flour was very expensive. So after the harvest we would ask the permission of the farmers to go gleaning in their fields. We would pick up the ears of corn and wheat which were left, and even the individual grains. This raw material could then be ground into coarse flour for baking the bread and sometimes cake for the family.

The baking wasn't undertaken in the home because we didn't have the luxury of an individual oven in the kitchen. None of the small houses in the village did. Instead there was a communal baking house beside the school used by most of the population, and it was a treat for us to be taken along for the evening baking session. Not only was there the possibility of newly baked bread or cake to eat and other children to play with, but also there was always news and stories to be heard. This is another area where there has been huge progress in my lifetime - communication. Just sixty-five years ago in Ochsenwang we were cut off for most of the winter and even in the bloom of the summer we didn't have regular newspapers and the radio was still in its infancy. Some radio 'Hams' (amateurs) did operate crude crystal sets, but the reception was poor and temperamental. So, it was important to listen to the stories which were being told, and the bakehouse was a good venue for this.

Another source of the news and of impressions of the outside world were the shepherds and the stone cutters. My friends and I wandered many kilometres away from home without fear or any anxiety. We spent many attentive hours listening to the shepherds and watching them as they brought the young lambs into the world. Similarly the stone cutters, working the small roads, were great raconteurs, some of them having travelled widely.

In 1925, we moved to Creglingen on the Tauber River. Creglingen is about 80 kilometres (50 miles) north-east of Stuttgart, between the historic town of Rothenburg and Bad Mergentheim. Father had applied for a job as a teacher in a fairly large school and was to be appointed as deputy to the Director (although at this time the actual term Director or Headmaster was not in use). There were four elementary grades and then three high school classes, with each of the lower classes having two levels of teaching within them.

It was a very traumatic time for me. I was looking forward to moving to a town and into the larger school, but I had led a protected life in many ways in the village and the shadows of the town seemed, to a seven-year-old, to hold many fears, not least of which was the problem of communication with other children. Although we were only moving about 200 kilometres (125 miles) the dialectal change was quite severe. We in the country spoke the strong Swabian farmers' language, but in Creglingen we had to get used to Franconian. It wasn't just a question of accent but of a very different language. Again I have to comment that today it must be difficult to accept these differences because the medium of radio and television has done much to eradicate the strong dialects and turn them more into accents. To young children, however, it was a major problem to overcome. I suffered much ridicule about being a farmer or a 'hay seed', children being the particularly cruel animals they are.

Early school photo - note mixed ages. I'm holding the flag, front left

My parents were labelled as 'social climbers' by some of the established townspeople. After all, they had come to Creglingen from a very small mountain village, and then begun to carve a place for themselves within the society. My father had been very active in improving the football field and training the teams. Soon they were regularly winning matches against other towns, and his notoriety began to grow. Not only was he responsible for the equipment and the managing of the team, but also for the preparation and maintenance of the field. As his energy and personal ambition led to the improvement of the field, he realised that, being close to the Tauber River and in a small valley, a natural Grandstand was provided for spectators and the games began to attract substantial audiences. Soon, in addition to the well supported football, he introduced athletic events like long jump, high jump and shot putting. All of this was good for the community as a whole, but proportionally raised the ire of Father's self declared enemies.

Mother, of course, was not to be left out of this and soon began her own inroads into the social side of the football club. First she began a class of gymnastics for the women and presented a new show for the Christmas celebrations. Tradition had it that there would be presentations, some extracts from the theatre and speeches. Mother's gymnastics class performing to music was quite new and innovative; it was also a great success. Then she began to form a mixed choir, and this too was soon fully subscribed.

Their successes were both a blessing and a curse. Their kind of talent, energy and organisational skill almost always makes enemies amongst those who lack some or all of those qualities. Within the town there was a sporting organisation known as the *Turnerbund*. This was attended by the higher class people of Creglingen such as the Mayor, the *Bürgermeister*, the doctors, the dentist and the chairman of the *Reichsforstamt* (Forestry Service). They found the success of the lower class club to be an embarrassment, and when Mother's choir won a competition against the choir which was coached by the wife of the Director of the *Reichsforstamt, Frau* Henning, what had been mere chagrin became a positive affront.

Christmas at home. Father on the extreme left and mother on the right.
I am sitting in the foreground complete with hammer and bow-saw.

36

All these problems passed over my head at the time and didn't affect my life too much. However, the future would change this dramatically. But, for the meantime, I busied myself with my very full life. For years it had been a joke in our family that I was forever fixing or dismantling things, particularly machinery. My sister reminds me that I was always to be seen, as a young boy, with a small hammer and a saw in my hands. This interest in things mechanical persisted, and in Creglingen I befriended the owner of the first small garage. At first I helped out by cleaning cars or motorcycles and would be rewarded with a few *pfennigs* or a ride on a motorcycle. After a while, I began to help with the removal and stripping down of motorcycle engines.

Very soon the mechanics began to trust me more, and I graduated to grinding-in the valves in the cylinder blocks. At this time most engines were side-valve with the ports located in the cylinder blocks (later they were to be located in the cylinder heads). I enjoyed the work and was often to be seen on the back of a speeding motorcycle or in one of the still very rare cars. Mr Unger, the owner of the largest store in town, once, when discovering that I had cleaned his car several times, took me for a ride in his NSU car the full 50 kilometres (30 miles) to Kunzelsau. He was very proud that we only had to stop twice to repair the tyres.

The problems which had been created by my parents' success were soon to be vested upon me. It is sad to remember that the adults who were involved didn't have the courage to challenge my parents directly. I wasn't aware of what was happening at first but soon I began to become the brunt of all sorts of unreasonable attacks by senior members of the community. In the first of these incidents I, and some of my friends, were riding bicycles down a steep hill at the edge of the Tauber Valley. We didn't know that we were being watched by one of the forestry employees. When it came to my turn, I came down the hill at some speed and he threw a rock at the bike, knocking me off. He then proceeded to give me a quite uncalled-for beating.

My parents were appalled by this violence towards me and decided to take him to court to answer for his behaviour. It seemed that my mother and father were still naive about the working of the town and thought that the truth would suffice in court. There was only one solicitor available in Creglingen and he quickly jumped to the defence of the forestry man. Therefore we had to hire a solicitor in Bad Mergentheim to represent us. On the day our side of the story was told, we found that the defence had produced three witnesses from Creglingen who swore that I was a hooligan and a vandal, that I was constantly running wild about the town and leading the other, more sensible children, astray. The judge at Bad

Mergentheim, where the *Amtgericht* (Public Court) was, looked at the weight of evidence and decided that the forestry man was vindicated and that my parents would have to publish an apology in the local paper. All in all, the experience cost us a lot of money and there was no way that we could repeat the action if I was attacked again.

Outside this incident many other, more subtle, tactics were adopted by these vindictive people. This was to make my life very stressful for a time until things came to a head. I was aware that the attitude of my parents was becoming more and more severe towards me. They had become very strict and punished me harshly for the most minor transgressions. I began to become very unhappy and confused. I really didn't know what I was doing wrong. Of course, at that age you still believe that your parents are infallible and therefore you have no choice but to internalise the stress. The only conclusion is that you, yourself, are wrong, perhaps bad inside.

Things got worse and worse until one day when my mother was supervising my piano lesson she began to beat me for the most minor mistakes. In the end she took off her shoe and took that to me as well. That was enough for me and I ran from the room to my bedroom, locking the door. I opened the window and threatened to jump out if anyone tried to open the door. I was so unhappy and confused that I think I would have done it.

This shocked my parents into reviewing this situation, and they told me that they had been in receipt of a constant stream of complaints about my conduct and behaviour about the town. When we discussed this in detail it became apparent that the accusations were, for the most part, unfounded. I was no angel - I was a normal healthy boy and, naturally, I got into trouble from time to time. But the story which had reached my parents showed a picture of a really bad boy dragging their reputation and standing within the community through the mud. They had believed the tales and had become unnecessarily aggressive towards me. Once we had discussed the matter their behaviour changed towards me and I felt much better. I think that this was probably the first occasion when I had a serious and adult exchange of views with my parents.

This ostracism of my father from the community, had, I think a profound influence upon his political views. In the very early days of the *'Die Partei'* [1] he became interested in their doctrines. Having been an officer in the First War he felt keenly that Germany had been stripped naked by the Treaty of Versailles. Hitler and the National-Socialists seem to have the drive and commitment to put things to rights, to put Germany back on her feet. That, combined with the pressures exerted upon him by the predominantly conservative upper classes of Creglingen, induced him to become a member of the Party, long before it became mandatory for public employees. At this stage in the development of the *Nationalsozialistische Deutsche Arbeiterpartei (NSDAP)*, their more sinister underlying policies were still well hidden. Had these been public knowledge earlier, I wonder how far they would have got?

In the meantime, I had reached the end of the third year of higher school education in Creglingen. Normally it would have been time for me to move onto the High School proper in Bad Mergentheim. But, as I was only twelve-and-a-half years of age, it was thought that I was too young to go into a *pension* for the school week, coming home for weekends. Therefore, it was decided that I would spend an extra year in Creglingen before moving on. This was a help in a way because I was able to concentrate on English.

After this extra year we once more came to the point where a decision would have to be made about my staying in a *pension* in Bad Mergentheim. A few sums revealed that this was going to be a great expense for my parents and we cast around for another solution. Just at that time the first cycles appeared with the *Hilfsmotor*. They were the first mopeds but quite inferior to the type of small motorcycle which we see today. Essentially they had a small petrol motor which was mounted in the frame of a stronger bicycle to give motorised assistance to the rider. This was the answer to the dilemma for us, or so I argued, as I could now ride the 30 kilometres (19 miles) to Bad Mergentheim every day, and save the expense of the *pension*. A little pressure from the owner of the cycle shop and my father agreed. So I became one of the first boys to ride to school on a motorcycle.

But it was only to last for about a week. A trait in my character was about to show itself. I seemed to have an inbuilt aggressive competitiveness which would, during my lifetime, prove to be both a blessing and a curse. The situation in this case was that I was riding my cycle home from school when I was passed by the Creglingen midwife on her cycle, also fitted with the *Hilfsmotor*. She passed me like I was standing still, and I wasn't about to settle for that. I gritted my teeth and set the throttle to full, catching and passing her after a few hundred metres. I was just congratulating myself on my skill as a rider when the motor seized. It hadn't been fully run in and the strain which I had put on it had been too much.

I had been really stupid to run the new motor so fast at that time. Our plans were thrown out and I had to ride the peddle cycle 18 kilometres (11 miles) every day to catch a train from Weikersheim to Bad Mergentheim. In good weather this was OK, but on occasions I got wet in the rain and then had to sit all day in wet clothing. That soon began to tell, and I developed a serious kidney complaint which confined me to bed for many weeks. Fortunately my period of illness fell towards the beginning of the summer holidays so I was able to recover without the loss of too much schooling. Quite a price to pay for the affront to my pride!

During the time of my illness the *Hilfsmotor* for the cycle was repaired and returned to us and to save money I fitted it back myself. I wanted to give it a trial run so I started up and rode it before I had fitted the exhaust and silencer. I rode it two or three times past the house of the Town Actuary and I was recognised. The noise from the cycle was apparently thought to be enough to warrant stern action. As I passed on my next circuit he threw a couple of logs at the cycle and one hit the front wheel, throwing me into the road. I wasn't badly hurt but the front wheel of the cycle was ruined. I don't think that it was being paranoid to say that it was another example of an attack upon me because of who my parents where. I wanted them to take some action but they explained that the first court case had cost them too much and they had learned a lesson from it. So I just had to take it.

I rebuilt the wheel, and finished the installation of the engine. This left us with a cycle which we really didn't need. After my illness it was decided that riding to school was out and my parents made overtures to the cycle dealer to buy back the machine. He wasn't prepared to offer a sensible deal and so the decision was made to keep it. Thus it was that I became one of the few young people in Creglingen to have a motorised cycle for my own use.

One consequence of my illness was that I was liberated from sports, whether at school or otherwise. Maybe as a result of this, I spent much more time at the piano and also began to experiment on the organ. I say experiment because I was still too small to reach the bass pedals and therefore I was not able to use the full range of the great instrument. The only organ available was in the church and it was there that I had to go if I wanted to further my musical education by practice. Being young, I loved to play bright music and practised the very latest dance tunes of the time. I soon discovered that the tango sounded marvellous on the church organ and played it and other dance tunes with great gusto. However, one of the protestant pastors who lived opposite heard this strange music coming from the church, and my organ playing was temporarily over.

At this time we had a very severe winter and I was fortunate enough to get my first real skis. For years I had practised on a pair made from two slats from a barrel, but they really only served to keep me from sinking into the snow, I couldn't actually ski on them. I took to skiing immediately and taught myself the Telemark and Christiana techniques from a book. Soon I was skiing with some of the older boys from the town and I think that the considerable improvement in my reputation and marked maturing of my behaviour owed much to their influence.

It was decided that because I had begun to improve my behaviour, I would be placed in a pension run by a *Frau* Adelman. She was known to my parents, having lived in Creglingen whilst her husband ran a café /konditorei. He, however, had taken to drink and she had decided to move to Bad Mergentheim and re-adopt her maiden name of Adelman. Her daughter, Liselotte, had been in my class in Bad Mergentheim whilst I had to wait an extra year, being too young at twelve-and-a-half to live in a *pension*. *Frau* Adelman had to make her living from the income from us lodgers, and so the food was far from extravagant, but we all got on well and enjoyed ourselves.

At Bad Mergentheim I had my first serious contact with the *Hitler Jugend* (Hitler Youth). I was approached by some of the leaders who wanted me to join. I took a look at what they had to offer, I even went along to help with the towline pulling for their early gliders, but I didn't like the personalities that I met. They all seemed to come from the same kind of background, having left school at the earliest opportunity to further a career in politics. There seemed to be a little too much of the bullyboy element present and so I, politely but firmly, declined.

First real skis

One person who became very important to me at Bad Mergantheim was our English teacher, a secondary school teacher, *Studienrat* Wobbelmann. He was very tall, about 1.96 metres (6ft 5 ins), and had lived in England. He told us on many occasions that the best thing in the world would be to hold a British passport. With this, he said, you could travel virtually anywhere in the world without the necessity to continually apply for visas. His overwhelming affection for the English people and their stoic determination and tradition left a strong impression upon me.

I did rather well in Class 5 at Bad Mergentheim and my parents were now in a better position to support me financially. Therefore, the decision was made that I should continue my education up to university level. This could not be done at Bad Mergentheim and so 1 was enrolled in the Friedrichs Eugen Oberrealschule in Stuttgart. I attended for the first time on 23 April 1933.

Once more, I had to live away from home during the school week but this time I was placed in a YMCA Hostel. In some ways this was a big responsibility for me. I was only fourteen and a half and the hostel was quite open. We could come and go as we wished, and if I had been half the hooligan that the good people of Creglingen had called me, I would have run wild. But, I was a serious student and, I think, fairly grown up for my age. I had an allowance of 50 marks to last me for the month and I saved what I could from that by skipping meals. This gave me a small fund which I could use for excursions to the cinema and so on. I didn't tell my parents though, or they would have worried for my health.

I enjoyed going out in the evenings, coming as I did from 'the country'. Being well on through the syllabus before I came to the school and, apparently, finding the work easy, did not help to integrate me with my classmates. Young boys are rather like sparrows in a way - they soon recognise anything that is different and swarm upon it to try to peck it and drive it away. In my case the pecking came in the form of regular trips to 'The Scaffold'. This was the tilting blackboard and I was forcefully held upside-down whilst dirty washing water was poured over me. I really was rather lonesome and lost at school and there was little relief from this in the evenings.

I'm not too sure how long I could have taken this, but a solution came at vacation time. Back in Creglingen I met a girl named Siggi who was visiting some friends. She came from Stuttgart, her father being one of the wealthier members of society. We soon became friends and she told me that she had a brother who wasn't doing too well at school. Together we hatched a plan to get me to live with them as in a *pension* and I would help her brother as well as being a friend to her.

Now it was up to me to call upon Siggi's father and put the proposal to him, man to man as it were. He was a rather nice person and seemed to be very genuine to me. Although he was one of the wealthier people in Stuttgart, he had been ostracized by the society set for marrying an Austrian girl, who he had met when studying there. I must have made an impression because he readily agreed and I moved out of the YMCA.

The move greatly enhanced my life. Living where I did gave me a different status at school. Outside school-time I lived very comfortably and had friends to hand. I lived up to my side of the bargain, working with Siggi's brother and coaching him in his weak subjects. We also soon became firm friends and entered into many adventures and experiments, once almost burning the house down. It also gave me a chance to look into another world; a whole new set of standards and values. It was a valuable part of my education.

Whilst all this was taking place within my small view of the world, massive changes were taking place in Germany. Adolf Hitler had seized power in 1933/34 and now his revolutionary changes were set in motion. I did not realise it at the time, but my future was now in the hands of others.

I had been approached by members of the *Hitler Jugend* again, but I had decided that I was more suited to the Y.M.C.A. However, things were taken out of our hands. Political decisions were made upon high and it was decreed that there wasn't room for two youth organisations. Therefore, with great ceremony and solemn celebration, we took off the green shirts of the Y.M.C.A. and donned the brown shirts of the Hitler Youth. For the first time I wore the insignia which, in later years, was to become synonymous with evil - the Swastika.

In 1934 my parents moved from Creglingen to Heutingsheim, close to Ludwigsburg. There had been many reasons for the move, not least of which was the mounting social pressure that was being brought to bear upon them. Coincidental with the move my father joined the *NSDAP*. I had very mixed feelings about this because the *NSDAP* was in direct opposition to the established social hierarchy in Germany. But many people who were oppressed by the establishment turned to the Party as a means of improving their position and to become part of the New Order. This was one of the reasons why Father joined, another being his very strong feelings about the way in which Germany had been treated at the end of The Great War. The attacks had not only come from the victorious Allies, but also from within. Upon returning from the front, he had been mobbed and almost beaten to death by the gangs of Communists who seized local power from amongst the turmoil.

Another reason why Hitler was to be held in high esteem was that in

1933 the salary of government employees had been cut by 10%. Their wages were paid in three parts during the month, which made for difficult home economics. This, coupled with substantial unemployment, had made the government very unpopular. After seizing power, Hitler brought about radical change, improving the lot of the working man in leaps and bounds and with this, his popularity rose in equal measure.

Because there was a High School in Ludwigsburg, which was of a standard equal to the one which I attended in Stuttgart, I was transferred to it. This meant I could live at home and commute by train the six kilometres to school every day. At school, my education proceeded smoothly and I seemed assured of a University place at the end of it.

I was now seventeen, and, like my friends, I began to attend dancing classes. Dances and dancing were much more an integral part of the social graces than they are today. Dancing formed the major part of one's social life and to be a good dancer was a distinct advantage.

It was in this environment that I first became aware of the bitter hatred felt for the Jews by some of the members of the *NSDAP*. We were allowed to invite girls to the dance classes, and one of my friends invited a Jewish girl to be his partner. This incensed the Party purists to the point where an article on this atrocity appeared in the little-liked magazine *Stürmer*, the organ of the Party. Pressure was increased and in the end she had to stop coming to the classes. Her boyfriend elected to leave because of this, although he remained in the Hitler Youth and in the same class at school. In view of this kind of distasteful behaviour my activities with the Youth were limited to an absolute minimum.

At that time the lower ranks of the *SA* and *NSDAP* were rife with intrigue and in-fighting, something with which I didn't want to become involved. They were a young party and this was all part of their political maturing, but at grass roots level it was very petty. I held on to the idea that it may be like this in the lower echelons of the Party, but surely the upper hierarchy would be free from it. If Hitler, Hess and Goring had rebuilt the dignity of Germany in such a short time, they must be free of all of this pettiness. We now know, of course, that this was not the case. In all probability their squabbling was worse, and the consequences certainly more dire. Witness the so-called 'Night of the Long Knives'.

As part of a concerted attempt to distance myself from the internal strife of the *NSDAP*, I pressed to join the Officer Corps. At first, I applied to join Infantry Regiment 13, which was the tradition in Ludwigsburg, but I was turned down. The excuse was that too many had qualified and there were too few places. I had my doubts if this was true. I believe that the long arm of Creglingen Society had extended and touched my career prospects in

Ludwigsburg. Indirectly, I suppose, this may have saved my life. The survival rate of the Infantry Regiment 13 was not impressive, serving as it did in Poland and France and then becoming a Panzer Regiment in Russia.

Early in the summer of 1936, the school had been visited by officers from the *Kriegsmarine* (Navy) and the *Luftwaffe* (Air Force). Both of them did a good job in promoting their services but I was electrified by the thought that a poor boy like me could learn to fly. I bombarded the officer with questions, even letting him know that I had been turned down by the Army. He told me that it didn't matter, that the requirements of the *Luftwaffe* were quite different from those of the Army. I also got the impression that, being a newer service, the *Luftwaffe* was largely free of the 'Old Boy' network which was so woven into the fabric of the older services.

I had to apply to the Headquarters in Berlin; everything was centralised in the *Luftwaffe*. To my joy I was invited, one of a party of fifty boys, to attend the selection centre in Berlin. With the invitation, the first concrete indication that I might get in, came the doubts and the questions. To be part of flying in those days would be like putting your name down today for training to man the Space Shuttle. However, at school we had a physics master who had been a flyer in the Great War and answered most of my questions and encouraged me to proceed. He even took time out to teach those of us who had been selected the rudiments of aeronautics.

All of this change came upon me very suddenly and I rolled forward on the crest of a wave of change. Above all was the nagging doubt - could a common lad like me from a small town like Heutingsheim really become a pilot in *Der Luftwaffe*?

Before I was due to report to the *Luftkriegsschule* at Berlin-Gatow, I travelled to Berlin. I was to stay with relatives there and to move into the *Luftwaffe* Barracks on the appointed date. At the station, I waited with my parents for the train. Mother was a little upset at my going so far away. Father had little to say apart from odd snippets of advice. Soon the train arrived and I found my seat. In true tradition I looked back out of the window as the first leg of the journey began. Quickly Heutingsheim was behind us and the train gathered speed towards Berlin.

The journey rolled on and I stared out of the windows of the train, trying to catch my first glimpse of Berlin. When we began to enter the suburbs it was slightly disappointing; it just seemed to be a larger version of Stuttgart. The station, however, was something new to me. So many platforms extended parallel to our own. Some with trains unloading like ours, others surrounded by a throng of people trying to find their appointed carriages and bidding friends and relatives goodbye.

All around us was evidence that the Olympic Games were taking place. Hanging from the vast roof and from the balconies and walkways were the flags of all nations. Central to the concourse was the five-ringed flag of the Olympics, hanging together with the huge red and black swastike banners and national flag of Germany. The emotional high I was already feeling was heightened even further by all of this - I cannot remember a time when I have felt so excited.

I was met at the station by my relatives and duly smiled and nodded as the introductions were made. There were the expected comments about breeding us big in the country, and, '...don't you look healthy, it must be the country air,' and then we were on our way to their home. All around me were interesting sights and, of course, new sounds and languages. It was an exciting and interesting time for me, although I tried to appear casual and unimpressed; I wasn't going to let these city types think that they had the edge on me.

On the date specified for me to report to the *Luftkriegsschule*, my relatives dropped me at the barracks at Gatow. Here, I met up with the other boys. There was a steady bustle of movement as we strolled here and there, exchanging greetings with friends and trying to appear casual and mature. Inside we all boiled with excitement, feeling rather important, having been summoned to Berlin. The majority of our parents had never been to the capital and had only speculated about what temptations lay in wait for us simple country boys.

The tests were scheduled to cover three days and were quite exhaustive. Intellectually we were evaluated with such exercises as speech and debate. We were each given a choice of three subjects and then asked to deliver a ten minute oration from the podium on the selected subjects. The audience comprised some *Luftwaffe* officers, who occasionally jotted down notes, and the rest of our group of examinees. After the delivery of the speech we had to lead a debate on the subject from our position in front.

I had chosen The Advantages or Disadvantages of Large Cities and had considered the current *NSDAP* line of Back to the Country. However, I chose to take the line of the cultural and spiritual achievements which could be made within the framework of a city. I developed the theme well as I went and surprised myself with my ability to think on my feet in front of such a formidable audience. During the debate I received plenty of flak from my fellow recruits but held my position well.

The second part of the evaluation was strictly physical, involving simple gymnastics and events to demonstrate stamina. This is where I thought my undoing would lay. The severe kidney-related illness that I had suffered at the age of thirteen had required that I be excused sports for some time afterwards. It was now that this lack of exercise was to tell.

Firstly, in the gymnastics, we had to perform a full sideways vault of the horse. I ran at speed towards the wooden horse, ready for the take-off, but just crashed into the side, moving the whole horse across the floor and against the wall. I wanted to try again, but the supervising officer took me to one side and advised me to pass on this exercise. I thought I'd failed right there and then, but it wasn't so.

In the field events I didn't exactly make up for my shortfall in the gymnastics. In nearly all the events I came in well down the field and in the 3000 metres the officer had actually closed his notebook and walked off before I staggered past the finish line. What had been doubt in the gymnasium had turned into certainty in the field. I couldn't see any way that I would be accepted on such a performance.

In any event, after two and a half days, ten names were read from a list as being the successful candidates. To my total surprise and immeasurable joy my name was read out. So far it looked as if I was to achieve the impossible - I was going to get into the *Luftwaffe*.

There was a last simple test of power of command which we had to pass before we left the *Luftkriegsschule*. This was simply standing in a back room and shouting orders to imaginary subordinates. Elated as I felt, I could have shouted the orders from Berlin's Funkturm (Radio Tower) and I'm sure they would have heard me in Stuttgart.

I had enough money to stay on in Berlin for a while but I didn't like the City at all. The streets were especially packed with visitors to the Games and everywhere was full of people. Really, I suppose I should have taken more interest, especially in the sports events, but I was very uncomfortable in the restricted environment of the buildings and people. I'd had this experience before in Stuttgart when the local *Turnerbund* had staged a grand festival. Again, I had the opportunity to stay but instead I had elected to go home to Creglingen and spend my school holiday there.

I was also absolutely bursting to tell my parents my good news and especially to tell my physics teacher, who had taken such a keen interest in our applications to fly. There was still one more set of physiological tests to be undertaken, but these were to be held at Bad Cannstatt near Stuttgart. After the rejection of the Infantry I was very proud to be able to return home with good news and the probability of a position as an officer in the future.

Bad Cannstatt was a chamber of horrors designed to test our balance, sense of direction and general physiological co-ordination. First we were moved around the building, floor by floor and had to give an account of the cardinal points of the compass. Then we were individually strapped into a device which resembled a stretcher. It was pivoted in the middle on a horizontal axis. When securely in place the stretcher was rotated at speed with the occupant effectively tumbling head over heels in the vertical plane. As if this wasn't enough, we had numbers shouted at us and we had to perform calculations, shouting back the answers to the observers. It wasn't the most pleasant experience of my life but I was one of those who stuck with it and passed that stage.

Lastly, and for reasons which still puzzle me, we had to hold two handles whilst a rising electric current was applied to the circuit. Some of the trainees didn't like this at all, quitting after a very short time. However, I was more stubborn and decided that I would rather pass out than let go and fail the test. I'm not sure how well I did against the others but the net result was that I was one of those who passed. There were no more tests, I had made it. I was going to learn to fly.

Notes on Chapter 2

1. *Die Partei* - The Party: It was not until I became a prisoner of war that I first heard the name *Nazi* Party. Therefore I will refer to 'The Party' just as that, in the way which I and most Germans knew it at the time.

CHAPTER 3

1936 – *Arbeitsdienst* to *Luftkriegsschule*

On the 3ʳᵈ September 1936 I received my letter of acceptance to the *Luftwaffe*, but there were conditions. Firstly, I had to obtain my passing out marks from school, then I would have to serve my *Arbeitsdienst* (Labour Service). Even after that there would be a six month probation period at *Kriegschule* (Military School) before my appointment would become official, assuring me, of a place to be trained as an officer. Despite all these problems, I was confident that I would make it. A whole new chapter of my life was about to begin.

From September 1936, my life seemed to change gear and rush forward at a pace which I hadn't thought possible. Germany was building up her armed forces and the priorities were men and machines. This was obvious when I was given my instructions before entry to *Luftkriegsschule* (*Luftwaffe* Military School). There would be no time for me to sit my final examinations at school in the usual way. Instead, my results would be formulated upon the average of tests set during the earlier part of the year. This, coupled with an assessment by the class teacher, would give a final result. I was sure I would get the required passes but I was interested to see how the 'human factor' affected my results. For instance, my physics teacher, who had been a flyer in the First War, gave me a grade 1.I was good at the subject and deserved a high mark, but I often wondered if his interest in my future didn't just ease that up a bit. In contrast to this, the chemistry teacher who had no apparent nationalistic feelings, gave me a grade 4 - a bare pass. I wasn't as good at chemistry as I was at physics, but I thought that I had earned better than that. 'Still,' I told myself, 'what you lose on the roundabout, you make up on the swings.' Overall, I qualified well enough to have been granted a university place in ordinary times, but the end of 1936 was anything but ordinary for me.

On my 18th birthday, 14th September 1936, I was automatically transferred from the *Hitler Jugend* to the *SA (Sturm Abteilung* – Storm Troopers - Brown Shirts*)*. I wasn't very interested in either organisation, but I did want to get the *SA Sportabzeichen* (Sport, Shooting and Marching Tests). Time was now short and I wasn't to have enough to get through the whole set of tests, but I did qualify up to *Reichssportabzeichen[1]* (I still have the qualification book). I thought I would be able to make the *SA* Shooting Tests just before I left for my labour service, but events were to conspire against me - that, coupled with youthful naivety.

The test was to be held on the Sunday before I was to leave. On the Saturday I had agreed to have a farewell party with my mates, we were going to 'paint the town red'. (Red was going to figure in the evening and the next day, but not in the form of paint). To promote certain vintages of local wines there had been declared a 'Day of Wine' in Ludwigsburg. The particular wine in focus was a *'Brackenheimer'*, a light red wine made from the grapes which were grown within the district of Ludwigsburg. The price of the wine was subsidised for the duration of the 'promotion' and presented a very cheap drink for a bunch of young people bent on having a good time. As usual, I thought I was immune from the effects of such a mundane thing as red wine and, with the willing assistance of my mates, managed to consume much too much. I don't remember how I got home, but my next experience was to wake up feeling indescribably awful, in a bed that was saturated with partly digested red wine and other unidentified substances. Fortunately, my parents were understanding and didn't make too much of it, other than making fun of my monumental headache and hangover.

Thus it was I missed the shooting section of the *SA Sportabzeichen.* I could no more have held and fired a rifle on that day than I could have flown unaided. I consoled myself that I would soon be doing things that were important to me and I could well miss the qualifications of an organisation about which I had the gravest doubts anyway.

Having passed my 'exams', I learned that such was the urgency behind recruitment into the services, that I was only to do two months of my six months *Arbeitsdienst.* This was good news indeed. I was straining at the leash to get into the *Luftwaffe.* Since passing my acceptance tests, I had thought of little else but the possibility of flying. I was impatient to make a start and things like my labour service just seemed to be unnecessary obstructions which were being placed in my way. Still, there was no way around it and on 1st October 1936 I reported to Schwäbisch Hall.

Again, I was to find that corners had been cut to expedite our progress through Labour Service. It was normal practice for the young people who were serving their time to be sent as far across Germany as possible. The object, apparently, was that a good mix could be achieved at this important stage in a young person's life. You have to remember that it was unusual for people to have travelled around too much, even in their own country. So it was decreed that the Labour Service youngsters would travel to experience other parts of Germany and meet fellow Germans. It was an interesting piece of planning on the part of the government. The regional differences were still very marked in both tradition and dialect. When we moved, as a family, from Ochsenwang to Creglingen, about 200 kilometres (125 miles), both myself and my sister found it difficult to communicate with other children, because they spoke Franconian, while we still used the slower Swabian farmers' dialect. Part of the philosphy of *Arbeitsdienst* was to provide a sort of cultural 'melting pot for the youth of Germany. Certainly many friendships were struck up which forged strong links across Germany.

So on the 1st October, I reported to Schwabisch Hall to begin my eight weeks of service. The quarters were in a converted barn which had been one of the outbuildings of the *Comburg,* an ancient and very robust castle, perched on the top of a hill overlooking Schwabisch Hall. The barn was a completely self-contained unit for us. Within it had been built a kitchen, mess hall, sleeping quarters and separate rooms for the supervisory staff. All the boys there were on their way to the various arms of the *Wehrmacht,* but only Werner Ruoff[2] (from Stuttgart and an aspiring Infantry Officer) and myself were on the short course. The staff were aware of this and ensured that we both got maximum 'benefit' from our time by giving us every extra and unpleasant job that they could. We only did our eight weeks but I would hazard that the two of us did more than we would have done, had we served the full time. This was relaxed a little when we formed a band which we called *Arbeitsdienst - Kameraden.* I played piano and Werner joined me on cello. Gradually, we collected together five or six of the boys and made a nice diversion from the drudgery of the day.

Ours was quite a small camp, only catering for one *Arbeitsdienst Kompanie.* Food was scarce but the camp leader had, on his own initiative, supplemented our diet by having a kitchen garden and raising pigs on the food scraps. It didn't provide an excess of food but at least we all had fresh vegetables and salads.

Our working day was started by reveille with military style bugle blowing at 05:30 hrs. At this time of the year, of course, it was dark and beginning to get very cold. There were just ten minutes for washing and dressing. Then it was outside in all weathers for thirty minutes of gymnastics.

51

To really enhance the morning scene, the farmer had unloaded a dung cart on the meadow where we undertook our exercises. This didn't encourage our leaders to seek a different venue, as I suspect the farmer wanted, but merely to *increase* the exercises that brought us into complete contact with the stinking ooze.

After the callisthenics we would double back to our quarters to change into our working overalls and to cram down some black bread and chicory coffee. Our wet exercise suits were hung up to drip dry beside our beds. With hardly a pause, we would be out at 06:30 hrs., spades shouldered like rifles ready for the march to town. However bad we felt in the morning there was a certain pride in our group and as we reached the outskirts of the small town we would break into song, something which I enjoyed. Then with great pride, and almost military precision, we would march through Schwäbisch Hall as if we were returning from some great victory, instead of being on our way to dig ditches.

Out of town we marched uphill to the area where we were working which was not too far from the *Luftwaffe Flughafen* at Hessenthal. Our work was nothing to do with the airfield, but many was the time I found myself looking at the lumbering Dornier Do 23 bombers and wondering what it would be like to join those elite men, the fliers. I was usually brought back to earth by the sharp bark of our supervisor extolling the virtues of physical labour.

Our task was to enlarge a small stream into a broader and deeper drainage culvert. The meadows on either side of the stream were very marshy and it was hoped that if we could sufficiently improve the drainage, then the meadows would be of more agricultural use. The main problem for us was that the water could not be stopped whilst we worked, and so we were always standing nearly to the tops of our boots in water. That is not to say that our boots were waterproof either, they were just the standard issue 'Jackboots' which are common in all of the German services. Being leather, they soon became saturated and offered no protection from the water. Really we might as well have taken our boots off for all the water they kept out. Each of us only had the one pair and it was left to our own ingenuity to dry them out at night, prior to the next day's hard labour.

I think my strongest impression of this short time was of being cold, wet, hungry and tired all the time. I am sure that Werner and myself did more than the others for the reasons which I have explained, certainly the lower ranking *Arbeitsdienstfuhrer* found us special tasks regularly. A favourite of his was 'searching for the angle of the slope'. This involved virtually lying in the ditch to 'better observe' the drop of the land to ensure a good flow of water. In the end Werner and I would just fall into the water on purpose to spoil their joke. It didn't help, we got wet anyway, but at least we felt that our pride had benefited.

I felt miserable; how I now longed for those happy days at school. Still at least there were two of us and it was only for eight weeks. Those were sustaining thoughts. After the first four weeks we were allowed out to the town and things began to be a little better. However, when our eight weeks were up I was heartily glad to wave goodbye to that barn and my labour service. Things must get better now, I thought.

There was to be no pause in my education, and the day after I returned home I was packed and waiting on the station for the train which would start me on the first leg of my journey back to Berlin. All of a sudden, travel and new experiences had become the greater part of my life. I could feel that I was beginning to toughen up inside as well. The labour service had slimmed me down a little and I could feel that my muscles were now in excellent tone. I felt able to face anything, but I was still a little apprehensive about actually going into the Military Establishment. Still, I thought, what could be harder than *Arbeitsdienst?*

Arbeits Dienst - I am second from the right

53

The journey from Stuttgart to Berlin took ten hours, mainly at night. In the morning I arrived at Anhalter Bahnhof and made the change to Potsdamer Bahnhof, arriving at 11 o'clock. There was a military bus waiting for me and other new recruits. It was in the charge of a *Luftwaffe* soldier who was also the driver. I tried to ask him some questions but he was very surly, almost aggressive.

Ditch digging. I am in the back row with the spade behind my head. Next right is Gromer and next is Werner Ruoff.

Two other boys were already on the bus and they told me to ignore him. Another train arrived and some more recruits got on the bus. The driver tried to impress them by telling them that they were late, still we sat and waited for another train to come in before we got started.

We really did look like a sad bunch of refugees, each clutching a cardboard box, not a suitcase or bag. This had been on the instructions of the *Luftwaffe*. Each of us was to bring a box with us, so that our civilian clothing could be sent home. I think we had all expected a welcome, to be made to feel important; on the contrary. We just moved around like so many dumb sheep. At Wildpark Werder we were all made to produce our letters of acceptance to make sure that we should be there. As if we would have travelled halfway across Germany without having the proper papers. I was getting my first insight into the slow workings of the military machine.

We were told that we would be the first intake through the new centre at Wildpark Werder. All the buildings were new and smelled of paint and plaster. Later, we learned that some of the buildings formed an entrance to Goring's underground command post, which was situated under an adjacent hill. Some of us wondered if we were in the right place. There were no hangars, no aircraft, just accommodation that looked like classrooms. We were plucked from our reverie as we were told to get out of the bus and line up - 'Quickly! You're in the *Luftwaffe* now!'

Now I really began to wonder what I had got into. In my naivety I had thought that going into the *Luftwaffe* would be like going on to higher education. After all, we had been selected from hundreds of other applicants and, by virtue of that, felt we were special already. Not to the military!

'Line up there! Where are your papers?' 'You're in room 8B!' Always shouting and everyone running.

An NCO shouted at me to get to my room and I ran for the stone staircase, the cardboard box under my arm. I tried to push my way through a sea of others, all with their cardboard boxes, some trying to get up the stairs, others trying to get down. At the landing there was an NCO shouting unintelligible orders at me to get back downstairs for reasons which I couldn't catch. At the bottom there were others shouting at us to get to our rooms. 'Didn't we understand a simple order?' 'Why the hell are you down here again?' It was madness! Just a mass of young men pushing in either direction, all clutching desperately to their pathetic cardboard boxes.

At last, a fellow newcomer told me that I should take off my tie. Apparently the NCOs were sensitive about the nickname, *Schlipssoldaten*[3], that had been given to the *Luftwaffe* by the other services. I duly removed my tie and folded it up. Then I approached the NCO and reported, in what I thought was my best military style, *'Bitte Herrn Obergefreiten, vorbeigehen zu dürfen'* (may I be permitted to pass?). A curt nod of the head told me that I had solved one of the first conundrums.

At that time, a lot of abstract thoughts were beginning to race up and down the staircase of my mind. Somewhere inside my head was a voice barking, 'Uli! What in hell have you got into?' I had never liked the kind of mindless loud bullying which I had seen in the *Hitler Jugend* and in the *SA*. I have always held the view that raising your voice is an indication that you are running out of things to say. Violence is, of course, reserved for when you have completely run out of logical argument. I had thought I would be escaping from this kind of treatment, once I got away from the small town atmosphere at home. It had, in fact, been this kind of brainless persecution which had led to my joining the *Luftwaffe* and not becoming an Infantry Officer Cadet like my *Arbeitsdienst Kamerad* Werner Ruoff.

Within the small community from which I had come, my parents had been labeled as 'social climbers'. They had both, energetically, addressed themselves to social activities and had made enemies as a result. Part of the social pressure that was brought to bear upon them was the accusation that my mother was having an affair with one of the younger teachers from the school at which my father was Head. Father was a member of the *NSDAP* and one of his junior teachers at the school was a senior official, in fact the *Ortsgruppenleiter* (local party chief), in the *NSDAP*. Apparently, the *NSDAP* man felt that his position in the party entitled him to the Headship of the school, and thus a slanderous campaign was begun, with the object of replacing my father with a more suitable and, 'morally' more stable, person.

It is incredible to think how seriously the 'affair' was taken. In the end, father was required to face an 'Honour Court'. He was cleared, but you don't throw mud at a wall without some of it sticking. Our family name had been tarnished for no real reason, and this had resulted in my being found as 'unsuitable' material for officer training in the Infantry, a fact which I suspect indirectly saved my life.

My father had become a Party Member, partly as a reaction to the ostracism of the established hierarchy in Creglingen, and partly because, like so many Germans, he could see Hitler overturning the vicious and uncompromising conditions of the Treaty of Versailles and giving our country back her dignity. My mother would have joined the National Socialist *Frauenschaft*, but she was of the opinion that this group had been well established around the female equivalent of the 'bully boy' faction of society.

Even in retrospect, the German people had fairly accurate views of the Party Leadership. Goring was a bit of a joke. His flamboyance and showmanship were seen for what they were, but the fundamental point, which many must have missed, was that, despite the fact we laughed at his transparent antics, he took himself seriously. Gobbels was the master of advertising and a genius at this trade. By virtue of his position he was also afforded some latitude in what were extreme views at the time. In close company with him was Julius Streicher who managed the awful magazine, *Der Stürmer.* For most, the paper represented a fanatical view and was not, therefore, much subscribed to outside the Party 'faithful'.

Rudolf Hess was the Deputy *Führer* and the Party purist. From all accounts it was he who tried always to keep the doctrines of the National Socialist pure and uncorrupted, the idealist. Over and above these individuals who formed the core of the Party was Hitler. He had no specific talent but an intangible abstract ability to weld the diverse aims of these individ-

uals into a common policy. To him would fall the task of guiding their energy and in manipulating and managing the political environment to further
their aims. He was a peculiarly charismatic character who, although not of
impressive physical appearance or stature, had a certain magnetic quality
about him. In the years to come I was to meet him and experience this first
hand. Since that time I have sensed it in others who were destined to
become exceptional people but never to the same powerful degree.

What, unfortunately, abounded in The Party was the 'bully boy' type.
This was something to do with the fact that the *NSDAP* was a new party on
the German Political scene and, to a degree, had to attract new blood in
vast numbers by whatever means. This led to many outcasts from other,
more established, organisations becoming welcomed into the Party 'faithful'. They, in turn, attracted more of their own, and so an unbalanced
organisation grew.

I thought, initially, that this was the reason why I had been confronted
by so many of the bullies in *Arbeitsdienst* and now on my first day in the
Luftwaffe. But since then I have discovered that this corps of loud, seem-
ingly ignorant people, is most people's introduction to military institutions
worldwide. Many servicemen in Britain remember the Welsh Corporal
who screamed at them from dawn to dusk, or the Sergeant Major who
could shatter your nerves at a 1000 metres with his phenomenal voice. We
had Saxon *Gefreiters* and an *Unteroffizier* who, we felt, had the power of
life and death over us. That is not to be too disparaging of these groups; it
is just a sort of abstract concept which is common to most servicemen's
experience.

I had come to Berlin thinking that I had left all the petty prejudice and
bullying behind. I didn't think the bully element would exist with such
strength within the military. If this first contact was anything to go by, I
was hopelessly wrong. My parents tried to impress upon me that I was a
talented young person with a good brain and a sound education to go with
it. What I had to learn, they explained, was to be more patient and to stop
requiring the world to come up to my expectations of it. I'm not sure that
I've ever completely embraced that view. Whatever my immediate problems, I had to come to terms with the fact that I had 'signed up' and that
there was no easy way out. First, I had to take the six month's infantry
training, and then, perhaps, things would change. Again, I found myself in
the position of wishing a part of my life away, so that I might arrive at a
time which would be more fulfilling. So, I had to address myself to the
immediate problems - *let's get up the stairs and then see what else the day
had in store.*

Soon we began to find out a little about our 'jailers'. There was a

Hauptmann (Captain) in charge of the *Fahnenjunker Kompanie (Officer Cadet Company)*. The *Kompanie* was sub-divided into three *Zugs* (Platoons). These in turn were led by either an *Oberleutnant* or a *Leutnant,* with an *Oberfeldwebel* (Staff Sergeant) or *Feldwebel* (Sergeant) as a deputy. The *Hauptmann* lived at home, but each of the *ZugFührers,* and their deputies, lived on the same floor as their *Zug*. We saw them all during the working day, but after five in the evening or at weekends, they were seldom seen.

The majority of these officers and NCOs had come from the 100,000 strong Regular Army, which had been retained within the terms of Versailles. The NCOs had almost all come from an Army background and had initially trained policemen. Now they had changed uniforms, but not their methods, to 'prepare' us for our future service. They were obviously aware that, all being well, we would be their superior officers in two years, but just now we were under their control and beholden to them. The lower ranking NCOs never missed a chance to remind us what power they had to scotch our careers by adverse reports. We all badly wanted our career and, in my case, above all, to fly. Thus it was that I was allotted the task of cleaning the shoes of my particular *Korporalschaftsführer,* the selfsame individual who had made me run up and down the stairs until I took my tie off.

The first day was filled with our reception and issue of equipment and uniform. Again, this was done in the noise and chaos which I had quickly become to view as a necessary component of my new military life. Items of clothing were literally thrown at you and pronounced as a perfect fit after the most cursory glance. That was the word of the day - 'Fits!' 'Helmet - Fits!' 'Boots - 'Fit!' 'Jacket - Fits!' 'Trousers - 'Fit!' Everything heaped upon you with the constant barking of the NCOs. 'Fits! Fits! Fits!'

Then the regulation stitching of labels into each and every item of clothing and equipment. Hardly any of the boys had any skill at sewing and the job seemed to take days. Always there were the *Gefreiters* stalking around, picking up finished items, then throwing them into the face of the unfortunate owner, ordering them to do it again. And again, and again, and again. They'd soon show us how an army should be run. My personal bogey was my water bottle. The stitching of the label onto the felt cover just seemed to defeat me. Every time I thought I'd got it right the *Korporalschaftsführer* would rip it off and order me to do it again. I was up to the twentieth time when we were given leave to go home for Christmas and I smuggled the bottle out for my mother to stitch for me. At last the NCO was satisfied.

Giving us leave was a welcome rest for us, but it also gave me time to reflect upon what was going on. I was very depressed about my first three weeks. I almost wept as I told my parents that I didn't think I could take six months of this kind of barbaric treatment. Really, it was father who managed to lift my spirits by telling me that it was always the first few weeks that were the worst. After that, things would become easier. He asked me to have faith and stick with it. He had survived his rough intro-duction to the Infantry and even managed to laugh about the antics of their NCOs, all those years ago. I felt a little better, but I still couldn't see that my present situation was anything to laugh about at all.

I returned after the break with a feeling of dread. Despite my expecta-tion to the contrary, things didn't seem to let up at all. In many ways they were worse! It was January, and the training grounds were wet with snow and slush. Every day we returned to the barracks with our dungarees plas-tered in mud and wringing wet. Amongst all the other things that we had to do, the overalls would have to be crisp, clean and white for the next day. Frequently we would be found, after lights out, scrubbing and washing in the laundry room. This was really very well equipped for laundry work with troughs for washing and scrubbing and an inexhaustible supply of hot water. However, it was strictly against the rules to be up that late, but it was the only way in which it could be done. Many of us would then go to bed with the wet overalls inside the straw mattress, so that they would be dry and pressed in the morning. It was normal practice to put our uniform trousers under the mattress to sharpen up the creases. Every now and then, the NCOs would catch us out whilst doing our nocturnal laundry, so that they could award the appropriate punishment and remind us that they were in charge. Punishment usually meant the withdrawing of one of our privi-leges, such as weekend passes out, confined to barracks for the weekend, scrubbing floors and cleaning up. Another little game was *Flagge Lucie*. This had been imported from the Navy and was usually sprung on a whole room (four recruits), rather than being a punishment for one. The NCOs would order the four of us out to the end of the corridor. Our *Stubenaltester* (room-elder) would report to them for instructions. They would then shout, for instance, 'Dress Uniform - three minutes!' We would then run like mad-men into the room and report back within the given time. The NCO would then inspect the room and woe betide the occupants of a room whose con-tents were not in perfect regulation order. What is hard to understand today is why we put up with it. On some occasions people did rebel and nothing happened. I can remember one time when the NCOs went over the top and pulled everything out of our lockers, emptied the straw from our mattress-es and mixed it all up in fantastic mess in the middle of the room. It was appalling. When the orders came to clear it up, one of my room-mates, who had come all the way from Peru to be in the *Luftwaffe*, suddenly took his bayonet and went after the *Gefreiter.* To our utter amazement, nothing happened. On another occasion one of the other rooms decided that they had had enough. When they heard that there was to be another *Flagge Lucie* to be pulled on their room, they rather indifferently appeared in the corridor and then went back to their room to finish some snacks they had been eating. The *Gefreiters* went berserk, shouting and screaming around the room - nothing. The *Feldwebel* was called and he did his share, without result. In the end, they just went away and the incident was forgotten. But, for the most part, the recruits 'played the game' and danced to the tune that was called by the NCOs.

We knew that although it seemed that all had been forgotten, the NCOs would get their revenge. So it was. There were longer periods of holding rifles at arms length, or bunny-hopping with the rifle held out in front with straight arms. Then, of course, there was always the NCOs friend and ally, the MUD! Every day that there was the smallest patch of mud or filth, they would see it and enjoy every minute as they had us down in the mud, up to attention, down in the mud... The officers couldn't be around all of the time.

Although we were young and fit, it was still exhausting. One weekend we were tired out and resolved to try to catch up on some sleep. It was no use just trying to stay in instead of taking a weekend pass. If you stayed in, there was always work to be done. It was no rest at all. So we took our passes and then locked ourselves in our room to sleep. At around 10:00 hrs. on the Sunday, we were startled by one of the NCOs banging on the door. We tried to brazen it out by being quiet, but he wasn't to be fobbed off so easily. He returned with the master key and caught us. For the rest of the day we were more gainfully employed scrubbing two floors with the brush, soap and floor cloth. We felt utterly miserable but we were determined to see it through.

One lesson I learned, very early on, was NEVER VOLUNTEER.! One day we were lined up for roll call when the *Oberfeldwebel* (Staff Sergeant) asked: 'Anyone who can play a musical instrument - one pace forward . . . March!' Well, thinking in my naivety that they might really want musicians to start a band, like we had during *Arbeitsdienst,* I stepped forward. That won me potato peeling for the whole of Sunday afternoon.

During all of these months, we only went out a couple of times, just to see something else. In the first few weeks before Christmas, we had to go out with a *Gefreiter so* that he could salute for us as we hadn't been trained to undertake that particular complex task at that time! It was such a performance and a great deal of time involved in the training of the military salute, if we'd had to learn the 'Hitler' salute as well we might never have finished training.

Eventually, we all qualified and could go out of barracks unaccompanied. Although we weren't very far from Berlin's centre, just a short ride on the '*U Bahn*' or the '*S Bahn*', I never ventured back into the city. I just didn't think it held anything for me and, frankly, we were just too tired. Closer to the barracks, in Potsdam, we had found a cheap little restaurant, which was run by a very good-natured woman. The favourite for us was *Bauernfruhstuck,* a mixture of fried potatoes, ham, eggs and corn. It had two other ingredients which were of paramount importance to us; it was cheap - one fixed price - and you could eat as much of it as you liked. It wasn't much of a social life, but it got us out of the barracks for a time, that's what counted.

Soon we began to start our weapons training, and here I found I liked the rifle best. We used the standard infantry rifle, the Mauser K98 *Kar*. It was a bolt action weapon which had no frills on it. At least I had done some competitive shooting with the *HJ* and the *SA*, prior to beginning my military service, and I took some pride in recording a good score. With the machine guns I wasn't so interested. There just didn't seem to be enough accuracy or technique involved. You just pointed the weapon towards the target and on continuous fire, the magazine was empty in just under three seconds. I found it very difficult to hold the gun as it bucked and reeled from recoil. We only had to reach a certain fixed score and then we were judged 'qualified'. The best feature of the shooting days for us was that it was a day out. A fairly long ride in the truck, followed by a day on the ranges. It was an almost 'normal' day, something to which we could look forward.

The other excursion which we enjoyed was to the Infantry Officers' School at Potsdam where, incidentally, Erwin Rommel was one of the principal tactics instructors. However, we were there only to swim. I was astounded how poorly some people swam, but then I had had the advantage of many summers in the River Tauber in Creglingen. Again, in typical military style, they had set an arbitrary standard. We all had to be able to jump or dive from the three metre board. I did this simply for pleasure, but for some of the poorer swimmers, it seemed to pose an almost insurmountable barrier. Then the Senior NCO would lay down the law. 'Either you jump, or you're OUT!' It was amazing to see how some of the more desperate souls entered the water. The more confident among us just sat at the side, trying to determine who, in fact, had made the most spectacular effort. In the end, we all 'qualified'.

By the end of May 1937 we had the last exercise to do to complete our training. This involved a 90 kilometre (56 mile) march from the barracks to the training ground at Doberitz. This was not just a route march, but part of the exercise. We had to advance like a proper Infantry unit, sending out forward patrols and securing the way as we went. We also carried our full complement of weapons, rifles, sub-machine guns and the heavy machine guns. Also thousands of rounds of blank ammunition, for we were to be 'attacked' many times on the route. Each man had his own full pack and complete equipment: rifle, hand grenades, entrenching spade, bayonet, steel helmet, gas mask and supplies. Altogether it came to about 20 kilograms (44 pounds) and we marched about 30 kilometres (18 miles) a day.

In the evening we would come to a predetermined village, where we would be accommodated for the night. About two kilometres outside the village we would be met by a band and they would 'play us in' with stirring military marches. After a hard day's marching and 'fighting', it really lifted the spirit to march in such style. In the evening there would be a *Manoverball* in the village hall or the largest guesthouse. Typically, there would be about three-hundred people there and the band would play good dancing music. It was not to be missed. We were the heroes, and badly blistered feet counted for nothing in the face of such recognition, at least not until the next day.

May 1937 - Infantry Training - our final march to the Truppenübungsplatz (training ground). Note the girls in the front row.

In the morning we were roused early to be ready to march out at 08:00. Once more the band would play us out and on more than one occasion, our first and last ranks were made up from the local girls, who had come to see us off. Many were the promises to return, few were the times that it happened.

At last we arrived at the *Truppenübungsplatz* (Infantry Training Ground) where we were to spend the next two weeks. Finally, the diverse training in the many skills of warfare came together, and it all began to make sense. Our 'finishing' included the very dangerous practice of throwing live grenades and, for the first time, the use of heavy calibre pistols. All over the training ground we had our 'wars'. We sweated as we excavated dugouts; we laboured to drag sufficient air to breath through the stifling filters of our gas masks; we practised the stealth of the sniper. We were quite good, but we all had in mind that we weren't going to be infantry, we were going to learn to fly and the infantry training was just a hurdle to cross; a view not entirely shared by our Regular Army Instructors.

One event which I will never forget was when one of the Staff Sergeants took real exception to the apparent fact that we were being treated like regular infantry recruits. On one occasion, he waited for a time when there were no officers around, then he ordered us out in full field kit. Steel helmets, gas masks, rifles and fixed bayonets. Once out onto the training area, we were ordered to *Achtungsmarsch* (Goose-step), as if it were a parade ground. We hadn't had time to fit dry filters in our gas-masks so very soon the visors steamed up and we couldn't really see where we were going. We obediently marched straight into the trenches, piling in, one on top of the other. It was a miracle that nobody was badly hurt. That was enough for us. Even in the face of deliberate disobedience of orders, and threats about the penalty for mutiny, we refused to do any more, and he had to march us back to barracks.

This was not the end of the matter either. Some time after this event we were back at Wildpark for a weekend exercise when this same Sergeant turned his platoon out for parade drills after midnight. At first they thought he was drunk, and for that they might have covered up, but it became obvious that the problem was more serious than that. A few brave hearts informed one of the officers and later, still in the dead of night, the sergeant was taken away to a mental hospital. We never saw him again.

The last week was the breaking point for a few. The pressure was really on with long distance runs, all-night exercises, night time orienteering marches and very exacting marksmanship. I was to have mixed fortunes during this period. I was fortunate that I missed a lot of it, but considering the alternative, I'm not too sure I won the day. During the manoeuvres I, like a lot of us, suffered blistered feet. A truck followed us on the longer marches and anyone could elect to take a ride in the truck if their feet became bad. Mine had begun to blister but, typically, I wouldn't give up. Doggedly I marched on with increasing pain in my feet until I felt the blisters burst and the raw flesh begin to rub. Once more, my tenacity was to cause me problems. I finished the march but when I took my boots off, my feet were in an appalling mess. I went to the sick bay at Wildpark and saw the *Sanitätsobergefreite* (Medical Sergeant). In typical military style the Medic decided that the loose flaps of skin should be cut away and then the feet liberally dosed with iodine. I warned him that I had a very dangerous allergy to iodine, but he dismissed this as my being babyish about the stinging of the iodine and applied the red solution with great relish. Within 30 minutes my skin had begun to erupt in flaming red and white hives, and my temperature had begun to rocket up. I told him to check it and there was considerable consternation as the mercury passed 40° Celsius. Then he called the doctor, who arrived in record time. The two of them really had their hands full for a while and all the other casualties had to wait whilst I was given complete attention. I was covered in white powder to help stop the itching and, gradually, over the course of about 24 hours, I came back to normal. I gathered, from snatches of conversation, that neither the doctor nor the sergeant were going to report the problem. It wasn't the last time this allergy would cause problems for me; even now I'm still scared to go into hospital for fear of what might happen.

Although I had missed the greater part of the last week, my grades had been good enough for me to pass along with the rest of the *Kompanie*. I suspect that the nature of my illness might have had something to do with this. If they had failed me, it would have necessitated them admitting why I had been in sick-bay for four days. So, in the end, the infantry training was over. During my last day of sickness, the whole *Fahnenjunkerkompanie* was moved from Wildpark across the bridge to Werder, on the other side of the Grosser Zern See. Werder, of course, was the military airport which was now part of the *Luftskriegsschule* as a whole. At last! We were going to begin to learn to fly. It had been a long hard road, but we all hoped it would be worth it in the end.

Notes on Chapter 3

1. *Reichssportabzeichen.* This is a National sporting qualification and existed before the rise of Hitler and is, in fact, still in existence today.

2. Werner Ruoff. He was one of the boys who was accepted in the Infantry Regiment when circumstances conspired against me. It proved to be a mixed blessing in that both he and his two brothers were killed in action very early on in the war.

3. *Schlipssoldaten* - Literally soldiers with ties. None of the other, more senior services, wore neck-ties - still retaining the older, high collar, military tunic.

CHAPTER 4

1937 - *Flugsschule*

Whilst I was still in the sick-bay, the whole *Kompanie* packed up its equipment and moved from Wildpark to Werder. I arrived on the same day as the rest of my peers, but in an ambulance. Right away the difference was clearly apparent. At Wildpark we had been selected to form three platoons before we actually arrived. With typical German thoroughness, the platoons had been made up according to height. Our medical papers had been examined and we had been grouped because of our physical height. Number 1 Platoon had those who were 1.80 metres or more. Number 2 Platoon (mine), had those who measured 1.72 -1.80 metres, and Number 3 had those under 1.72. It may seem to be an almost laughable selection but, on the parade ground, the nicely reducing height of the platoons finished off a smart parade to perfection.

At Werder there seemed to be a more relaxed atmosphere and no perceptable structure to the selection. There seemed to be a good mixture of the many German 'tribes', but then, with such a wide selection of candidates, this would have been unavoidable. There was nothing wrong with mixing us up as in *Arbeitsdienst;* it seemed to help us all to realise how big the country was and how divided we, as a people, still were in many of our views and traditions. Our 'losses' were also made up. We had lost some ten men during the training who had, at one stage or another, failed to qualify. So we had some new boys brought in who seemed to have had an easier time, being given their basic training at other flying units.

At Werder, the quarters were much more comfortable. There were only three or four of us to a room and only two rooms using a bathroom - luxury! It was whilst sharing a room at Werder that I first met Hinnerk

Waller, who was to become a friend over many years and many, many adventures. He, like me, was now promoted to *Fähnrich* (Ensign - First Class), as was our other room-mate Willy Hofmann. Both Hinnerk and Willy came from Northern Germany and spoke the *Plattdeutsch* (Frisian) dialect. I, of course, came from the south and spoke *Swabian,* totally different from the heavy accent of the north. Often the two of them would lay in bed after lights out and exchange jokes in the incomprehensible dialect. Abruptly, one or both of them would break out into gales of laughter. I found it frustrating being able neither to sleep nor share their joke. At times it was irritating, but it at least illustrates how the advances in communication have broken down the internal traditions and barriers of countries like mine. Sadly, I have to observe that other, more tangible, barriers were erected in their place, particularly in Germany.

Hinnerk, right from the beginning, was very ambitious. He was the son of a farmer who seemed always to count himself so lucky to have been accepted into the *Luftwaffe.* Certainly I felt privileged, but Hinnerk felt something deeper than this, almost beholden to the government for offering him the chance to serve as an officer. Willy Hofmann was a really 'happy-go-lucky' lad, always in the highest of spirits, taking the hardest knocks with good humour. He also seemed to have an inexhaustible supply of poems, both classical and, of course, those that were a little crude. He even made some up of his own, and these too seemed to be of a high standard and very popular as an evening diversion. Willy's father was a train driver for the *Reichsbahn* (State Railways) which, if you consider the mixture in just our room, demonstrates the truly classless selection of the *Luftwaffe.* It was a case of the best man for the job, and this was to be carried on later, even under combat conditions. However classless the selection, I have to comment that I think Willy was badly suited to the *Luftwaffe,* perhaps not having enough concentration when flying. Often he would sing at the top of his voice, whilst heading for some potential catastrophe.

Early on in the course we were being given a lecture in navigation by a *Luftwaffe Major,* who put a question to Willy: '*Fähnrich* Hofmann,' he said, 'you are in a blind flying situation and in command of the aircraft. In flight, your radio operator tells you that the radio fuse has blown and that there is no spare. What do you do?' We all knew that Willy had no technical sense at all and could see that he was completely lost. Well, as Willy was standing out in front of the class and facing us, and the *Major* was watching Willy with his back to us, we all started to make signs to him, indicating smoking and opening of cigarette packets. What we were trying to get across was that he should use the aluminium foil from a cigarette packet to mend the fuse. Suddenly there came the dawn of realisation over

Willy's face. He cleared his throat with great ceremony and with ines-
timable pride said, 'I would, *Herr Major,* with complete calmness, smoke
a cigarette whilst I further considered the problem.' As can be imagined,
the class dissolved into helpless laughter, the *Major* included. He just
shook his head in defeat and simply said, 'You've passed!' It might be that
this was not a favour for Willy as later, in the early days of the French
Campaign, he was killed in a '109. I often wondered if he had been
singing, or maybe he was admiring the clouds, when the shells hit his
plane and snuffed out his carefree life. He was never cut out to be a soldier
and both his youth and his talent were squandered for nothing.

At that time we weren't thinking too much about future dangers. We
were conscious that we were training to be pilots and that one day we
would fly the fighters and bombers of the *Luftwaffe,* but I don't remember
that we much considered what horrors a war might hold for us. Right then
we were just an energetic bunch of boys on the edge of a fantastic adventure and every day took us closer to the realisation of our dreams.

Before the next phase of our training began in earnest, we were given
leave to visit our homes. What a contrast this visit was to the last one when
I'd still been in the early days of my basic training. I was brimming full of
excitement about flying school and frankly, I couldn't wait to get back to
barracks. There was obvious relief from my parents that things were now
going well and it was with a really light heart that I returned to Berlin.

Werder, the little town near to our airport, was famous in its own right
as a resort for the Berliners. The pride of Werder was its *Baumblüte* (flow-
ering trees), cherry, peach and plums. Meanwhile, on the ground, there
were masses of strawberries. In the season, it was a paradise of different
scents, a real wonder. The local farmers would sell their goods both whole-
sale, to the traders, and retail, to those who wanted fruit for jams and wine.
During the four weeks from the middle of May to the middle of June (varying by a few weeks according to the weather), the Berliners would come
out in droves to experience the *Baumblüte* and to drink the local wine made
from the cherries and peaches - very unusual. It was very sweet and quite
strong, resulting in many headaches the next day.

During 'The Season' we weren't allowed out too much, and even when
we did go out we had to wear civilian clothes. These we had brought back
from our leave for the purpose. On the whole, we weren't too worried
about not going out during *Baumblüte* because there were so many people
about and too many drunks. You couldn't go anywhere without someone
wanting to pick a fight with you, or just messing up the evening by behav-
ing badly. We were glad when all the invaders went off back to Berlin. The
only advantage was that there were many more dances and lots of girls

about who soon got to know us well.

Back at the school, we were amazed how the attitudes had changed. We were actually treated like humans and not like a low form of life. We had completed some of our theory and soon it was time for us to take our first, however faltering, steps towards the aircraft. For initial training we used two types: the Heinkel *Kadett* He 72, a biplane which had a 140/160 h.p. radial engine and two seats in tandem, the pupil sitting at the front, and the Focke Wulf FW 44 *Stieglitz* (Goldfinch), which was similar to the Heinkel, both being certificated for full aerobatics.

When the day came for the first flight we were all nervous. I suspect that most of us were having the same thoughts, having come so far and hoped for so much, what would happen if we were frightened? How could you face your comrades if you were airsick down your flying coat? We were all sure that we wanted to fly, but could we do it when the time came?

On the great day we were all too busy to feel too emotional about the forthcoming event. There was a great bustle as we grouped up ready for the flight. The aircraft were being run up by the instructors and the ground crew. When they were ready, they waved the first candidates over to the cockpits and waited for them to strap in. At the drop of a flag, the instructor would take the aircraft up for about five circuits and land, ready for the next candidate. When it was my turn I doubled across to the plane and saw the grinning face of the previous pupil as he passed me, *'It can't be so bad,'* I thought as I stepped into the blustering prop-wash from the idling radial engine. I climbed up and dropped into the cockpit, feeling for the straps to secure me with shaking hands. Then I felt the engine falter for a second and then roar into full life. The wind buffeted the short screen in front of me as I struggled to see past the engine that rose in front of my eyes. The whole airframe shook as the power was applied by the instructor and then the aircraft began to move. Slowly at first, as it veered left and right to allow the pilot to see forwards, then the short wait for the 'all clear'. Abruptly, the engine's note rose to a new high and the plane surged forwards, gathering speed at what was a phenomenal rate in my experience. For someone like me, who had only ridden trains and some very basic cars, this surge of power and the experience of such acceleration was unique. However, this would be nothing to the pure exhilaration which I later felt when releasing the 1175 h.p. of the Daimler-Benz engine of my '109 E.

Quickly, the tail came up and I could see clearly ahead through the silvery blurr of the spinning prop. Then I had a sudden feeling of lightness and I realised that I was flying. In an instant my anxiety was gone; this was where I wanted to be. We gained height and I didn't know where to look next. I could see outside the airfield and many of the roads running far off into the distance. I could feel the little plane rise and fall in the air, and was conscious of the adjustments to the engine speed that were being made by the pilot. Between my knees I could see the joystick moving as he controlled the aircraft and, down by my feet, the rudder bar moved in eerie autonomy. I wanted to start right then and there, but it would be a couple of days before I took those controls for the first time.

The flying instructors had nothing to do with the military establishment and the Chief Instructor of our *Fluggruppe* was also civilian, *Herr* Harms. He was a very nervous type of individual and we were told that he had already been involved in several air-crashes with students. Apparently he had been injured on several occasions, sometimes seriously and, as a souvenir, still had a silver plate in his head. He had three instructors and each of these would be assigned 10-12 men. Ours were *Unteroffizier* Haberkorn, *Herr* Grote and *Graf* (Count) Perponcher. We didn't have fixed instructors at first but later, after some doubt had been registered about the quality of instruction, it changed.

After a very short period of dual flying and very limited theoretical training we were expected to go solo. This really was nerve racking in the extreme, especially when you see several of your colleagues having very near-misses before you. Many seemed to have the same problem. They would open the throttle fully for the take-off run and then inexplicably make a very sharp left turn. Careering across the airfield they would make for the barrack block which was a very substantial, two-storey building with a high, pitched roof. One fellow managed to cut the engine before he became fully airborne but another took off and missed the top of the roof by a few metres. He then disappeared from our view as he dived into the court-yard behind the barracks. Then, with a roar of the radial engine he soared up again as close to a complete stall as you could fly. He then completed his circuit and landed. I don't know who was most shaken by the experience, us who watched, or the chap that flew.

Soon it was my turn and, having seen my friend's close call with the barrack roof, I was more than a little nervous. I had flown about 40-45 circuits with the instructors, but I didn't really think that I was ready for a solo yet. This was a problem with the constantly changing instructors. Nobody had a really accurate idea of each individual student's capabilities. It was just a case that if the instructor on the day felt that you were ready, you did your first solo.

As I sat alone in the cockpit of the aircraft, it was more than the vibration of the engine that made me shake. My mouth was dry and I found that I was gripping the joystick as though it was life itself. Feet on the rudder bar and left hand on the throttle, I was as ready as I could be. Then the flag was dropped and slowly, but firmly I pushed the throttle lever forwards. The engine missed slightly, then began to run up smoothly adding more power to the propeller and I began to roll.

Before the aircraft reached take off, the only controls I had were the individual brakes on each wheel and the throttle. I had to wait until I had enough speed to get sufficient air flow over the rudder to give any real steerage from the rudder bar. Now came the big surprise for me - I had to exert a massive push with my legs to get the rudder to respond at all. This had been one of the problems which had been brought about by our instructors. It seemed they had never really trusted us to take complete charge of the aircraft on take-off. Apparently, they had always taken most of the rudder control and thus we had never really felt the full weight before. I soon learned to be brutally assertive with the aircraft, I really took command and managed to fly the machine rather than respond to its apparent wants. After the first, almost disastrous, solos the system was changed and we were allocated, in small regular groups to one instructor. In this way he became much more familiar with our strengths and weaknesses and, as a result, we began to do much better.

My first solo - note the barracks to the right of the picture with which many of us nearly collided.

The first hurdle for the young pilot was the A-2 licence. This required a given number of solo flights, the practising of emergency landings both with and without the instructor. On the occasions when we were to make emergency landings solo, we would fly to a designated field out in the country where one of the other instructors was waiting. At about two-hundred metres we would cut the engine by switching off and glide down to about 2-3 metres from the ground, before cutting the motor in again. The instructor would either signal that we had passed or that we were to do it again.

Another exercise like this began at about seven-hundred metres above the landing cross. Here, once more, the engine would be cut and we had to glide the aircraft down in a spiral circuit to finally line up and land close to the cross. This had to be achieved without *Schnirpsen* (light and carefully applied touches of throttle). Some of us became very dextrous at applying the delicate little touches of throttle to better control the aircraft and to give a little lift, without the keen ears of the instructors picking up any engine noise. It was fair game to try to fool the instructors, but it was a matter of honour to own up to *Schnirpsen* to the other members of the group, once the instructors were out of earshot. The training was good and developed the skill of side-slipping, this was to prove very useful later when landing the '109 under adverse conditions.

The A-2, if I remember correctly, required 2,000 kilometres (1,250 miles) of *Überland* (cross-country) flying. I remember my first flight to Magdeburg where I was to make a landing on the very much enlarged airfield. It was the first time I'd ever been there and would, therefore, have no idea of landmarks. Before take-off we had to get the weatherman to give us his forecast and to stamp our *Bordbuch*. Then the instructors would check the barograph in the tail of the aircraft so that, upon our return, they could see if we had been flying level and at the correct height. You must remember that we had no radio and there was no such thing as air-traffic control. Similarly, if we got lost, it was our (illegal) practice to find a railway station from the air and then to dive down low enough to read the station sign and find out where we were. This too would show up on the barograph and earn the unlucky pilot a heavy rebuke from the instructor.

My first long distance flight to Magdeburg was to be a real education for me. It was a case of trying to consolidate all of the theoretical work into a practical result. We had had some time to prepare our routes at our desks, taking into account wind speed and drift, air speeds and fuel consumption. The flight plan had been checked and approved and it was with confidence in the navigation but apprehension about the flight, that I started up and taxied ready for take off. I was soon airborne and knew that I would have to adopt my first compass heading. There was the first problem, the compass wouldn't settle. In theory you just glanced at the compass, which would read 270° (Magdeburg) and follow that course. In practice it swam before my eyes varying by tens of degrees. The result was that I very soon became lost and had to find my way back to Werder. There, I started out once more, and this time I flew a little steadier, cutting down the compass swing.

In formation in an early cross-country flight.

Learning to fly long distance solo was a very sobering experience. If I had to say that there was one single part of my training where most things came together and I learned most, it would have been there, in that lonely, windy, cold cockpit. It really was a kind of maturing for us, and for some the effect was much more dramatic. From our *Kompanie* (120 men) we lost about 10 trainees whilst they were accruing kilometres, *Überland,* for their A2 and B1 licenses. Ten men and ten aircraft - a staggering price. Young hopes, dreams, lives and potential obliterated in a few seconds. Their epitaph, a tangle of aluminum, wires, oil and fuel, mixed with the wreckage of a body which had once served the soul of a friend and colleague.

It was not only on the *Überland* that we lost our pilots. More often it was due to the practice of unscheduled aerobatics at a time when we had not been fully trained in control. Looping-the-loop was a popular manoeuvre as were short periods of practice Dog Fighting. These extra-curricular activities were difficult to monitor by our supervising instructors when we were just a group of trainees out on a Squadron Strength *Überland.* Five to seven of the little bi-planes would take off and form up, making for a common objective. During the flight it would become obvious that one or more of us was ready for a little unscheduled activity. Before long, each of us had become involved in dangerous manoeuvres and, unfortunately, sometimes the consequences were fatal. Then, for a few days, we would all become model trainees, but it never lasted long.

The trouble was that the instructors didn't fly with us at all on the *Überlands.* We had to fly the nest sometimes and, unless we were observed, they had no idea what we were up to. During the flights, the unscheduled descents to read rail station signs or directions on the motorway would be spotted on the barograph record. But, manoeuvres, whilst airborne, did not show up. There would be a slight climb, then a drop in altitude and a slight climb. On the barograph it was just an apparent reaction to turbulence. In fact, it had been a high speed loop which had stretched the control of the trainee to the limit. Young people will always stretch themselves to their limit, it is all part of growing. The trouble with doing this in the air is that nature is completely unforgiving of this youthful folly. If you lose control, you can't just pull over, recover your wits, then have another go - you die.

Recognising that it was the unscheduled aerobatics which caused most of the fatal accidents, the instructors tried as best they could to limit our games. They soon realised that many accidents had taken place in the vicinity of a pupil's parent's, girlfriend's or relative's home. The cause was apparent - showing off. Soon they had a register of all 'significant sites' for the pupils and training routes were designed to avoid this kind of temptation. I, for instance, had a statutory ban imposed upon me from crossing the Main River, to the south of Stuttgart, let alone getting near to the town itself.

I didn't have too many narrow escapes. I don't know if I was naturally more skilled than the others or more cautious, I don't think that either was the case, maybe I was just lucky. Those that did occur were usually beyond my control. The closest I ever came to death during the early days of my training was a case in point. When I recall the memory of this, even after all the years that have since passed, I still feel the knot of panic in my stomach, the smell of petrol, shouts of alarm and willing hands trying to pull me from the twisted mass which had, seconds before, been my aircraft.

Accidents happen when you least expect them; that seems to be a fairly universal rule. This day was no exception. I remember that it was sunny and clear with a light wind, ideal flying weather. We were all flying circuits and bumps, that is, take-off and landing with one circuit of the airfield. There was a strict control by means of flags and, when danger threatened, by use of flares, either red or green.

I had finished four or five circuits and was making my way back to the neutral zone behind one of the other trainees. I was keeping a very close check on our spacing, ensuring that I didn't run into his tail. With the tail of my aircraft down and the engine rising in line of vision, this was only achieved by swinging the aircraft left and right on something of a serpentine course by using alternate brakes. This, of course, required concentration and we tended to rely on the other pilots to play their part and to avoid us in turn. As we made our way across the field I concentrated on the front left because this was were I could see the aircraft in front. Quite why I don't know to this day, but I suddenly looked to the right, towards the take-off line. To my horror, I saw the silvery spinning blur of a propeller and the menacing outline of an aircraft as it hurtled towards me on a collision course. I had less than a second's warning. It must have been sheer instinct which made me duck down into the relative safety of the cockpit, just before the shattering impact of the propeller. I was thrown sideways and felt the pressure of the mangled wreckage pressing down on me.

There had been a tremendous rending of metal and splintering of wood, but I was still aware of regular high speed impacts as something, which I took to be the propeller of my aircraft, continued to beat. From the overwhelming experience of the initial collision, I gradually began to be able to sort out different sounds and feelings from the overall trauma – the vibration and hacking of the prop, the tearing and crushing of the structure of the aircraft and the knowledge that I must act. 'Ignition Off!' was the phrase which burned in my mind. 'Must get the ignition off.' Bent over the joystick, I was aware that the instrument panel was above my head. I felt

75

upwards, cautiously, to where I thought the switches might be, and found the toggle switch which controlled the electrics. I switched off. Then I became aware of a metallic pinging sound as hot metal cylinder fins and exhaust manifolds began to cool and the menacing ptsst... ptsst... ptsst... as fuel from ruptured feeder pipes dripped onto hot metal. I then became conscious of the shouts of my friends and colleagues as they made their way towards the tangled mass. Over the top of the others I could hear the almost hysterical voice of Mr Harms as he shouted, 'Get out! Get Out! ... Fire! ... Fire!' I suddenly came fully to my senses and tried to move, but I was firmly held. I was still in my harness and one of the cylinders of the radial engine of the other plane was pinning my shoulder. My stomach knotted with fear as I imagined the sudden explosion and fire; the horrors of slowly burning to death erupted into my mind. I had to swallow a scream and try to think calmly.

Willing helpers reached into the tangled mass and pulled at my clothing, nearly wrenching my arms from their sockets, but still I was held firmly. In what was actually only minutes, but seemed like hours, enough help arrived and the two aircraft were physically ripped apart and I was released. As I looked back at the tangled mass of wreckage I felt fortunate indeed to have only suffered minor injuries. There had been no fire. Luck must have smiled upon me that day.

The aircraft which had collided with mine was piloted by an army captain who was training for the *Luftwaffe* and his A-2 licence. He was loosely attached to our training cycle, but got much more solo flying than us and was allowed to be much more his own master. On this day, because flying conditions were ideal, the field was very busy. That, in itself, need not have been a problem, but it didn't leave much of a margin for error. In this case the captain had mistaken two of the flags on the field for those of the take-off line. He had been sitting in line with three other aircraft, awaiting the signal to begin the take-off run. When it came, he opened the throttle and began the run. However, probably because of the yawing of the aircraft as the tail lifted, he aligned himself with the wrong two flags. One was the small flag that marked the middle of the neutral zone and the other was the last flag on the take-off zone. The result was that he accelerated right through the neutral zone where I was, quite legitimately, manoeuvring to get back to the take-off line. I had been very lucky to survive the collision, the margin had been slim indeed. The splintered wooden propeller of the captain's aircraft had sliced through my helmet just above my ear, just breaking the skin. The rocker covers of one of the cylinders of the radial engine had caught my shoulder and broken one glass of my goggles, but nothing more. Just inches more and the collision would have been fatal. As it was, I was taken to Postdam for x-ray and a check up. The only injuries were the cut on the head and a sprain of one of the smaller bones of the hand. The army captain was not allowed to continue training at our field. I suspect that it was his rank that had prevented more serious action being taken.

That evening, as was the tradition, the *Zugsführer* threw a grand party with lots of Sekt (German champagne). The party was a simple device to make you turn potential tragedy into triumph. It must have worked because, after all of these years, I find it easier to recall the ebullience of the party than the terror of the accident. This was the case with much of the emotion we felt during those heady years. I have to search for the feeling of tragic loss for each of my friends who were killed or mutilated during the training, but the good times flood back.

One of my most vivid memories was of a party when our team-spirit really came to the fore. As platoons we soon identified ourselves as being of one tribe or pack. Our individual *Zugsführer Leutnants* would be the pack-leaders and we soon felt close enough to them to hatch practical jokes. One time, under the leadership of Hans Rudel[1], we physically carried the small DKW car of the *Zugsführer* of another platoon up the staircase to the officers' mess. There it was left and, as the next day was Sunday, it fell to the *Fahnriche* (NCO Cadets) to bring it down, in full daylight, to the catcalls of the 'erks' who were about.

Besides flying there were other activities which became more of a recreation, such as sailing. We were introduced to sailing in the Olympic *Jolle* and soon learned the rudiments of the art. Hinnerk Waller really had the edge on me as far as the sailing went. He had come from the north coast of Germany and was familiar with the crafts of the water, whereas I had had little time to study sailing, living at the top of the *Schwäbische Alb*. Apart from the fact that the sailing was an enjoyable part of our training, we could also develop it as a real recreation at the weekends. On the huge Havel lake, south-west of Berlin, we hired sailing boats and spent many relaxing hours tacking up and down the great lake. To be sure of a sailing boat we would book in advance but, if on the off-chance we went without booking, we could always get canoes if there were no dinghies available.

At the Potsdam end of the lake was a stretch of water known as the *Zeppelinhafen*. Here there was a superb cafe and restaurant where we could take five o'clock tea; that was the name given to the afternoon to early evening dance. Thus we could enjoy an afternoon's sailing on the lake and round it off with a few hours dancing. I have very warm memories of those days.

*The party - following my flying accident.
I am in the centre with bandaged head.*

Other training was in driving, right up to and including heavy goods vehicles. At that time there was a special licence for lorries, but the *Luftwaffe* insisted that we learned the proper technique, although we would probably rarely sit behind the wheel of a heavy lorry again. That was all rather mundane, though it did have its moments.

More interesting by far, was our introduction to motorcycles. Being young, the powerful motorcycles better suited our temperament. Again we were to take a full course on the machine and this included cross-country riding and some very hair-raising downhill slaloms. On the open road the competitive spirit of youth would bubble up to the surface and cadets would speed past the instructors, only to come to grief on wet leaves on a corner, or more often simply, 'run out of road'. The net result was that we soon had a number of trainees in the hospital with broken legs and other injuries. The authorities quickly decided that we were all of a standard to 'qualify' with a minimum of experience; we all got our motorcycle licences first.

Back at Werder, the training in the air was progressing with many accidents and incidents, one of which involved a friend of mine, an Austrian named Fischer. Every Thusday from 16:00 hrs to 18:00 hrs there was *Kasernenabendstunde*, a kind of religious sermon, which was given one week by the Catholic Priest and the next by the Protestant Pastor. Both of them came to us from the nearby Garrison Church at Potsdam. The first hour was a formal military-type service but afterwards there was the opportunity to debate with the priests the many facets of religion, as it affected their particular dogma. I was from a Protestant background and Fischer had been brought up as a Catholic, but we both shared the desire to quiz the priests on their convictions. One idea in particular was the cause of much heated argument with them - the subject of how best to behave to ensure that you went to Heaven. Both of the priests received the same spirited attack from myself and Fischer but it is fair to say that the Catholic seemed less able to accept our questions and to enter into free debate. He obviously disliked our apparent irreverence, and more than hinted that our attitude, for instance, was a fairly sure way to eternal damnation rather than the bliss of Heaven. I could accept that view I suppose, but I wasn't prepared for the ruthless way in which he was later to try to drive the message home.

The opportunity for the priest was offered by an accident, which is often the case. A clear, bright day offered good conditions to get many of the pupils into the air. I was on the ground, as two aircraft began to approach the field. Naturally our attention was taken by the sound of the motors and we turned our heads to watch the approach. To our horror we could see that the two aircraft were on a collision course, one above the other. The pilot in the lower aircraft was concentrating on his approach and had not checked the six o'clock high position behind him. To be fair, it was a very unusual area for another aircraft to be, except, of course, under combat conditions. The pilot of the higher plane would have his twelve o'clock view obstructed by the engine and fuselage and to the sides by the lower main-plane. The higher man was descending faster than the other and collision was inevitable.

For a few seconds we were struck dumb, not knowing what to do. Then Mr Harms ran out firing red Very Pistol signals in warning. The pilot of the lower aircraft saw the warning and pulled back hard on the stick, not realising that the danger was above him. There was a sickening impact as the propeller of the top plane smashed into the cockpit of the other aircraft. Inextricably tangled together the two fell to the ground. We raced across the grass in record time, myself in the lead, probably spurred on by the memory of my recent experience. As I ran I wished, 'Don't burn! Don't burn!'

I was the first to arrive, my chest heaving from the effort and my mind racing. It was encouraging to see that the wreck didn't seem too bad, but when I looked into the damaged cockpit I found myself looking into the open neck of my one-time debating friend Fischer. The slicing propeller had virtually decapitated him, exposing the ivory white bones of the spine in stark contrast to the frothy red of the torn flesh and blood. The sight was like a hammer blow, I staggered back, I couldn't look any more, but the vision was burned in my memory, as clear today as it was all those years ago. I was profoundly shocked by this experience and thereafter I tried to avoid seeing the aftermath of accidents of all kinds. I couldn't stand the thought of repeating the horror of that day. Although the other pilot escaped virtually unharmed, there was no *Sekt* Party that evening. The outcome of the enquiry was that it had been an accident. There had been no other way of warning Fischer of the danger from above. Without radio communications we relied completely on visual signals and these could be interpreted in different ways. In this case, Fischer had probably thought that something which he couldn't see was wrong and pulled up and away from where he thought the danger could be. However, even after the full military funeral of Fischer, the case was not closed for me.

At the next *Kasernenabendstunde,* the Catholic Priest decided that he would capitalise on the death of this atheist and preached powerfully about the fate of non-believers, stating clearly that there was little or no chance that the likes of Fischer could ever get to Heaven. I couldn't believe what this 'Man of God' was saying. I shook with anger inside and slowly got to my feet. Without asking any formal permission, I started to leave the room. I was so choked with my contempt for the man, that I hardly noticed that the rest of the trainees felt likewise. Outside the hall I looked back and found to my surprise that the priest was alone, everyone had walked out on his 'lesson'.

We took a vote and elected a speaker to represent our feelings to the officers, but nothing was done. Therefore, we had no choice but to take the law into our own hands. Risking Court Martial for disobedience of orders (virtually unthinkable in the German Military Machine), we refused to enter the hall when this 'Holy Man' was present. After the second mutiny, he was replaced. As the years have passed I have wondered if he and Fischer ever met again, and if so - where?

When I look back to those very strict military days, I'm amazed that I didn't get into more trouble. I have always been of a fairly strong nature and not afraid to voice my opinions. This, of course, is not desirable behaviour within the inflexibilities of the military. Mr Harms was already a bag of nerves and my appearance amongst his trainees did little or nothing to help his condition. *Graf* Perponcher became my principal mentor, although he didn't behave like most Prussian noblemen. However, he still liked to be addressed as '*Herr* Graf'.

We seemed to get on very well; he had more faith in my ability than myself, however confident I seemed to be on the outside. Sometimes it seemed to me that he pushed us too far, too fast. I had progressed to aerobatics and found I could perform the manoeuvres without undue distress. Climbing spirals, both left and right, spinning and spin-recovery and basics like loops were all part of the programme at this level. Again, we seemed to reach a watershed for some of my peers - the aerial aerobatics were too much for them. For days they tried to hang on in, but they were being airsick and feeling nauseous even hours after flights. They would lose weight and finally they would have to come off the course. Most of them went to *Luftwaffe* Anti-Aircraft Units. I felt very sorry for them, all of us having come so far.

Back, in shirt and tie Graf Von Perponcher - next right
Uffz Habberkornand next - sitting on the ground Fischer.

It was about here that *Graf* Perponcher decided that I would fly the Arado 66, an aircraft which I hadn't expected to meet for a while. It was a step to the B1 licence which I would have to take, but I thought it was a bit of a leap forward for me. A couple of the top cadets in our platoon had already been in the Arado for a couple of days but I hadn't expected to 'graduate' yet. I'd had a few problems with the vertical climbing roll (part of the *Kunstflugschein 1* (*Kl* - Aerobatics 1) and had only just begun to master this when I was offered the chance to fly the Arado.

Perponcher took me up in the Arado, did one circuit and landed. Then he handed over to me and pronounced that I was ready for my first Bl solo. I didn't share his confidence, but I was willing to try. It was a complete surprise and I suddenly found that I was alone in the cockpit staring at a totally new control and instrument layout. Although I was nowhere near confident, I just couldn't say 'No'. My gut feeling was that I wouldn't make it, but something, maybe my pride, wouldn't let me step away from this challenge. I was equally sure that this must be the epitaph of many young pilots. There I was and there I was going to stay.

Fischer's funeral

I manoeuvred the big bi-plane onto the takeoff line and then shouted to the fellow who was holding the flag. 'Arndt! Arndt, now that the big fellow has got out, how do I change the trim to be a little more forward? Is there a handle or lever for that?' He only just heard me over the steady thump of the 240 hp engine. He thought for a moment, then, cupping his hands around his mouth, he shouted back, 'A small round button to your left, push it forwards a little.' I gave him the 'thumbs up' and made the adjustment. Then, heart in mouth, I looked up to see Arndt drop the takeoff flag and I pushed the throttle fully forward, full power. Quickly I gathered speed with the big aircraft bumping majestically over the grass and gradually lifting off. I felt like a real king, to be able to complete this exercise without mishap. Ahead of me lay the lake, which was in the direction of take-off that day, but I was still too full of my success to worry about anything going wrong.

That is exactly the time things go wrong, of course, when you least expect it! At 150 metres and still climbing I had eased the throttle back a little, but suddenly the big eight cylinder motor started to splutter and cough. Then it quit. I went from the exhilaration of my success and the roar of the engine, to the lonely isolation of the cockpit with the only noise being the wind shrieking through the wires and over the surfaces. 'Oh boy!' I thought to myself, 'My first Bl solo and I've got a real emergency to cope with.' The training took over and the instructor's voice started to bark from my memory, 'Look for a good field! Select one and then stay with that decision! Even if things turn out worse later.'

I estimated that I would make it across the lake and I could see a good-sized field close to the shore line. I brought her around on a suitable glide path and made my approach. All was going well until I saw a power line, strung across my approach. I had to bring the nose up a fraction to hold height and managed to clear the lines, but I had now encroached on the available landing ground. I had to lose height and get her down soon or I'd be out of field. Sideslipping in a strange aircraft wasn't easy, but with a little rough treatment of the stick I got her down and we came to a halt in about a hundred metres, nearly standing the aircraft on its nose. The ground was very soft and the wheels had almost sunk in. I'd been lucky. I was very proud of my flying; first time out in the Arado and I pull off a successful emergency landing!

Unstrapping myself, I hopped out of the cockpit and made off to find a telephone. This was our next instruction. Get to a telephone, let us know where you are and give us some idea of what went wrong. Damn! In my welter of self-congratulation I had forgotten to look over the plane and see if I could determine why the engine had failed. Still, I'd only been walking for five minutes or so and I quickly back-tracked to have a look at the Arado. I climbed back into the cockpit and switched on the ignition. All of the instruments jumped into life and I began to see what story they told. It didn't take long, fuel pressure 0! I took a look down to the left where I had altered the trim and found that there were two round buttons! One black one marked 'Trim' *(Vorwärts - Hinten)* and a red one marked *Brandhahn* *(Auf - Zu)*. Very smart indeed. Before take-off I had closed the fuel supply. My great self-esteem and pride at handling the landing so well drained out of me into the wet marshy ground. I pushed the red button back to the 'On' position, and self-consciously made my way to a farm house to telephone. This time I didn't hurry, I wasn't looking forward to making the call.

I couldn't own up to my fault on the telephone, so I just said that I'd lost fuel pressure. I was congratulated on my successful landing and told to return to the aircraft. A truck was already on its way with some fuel, a mechanic and so on. Other aircraft in the circuit had seen mine and reported the location. Also, two instructors were going to fly a Stieglitz and land it close to the Arado. I dawdled back with little enthusiasm for the next few hours. I knew that no mechanical fault would be found on the plane and then I'd have to tell them what I'd done. I really felt foolish.

When I got back, the Stieglitz was already neatly parked near to the Arado. The instructors had checked the instruments and controls over and had nothing but praise for my landing; but they were mystified as to why the engine had cut out. All indication was that there wasn't a fault. I couldn't lie to them, so I just told the truth and waited for the bawling out, which I felt would follow. But it never came. They didn't seem to mind too much, it had been an accident and no real damage had been done, apart from my pride, of course.

When the truck arrived, we all got together under the wings around the fuselage to lift the heavy Arado out of the mud. This done, one of the instructors started her up and back tracked to the edge of the field. When he was sure that all was running well he decided to taxi the length of the field to check that he could reach flying speed before taking off. But things must have gone better than he thought and he simply gave the Arado a boost of throttle and she rose out of the field and cleared the hedges with ease. The Stieglitz wasn't so heavy and posed no problems, in a few moments it was airborne, following the Arado back to base. I had the ignominious reward of a ride back in the back of the truck with the mechanics and other personnel. But that was after the farmer had given us a first class lunch. He thought it was quite the most thrilling thing to happen on his farm for years!

Although my emergency landing had been of my own making, it was still an excellent piece of flying for a cadet, although I could never really congratulate myself, having caused the problem in the first place. Other accidents were avoided by sheer dint of good flying by pupils. A case in point was Martin Lensch. He was at a more advanced stage of training, already up to his B2 and flying the low wing monoplane, the Junkers W 34. Again we were on the ground and saw him take off but all was not well. Whilst bumping over the rough grass one of the undercarriage legs had come loose and was hanging down. There was no radio and so we had to rely on crude signals and hope that he would read the right message.

After a five minute circuit Martin came back to the field for a landing and saw the red Very Signals which were fired up close to him. He retracted the flaps and made a low pass to see if he could get a clue as to what was wrong. We held up a round plate, about one metre in diameter, to indicate 'Wheel' and he indicated that he understood by waggling his wings as he climbed away for another circuit. By the time he returned, we had another board with 'R' (to indicate *'Rechts'* - Right') and, again, he apparently read it correctly, waggling his confirmation. On the next circuit he had slowed and was making a landing approach. We held our breath as he flew close to the ground with the right wing held high - it was a practise run. Then, around he came again, this time very close to the stall speed of the Junkers. Right wing still held up, he managed to get the left wheel down and slowed the aircraft so well that, at last, when the right wing came down, there was no damage at all. He was carried shoulder high from the plane and not without due cause, for the same aircraft was up in the air the very next day, such had been Martin's skill. That evening there was a huge party with many bottles of Sekt.

I had established a kind of friendship with *Graf* Perponcher and learned more about him. He had made a substantial amount of money by delivering a Junkers 160 (the main competition of the time to the Heinkel 70 'Blitz') via Russia to China, no mean feat in those days. The Junkers was an advanced aircraft, low wing monoplane, all metal with retractable landing gear. He was a very experienced pilot and a good instructor. He had quite forgiven me for almost crashing the Arado 66. I think that he felt a bit guilty about bringing me on too fast perhaps. We pressed on and soon began the night exercises.

To reach the B2 standard we had to perform 20 night landings on the Junkers W 34. This was a really hefty aeroplane with very heavy controls. I thought that it was more like driving one of the big trucks than flying. The previous day *Graf* Perponcher had told me that I would be checked out on night landings the following evening and should report to the field for 20:00hrs. I had done enough daylight hours on the '34 and so I took off and began the wide circuit of the airfield. About halfway around *Herr* Graff took over to show me the correct approach. We came around and lined up on some lights and then began a descent. I thought that he was just demonstrating the alignment on the lights and setting the aircraft up for a landing, but it became increasingly obvious that he intended to land. I cleared my throat and said in the calmest voice that I could manage.

'*Herr* Graf, excuse me but those are not the landing lights for the field, they are the lights of the main street of Werder!'

He grunted an acknowledgement, 'Here,' he said, 'you're much better at this anyway, take over.' It was then that I caught the strong smell of whisky on his breath.

He slumped back in the seat beside me and left me to it. So I virtually did my first night landing on my own. When we got down *Herr* Graf got out, and one of my peers took his place, and I went on to complete another six landings.

The spring and summer of 1937 were very good days for us. We were flying and even whilst on the ground we had plenty of sports to keep us fit and active. We had Olympic standard instructors, and many interests in new sports were started at *Flugsschule*. Hans Rudel, for instance, became interested in the shot-put, a sport which he practised at every opportunity. Later, even during The Battle of Britain, he kept the heavy shot beside his Stuka so that he could practise during stand-down time.

All around us there was a new vigour and vitality, Germany was beginning to grow again, to regain her pride. After the First World War Germany was morally and spiritually devastated. Most of her menfolk had fought a war they felt they should have won, had the leadership grasped the initiative at the right times. But instead, they had become bogged down in a war of attrition that could only have had one result, given that one side had the support of the whole British Commonwealth and the formidable industrial power of America. Following the armistice, the soldiers found their way home. There were no parades or marches, just a lot of tired and injured men, sick of war.

My father had fought in the infantry and later transferred to a heavy machine gun unit. He had been commissioned and returned home as a decorated officer. But there was no warm welcome for him from the people for whom he had risked his life, only gangs of communists who tore off his rank marking and decorations and beat him badly. Thereafter had followed the internal problems of the nation, trying to rebuild the economy and industry whilst straining under the yoke of the *Versailler Diktat* [2] . East Prussia had been estranged from the rest of Germany as the Polish Corridor was allocated from Poland to the coast. Alsace and Lorraine in the Rhineland were taken by the French, as were the phenomenal reparations. Germany was being bled white by the victors. It may have been that the first war was avoidable, but the conditions at the end of it, and the subsequent punishment of Germany, probably made the Second World War inevitable.

The inflation of the twenties, the thousands who starved to death, the uprisings and political strife within Germany were well documented. But what, perhaps, is not so well recorded was how this offered the chance for Hitler and the National Socialists to come to power. And once having gained power in 1933, they began to reshape the nation. We became part of the building process. Having seen the privations and heard them discussed at length by friends and relatives, we were proud to be part of the building process. The *Versailler Diktat* limited Germany to a 100,000 man army and forbade her to have an airforce. Hitler flew in the face of that and developed an army in secret - in Russia. Then came the airforce, which I was to become part of. We searched for clues. Were we doing the right thing? Was it right to build up forces in contravention of the Treaty?

The Rhineland, always part of Germany, had just been sliced away, acquired by the French. East Prussia was now cut off on the other side of a vast tract of what was once German soil. We had to ask the Poles for permission to visit our own people in the annex of Germany. And the Germans who lived in the occupied zone - all the time we heard reports of the mistreatment by the Poles, driving them from their farms and beating them up in the towns. Reports in the newspapers and short news films at the cinema verified this.

Lastly the Austrians - they seemed to hunger to be part of Germany. In Vienna, what was swish or chic was German. The styles, the dances, the music were all German. Many, many, young men like my debating friend Fischer had left the Tyrol to come to Germany, to join her armed forces to fight, if necessary, for another land. Every clue we could get seemed to clearly state that we were right.

I'm sure most of us knew that we would go to war in the end, but war with Britain or America seemed to be a very remote possibility. More likely we would clash with France or even with the Russian Soviet, but thoughts then were more of defence than attack. Only later, as confidence grew, were plans laid to repossess what we saw as ours. In the meantime, in 1937, the talk was of the Spanish Civil War and how a fighting unit from Germany was to be sent to fight with Franco. It was to be called the Legion Condor.

Notes on Chapter 4

1. Hans Rudel (see page 65) - became an outstanding Stuka pilot, destroying over 700 tanks and armoured vehicles in Russia.

2. *Versailler Diktat* - The Treaty of Versailles was never accepted as being fair in Germany. It was therefore referred to as a *Diktat* - an order or instruction.

CHAPTER 5 - 1937

Der Reichsparteitag in *Nürnberg*

As is always the case, the youth of the country cannot see the dangers of impending war. To us there was no doubt that Hitler, together with *Reichspräsident* Hindenburg, Fieldmarshal from World War I and hero of Tannenberg, were on the right course. It was patently ridiculous to have French Troops in the Rhineland, seventeen years after the signing of the Treaty of Versailles. Hitler was the first politician to speak up clearly and to voice what so many of the people felt about the Treaty. It was no wonder that he had the backing of the people when he began to attack it. In spite of the human problems which were generated by the Polish Corridor, Alsace Lorraine and the Rhineland, none of the preceding governments had wanted to act. When Hitler, with his highly emotive speeches, explained how much to the advantage of the victors the maintenance of the Treaty was, he won applause and more votes.

There was hardly a voice to be heard against him, so cleverly did he and his colleagues present the case. The *Reichspropagandaministerium*[2] was brilliantly managed by Dr Göbbels, releasing the appropriate stories to the papers, rewarding and encouraging those editors that extolled the Party line by placing them high on the list for further confidential information, whereas those who did not print the truth were systematically frozen out by lack of material. Similarly well orchestrated were the Olympic Games, when the eyes of the world were on Berlin. Many hearts and minds were won there by the skilled presentations and tactics of Dr Göbbels and his staff.

The obvious risk of building up the armed forces didn't worry us too much. We knew that it was a risky enterprise, especially with the *Luftwaffe,* but it was the only way forward. The invasion of the Rhineland had been a real bluff. Most of the *Ju* 52s were loaned civilian types and the majority of the fighters didn't actually have any armaments at all. Still, having overcome the first of the thorns in our national side, it was time to address ourselves, one by one, to the rest. We applauded this action, every step gave Germany back some of her land and much of her pride. If only the French, for instance, had known how weak we were and retaliated, we wouldn't have stood a chance. Virtually all military units had the same standing order, 'If any resistance is met - withdraw.'

After each campaign every unit had the same litany read by the commanding officer at a full dress parade. All personnel would be fully armed and in field kit. The band would be playing as they assembled and then the CO would read his prepared speech. The same speech was read throughout the services, no local improvisation was allowed;

'Once more we have been instrumental in the rationalisation of a compromising situation, inherited from the destruction of Germany and the Austro-Hungarian Empire, to the advantage of the German people. Towards the progress of the economy and, most importantly, towards the progress of Europe.'

Now who was to safeguard this for the future? It was the *Wehrmacht,* the Army, the Navy and the Air Force. It was us who would provide the cutting edge for the sword, with which Hitler would achieve ultimate justice and freedom for the German people.

Everywhere we looked we could see that things were improving. No more deaths from starvation, no more inflation and no more unemployment. We had begun to lead in Europe again. Germany was the first to build the *Autobahns.* German Mercedes and AutoUnion cars were first over the line in the major European car races. Aircraft from Junkers, Heinkel, Dornier and Messerschmitt were flying higher, faster, further and more economically than any others in the world. The economy was booming and with the formation of groups like *Kraft durch Freunde* (*KdF* – Strength through joy), people who worked hard began to travel outside Germany on cruise ships, returning with first hand experience of the plight of other parts of Europe and extolling the virtues of the German way. A great national pride had been restored and we backed further progress all the way. The quicker we build up and consolidate, we reasoned, the less chance there will be that we might lose it all again.

The Nürnberg Rally was one of the means of re-enforcing the power of the Party in the minds of the people. Every year the great rally took place and the newsreels and newspapers were full of it. With such scenes, how could we possibly fail in the future? Although the thought of being present at such an event was thrilling, it was cooled by the practical fact that if we were chosen to participate, we would fall behind in our flying time. And really that was all we wanted to do, fly more and more and get onto the powerful fighters and bombers as soon as we could. Then it was made clear to us by the platoon leaders and *Hauptmann* Pilger that anyone who volunteered and was selected for this period of substantially harder drill instruction would have their flying time made up double after Nürnberg.

We would have priority over all other pupils until we had caught up on our hours and gone in front by a comfortable margin. That was a good incentive. The other was pride. We were still treated as second class soldiers by the other two, more senior, arms of the *Wehrmacht*. We still had to suffer the cat-calls of *Schlipssoldaten* whenever we were in the company of the army or the navy. Similarly both the army and the navy were naturally proud of their traditional mastery of military drill. Our instructors confided that it was the intention that we should put the senior services to shame by producing an outstanding show of marching and drill.

I had wanted to participate, always having had a liking for these exercises. It had only been the thought of losing out on my flying-time that had prevented me from volunteering right away. There was something very satisfying in being a member of a crack drill unit. I don't think it is anything to do with it being a military exercise, I've never really been a militarist, but something about being part of a well-trained team. Precise and well-executed drill looks good whether you are soldiers, Boy Scouts or the Salvation Army. There is some kind of pride and spirit which you see creep into a raw platoon, the first time that they march in harmony, the first time that all the boots come to attention together and not as it has been for weeks, 'like the sound of a cow shitting' as many of our *Gefreiters* would have it. (Corporals worldwide seem to have a knack of expressing the vernacular in the most apt and colourful way). I don't know what the mechanics were, modern psychologists might call it 'group reinforcement' or similar, but at the time it was just a good feeling when 120 rifles were slapped in unison to *'Präsentiert das Geweeeehr!'* (Present Arms) or the united crash of the same number of boots just two full paces after the order *'Kompanie Haaaaalt!'*

There was to be one platoon from Werder - and the whole *Kompanie* was tested as individuals before the final selection for training was made. One platoon out of each of the *Luftkriegsschule*, Gatow (also in Berlin), Dresden and us at Werder. The three platoons would make up one *Fähnrichskompanie*. Just one company, a third of the *Luftwaffenbatallion* that was to represent the new arm of the *Wehrmacht* at Nürnberg. The other two companies were drawn from the *Fallschirmjaeger* (paratroops - an elite unit, tasked with guarding only the most sensitive installations and personnel of the *Luftwaffe*). We were to take on the tradition and expertise of both the navy and the army and to try to beat them at their own game.

There would be a flypast by aircraft of the *Luftwaffe*. There would also be a representative parade of machines from the army, so there was no real competition there. But to take them on at their own game was the challenge. I managed to qualify for selection by the individual tests and then our training began. It wasn't too bad, but our flying really suffered. It almost became a treat to climb into an aircraft for a short flight, to feel the freedom of the air again. Very soon we were off to Nürnberg, hoping that our mission would be a success.

We arrived by train in the middle of August 1937 and were conducted to the Zeppelinfield where a small city of large and well-ordered tents had been erected. Like everything at Nurnberg it was on a grand scale, a show-piece. From there we would be transferred every day to the practice ground where the rehearsals took place. It soon became apparent that we were better prepared than the competition and it was many of the army *Feldwebel* who raised an eyebrow to see the *Schlipssoldaten* march and drill.

Nürnberg Zeppelinf eld - our tent city

At first the idea was that we would march past in *Kompaniefront,* that was with a whole platoon (thirty) in a row, three rows to the *Kompanie.* The aim, apparently, was to reduce the actual time that it took the whole parade to pass the dais. The idea was fine for marching in straight lines, but when it came the wheeling right or left - the men on the outside couldn't keep up - even if they broke into a run. The result was chaos. The Infantry Commander almost wept as he saw the mess, he couldn't seem to understand why things didn't work, 'But they are all hand-picked men!' he would shout. Soon, the plan was changed and we reverted to a more workable formation, *Zugsbreite* (platoon after platoon), each in three rows of ten.

Our tent - I am standing in the doorway.

First would be the Navy, then the Army, followed by the three platoons from the arms of the *Luftwaffe.* We, the Ensigns, would be bringing up the rear, the *Fahnriche.* The whole parade was orchestrated to military music, via a complex network of loudspeakers. As we approached the parade line we knew that we were being watched by Hitler, Göring, Hess, Göbbels, the whole crew. We couldn't pick them out, of course, they were amongst the vast crowd high on the *Tribünen.* The order *Achtung* was called on the right foot and we would then have two clear paces before we all stepped up into *Achtungsmarsch* (goose-stepping) as one man. Then there was about 150 metres to be covered in the highstepping traditional march, before we could revert to normal. Now came the plan - our *Kompanie Kommander* had decided that we would try to steal the show and so, after passing the *Tribunen* and all the celebrities, we completed the 150 metres specified but did not relax as the other units had. We marched in superbly polished style all the way to the end of the stadium. The effect on the crowd was electric, raising a huge roar of approval as we, in our own way, saluted them. In a second they were on their feet in thousands and clapped us until we were lost from their sight. The manoeuvre had been a success, the *Schipssoldaten* had come of age.

Still high on our success we handed in our rifles and were released to enjoy ourselves for the rest of the day - we had earned it. We roved around in a group, proud of our pale blue uniforms and yellow collar patches. Even the tie didn't seem so bad any more. A drink was in order and so we marched into 'Robert Ley[3] Halle'. There we found a real festival atmosphere, like the *Münchner Oktoberfest* or the *Berlin Weissbierfest;* good 'oompah' bands and lots of beer, all served at long wooden tables. We took over the larger part of one of the tables, joining an elderly couple who, when seeing our *Luftwaffe* badges, congratulated us on our performance in the parade.

The place was filling up and the tables getting full when a group of *SS Junkers* came in, arrogant from the outset, in their field grey uniforms and sinister black collar patches. Right away they began to throw their weight about, demanding the places where the elderly couple and their friends were sitting. We decided that this wasn't on and stepped in. Very quickly the situation became heated and more than one of us was reaching for his short parade bayonet. Bloodshed looked inevitable; there was no reasoning with these SS cadets.

Fortunately, an arbitrator was at hand in the form of a senior *SA (Sturm Abteilung* - Brown Shirt) who stepped in to calm the situation. It was obvious from his badges of rank that he was a very senior official, a real *Goldfasan* (golden pheasant) and both sides respected his seniority. He seemed to be an intelligent man and a great diplomat. Soon the situation was resolved with the old couple and their friends staying, we even had a beer with the *SS*, but they soon melted away, leaving us to enjoy ourselves. It had been our first contact with the SS and not one which recommended them well in our minds. They were just young cadets like us, drawn from all over Germany, but already their attitude was insufferably arrogant and extreme. Certainly we didn't want to have anything more to do with them whilst we were in Nürnberg.

After the drill parades and march pasts were over there were the 'military might' demonstrations, which we were able to see. They took place at the Zeppelinfield and for many of us it was the first time we had seen simulated attacks. It was most impressive. Co-ordinated infantry and tank attacks were supported by fighters and dive-bombers. Actually a little old fashioned by later standards but at the time, a frightening demonstration of military power. The dive-bombers were still the HS 123 biplanes and the fighters, a mixture of He 51s and Me 109s, but with the 123s screaming down making a hell of a noise and the fighters beating in at zero feet over the crowd, you couldn't help but feel the military might that was stirring in the heart of our country.

The Luftwaffe flypast at Nurnberg

In many ways we were sad to leave the spectacle of Nürnberg to return to the routine of training. But our officers and comrades honoured us upon our return. The newspapers had carried favourable reports on the *Luftwaffe,* and we had certainly done much to bury the derisory *Schlipsoldaten* with which our senior services had tried to label us. Also, the officers were true to their word and the Nurnberg veterans were given priority in flying and training and soon we were qualified for the *Militarflugzeugführerschein*[4] which, amongst so many other things, meant that we could wear, for the first time, the treasured *Flugzeugführerabzeichen*[5] (wings). Now we felt like pilots, although we still had a very long way to go.

The next part of the training was to be attached to a real *Luftwaffe* unit. In my case it was to a bomber unit equipped with Do 17s located at Schwäbisch Hall where, by coincidence, I had served out my *Arbeitsdienst* a year or so before. Again, we were mixed so that we would get to know the trainees from other two *Luftkriegsschule*. So there were five from Werder, five from Dresden and five from Gatow. This had been done with the Hollerith punch card machine and we all had names which began with 'S'. Thus the group was made up by Steinhilper, Stendel, Strehl, Stangl, Staiger, Schmidt, etc.

The contrast from flying school to a combat unit was really striking. I felt really honoured to talk to a battle hardened *Oberfeldwebel* who had done a nine-month tour in Spain with the Legion Condor. They talked real tactics, learned from experience in the front line, and we young lads sat entranced, hanging on every word. It was both thrilling and frightening to realise that what we were really training for was a shooting war where only our skill would tell if we survived to tell our stories or not.

Up to that time I hadn't had too much experience in what could be called front line aircraft. I had done aerobatics and even flown a few hours in an He 51 at Werder, but that was already obsolete as a fighter, the 109 was years ahead of it in all respects. Similarly, we had not really come into contact with any of the new generation of bombers. I had flown the lumbering Junkers W 34 single-engine and the twin-engine FW 58 *Weihe*[6], but not the Do 17, this was something new again[7]. Firmly strapped into the cockpit of the twin-engine bomber we were treated to a hedge-hopping cross-country flight and participated in both high and low level bombing exercises on the nearby range.

All of this was done as an observer/navigator, the Do 17 being of a different class for young pilots like us[8]. I did, however, manage to get a unique experience on a Heinkel *Kadett*, which had been fitted with skis. We were now well into the beginning of the winter and the weather conditions had been consistently poor for flying. I was beginning to feel that I'd never get back into the air again. Then, one very icy day, I was offered the chance to take the little *Kadett* up. I was so anxious to get back into the air that I wasn't too worried about the strong winds. I climbed in and fastened my harness, but I had hardly pulled the straps down firmly when the howling wind really took hold and I was sliding along out of control. For a moment I was completely lost. There were no brakes to apply, and looming large were the huge steel doors of the hangar. In desperation I pushed the throttle full into the firewall and, at last, I felt some side pressure on the rudder; I had control again. The concrete apron of the hangar was just sheet ice and the wind still toyed with my little *Kadett* as I tried to keep what little control I had. I was so anxious to fly again that I just rode it out until I could see my way clear and then just let her go. With a few bumps and the rumbling of the skis I felt the lightness which comes as the plane breaks contact with the earth, and I was up into my medium again, the freedom of the sky.

Landing was exciting in the same way, but I had learned a lot about the feel of the aircraft by then. Still, there was no way I was going to get it back into the hangar unassisted and so I cut the motor and, with the help of some mechanics, we manhandled the Heinkel back into the comparative shelter of the hangar.

Training with the squadron was alright but I wasn't too keen on the very heavy drinking in the mess. There was a hard core of aircrew and pilots who had served in Spain and they seemed to be really well-off financially. Spain had been an outstanding experience for them, a new lifestyle, and they seemed to feel that drinking was an integral part of their status as 'veterans'. We had to spend many of our evenings in the *Kasino,* as the officers mess was known, mainly, as we were told, so that we would learn and improve our social graces. The weather played a significant part in the drinking activity at night. The worse it was, the less flying was done, the more morose the pilots got, and the more they drank. This affected us badly, being the butt of some of their more unpleasant drunken behaviour.

We, the *Fähnriche,* had our meals in the *Kasino* and often got involved with the Spaniards when we didn't want to. On one occasion about twelve of the fifteen ensigns were present in the mess and were ordered to stand in a line in front of the audience of experienced officers. They had decided that we hadn't been correctly 'tanked up' and orders were issued to the white-coated *Ordonnanzen* (mess orderlies) to supply glasses of beer to us. Then one of the officers would order *'Gewehr über!'* (literally weapons up - present arms) and we all had to empty our glass. Then, before the beer had had time to reach our stomach, the orderly was pressing another foaming glass into our hand.

This lasted until we could hardly stand up anymore, or still worse, like myself, we began to vomit. It was an awful spectacle, twelve young men, the product of a year's intensive training, the cream of the new officer corps, vomiting and crawling over each other like animals. The officers thought it was a great joke, telling us that we'd still got a long way before we had finished our real battle training. I have never known what to make of that kind of initiation. At one time I thought that it might be a process of toughening up for the potential hardships and horrors of warfare. But now I think I might have been too generous and, in fact, it was nothing more than rather childish bullying. Later on, I never imitated the same sort of behaviour myself, nor did I support that type of humiliation when I was an officer.

Rarely did anyone stand up and challenge the orders, in my experience only one, Stangl, with whom I shared a room, who really hated these parades. When it happened again he took it for a while then he refused a beer from the orderly. Tottering uncertainly to attention he announced that, 'If this bloody game is a prerequisite to becoming an officer I'll shit on it!' The audience was stunned into silence, the only sound being Stangl's boots on the floor as he staggered an uncertain course to the door, slamming it shut as he left. In horror we waited for the storm to break, but nothing happened. Once again I learned that you only have to stand up to that kind of thing and it stops. Maybe it's no fun anymore for the perpetrators.

Most of the Legion Condor men had good cars, they'd earned a lot of money in Spain. Traffic rules didn't really exist and nobody was too worried about drinking and driving. A visiting circuit usually involved many of the local *Gasthäuser,* with the crew getting steadily more and more drunk and outlandish as they went. Even in public some of them didn't seem to observe any protocol. The local population was very understanding, dismissing some of their revelry because, 'They had such a hard time in Spain. They must have seen the most awful things. Let them blow off a little steam.' One *Hauptmann* was famed for never running out of beer. Unlike the other Spaniards he had not bought a top of the range car, only a little DKW *Reichsklasse* with two seats and a large-lidded boot at the back. Over the weekend he would put a barrel of beer in the open boot of the car and make a tour, offering people, who he met along the way, a drink. Often he was joined by some of the others and they would tour as a convoy. I suppose it was harmless in a way, but did little to improve the reputation and standing of the *Luftwaffe.*

After the incident with Anton Stangl[9], we were not required to attend the *Kasino* so often. Instead, we were allowed out of camp to the town of Schwäbisch Hall, something for which we heartily thanked the guts of our comrade, Anton. Although it was a forty minute walk, it made a change to get away from the airfield. It was now January 1938 and *Faschingszeit* - a kind of celebration with extra dances, parades and many costume parades, etc. It was a nice time for us. We had discovered a special place called *Ritter* which, no doubt, our officers would have found to be below them. That, for us, was a positive endorsement of an establishment. There was good music, a small dance floor and we could meet a few of the local girls. Best of all, it was within our price range.

In the middle of the floor was an old wood burning, pot-bellied, iron stove which was the only means of keeping a reasonable temperature when it was below freezing outside. One evening, for no apparent reason one of our number went berserk and attacked the stove with his bare hands. He wrenched the angled stove pipe off the back, burning his hands in the process, and releasing the flames and smoke right into the room. Suddenly people were screaming as some of the paper garlands caught fire, and for a while all hell broke loose. We managed to get him under control and to put the fire out with buckets and fire extinguishers. Soon, all was back in order and our poor comrade couldn't remember a thing that had happened or why. Maybe it was just an accumulation of stress and alcohol which had to boil out in some way. The net result was that the owner called the police and they took his name. We reported it to our Group Commander and he wasn't unduly worried, but it must have come to the ears of the Base Commander, who had already had a lot of trouble with the mayor, and that was the end of our friend's career as an officer. It was especially sad in his case because he had worked his way up from the ranks and was proud of his achievement. We argued on his behalf but it was no use. He handed in his equipment and was on his way back to his old unit, a very disheartened young man.

On a lighter note we were invited to participate in one of the parades which are part of a *Fasching*. We had permission from the base to decorate one of our trucks as a float. There were lots of local bands and one from the *Luftwaffe* which provided traditional music along the whole of the route. We youngsters caught the eye of many of the housewives and they threw candy to us from the windows. Later, we received many invitations to households for tea and to meet the family, especially when there was a young daughter approaching a marriageable age. It was refreshing to be with a family again and to meet the girls, but not much else happened in those days.

When *Fasching* was over, so was our time with the bomber group. As we packed up the decorations, so it was time to pack up our kit ready to return to Werder where stage three of our training awaited us. That was how it was planned but we were the first course and nobody really knew what we were to do during the next nine months. Then, as though it had always been part of the carefully planned curriculum, it was announced that we were to be sent skiing - to improve our health and fitness. I thought that it was a great idea, having grown up on primitive skis on the Schwäbische Alb. During our time together we had already exchanged many personal details and I knew that it was only myself and a chap called Sigi Gruel who had any experience. So, not for the last time, I was appointed as ski instructor along with Sigi.

I had learned to ski in Ochsenwang as a child[10], but Sigi had been a ski instructor. After finishing high school, he had taken some time out to earn some extra money. In the summer he was a tennis coach and in the winter he taught skiing. Certainly he was an excellent skier.

Our officers had arranged for the loan of a mountain hut from an infantry regiment for a month. All three platoons would be rotated during that month, us being the first. Sigi and I had been sent forward as the advanced detachment, to get things set up for the rest of the platoon. The hut itself was ideal for us, really out in the wilderness, a complete break from the strict routines of flying school. It was situated near to Oberstaufen/Steibis, but there was nothing really local at all. An infantry *Feldwebel* was in charge of the hut along with two cooks.

The Skiing Trip: Lower left Leutnant Möckel. Right from the third
set of skis from the left Willi Hoffman, myself, unknown,
Siggi Gruel - in the white jacket at the back.

They had things well organised, ready for their first guests from the *Luftwaffe*. Straw mattresses were laid out, together with clean linen. Everything was prepared. We wondered if things were always done this well or if instructions had been issued to show these *Schlipssoldaten* how the army didn't do things by halves.

Sigi was an excellent skier and teacher. Although I thought I could hold my own on the slopes, he taught me a trick or two.

Even here, in the snow of the Alps, the army seemed to want to attack the *Luftwaffe* personnel in any way that they could. Always when we met them on the slopes, whether by accident or because the *Gebirgsjäger* (Mountain Troops) were deliberately crossing our path, there would be a little contest. Not that the army were much competition, most of them being Flatlanders who had been taught to ski in the services. Usually the *Gebirgsjäger* would set off, showing us the way it was done. We would gasp and feign being impressed with their skills, then Sigi would set off, leaving nothing but stunned silence behind.

We had three good days together before the rest of the platoon appeared, led by *Leutnant* Möckel, our platoon leader from Werder. He was a pleasant and easy going officer and this was good news, because he wasn't known for his formality and adherence to the rules. Virtually none of the platoon had skied before and were anxious to start. Willi Hoffman, for instance, had never worn skis in his life, but he soon strapped them on at the top of a huge slope near to the hut. It wasn't until he had acquired prodigious speed that he shouted out for instructions on stopping. We tried to help him but it was too late, there was a huge cloud of snow thrown into the air as Willi lost what control he had and came to rest. Typical of Willi, he was up on his feet laughing like a drain, brushing the powdered snow from his clothes. All he wanted to do was to get going again.

It was a happy time for us all. What could have been better than to be skiing with your comrades in perfect conditions after the rigours of months of flight training. It really was a chance to blow off steam. Even in the evenings we were allowed out after a hearty supper. Although the hut was some 500 metres (1,600 feet) above Steibis we would still take a night ski run down to socialise. About halfway down there was a hollow filled with snow. On a moonlit night we had a chance to slow down before plunging into it, but more often than not we would just hurtle into the soft snow on the far side with a gentle flop. As we struggled out, and brushed the snow off, we could here our mates on either side, flop, flop, flop. Luck must have been on our side because nobody was ever badly hurt.

We would use different *Gasthäuser*, but one occasion sticks in mind, and that was when we had chosen to spend the evening in one of the more rural of them. Sigi decided that he was going to get into a competition with a group of local lumbermen, I have no idea why. Soon they were smashing wooden boxes with their bare hands. Surprisingly, Sigi could hold his own. Then, after several other tests they turned to the inevitable drinking bash.

Sigi challenged the lumbermen to a 'Vic' of Enzian (Schnapps). This meant a squadron formation in the form of a 'V' of nine glasses were lined up and the combatants would throw the rough spirit down their throats, each glass in one, Sigi racing against about four of the lumbermen. We tried hard to get them to stop. After all, it would be us that had, literally, to bear the consequences in the form of Sigi's drunken body. But, with the confidence that a few drinks give people, they went on. It got worse as Sigi upgraded the stakes to a *Gruppe* (three squadrons), adding the wing commander's flight (three) to round up to thirty glasses.

Who won, I can't remember but we had, as predicted, to carry Sigi's virtually inert body up to the hut. Very soon he was losing his Enzian through every orifice and was obviously a very sick young man. A few of us appreciated how potentially dangerous his intake of alcohol had been and woke *Leutnant* Möckel. He could do nothing, there was no doctor and by the time we got one up to the hut he would have been issuing a death certificate, not medication. Fortunately, the army *Feldwebel* was a seasoned old campaigner and understood how to treat Sigi. Under his instructions we stripped Sigi naked and then buried him up to his neck in a heap of cow dung outside the hut. The core temperature of the heap was somewhere around 50°C and caused Sigi to sweat profusely, drawing the alcohol from his body before it destroyed his liver and brain and the pungent smell of ammonia stinging his senses back to life. It worked. After a few days Sigi was on his feet, although a little incredulous about his adventures. Personally, I've never been able to take the smell of Enzian since.

It is sad to reflect how many of these intelligent, happy, vibrant young men died in the war that was to come. Just from that group, Willi Hoffman was killed in a '109 during the French Campaign and Sigi, my good friend was a casualty of the Battle of Britain. The majority of the others would not see the end of hostilities either. In all about 10% were to survive.

Notes on Chapter 5

1. *Der Reichsparteitag in Nürnberg* – The Annual Party Rally held in Nürnberg.

2. *Reichspropagandaministerium*-Propaganda Ministry. Although the Treaty allowed a limited Army and Navy, there was a total embargo on an airforce.

3. Robert Ley (see page 90) - Leader of the *KdF*.

4. *Militärflugzeugfuhrerschein* (see page 95) - A certificate like a driving licence which permitted us to fly all military aircraft up to B2. This included equivalent civil types.

5. *Flugzeugführerabzeichen* – Wings (see page 95)

6. *FW 58 Weihe* - Later fitted with floats and used in Air-Sea Rescue (see page 96).

7. To fly the Do 17, He 111, Ju 88 or Me 110 it was necessary to obtain the Cl & C2 licence which included blind flying. This could not be obtained at *Luftkriegsschule*.

8. It was often the case that the bomber was commanded by the navigator/observer who would be an officer, the pilots mostly being NCOs. The observers would wear a golden eagle type 'Wings' which was nick-named the *Weder-Noch* (Neither-Nor) because it didn't really qualify the officers as one thing or the other. In most cases the observer officers had to treat their NCO pilots well or they would find that their bomb patterns suddenly became erratic.

9. Dr Anton Stangl - Shot down in the Battle of Britain (1st September 1940) and now a leading Psychologist.

10. My first skis were slats from a wooden barrel (see page 100).

CHAPTER 6

1938 -1939 The Gathering Clouds

I had achieved the *Militarflugzeugführerschein* and I felt that something had changed inside me, a maturity. I had actually done something which, a year and a half before, had seemed impossible. Even during the infantry training, I had wondered if I would be intelligent enough to make the grade and to live through the apparently mindless behaviour of the NCOs and their exercises like *Flagge Lucie.*

Around Easter of 1938, things were so much different. I spent a few days with my family at Heutingsheim. Helga, my youngest sister was now four and Trude (Gertude) was sixteen. How proud they were of their big brother in his colourful uniform. Best of all were the 'Wings' on my breast pocket. And there were other aspects of my new status as a pilot and officer candidate in Göring's *Luftwaffe* which pleased me. My father's position as Headmaster of the school had been a little tenuous for some time. One of the other teachers held the high rank of *Ortsgruppenleiter* (local party chief) in the *NSDAP* and felt that this entitled him to a position senior to my father in the school, irrespective of his experience or qualifications to teach. However, my appearance seemed to mollify his superiors in the *NSDAP* and, for the time being, Father's position was secure.

All of this helped my self-confidence; I had set goals and I had attained them. In retrospect, those first few concrete steps did much to shape my approach to the problems and challenges that were to come.

I wasn't interested in politics, but what I saw and heard only helped to convince me that I would be part of putting my country back in its proper position in world affairs. All my reference points told me that we were on the right course for the right reasons. The state had figured large in the backgrounds of both my parents: Father had been raised in an orphanage and Mother had received a substantial part of her education via government scholarships. This gave rise to a mood in the home that the government was a generous benefactor and that it was generally right. Germany was now beginning to stand strong, with full employment and a fast growing economy. On the radio, and in the newspapers, everything was success and growth. Hitler had broken the chains of the Versailles Treaty; the new German Eagle was no longer a fledgling.

In the services we remained quite detached from the rest of the population by virtue of our military status. The airfields and barracks were always a little remote from the large towns - generally, 5-15 kilometres away - and were under guard, offering little opportunity for social interaction outside. Sometimes we would go out to local cafes and restaurants by public transport, but even there we stayed in a group, rarely cultivating any local friendships. Even if we did, it wouldn't last long because we were constantly on the move. Sometimes though, friendships did form.

Back in the winter of 1937/38, during our Course 3 at Wildpark, we had to attend dancing classes at Potsdam - platoon by platoon. The idea was to finish us off as potential officers and gentlemen. The girls with whom we danced were an interesting group, mainly from the good class families in the area. It was here that I met Gerda Havemann.

She usually attended some of the other classes but, by occasionally swapping attendances with other girls for various reasons, we came into contact. Once she came with a person who I took to be her older sister and we managed to stay together as a group for much of the evening, having a wonderful time. At the end of the evening I accompanied the girls to the station at Potsdam and, being very excited about the whole evening, I even jumped up onto the running-board of the train to snatch a kiss from the older sister as the train pulled out.

A while later, I was invited to visit the family at their home at Babelsberg, not far from the German UFA film company studios. As soon as I arrived I was whisked aside by the older sister who explained that she was, in fact, Gerda's step-mother. That, of course, terminated my interest in that direction, but Gerda and I got on well enough. Professor Havemann, then in his fifties, had been the composer of the music for the 1936 Olympic Games and for the musical score for the film of the event. This had greatly ingratiated him to Dr Göbbels and the other members of the government, resulting in his appointment as *Reichsmusikdirektor.* However, he didn't fit in with the fawning 'yes men' that surrounded the political leaders and was never shy to speak out regarding music and the direction which German music would take. He maintained that he was an artist, a musician, not someone to blindly follow the orders of people who didn't have his depth of knowledge. Consequently, he withdrew from the post and concentrated on his own work.

Around June, Gerda went off to work in a forester's house near Grünberg in what was then Silesia (now Poland). We wrote to each other for a while and it was obvious that she was lonely. I learned that the forester took guests at the house and so, at Whitsun, I made arrangements to stay at the house, without telling Gerda. She was really overjoyed to see me but we couldn't spend too much time together because she had to work. There wasn't much for me to do so, by the end of the week, I was really glad to get away. We kept up writing for a while and when she transferred to a farm that was nearer I saw her again, but then we drifted apart.

During the third phase of our course the flying, unfortunately, took a back seat. Every now and then we'd be taken to Werder to fly B2 class aircraft, the Junkers W34 and sometimes the Heinkel 51 but we still didn't get any combat training. All of that, we were told, would be done when we joined our unit. Although we were busy most of the time, it was clear to us that the *Luftwaffe* had not yet geared up to train pilots and officers *en-mass*. The curriculum was constantly changing and it became obvious that they were really 'flying by the seat of their pants'. Ours was one of the first courses and the others would be shaped by what they learned with us.

It was difficult because we were training to be both officers and pilots, the officer training being substantially greater than the pilot training. There was the added complication that the German military machine was tuned to the army tradition and, as officer cadets, we had to laboriously learn the administrative systems which ensured that the paper-work flowed in the regulation manner. The *Luftwaffe* was a new arm of the *Wehrmacht* and a lot of the traditional styles of report were entirely inappropriate, but we had not developed to the point where our own administrative culture could take over. The range of work was also quite formidable, including courses on how to write orders, *Kartenwesen* (interpretation of maps), *Bildwesen* (photographic charting) and, of course, *Verwaltungswesen* (admin.); all this time spent teaching us the rudiments of paper-work, but no time on subjects like communications or blind flying. We hadn't a clue how fighters were supposed to communicate or what ground-to-air communications existed. This was because it was a new technique and couldn't be handed down by the army-based teaching staff.

We soaked it all up and tried to make life as interesting as possible, given the constraints. I had become friends with an Austrian, Otto Vlach, who was to open my eyes regarding the attitudes of the Austrian people as they were annexed by Germany. We also shared some odd experiences together, particularly involving *Oberltn.* Schmidt, our platoon's guiding officer. He had not become an officer through the usual route of selection, but had been promoted from NCO whilst serving with the Legion Condor in Spain. Apparently he had been involved in some difficult bombing missions as an observer, and, as a result, he had been promoted to the officer corps. He was obviously not as bright as the other officers and seemed to try to make up for his apparent lack of intelligence by complete adherence to the rules. It has been my experience since that a lot of people who don't have the flexibility of an agile brain take refuge within the structure of whatever rules and laws may be applied. I suppose it really is a case that, 'Rules are for the guidance of wise men and the obedience of fools.' In any event, in our judgement, Schmidt did some foolish things and that would have been OK in itself but, later, I was to discover that there was an ominous side to this man which would directly affect me.

We started to have problems one Sunday when Vlach, myself and another friend decided to stay in barracks over the weekend. We didn't have enough money to go to Berlin and so we bought some bottles of cheap strawberry wine for the Saturday night. On Sunday we didn't dress, but sat around in our pyjamas and dressing gowns, trying to cure our hangovers by finishing off the remains of the wine. Other officers in barracks would not have thought of room inspection on a Sunday, wishing to relax themselves; but not Schmidt.

His quarters were close to our room and he decided to come in and see what we were doing. I suppose we weren't as attentive as we could have been - after all it was our day off. To add to this, I had become a little more relaxed since I had qualified for my pilot's licence and didn't see myself having an extensive military career. I thought I would fly about the world taking photographs for magazines and books rather than being a soldier for the rest of my life. We were also a little tipsy from the wine and the net result was that Schmidt must have been offended by an apparent lack of respect. I answered his questions about us not going to Berlin by saying that I couldn't afford it; that I, as a habit, only went out one weekend in four, preferring to budget my small amount of money than spend it. He didn't like that, it didn't fit his model of a cadet and he inspected my locker, checking my money bag. This just verified my statement because there were only seven pfennigs there. That would have been alright, but in the room was a very good quality radio which was playing beautifully clear music. When I told him it was mine he was confused - here was a cadet who couldn't afford to go to Berlin, but who had a better quality radio than himself. In his mind it must have marked me out as being different and that, to the inflexible mind, made me dangerous. The fact that I had chosen to budget my money and to buy quality things for myself, rather than spending it all in Berlin, didn't fit for Schmidt. The consequences of that encounter were to be more serious than I could have imagined.

*The Sunday morning 'Hangover' session when Schmidt came
in to inspect our room. Left to right - Steinhilper, visitor
(Austrian with German pilots 'Wings') and Vlach.*

I had learned early on to handle my financial affairs positively. That has worked out well and I can confidently say that I have never really had trouble handling my money. Although I only had a little then, about seventy Marks boosted by my one hundred Marks per month *Fliegerzulage* (Flight Pay), my parents had said that we should make it a rule that when I wanted to buy something like my radio, or essentials like my uniforms, they would pay half and I would pay off the rest in monthly instalments. It would be a matter of principle for me to meet the payment and I never once missed. This applied to everything, even my little DKW car which I was to buy later. My parents were happy to contribute, realising that my military career was going to be a good deal cheaper, in the end, than if I had gone to university.

Oberleutnant Schmidt didn't credit me with such planning and merely, I think, imagined that I was making fun of him. This was further reinforced by my next run in with him. Our rooms were on the ground floor and just outside was the path which led to the classrooms. One afternoon, after lunch, I had taken a nap and overslept. Classes started at 14:00 hrs and it was already well past that time. I knew that if I went out of the room on the normal route, Schmidt, if he was in his room, would see me and there would be hell to pay for oversleeping. I decided to shut the door from the inside and hop out of the window. As my feet hit the soft grass beside the path, I looked up to see Schmidt standing there. He stood me to attention and ordered me to write a report on why an Ensign should not jump out of a window. *'Jawohl, Herr Oberleutnant!'* was all I could say. I'd been caught red-handed.

The subsequent report is translated here:

Luftkriegsschule

Wildpark, 5,13th 38.
W i l d p a r k
Werder   111
Course 1938/39
Platoon   F
S t e i n h i l p e r,
Fähnrich.

Task: Why an Ensign should not jump out of a window.

Report for Herr Obltn. Schmidt.

To jump out of a window is an activity which sometimes may be the duty of a soldier, especially at war when it frequently may become necessary. But, just as the individual soldier is not permitted to fire shots at will, he is not permitted to jump out of windows when there is no reason other than his own desire. When he decides to act without reason, he will always be reprimanded for it. Where would we be if everybody just jumped through a window when they felt like it? When an Ensign jumps through a window it is an indication that he has not only lost his good up-bringing, but also his military discipline. Should such behaviour be observed by the lower ranks, it would serve as a bad example in their education.

However, there are circumstances which might require such action - for instance: If a Fähnrich has overslept, he may only prove his zeal by jumping through the window, especially when living on the ground floor. - When a Fähnrich gets into a desperate situation: To reach his goal when there are two roads to take. One is closed and the other is the window - In such a case there is a great temptation to jump. Tactically it is not too smart, when the latter route is under observation and the goal can only be reached with heavy losses.

In such a case it would be quite objectionable for the Fähnrich to jump through the window - he takes a chance that he will damage the window-frame and instead of succeeding, he fails.

As you can see, I had little respect for Schmidt, and a report like this was going to do nothing to ingratiate me to him. Nor was the way in which the report was presented by me.

Two days after the incident I was due to present the report. Schmidt was to teach the class and we had assembled in the classroom before his arrival. All of my mates knew, by now, what had occurred and were interested in the outcome. I decided to read the report out to them from the front of the class, doing my best impersonation of Schmidt. As you can imagine the report was met by howls of laughter and I became so enthusiastic that I didn't notice that the laughing had stopped and all eyes, except mine, were on the doorway. Too late, I looked up and saw that the infuriated Schmidt had entered the room during my recital. He could barely contain his anger as he took the report from me. Two days later I got it back, simply initialled 'Sch'. What I didn't know was that my rather immature goading of Schmidt had resulted in a lengthy report on the unreliability of *Fähnrich* Steinhilper being placed in my personal dossier. It would be some time before I discovered how Schmidt had deliberately poisoned my record.

Around July 1938 the rumour started to spread that we were to be posted to active units before the scheduled date for the end of our course. We were anxious about how the selection procedure would work, but in the end it was simple. Most of us were sent to either Fighter or Stuka units. That was because our B2 rating was sufficient for this purpose, not requiring any more training. Some of the former NCOs had higher, C2, qualifications from reconnaissance or bomber experience, and they went off to more specialised work. We got the impression that the big build-up was in the fighter and Stuka wings and not so much with the bombers. Most of us were happy with the thought of flying the fighters and even the Stukas; we didn't know how vulnerable they would be when met by a skilled and determined enemy.

From the routine of the school, all now suddenly changed. We were packing and saying our farewells as each left Wildpark for his unit. I was happy with my posting - Bad Aibling, near Rosenheim, south of Munich, only a few miles from the Bavarian Alps and not too far from home. The company was good too with two of my friends, Hinnerk Waller and Rudi Schmidt (no relation to *Obltn.* Schmidt), who were posted there too. There was good luck and bad too. We were all desperate to qualify on and fly the modern Me 109, led by *Oberst* Max Ibel, a veteran of World War I, and some Legion Condor flyers like *Obltn.* Pitcairn and Priller. Hinnerk and I were assigned to a still-unnamed group of new pilots consisting, in the main, of *Fähnrichse* and NCOs. Rudi was soon flying the '109 whilst we sat around, not even knowing if we were a squadron or who was in command. We counted ourselves lucky that Rudi still deigned to talk to us at all. The problem was that the *Luftwaffe* was expanding at such a rate that we were always ahead of the industry's capacity to supply modern planes, and the *Luftwaffe's* ability to evolve a balanced structure of squadrons and appropriate personnel. Everyone was 'pulling strings' to get aircraft and equipment and it was those who had officers with the best connections who got the cream of the supplies and personnel.

There was no consolation in being able to fly either. Even the most basic of aircraft were in short supply, but we did get some time in on the Arado 68E, a biplane like the He 51 but with the more up-to-date Junkers Jumo 210E engine which delivered 640 hp. The Arados were supposed to have two fixed guns, but most of ours were without any armaments and devoid of any oxygen equipment.

Nobody even talked about radio communications, let alone see them fitted to an aircraft. I just wanted to fly, so I didn't bother too much with the waiting list for the Arados; I took the alternative. There were a couple of Focke Wulf 56 *Stössers* (Hawks) which had been built for aerobatics and fighter training. They were high wing monoplanes with a fixed undercarriage and the Argus As 10 inverted V8 engine developed 240 h.p. It was a lovely little aircraft to fly.

The officers weren't much help to us at all. They spent most of their time trying to get posted to the more established veteran units. It was mostly left up to us to organise aircraft and to get what flying time we could. But there was still no tactical instruction, though sometimes an NCO, a Condor Veteran, would offer to talk to us about dogfighting. I managed a few hours on the Arados, but still with no gunnery. The flying was great, going up and down the slopes of the mountains and chasing the sailboats on the nearby Chiemsee. Some of the Veterans claimed to be able to blow boats over with their prop-wash, when passing so low over them. I was simply amazed that there weren't any accidents, or at least none I can remember. I had a near miss which taught me how unforgiving nature can be. I had the use of the *Stösser* which was particularly good in the climb, practically hanging on the prop. I was having a great time when I saw some thunder clouds and decided to explore the inside. I built up the airspeed nicely and began a climb right through the centre of the clouds, enjoying the shaking and turbulance immensely. Then, to my horror, I felt the airspeed fall off dramatically and, looking at my instruments, I could see that the aircraft was losing height - instead of climbing I was falling out of the sky. Suddenly, I dropped into the warm summer air again and was surrounded by a cloud of flying ice shards and crystals as it was stripped from the *Stösser* by the warm summer air. I had never thought there would be ice in the summer sky.

As we were really reserve pilots, as far as the rest of the organisation seemed to be concerned, we sometimes got interesting ferrying jobs to do. They were the kind of assignments we all wanted, in the absence of actually joining a fully equipped fighter unit. This one was for Hinnerk Waller, *Fähnrich* Kahse and myself to take the train to Cologne, to pick up three Arado AR 68s. It was over the range of the Arado and so it would mean at least one stop for fuel. It was very short notice but I still arranged a train stop-over in Stuttgart which would allow us to catch the local service to Heutingsheim and visit my parents. The only real problem was our parachutes but, with a few smiles from the railway staff, we checked them in at Stuttgart station as left luggage. It was worth the effort as the three of us enjoyed my mother's speciality, *Sauerbraten.*

We arrived at Cologne on the Saturday, ready to fly out on Sunday morning but the weather officer refused to rubber stamp our flight plans because of threatening thunderstorms. I remembered my earlier experience with storm clouds and was content to wait. But as it was, an alternative route via Giessen was suggested, which would circumnavigate the area of storms. To ease the strain of having to fly and navigate at the same time, we agreed to fly in 'V' formation, with the leader setting the course. We would change around, each having a turn at the difficult task of squadron leader.

The first lap fell to Hinnerk who kept us on course through bad conditions. The Arado was, of course, open cockpit and it was raining heavily - very unpleasant indeed. Hinnerk must have thought to land at Frankfurt but we could see that the sky that way was nearly black and so we stuck to the plan, landing at Giessen. After refuelling, we got permission to proceed if we took another wide detour to land at Karlsruhe, which lies in the flat Rhein Valley. Kahse was to take the lead but soon after we had taken off he began to gesticulate wildly, making signs which we didn't understand at all. Not knowing what else to do I pushed forward, making it clear that I would take the lead. I felt confident to do so as this was on the edge of what I saw as my homeland. Hinnerk seemed happy to follow my lead and Kahse slowly came to form up on the other side of me.

Soon the weather improved and we could clearly see the Frankfurt - Karlsruhe *Autobahn*, and I dropped down rather low, about one hundred metres above the cars and lorries. I saw Kahse drop down even lower, apparently comparing speeds with the cars, then I lost sight of him, but I wasn't too worried as he would only have to follow the *Autobahn* to find Karlsruhe. Hinnerk and myself landed without incident and soon heard the approach of Kahse. He landed and taxied the aircraft right over to the repair workshop. Thinking that he might, after all, have had a mechanical problem, we walked over in the pouring rain to see what was up. Kahse was really mad with me, saying that I'd led them into a thunderstorm and that his Arado had been hit by lightning, forcing him to fly too low. I was shocked, but that didn't last for long. We had only been there a while when a report came in of a bi-plane hitting some power lines which ran across the *Autobahn*, just north of Karlsruhe. Two villages had been blacked out and Kahse had had a very lucky escape.

When faced with this Kahse admitted what had happened, which was obvious from the cuts and burns in the leading edges of the wings. There was no chance that anyone was going to believe the lightning story. We were really mad with him for trying to blame us and left him to it, not bothering to have anything more to do with him. He stayed at the airfield, trying to get the emergency repair crew to patch up the aircraft if he would pay for it himself.

Before taking off on the Monday morning Kahse told us that his aircraft would be ready in two days. The repair shop was only going to make it fit to fly - the full repairs would have been too expensive for Kahse. He asked us to report the damage but we promised that we wouldn't reveal how it happened, we'd leave that to him to explain. We set off on the next leg of the flight which, to me, was the most important. I had originally agreed to lead on this leg because it was over my ground and my mother had told us that she had organised a *Sängerfest* (a local competition for choirs) in Heutingsheim. It was to begin on the Sunday but it also included the Monday which, traditionally, was the children's day. I had hinted that if all was well, we might pay them a visit.

I easily found the site and Hinnerk and myself made a few circles around the area to let them know that we were around. It was exciting to see the mass of people that suddenly erupted from the big tent, all scanning the sky, looking for us. We put on quite a display, diving at full throttle and making hard banking turns, returning at ground-zero to beat the place up. Unusually for Hinnerk, who was a bit of a stickler for discipline, he followed me, adding much to the display which was really quite impressive for such an isolated village. Maybe he felt that he should repay the *Sauerbraten*. After five minutes we took our leave of them and continued on our way. The wind was on our tails and so we decided to bypass Augsburg, and made it back to Bad Aibling in one hit. We waited anxiously for a few days, but no report of our unofficial display came in. The day after our return we reported to our new Squadron Leader, *Obltn.* Robitzsch, that we had lost Kahse due to mechanical problems and that he'd be along in due course. When he did arrive and the truth came out we got a royal dressing down and he was confined to barracks for a week and had an entry made on his dossier.

Bad Aibling was a very pleasant place to be, with swimming and sailing available on the Chiemsee, and we were close to the beautiful and historic town of Rosenheim. I had a new girlfriend, Ruth Schubert, who was living with her foster parents, White Russians, who had exiled themselves after the Revolution. I got to be friends with them and even experienced a traditional Russian Goose Dinner, with lots of vodka to ease the digestion. It was quite a feast.

For the most part we were still part of a military unit and the social side of our lives was secondary to our work and training. My next real assignment was to provide air attack experience for the *SS* regiment *Feldherrnhalle* whilst they were on manoeuvres. I don't know if it was the fact that they were an SS regiment, but there was no problem at all in our squadron getting aircraft and fuel for the exercise. We moved to Neubiberg, north of Munich, for the day and because of this we couldn't take our mechanics. We had, therefore, to learn to start the aircraft on our own. This entailed stepping onto the wing with the cranked starting handle and winding up the starter fly-wheel to a fairly high speed. You then stepped back into the cockpit and engaged the starter, hoping that there was enough momentum in the flywheel to turn the engine over fast enough to fire. If you were lucky it worked first time, but if not, it was a case of try, try, try again. In the warmth of the summer you would really start to sweat in the heavy flying overalls.

Once the engine had fired and could be kept hot, the starting was no problem. To help with this, we generally kept the radiator shutters closed to prevent cooling. This had helped me when our scramble came and my engine fired first time, and I was soon in the formation, ready to attack the *SS*. I suppose this was my first experience of any kind of combat, and a whole host of thoughts went through my mind as we dived on the marching columns and vehicles, watching them dive for the ditches and loose off all manner of blank charges from a whole arsenal of assorted weapons.

Then it started to rain, first lightly, and then, apparently, much harder. What I didn't realise was that the larger part of the liquid which was obscuring my vision was coming from my own engine. I'd just assumed that the rain had become heavier, although the alarm in my mind had started to ring, as I found the peculiar taste of boiled-off coolant beginning to coat my tongue. It was my wingman, who flew towards me, giving the cut-throat sign to indicate that all was not well, that really galvanised me into action. The first instinct was to check the instruments, and I saw right away that the engine coolant and oil temperatures were way into the red. Then I saw that the radiator shutter was still indicating closed. In my excitement to take off, and in the new experience of the attack, I hadn't opened the radiator shutter, and now my engine was close to seizing up.

I opened the shutter and, to my relief, the temperatures dropped. Because the engine stopped boiling the 'weather' improved as did my visibility and we continued our strafing attacks on the helpless Regiment *Feldherrnhalle*. I had only made a few dives and climbs when the temperature began to go up again. I must have boiled off too much coolant when the engine was hot, and now there wasn't enough to take the heat out of the engine properly. I remembered the instruction for this kind of case and decided that the risk of minor damage to the airframe during an emergency landing was preferable to a blown up engine. I cut the ignition and selected a suitable field, remembering my flying school instructor's words, 'Once you've found the field in which you are going to land - stick to it - never change your mind at the last minute.'

This was a case of the last minute, but I stuck to my decision. I had made my approach up-wind to reduce my airspeed and was on course when I noticed, too late, that the field, in fact, sloped downwards in the direction of landing. Well, I was committed and touched down, trying to use the brakes as much as possible to slow up. It didn't work and, still moving quite quickly, I rolled into a ploughed field. Ahead of me lay a ditch. I couldn't risk losing the undercarriage there so I applied the brakes harder and, slowly but surely, the wheels began to dig into the soft earth and the tail began to rise. With a final lurch the tail came right up and the propeller sank deep into the soil. It felt very odd to be that far up in the cockpit, but I climbed down to inspect the damage. I was really depressed now, this was the second accident I'd had and I couldn't help but think that the consequences might be serious.

Taking out my pocket knife, I scraped away the clay and earth from the propeller and was encouraged to see that there seemed to be little damage. Similarly, the rest of the aircraft was sound. Thoroughly depressed I trudged across the muddy fields in my boots and overalls, the rain now returning to make conditions even worse. Every now and then I would have to stop to kick the heavy accumulation of clay from my boots which made them very heavy and walking difficult. When I reached the farm, the owner was completely surprised, having heard nothing. I was able to tele-phone Schleisheim airfield and report my location, asking for fuel and coolant for the engine and also for another pilot because I was too dirty to get back into the aircraft.

After that I set off back to the aircraft with the farmer. He loaned me a huge butcher's knife and with it I carefully excavated the propeller, paring the heavy clay away from it. Then, when all seemed to be clear, we man-aged to get the tail down and things didn't look half as bad as they had. Just as we had finished, the truck arrived and it didn't take them long to find that there hadn't been a leak from the cooling system. It was obvious that the radiator had overheated. We topped up the fuel and the NCO pilot gave the engine a full run up to test that it was ready to fly and could find noth-ing wrong. With our help on the wings, he pushed the throttle fully for-wards and the aircraft was in the air again in no time. When I got back I claimed that I'd had a radiator shutter sticking, half closed, and Robitzsch believed me. In view of the fact that I'd taken measures to prevent further damage and performed a credibly good emergency landing, without dam-age to the aircraft, there was no further action. I was relieved to be off the hook once more.

Rumours had been circulating for a while that Max Ibel was none too happy with the number of squadrons that were operating from Bad Aibling. Two whole groups, six squadrons, were just too much for the lim-ited resources. He got his way and we were soon on the move to Herzogenaurach, just north of Nürnberg. It had been a training centre for basic flying, but that was being run down: the important thing was that we got an official name - we were *1/333*. The Group Commander was *Major* Stoltenhoff and Robitzsch remained as our Squadron Leader. We were joined by another influx of new faces, some were *Fähnriche* direct from the schools and others had been drafted in from other groups. Overall, the situation wasn't a lot different, too many pilots and too few aircraft. At least there were some 109s in the group but none were with our squadron.

Very soon after the move the order came through to promote all the *Fähnriche* to *OberFähnriche*. That was very important because it brought the pay up to the same level as a *StabsFeldwebel* (staff sergeant), which was only one level of pay below the *Leutnant*. All were promoted with the exception of three, *Fähnrich* Helmut Wick[1], who had joined us from another unit, *Fähnrich* Kahse and last, but by no means least, *Fähnrich* Ulrich Steinhilper. I was desperately disappointed, not knowing why I had been left out. At the time I didn't know too much about Helmut Wick's background, but it was obvious why Kahse had been singled out. I was aware that I'd made a few mistakes and had a couple of near-misses but I couldn't reconcile any of those with this sanction. I couldn't get a firm answer from my Squadron Leader and was left to brood about it on my own. One thing which did come from this was that Helmut Wick and I became firm friends, and he revealed to me why he had been picked out for special treatment.

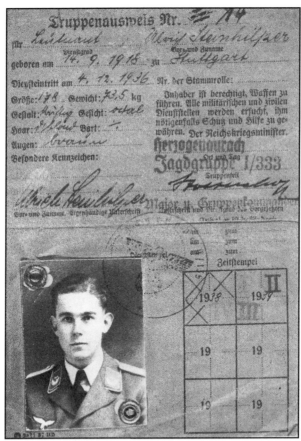

My identity card for my first posting
to Jagdgruppe I/333

117

He said that he had a fiancée whom he wanted to marry at any cost. However, when he had applied to the Officers' Committee for permission to marry they had refused him on the grounds that:

(1) He was too young.

(2) He should forget the woman to whom he was engaged.

Apparently she was a divorcee and the officers didn't want any hint of scandal attached to their cadets. Actually, there are many people today, even in Germany, who don't know of the tradition in the Officer Corps that the committee had the facility to vet potential brides-to-be.

I don't know what he'd said at the time, I presume he must have agreed, but he was determined never to give up this woman. He told me that when the fighting started he would show them all up by becoming an *Expert* (Ace). 'Then', he said, 'they won't talk to me like that any more.' Certainly Wick became a very hungry hunter when the opportunity arose and had the reputation of being a young man 'with a very sore throat'[2]. It is interesting to be able to see, in retrospect, what may have motivated one of the *Luftwaffe's* most successful pilots.

This obviously explained Wick's problems, but I could think of no good reason why I was apparently being discrimated against. I tried everything I could to find out what was wrong but to no avail. I asked Robitzsch and even applied to see *Major* Stoltenhoff, but there was no result. Robitzsch reassured me that I'd be alright in the end, but this was no real help. I felt somewhat ashamed of what I saw as a slight on my character and decided not even to tell my parents. The mystery was only solved about a year later when I was a full *Leutnant* with *1/JG52*. The whole *Gruppe,* under the command of *Hauptmann* Graf von Pfeil and Klein Ellguth, had left Böblingen for gunnery training on the island of Wangerooge in the North Sea. I had been left alone as communications officer and jack-of-all-trades, but as a consequence, I had access to all the personnel files. I took the opportunity to look at my dossier and there, dating back to Wildpark, was the report of one *Oberltn.* Schmidt, detailing his strong doubts about my potential as an officer, 'Wastefulness and an inability to handle money' and, of course, there was subtle reference to the window incident, 'Weak in discipline, a rebel . . . Steinhilper is not the kind of fellow that others are likely to follow . . . etc.' It was a good job that I was already a *Leutnant* then - or I might well have gone looking for Schmidt to make his worst fears for me come true.

Oberfähnriche Helmut Wick (after his eventual promotion)

As it was I still didn't know what I had done wrong, but things were beginning to hot up over the problems of the Sudetenland in Czechoslovakia and the possibility of war galvanised all military units into action and helped, at that time, to take my mind off my problems.

The successful *Anschluss* in Austria had led Hitler to look at Czechoslovakia as the next extension of his expansion of Germany. Czechoslovakia had been created out of a part of the old Habsburg Empire, following the end of the First War in 1918. It was another piece of the

Treaty of Versailles which so offended the German people. The original concept of Tomas Msaryk and Eduard Benes, two exceptional Czech intellectuals, had been to create a system of cantons like Switzerland, complete with its neutral status. To do this, they had to cobble together a people made up of several ethnic races also, historically, like the Swiss. It was the minority groups that would cause the internal problems within the fledgling state. There were, amongst others, one million Hungarians, five hundred thousand Ruthenians, and three million two hundred thousand Sudeten Germans, all of whom looked to the motherlands for guidance.

Early days. I am laughing at something which
Hinnerk Waller has said.

The country was internally unstable as the groups fought for power and to influence the course of the country to the best advantage for their particular race. This was inevitable in any such new creation but Hitler was to use it to attack this part of the hated *Versailler Diktat*. When he became Chancellor, in 1933, Hitler had extended the hand of friendship to the Sudeten Germans and, as a result, a brother party to the *NSDAP* had been formed in Czechoslovakia, the *Sudeten Deutsche Partei* (Sudeten German Party - *SDP*) under the leadership of Konrad Henlein. By 1935 the German Foreign Office was bleeding 15,000 *DM* per month into the funds of the

SDP. Two weeks after the annexation of Austria, Henlein was called to see Hitler and, apparently, plans were made to further destabilise the government of Czechoslovakia by causing the large German minority to formulate demands which could never be met. Exactly the same tactic was used a year later to foment unrest in Poland over the so-called Polish Corridor and the seaport of Danzig.

The German people didn't know anything of this at the time and just saw, with pity, that their fellow countrymen were having a hard time trying to assert their rights in Czechoslovakia. This, of course, was cleverly orchestrated by Dr Göbbels, reporting more and more terror attacks against the Sudeten Germans by the Czechs. In the end the question on everybody's lips was 'When will the government act?' not, 'Should the government act?'

* * *

As the crisis grew so did our state of military preparedness and my personal anxiety about going to war. Our squadron was still woefully badly equipped and we still had not undergone any tactical or weapons training. We had Arado 68s which were capable of being armed, but only a few had guns fitted. Not that this really mattered because we didn't have any armourers to load and maintain them. As the troubles began to peak in mid-May we moved to Straubing near to the Czechoslovakian border, where we were grouped up with some very old Dornier Do 23s. These were known by the pilots as 'The Flying Coffin'. With maximum airspeed of 260 kmph (161 mph) and cruising speed 210 kmph (130 mph) and an open cockpit, it's easy to see why.

It was with great relief we heard that again there wasn't to be any fighting. Apparently the demonstrations of military might - squadrons of fighter and bombers cruising up and down the border between Bavaria and the Sudetanland, and twelve full Divisions of the Army standing in plain view - had been enough to convince the Czech government to accept the help of the German nation to stabilise the internal strife. To help impress the Czechs, and probably to ensure that reports of great military strength were sent back to the British and French, all available units were flown into Czech airfields. We moved to Eger to form part of the occupation force, leaving the Dorniers behind.

The flight well illustrates the 'state of the art' as far as our ability to bring Czechoslovakia to her knees was concerned. We took off from Straubing for the 150 km (93 miles) transfer flight to Eger. There were no armaments, no radio and only one map - for the squadron leader. We formed up in three 'Vics' with *Oblt.* Robitzsch in the lead, we were so close together that we could see each other's faces. The weather wasn't too rosy, but at least the mountains weren't hidden by cloud, waiting to destroy any wayward flyers. After about an hour it became clear to us all that we were off course; we had to be, or we'd have been close to our goal by then. We could see the *Oberleutnant* constantly looking down into his cockpit, checking the map, and then looking over the side, trying to get a good land-fall. Pretty soon he pointed to the map and then threw up his arms in despair. We were well and truly lost.

What a situation, only fuel for about fifteen minutes, no map, and close to the border. We had no choice but to scatter, each going his own way and trusting to luck. In this case I was one of the lucky ones, soon seeing an airfield with trucks upon it. I was careful to make a low pass and make sure the trucks were German, before I entered the circuit and landed. Amongst their vehicles they had a tanker and, fortunately, they were happy to refuel my aircraft without any red tape. They then pointed out the direction of Eger and said that if I pulled up in a climb, I'd see the airfield with no problems.

It took me fifteen minutes to land at Eger but it took the squadron two more days to assemble fully. A few, like Robitzsch and *Leutnant* Rott, had made it first time; others were down on soccer fields, in meadows, any-where there was enough grass. Fortunately Eger was full of aircraft and very busy with constant movements, and the commanding officers didn't really have much time to question the ragged arrival of yet another rag-tail squadron for the 'Front'.

It is interesting to reflect now and to hear the comments of many histo-rians who record that the modern and well-equipped forces of the German *Wehrmacht* marched into Czechoslovakia and that resistance would have been pointless and hopeless. Certainly from my perspective, and that of very many others, we were just a hotch-potch of personnel of very varied experience and training, in aircraft which either belonged in a museum or weren't armed anyway. Another gigantic bluff had come off.

At Eger all was bustle and chaos. It took me a while to find Robitzsch and when I did, although he was pleased to see another of his pilots, he didn't have time to issue any instructions for me or the others. He was too busy trying to locate the stragglers. We were just told to go to town, report to the *Quartiermeisters* (Quartermaster) Office, and to be back at Eger airfield the next day. We took a military bus from the airfield and arrived at the school where the *Quartiermeister* had made his HQ. Our accommodation was to be, inevitably, in a classroom, with straw palliasses on the floor. We had each brought a bag with our toilet requisites, clean underwear and a better uniform. We decided that it was time for us to stage our own invasion and to step out in town.

It was very strange for me and most of the others to be in a foreign town for the first time. Although there was a very substantial German minority in Czechoslovakia, based mainly in the Sudetenland, there were still many shop signs written in Czech. Many of the people had the high-boned facial features of the Slavs and every now and then you'd catch a snatch of a foreign language.

We had German money to spend or it could be changed for Czech at the *Quartiermeisters*, but on the whole it didn't matter to the local traders. Virtually all the guest houses and restaurants were open for business, and there was good beer and tasty food available right away. There was something of a party atmosphere as the *SDP* staged grand celebrations all over the Sudetenland.

Every day there was a lot of flying. There would hardly be a moment when there wasn't a German aircraft in the sky over Eger. Then came the main flypast. The day wasn't ideal, with lots of turbulence, but the chance was taken to put a hundred aircraft into the air. The bombers and Stukas came over the border, but the fighters, including us, joined them from Eger and from the nearby base of Karlsbad. We had never flown in such tight formation, the up and down pitching of the aircraft bringing us with two metres of each other. In this situation I had to give my full concentration, my hand tight on the throttle lever, constantly adjusting the speed of my aircraft. But for brief moments I was able to feel what it was like to be part of such a huge formation which, had it been armed, would have had awesome destructive power.

The flypast was a success and we all landed back at Eger in good order. Jumping down from our aircraft, we dashed in to change and get into town for Hitler's parade. For the best view we stepped into the cordon which was there to keep the crowd from the roadway. Although we just took our place in line with the army boys, we really did stand out in our better tailored uniforms and colourful badges. Before Hitler and his acolytes swept past in the huge black Mercedes, some of the local girls had spotted the few of us Fähnriche in our officers' uniforms and gathered behind us to chat, apparently relishing the opportunity to speak German with Germans. They were very pretty, and it wasn't long before we became friends.

One girl, Traudl Hahn, wanted to know where Hinnerk and myself were staying and was horrified when we said that we had a palliasse each on the classroom floor. She said she thought things could be better than that and explained that her mother had been providing billets for *Luftwaffe* Officers.

There had been two *Leutnants* there, but they had left, unexpectedly, to go back to Germany. Traudl said that if we were quick, we could probably secure the places at her home.

Eger was crowded with all kinds of aircraft typical of the hotchpotch at the time of the Czech Campaign, From the left: Me 109 E, Me 109 B, He 51, Me 109 B Arado 68, Me 108 Taifun.

We had both had enough of the schoolroom floor and in no time at all we were back at the *Quartiermeisters*, asking permission to board out. To our amazement it was treated as routine and as soon as we could pack our bags we were on our way to the Hahn household. It was only in the evening, when Traudl came home, that her parents became aware that we had met before. It was great to be part of a family once more. The Hahns were all in favour of the Sudetenland becoming part of Germany again, but Traudl's two brothers were anxious about their future as they were, at that time, well into their courses at the University of Prague.

The accommodation was excellent and the food top rate, but more than anything, it was good to be away from the Military whenever we weren't actually at the field. In the evenings we went out, most of the time with Traudl. Hinnerk had been made a full Oberfähnrich at the time when I had been passed over and he now wore the full uniform - much more impressive than mine. But that didn't seem to affect Traudl's choice, she seemed to want to spend her time with me. Maybe I was a better dancer, I don't know, but it was nice to be the subject of someone's choice. However, it caused some whispering and a few friendly warnings about the *Taschentraualtar* (pocket marriage altar). Although we became close and I got on fine with her family, it never came to serious plans to marry. After two weeks we were moved out, but I wrote to Traudl for a while; but then we drifted apart eventually. I was learning the soldiers skill of making and breaking relationships.

After the 'Invasion' of Czechoslovakia the locals were pleased to see the Germans back in control. Here the girls cheer. I got to know the girl in bottom left of the picture, Traudl Hahn, quite well. This photograph also appeared on the front cover of the Berliner Illustrierte.

We moved to Herzogenaurach at the end of October, and all of us were promoted to full *Leutnant*, effective from 1st September 1938. I could never understand why they had, at first, so badly disappointed me and then acted as if nothing had been wrong. But then I thought the important thing was that I'd made it in the end and there was no point in brooding about it. (At this time, of course, I still didn't know about the reports made by *Obltnt*. Schmidt). I was just happy to give 5 *DM*³ to the first sentry who presented arms to me as a *Leutnant*, as I walked through the entrance gate of the *Fliegerhorst* at Herzogenaurach.

As a squadron we were still short of aircraft and I hadn't had much leave for a while so I decided to apply for a little time off. There were two urgent things I had to do. First I had to order all of my new uniforms and equipment. This was quite a list, and included my normal dress uniforms, a white summer uniform, formal mess uniform, leather overcoat, jack-boots, etc. Quite a list. It all came to 1500 *DM*, but that was no problem. I just had to sign for it and the *Luftwaffen Kleiderkasse* (clothing fund) would pay the bill. Then they just recouped a small amount from our pay each month. The second major purchase was to be a small car.

I approached my parents with my woeful story of how we were always on the move, staying in remote barracks, miles from any social life. I claimed that if I was to have anything like a normal existence, I would need some transport. They were a little reluctant, remembering the accidents which had occurred when I owned a small moped, but in the end they agreed. They had, themselves, put their names down for a Volkswagen but, at that time, neither of them had made any firm steps towards getting their driving licences.

That was the first obstacle overcome, but then there was the question of actually getting a car. Because of Germany's new-found expansion and rate of economic growth, demand for cars had outstripped production and there was a substantial waiting list for Opels and DKWs - the kind of cars which would be within our price range. Quite by chance, I saw an advert in a Stuttgart newspaper for a DKW. It was not too far from Stuttgart, about 30 km, at Schorndorf, so I decided to take the train and look it over. The car belonged to the owner of a waffle factory and it was a real beauty, I couldn't believe my luck! It was a DKW Meisterklasse, 900cc, twin cylinder two-stroke motor, with wooden bodywork and fabric covering. The upper part was black but the lower panels had been painted a lovely green. It was only three months old and had done just 2,000 km.

I went to the receptionist in the factory and told her that I was interested and the owner, *Herr* Mossle, explained that he, too, was a flyer and that he would be more than happy to sell the car to a *Luftwaffe Leutnant*. He said that he'd just bought the car for fun, to see how it went. He, himself, had a Mercedes and, having a strong national conscience, thought it was too much to have two cars when so many were waiting for one. He wanted a fair price, 2,000 *DM*, and, after just filling in the details of my parents' signed cheque, I was driving home to Heutingsheim in my first car.

Taking my mother and youngest sister out for a trip.
Notice that the seats were removable.

My parents were far from wealthy, but as their treat they said they would meet half of the price of the car and I could pay off the rest to them at 50 *DM* per month. At that time I was drawing about 300 *DM* per month, including my *Fliegerzulage* and I thought I could afford just one more purchase. I traded in my radio for a portable Blaupunkt and this too turned out to be an outstandingly good investment. It was a very heavy thing because it contained a 120 volt accumulator type battery and a mains lead but, with the aerial raised, we could receive many national radio stations and some from France. I used to have it on the back seat of the car when I was travelling and, when I got back to Herzogenaurach, Hinnerk Waller and I used to take it to a café and use it there. At first the people didn't like it, but when we regularly had dance music at five o'clock, and more customers started to come in, we didn't have to pay our bills anymore.

That radio stayed with me right into the action that would follow and, when we were moving around in France, the squadron got better intelligence information through that than through official channels. My little car served me well indeed and was often to be seen en-route to a town or village, hopelessly overloaded with young airmen. It was wonderful in those days and I'll always remember my first car, much in the way you always remember your first real love.

Things were much more stable for us now. The crowd of young *Leutnants* was constantly changing. Helmut Wick managed to get a transfer to be closer to his fiancée but Kahse and Hinnerk Waller stayed. Hinnerk and I were really close friends and we wanted, if possible, to stay together. But we never knew what the military machine might want. When it came to it, personal circumstances and preferences would not be considered. We just trusted to luck that we wouldn't be separated.

Hitler had undone another part of the Treaty of Versailles and Germany had survived. We could not see that this was just another step in a plan that was aimed at completely destroying the Treaty, paragraph by paragraph. Hitler and the *NSDAP* had seen how the Treaty had wounded Germany and what suffering it had caused. If there was one thing they wanted to achieve, it was the final and irreversible destruction of the *Versaillier Diktat* and all it had stood for in post-war Germany.

Notes on Chapter 6

1. Helmut Wick: Quickly rose to fame, being promoted to *Major* by September 1940 and Commander of *JG2*. The circumstances of his death on the 28th November 1940 have been the source of much debate. It is generally agreed that he was shot down over the Channel by Flight Lieutenant John Dundas DFC who was, only seconds later, hit by Wick's wingman.

2. 'Having a sore throat' (see page 118), was common *Luftwaffe* slang meaning that the subject of the reference was apparently desperate to win the Knight's Cross of the Iron Cross. This decoration was worn at the throat and those who coveted it were said to have a throat that was sore - awaiting the cure of the Knight's Cross.

3. Giving away 5 *DM* - (see page 126) German military tradition. All newly promoted officers are duty bound to reward the first sentry who salutes their rank.

CHAPTER 7

Obstacles on the Approach

Sometimes Hinnerk Waller became homesick, which was understandable because he was based a long way from home, and, therefore, he wasn't able to get away as often as myself. I, on the other hand, was based about as locally as I could get. Because of this I would often change duties with him so that he could take advantage of a few days' leave. At Christmas 1938 Hinnerk had been assigned to duty, but he was desperate to be with his family for the festivities, and so I took his duty.

Initially, far from being a task, I found that I rather enjoyed my time at the base. The nights were cold and crystal-clear with thick snow which crunched under the boots. I would make my rounds of the airfield with all of the sentries calling *'Halt! Wer Da?'* Then they would jump to attention and report as I gave the password and stepped out of the shadows. After midnight all of us who were on duty would have *Glühwein*[1] and, really for the first time, I began to feel the comradeship of serving with and commanding a group of men, one of the more attractive facets of a service life.

By New Year it was my turn to go home and I spent New Year's Eve in the elegant Traifelberg Hotel, high on the Schwäbische Alb where there was plenty of snow for skiing. I also met old friends and made new ones. Wilfried Roser was there, having now grown a lot and finished with his school examinations. And it was here that I met *Herr* Rose from the Zeiss Ikon factory near Stuttgart. He took a liking to us and impressed upon me that I should buy an 8mm cine camera, a recommendation which I later followed, and which was to have some interesting results.

We all managed to stay friends, even if our youthful high spirits did run away a bit at midnight. We had circulated through the crowd like a hurricane, removing the fashionable hats from the ladies' heads and then taking

them to the yard. Here we proceeded to blow them up in the air with fireworks - the more fashionable the hat, the bigger the charge that went under
it. I wonder how differently we would have celebrated, had we realised that
it would be the last New Year's Eve where a whole Germany would see
peace.

Later in January, an order came through to join another fighter group,
I/JG 433, which was working up at Manching near Ingolstadt. Several of
us young *Leutnants* were to be moved at the same time, and so we would
be with people we knew. We were leaving Nürnberg and Erlangen and that
had been quite attractive, besides nothing much seemed to happen around
Herzogenaurach. Our experience there had shown us that as a fighter
group, *1/333* was a complete non-entity. We were young and keen and
wanted something that at least had the feel of action about it.

We weren't disappointed; life was better right from the start at
Manching. Our quarters were almost luxurious - each small flatlet had two
bedrooms and a bathroom, with the barracks as a whole set into the woods
of the *Fliegerhorst* (aerodrome). The Group Commander, *Graf von* Pfeil
und Klein Ellguth (Pfeil as he was known for obvious reasons) was as
impressive as his name, and certainly set the style of the new outfit. After
1/333, this *Gruppe* really had the feel of an experienced unit that had teeth
to bare. The Squadron Leaders were all ex-Legion Condor men, *1/JG433* -
Obltn. Galland, *2/JG433 - Obltn*. Ewald, *3/JG433 Obltn*. Klein and *Obltn*.
Woitke - *Stabs Kompanie* (Staff flight). The fact that these were all
'Spaniards' was going to help the Group no end, there was no doubt about
that. We had already learned that within the *Luftwaffe* there was a brotherhood of Condor veterans, a kind of old-boy-network, through which it was
possible to get equipment and to get things done. They also exerted a stranglehold in many other ways, which was to become more apparent later.
But, in the meantime at Manching all was movement and action.

Hardly had we unpacked when a meeting was called to allot us our positions within the squadrons. The Group Commander, *Hauptmann* von Pfeil,
and the Squadron Leaders were there as were some other, slightly senior
Leutnants. Altogether there were ten new *Leutnants* from the class of
September 1938, all looking very much like the new kids in school. The
established officers sat around, slouched in chairs, looking us over with an
air of nonchalance, Galland smoking one of his cigars. *Graf v*. Pfeil read
out our names as we were assigned: *Ltn*. Kirchner *T.O*. (Technical Officer)
1st Squadron. *Ltn*. Geller z.b.v (Adjutant) 2nd Squadron. *Ltn*. Göbel *T.O*
2nd Squadron. *Ltn*. Waller *T.O* 3rd Squadron, and so on. I had barely been
assigned as *z.b.v.* to the 1st Squadron with Galland, when it became obvious that one post had not been filled - that of Communications Officer for

the *Gruppe. Graf v.* Pfeil offered the job around, but as nobody knew what it involved there was silence. 'It has to be filled,' he said, 'any volunteers?' Again there was silence. 'Alright, who is the youngest?' I realised with some trepidation that I was and answered up feeling more than somewhat self-conscious. But I wasn't so overawed by the company that I wouldn't stand my ground a little. I was there to fly the '109 and I wasn't, if I could help it, going to become pilot of a desk only. I asked respectfully if I could retain my position as *z.b.v.* with *I/JG 433* for flying and still discharge my function to the *Gruppe*, whatever that might involve. Pfeil thought it over for a moment, glancing at Galland who nodded his approval, and it was agreed. Thus it was I became *Nachrichtenoffizier* (Group Communications Officer) for *I/JG 433*. Another piece in the jig-saw of my destiny was pressed into place.

After the meeting, we junior officers all got together and fed upon our own enthusiasm. This really did look like a fighter group in the making. '109s were about in numbers and all the squadrons had delivery dates for more in the near future. Also available, and of more immediate interest to us rookies, was an Me 108 *Taifun* - Willi Messerschmitt's predecessor of the '109. It was a four-seater and still in its bright blue civilian livery, but it also had retractable landing gear, flaps and the new and innovative leading edge slats, which operated automatically at slow speeds, changing the wing configuration. It was an ideal aircraft on which to train for the '109. We had the luxury of time with which to be fully experienced before converting to the front line fighter. But later on pilots were introduced to the '109 with precious few hours and with a resultantly high attrition rate. With enough experience, the '109 became malleable and stood up well to the roughest conditions, but it could be quite unforgiving as I was to find out.

Our conversion was done in the '108 under the tuition of the NCO pilots. I don't remember the name of my instructor but my impression is of a soft spoken and competent pilot. I was far from the first to get training and was a little apprehensive, having seen some of the others before me. Many had had problems and these had resulted in broken undercarriages, smashed propellers, bent crankshafts and structural damage to the aircraft: all mechanical - we were fortunate that the damage in human terms was minimal with few, if any, injuries. I was still desperate to fly, but I had to be patient.

As the *Nachrichtenoffizier* I was actually part of the *Stabskompanie* (Group Staff Company), together with the Group *T.O* (Technical Officer) and the Adjutant. But *Hauptmann von* Pfeil wasn't a Condor veteran, nor was he an expert on the '109, and subsequently he wasn't keen to fly with his own *Schwarm*[2.] Neither did I occupy a strong position as the titular adjutant of Galland's squadron. I was heading towards being a military jack-of-all-trades with the usual result. Nobody was making too much fuss to get me trained up and I would have to wait a while but, in the meantime, there were other diversions to occupy us.

Late in January a great event took place. All the young *Leutnants* from the 1938 courses were to be invited to The *Reichskanzlei* in Berlin to meet our country's leaders. The invitation was to the young officers from all arms of the *Wehrmacht* (the army, navy and the airforce). It was the first time that such an event had been planned and was typical of some of the rather advanced management which was used by people like Dr Göbbels. It was all calculated to help bond us to the national leadership and into a homogeneous armed service.

The human chemistry worked - the building was breath-taking and the organisation outstanding. Hitler gave an inspiring speech which set our emotions racing. Then, all as one body, we had to re-affirm our loyalty to *Der Führer* and the German nation. As we lined up in solemn parade, this slight figure stood in front of us, his eyes steady on ours, giving the feeling that he knew us personally, and if we were to let the side down he'd know. It was very emotive and certainly created an impression which was to last - exactly as it had been calculated it would.

The *Luftwaffe* had been the last to be presented and, in the meantime, we began the chant of 'Herman, Herman, Herman!' Göring was there of course, wearing one of his fancy uniforms and beaming like a fat school-boy who had stolen the key to the tuck-shop. Surprisingly he didn't take too well to our salute and left before the formal presentation. He wasn't missed; there was too much to do and see. There was a plentiful supply of Sekt and there were lots of old friends to meet, many of them now in the other services. I saw loads of people from my Ludwigsburg School and from my class in Stuttgart. Werner Ruoff was there as a *Leutnant* in the Infantry and many others whom I hadn't seen for over a year.

So much had happened in just a year and yet this was nothing compared to what would befall us in the coming few years. How tragically depleted that throng would have been if reconvened in the wreckage of the chancellery in 1945; how few of us would have been there in the tatters of our uniforms. But then the future was bright and as bubbly as the glasses of Sekt. Nobody seemed to be interested in closing the party, and so it went on into the early morning. It was a memory which lived with all of us for many years.

One thing I did discover whilst 'talking shop' in Berlin was the sketchy outline of the duties of the *Nachrichtenoffizier*. Many colleagues had been given the same job, and at least I got some idea of which books and manuals to read to get the full specification. The more I read, the more I began to realise what was involved. The *Nachrichtenzug* (Communications Unit) should be a unit of 75 men, equipped and trained to operate two 1.5 kilowatt radio stations, together with two field telephone units, mounted on trucks and complete with switchboard, cables and telephones. The purpose of this was to enable each fighter group to be an independent unit which could move at will. There were three platoons allocated to the *Stabskompanie*: the *Werftzug* - the maintenance unit, which was equipped with spares and tools, even lathes, to keep the aircraft and motor transport functioning; the *Nachrichtenzug* - to provide ground-to-ground and ground-to-air communications and to plug into the national telephone circuit; and lastly the *Stabszug* (Staff platoon), who dealt with all administrative matters.

The reason why the *Nachrichtenzug* had most of its equipment duplicated was so that at times of movement half of the unit could be moved in advance to set up communications at a new base, whilst the other half maintained services at the point of departure. The advanced party was transported by air in our own *Tante Ju* (Junkers Ju. 52-3M) which was attached to the *Stabskompanie Staffel* (Staff Squadron). We had the transport, and now it was time for me to appraise my personnel, and this gave me quite a shock. Instead of 75 trained operators I had just 17 raw personnel. The highest rank was *Obergefreiter* and he had served no less than three weeks in 'The Glass House' (military prison). The rest of the men came from various places such as Wiesbaden-Erbenheim, Bad Aibling and Herzogenaurach. They had one thing in common - they had all served time in military prison, none less than seven days. What a bargain I had got! It soon became clear that the supply units had taken the opportunity to clean house at my expense. What a hand-picked and highly motivated workforce I had! We had an aircraft to move the unit when necessary, but instead of 75 trained operators, three *Unteroffiziers* and many specialist *Gefreiters*, I had this motley crew of misfits. And as for equipment - that really consisted of my own Blaupunkt radio - nothing else had been thought of. It wasn't the ideal proving ground for a young officer for whom this was the first experience of man-management and logistics.

I went to *Graf von* Pfeil and discussed the situation. He naturally consulted the 'Spaniards' and here we got a taste of what was to come -indifference. 'Why all the fuss?' they asked, 'We did OK in Spain without a *Nachrichtenzug*. Communications was a job for the *Luftnachrichten* units (air support groups), so why try? There was no need to clutter up a fighting *Jagd-Geschwader* with that kind of nonsense.' I could see that I was really going to be up against it here. And things were to get even more difficult when my 'Spaniard', *Obltn*. Woitke, chose to take command of a new fighter squadron which was being formed at Eger. Woitke had at least been prepared to listen to me. But the new commander of the *Stabskompanie*, *Ltn*. Möllenhoff, was only senior to me in service and, being only a Leutnant and not a Condor veteran, the others wouldn't listen to him whether he was interested or not.

It was a Herculean task for an inexperienced 20-year-old to try to convince his group commander that change should occur but, with the help of the manuals and lists of equipment, I began to make progress. I even tried to convince him to report to *Luftgaukommando VII* in Munich that his fighter group was inoperative without any communications, but that was too big a pill to swallow initially, although I didn't feel that I had completely lost the day.

Here I will make some detailed comment on communications and the *Luftwaffe* which is the result of some in-depth research and my own experience. I don't think there would be much argument that the most valuable thing that came out of the Spanish experience was the tactical invention of the *Rotte* and the *Schwarm*. This was evolved by Werner Mölders (know affectionately as *'Vati'* - father[3]) and was to give the *Luftwaffe* the edge in combat for a long time to come. However, I am sure this was somewhat negated by the lack of ground-to-air and air-to-air communications. I have concluded that, at least in the Spanish Civil War, this lack of communications was because the Legion Condor was a clandestine unit and a recording of German language on the radio could have been held up internationally as proof of our participation. But the result was that the 'Spaniards' got used to coping without good communications, using wing signal etc, and these practices became part of the combat tactics. Again, as the 'Spaniards' exerted a stranglehold on the *Luftwaffe* it was extremely difficult to convince anyone that good communications were of paramount importance.

Even today I find the issue very frustrating and it becomes exasperating when I read in *Jagerblatt* (the newsletter of the German fighter pilots' association)[4] June/July 1985 - Adolf Galland's comments about communications in an article entitled '45 Years ago - At the Channel'. He writes, 'Looking back at the Battle of Britain, there was no direct radio communication possible with the bombers, due to the differing frequencies. A situation almost unbelievable, which amongst others had serious consequences when rendezvous points were missed or escorts/bombers were a little late.' When I read this now it still turns my stomach when I think of all the frustrations I had with this man when trying to sell good communictions to the squadron leaders. He and our other 'Spaniards' were so entrenched in their views that they, collectively, put the *Luftwaffe* well behind and may even have cost us the Battle of Britain by their inflexibility. Adolf Galland was against progress in all forms of communications within *I./JG 433* and later *I./JG52*. He could apparently see no reason at all to have *Funkgerate* (FuG) (radio equipment) in a fighter aircraft. Wing signals in the air and a telephone briefing would be sufficient. After all, they had won in Spain, hadn't they? What motivated this apparent obstinacy I don't know but maybe it was a desire to be free in the air, unfettered by a ground-based commander or directions from a bomber group. Equally, it could simply have been a complete lack of foresight; one can still only speculate after such a long time. But it still angers me to read comments by a man who, along with his colleagues, was at the root of our poor communications.

Not everything was negative though. At each *Fliegerhorst* there was a *Nachrichten Kompanie* in residence. They weren't attached to any of the units present, but were responsible for the communications of the field as a whole, including air-traffic control (such as it was), morse, and direction finding equipment for blind flying. The personnel were drawn from the navy and army and were experienced in their role, unlike my hotch-potch of rejects.

As a token of good will one of their NCOs was seconded to me as my *Gerateverwalter* (stores officer). He at least knew the procedures, how to order equipment, where from, and most important, what it was we needed most. Soon a mass of material began to arrive - trucks with huge transformers inside, transmitters, receivers, drums of cable, staff cars and motorbikes. *Graf von* Pfeil was suitably impressed and began to interest himself more in the frantic ministrations of his young *Leutnant*. Now that equipment had begun to appear it demanded attention, he couldn't miss it. I now had four heavy transmitter and receiver trucks, together with trailer power units, two trucks to carry telephone equipment, two 750cc Zündapp motorcycle combinations, two BMW staff cars and two Kübel Wagens to lay out field telephone wires. There were two antenna trucks to come that had outboard 10 metre masts but, in the meantime, I was very proud of my little outfit. All the vehicles, except the two cars, were brand new and caused more than a little curiosity as they were parked up in one of the hangars.

Soon the covetous eyes of the squadron leaders fell upon my small fleet. I still didn't have the staff to man the vehicles and had to borrow drivers from the Horstkompanie and from the squadrons just to collect the vehicles from the depot. 'As this bloody *Nachrichtenzug* has no use for them,' they argued with *von* Pfeil, 'why can't we take them for the squadrons. At least they'll be of use there instead of sitting around in the hangar until God knows when.' The whole tone was that the *Nachrichtenzug* was never going to be used - not if they had their way; the opposition was building, led by Adolf Galland. It wasn't only with the squadron leaders either - my own peers, the young *Leutnants*, were also courting favours from me. All sorts of emotional blackmail were used, pointing out that it was only the 'Spaniards' who had cars except me who was 'lucky' to have my own DKW. I could have screamed. It was nothing to do with luck and if they'd managed their finances positively they might have a car too! But they persisted with 'the old pals act'. 'Surely, it isn't too much to ask of an old chum to lend out a BMW for a weekend. After all, it isn't even yours.' There were all kinds of entreatments which came my way. But, with the help of *Leutnant* Möllenhoff and the determination of *von* Pfeil, I managed to keep the unit intact.

On a 750 cc Zündapp of the Nachrichtenzug, in the background a '109 E with machine guns in the wings (not yet cannon).

Digging my heels in like this did little to ingratiate me with the squadron leaders and other officers. Besides I didn't frequent the *Kasino* (Officers' Club). Because Manching and Ingolstadt didn't have much social life and Munich was only really a practicable journey at weekends, most of the officers spent their time in the *Kasino*, drinking beer and playing cards - sometimes all night. Hinnerk and I had the use of my little DKW and it proved to be a delight. We enjoyed a simpler but, I think, fuller life by eating out in the local towns and joining in with *Fasching* parties. You always found new friends that way. For instance, on one evening we came out of a dance hall to find that my car wouldn't start. I'd had a few drinks, but not enough to cause a problem on the roads in those days, and I didn't notice that I had parked with the exhaust pipe in a snow bank. The crowd was leaving the hall and someone stepped forward and cleared the snow from the pipe and she fired up. I was so pleased that I offered everyone a lift home. They all piled in and, in the end, there were nine assorted males and females, with Hinnerk and myself. Instead of the direct route we went on a midnight sightseeing tour of Ingolstadt, laughing and singing as we went.

We made lots of friends by getting out into the community instead of drinking at the Fliegerhorst, but it didn't help our careers much. If you didn't share the tastes of the majority you became an outsider and didn't attract any favours. My relationship with Galland as my squadron leader became progressively more strained and my flying suffered as a result. I didn't get a single hour's instruction from him; he always had more important things to do.

In the meantime, *von* Pfeil, in spite of the resistance of the 'Spaniards', became more active regarding the *Nachrichtenzug*. He called *Luftgaukommando* (area headquarters) in Munich and explained his communications problem. Apparently the answers were evasive - 'Try to do the best you can - you're not the only unit with problems.' etc, but he kept on trying and began to call some of his friends in the higher echelons of the *Luftwaffe*. It soon became clear that the rapid build-up of the *Luftwaffe* had left much reliance on good friends for progress. There hadn't been time for too much consideration, and neither promotion nor good assignments necessarily went to those with dedication, ability or a proven work record - it had mainly been done on personal recommendation. This is why the 'brotherhood' of the 'Spaniards' was so dominant in the early days. Things were expanding so quickly that it was often the dog that barked loudest who got the bone or, at least, the dog who knew someone who knew that he needed a bone. I received great help and encouragement from the *Nachrichtenzug* of the *Fliegerhorstkompanie*. With their assistance I drew up daily schedules of training for my personnel and, as I hadn't anyone qualified to train them, the *Horstkompanie* did much of the actual instruction as well.

We were making progress, but things were too slow for my liking, I hadn't enough personnel and I was desperately short of NCOs. It didn't help much when I was dragged away on other business such as the case of *Gefreiter* Huber.

Most of our equipment came from a depot at *Oberpfaffenhofen*, which is north of Munich. The driver of one of the trucks, *Gefreiter* Huber, had signed for a full load of cables and cable racks, but upon his arrival at Manching one rack, complete with cables, was missing. Huber couldn't explain how the loss had occurred so, for the time being, he was cautioned to be careful. As was the practice, I was required to report the incident in a government periodical which was circulated throughout Germany. The entry carried my name and unit.

Thus it was that one day I was called to answer my telephone to find that I was speaking to a policeman from Donauworth - was I *Leutnant* Steinhilper? Was I looking for some cable drums? I agreed I was and was curtly informed that the police had the drums and they were anxious to interview the driver of the vehicle from which they had fallen. A local farmer had been killed whilst riding home on his bicycle and the cable drums had been found with the body. I really didn't need this kind of problem at the time, what with things being so difficult with the *Nachrichtenzug*, but it would be a valuable experience to appear in court as the defending officer for the airman. However, it was yet another complication which I could have done without.

When the whole truth came out, the story was that the driver had not seen the farmer on the bicycle until the very last minute because it was night-time and there were no lights on the machine. The driver had pulled the truck violently to the left to miss the cyclist and thought that he'd passed him alright. Apparently he didn't realise that the drums of cable had fallen off or, more importantly, that they had hit and killed the unfortunate farmer. The *Gefreiter* was busted to airman, but otherwise he escaped any real problems.

That didn't apply to me though. The 'Spaniards' took it as ammunition to use against this uppity young Leutnant who wouldn't let them play with 'his' cars. 'Now the bloody *Nachrichtenzug* have killed an innocent farmer! Dragging the squadron's good name through the courts and the mud!' On reflection it all looks rather pathetic now, but at the time it really upset me. When I look back at the responsibilities which were loaded on my young shoulders, compared with what, in my later business experience,

I expected of twenty-year-olds, I am amazed that I didn't have some kind of breakdown.

Slowly I was beginning to grow in confidence. *Von* Pfeil and *Leutnant* Möllenhoff were behind me, advising me not only to request the cooperation of the squadron leaders, but to try to go out and sell my product, to convince them of its value. I thought that I'd be a little more subtle and try to win over other members of the personnel first and started to talk with the *Funkwarte* (Radio technician) on the squadrons. They had *FuGs* (*Funkgerate*) in stock, ready to fit to the '109s. Some were trying to fit them in secret, such was the opposition. I worked hard on the *Werkmeisters*[6], getting them to change the frequencies on the quartz crystals, but they were very wary in case the squadron leaders found out, and they told me what I already knew - I'd have to convince the 'Spaniards' before any real progress could be made. I knew that it wouldn't be easy, but it was the only way ahead and I decided to beard the lion in his den. So I went looking for the squadron leaders.

Hearing that both Ewald and Galland were in the same office in one of the hangars, I decided to see if I could speak to them both at the same time. I knocked on the door and entered, my sales patter already running in my mind. But what I saw took my attention immediately and I forgot my best pitch. Tied up close to a very hot radiator was Galland's dog. Being keen on hunting and in particular shooting, Galland always had a retriever of some kind[7]. The dog was stock-still, concentrating on a piece of sausage which had been hung up a few inches from his nose. He couldn't reach it and was probably very uncomfortable - being so close to the hot radiator. My attention now taken by this scene, I asked Galland what was happening and he explained casually that the dog had behaved badly at its last meeting with a sausage and that it would have to learn to modify its instincts. He had sentenced the hapless animal to two hours in its present position. I tried to talk 'radio' but the strange scene had knocked me off balance and I really couldn't recover. Perhaps if I'd known just how influential Galland was, I would have tried harder.

Later, one day when I was least expecting anything radical to happen, I had a message from *von* Pfeil to change into my 'number ones' and report to his office. Then, without any further briefing, I was driven in his Wanderer staff car to the *Luftgau* Munich, the *Luftwaffe* District Headquarters. I arrived in the afternoon and reported to the guardhouse and was immediately ushered up to meet *General* Martini, the senior ranking officer of the *Luftnachrichten Truppen*. It was almost like a dream (or a nightmare) for me. One minute I was employed on my day to day tasks then, a few hours later, and with no briefing or time to prepare, I was standing in front of a general. Like many people who have risen to high rank, he was very approachable and not half the ogre I thought he might have been. I soon felt at ease as he listened attentively to my story, detailing to him how I saw the role of the *Nachrichtenzug*, both in defence and attack. He nodded his head in agreement to many things that I said and then he told me he knew that I had some problems, although he never actually related how he came to learn of them.

As the General listened, and occasionally asked pertinent questions, I reviewed the situation at Manching: there was no shortage of equipment, the hardware was first class; what I lacked was personnel and the skilled technicians to train them. I suppose it was part of the man's skill that he made me feel important and, as a consequence, quite bold with my remarks, especially when it came to the behaviour of the 'Spaniards'. Again he took it all in and assured me that I wasn't alone in my problems. Most of the newly allocated *Nachrichtenoffiziers* were new to their task and had no experience. Also that I was far from alone in my problems with the Legion Condor Veterans[5]. In return for my candour, I was told that things would soon be changing for the better and that my fully-trained personnel would soon be arriving. As a bonus most of them had been drawn from *Abiturienten* (high-school graduates) and the majority of them would have amateur radio backgrounds. But as for NCO Training Officers, he couldn't promise too much. The new communications arm of the services was expanding as fast, if not faster than the *Luftwaffe* and there just hadn't been time to build up the kind of background experience to produce experienced and capable teaching staff. Anyone who showed promise was usually quickly transferred to aircrew, but I was assured that I would get at least one capable NCO and all the help that they could manage from the *Fliegerhorst-Nachrichtenzug*.

After just fifteen minutes, the meeting was brought to a close. In that time, which had seemed to be much more, we had exchanged a huge amount of information and I felt as though things would change for the better. The *General* advised me to try to keep selling the idea to the 'experts' and not be discouraged, things would change in time - they would have to; after all we were on the brink of the nineteen-forties. It was obvious there was a technological revolution going on which was apparent in our aircraft, our cars and, in particular, in the *Wehrmacht*. Communications would have to improve; we would not be able to carry on like a group of small boys with empty tins tied together with string!

Communications would be the key to the future. It would be a tragedy if we were to let the 'Spaniards' continue to live in the past.

With the assurance that within one month a new and much improved course for *Luftnachrichtenoffiziers (NOs)* from the fighter groups would begin at *Luftnachrichtenschule* in Halle, I left feeling that, at last, I was getting somewhere. But I didn't let this go to my head or to hope for too much, I had already been disappointed too often for that. During the journey back to Manching I turned the whole experience over in my mind and prepared myself to brief *von* Pfeil first thing the next morning. I was now hopeful, but it just sounded too good to be true. I thought I'd just wait and see.

General Martini turned out to be a man of his word. Within two months I got over fifty young and highly motivated young recruits, most of whom had exactly the right background. They had spent hours at their homes trying to contact friends on the amateur frequencies, either with the crude crystal-set or, in some cases, with the home-built valve sets. They couldn't wait to get their hands on the shining new equipment which had power potentials of which they had only dreamed. And, true to his word again, I got an experienced NCO, *Unteroffizier* Krehe. He was a good all-rounder with experience of short, middle and long wave transmissions. He was even disappointed that operational fighter units didn't have any plans for direction finding equipment. He was familiar with its operation and considered that it was essential for a fighter group, whilst I was still struggling to get the field-telephone accepted. Here was the only problem, until I could work the unit up as a whole, I couldn't give them a freehand with the equipment. So here I had these very intelligent young men full of technical knowledge and energy, and I had to make some of them sit and operate the switchboard. That wasn't the kind of challenge or stimulation they needed, but it would have to do until we could move forward under control.

Things now began to move on at a pace. Barely had I begun to get to know Krehe and to get him introduced to my friends within the *Fliegerhorst-Nachrichtenzug*, when I was ordered to attend the *Luftnachrichtenschule* at Halle/Saale. The course I was told, was to be of four week's duration and had been specially designed for the *Nachrichtenoffizier* from the *Jagdgruppen* (Fighter Groups). The invitation was also addressed to the individual group commanders who were cordially invited to furnish their attending numbers with aircraft. They would be required to take a '109 along from the group and to undergo practical radio training whilst also providing a live target for the trainees. Halle had a serviceable airfield but no aircraft or pilots of its own. *Von* Pfeil gave his permission for me to take one of the '109 Ds which had been assigned to his staff flight. Things were really looking up for me, I was getting quite excited, but I had begun to learn that this is a dangerous sign. Most times when things began to look so good, there had been a disaster just around the corner and this was just such a case. I didn't know what was waiting for me, just a few days away.

Just before my departure, on the weekend of the 18/19 February, it was my turn to be duty officer. I was the youngest officer and had some knowledge of the operations of the tower from my time with the *Fliegerhorst-Nachrichtenzug*. I'd also had some dealings with the *Wetterwarte* (meteorological service) and ground operations. It was difficult, therefore, to resist pressure when the majority of other officers wanted the weekend clear. I was junior-buck and was capable of doing the job. Senior rank had its privileges, and dumping the job on me was one of them. So it was that some of the officers drove out to Munich, whereas others wanted to get to Berlin. *Obltn.* Klein and *Ltn.* Möllenhoff, my immediate senior, badly wanted to get to Berlin; the official reason being that they wanted to view the Berlin Motor Show because there would be some new military vehicles there as well as the civilian models. We had known all week that our *Tante Ju* would be going to the capital with a night time stopover. Many of the station staff were lining up to get on the Junkers because they had family or girlfriends in Berlin, and this was an opportunity not to be missed.

Now it was Saturday morning and from the tower I could see the Junkers being prepared for flight, but I didn't think it would be going anywhere. The weather was bad and looked like getting worse. It was cold with a low and heavy cloud base and snow flurries in the wind. I kept ringing for the weather but there was no sign that it would improve in the near future and there was also the possibility of icing. It seemed as though every few minutes some hopeful would come in to see if things were improving, but realistically they weren't. There were 450 km between us and Berlin and there was no chance that this could be done without a substantial amount of blind flying. Most of the pilots with a blind-flying rating went to bomber and transport squadrons straight from the flying school, and we didn't have many pilots with the right rating. I had, therefore, to refuse the permission for the flight to proceed. Once more pressure was brought to bear upon me to let them go, another touch of the old pal's act. And again I was in an invidious position, being a junior officer and being the youngest, but I stuck to my guns and kept the Junkers on the ground. Finally *Obltn.* Klein came in to tell me that he had discovered that one of the *Unteroffiziers* on the flight had an IMC (Instrument Meteorological Conditions) rating. That was it - they could go, and in a way, it was a relief for me!

At noon the Junkers 52 lumbered down the runway with its eleven passengers and crew and gradually climbed away into the dark and forbidding sky. Gradually the drone of the three 600 h.p. BMW Hornet engines faded away and I got on with my routine bookings and checks.

Later that evening, whilst I was in my quarters, the tower called me to tell me that the Junkers had not reached Berlin and that it had been classed as 'overdue'. On the Sunday morning the confirmation came, it had tried to clear some hills north of Eger in a snowstorm and, with heavy icing, it hadn't made it. Our old *Tante Ju*, together with eleven men whom I knew and with whom I had worked were now one tragic mess of human and man-made wreckage. The confirmation of the crash and the fact that there were no survivors hit me like the icy blasts of wind which now screamed across the empty apron. I felt the pressure of it all being dropped onto my young shoulders.

On the Monday I had the unpleasant duty of informing everyone of what had happened. It was a kind of punishment I thought. Initally *von* Pfeil had seemed to blame me for the whole thing: Why had I let them take off? Didn't I know that the last word lay with the duty officer? Once more I had to hold my ground against a verbal assault from a senior officer, but hold it I did. I told him about *Obltn.* Klein and the *Unteroffizier* with the IMC rating (which subsequently proved to have been a lie) and asked what chance *von* Pfeil thought I had against an experienced *Oberleutnant* and my own immediate superior, *Ltn.* Möllenhof. I couldn't call them liars, and the rules were clear that they could go if they had a man in the crew with the appropriate rating. Gradually things began to get less fraught and we could proceed with the inquiry in a more logical way, and this is where the true scale of the loss began to come home to us. Old *Tante Ju* had had a valuable cargo in her belly. One *Oberleutnant* Squadron Leader with the experience of the Legion Condor behind him; the *Stabskompanie Leutnant*; the entire crew of the aircraft; another experienced technical man, the *Schirrmeister*[8] *Feldwebel* Lohlein and another four personnel - one of whom had not been on the passenger list at all, but he had been seen boarding the aircraft.

It was with this extra fatality that involvement with the personal side of this tragic affair began. The *Unteroffizier* was not really classed as missing on the Monday, when he didn't return from leave. It was only then that we knew for certain that it was him. It was further confirmed when we got a call from his girlfriend enquiring as to why he'd not arrived as he'd promised her he would. We had to tell her that he'd died in the crash, and it was then that we discovered that she was in an advanced state of pregnancy. She didn't take the news too well. I then tried to negotiate with her and the boy's mother to try to get them together in their mourning, but the mother only wanted to talk about compensation and to ensure that the girlfriend didn't get any money from the *Luftwaffe*. I really made myself some work there, but in the end the mother was happy to stay out of the courts and actually warmed to the girl once she produced a grandson from the mother's only son.

I had my fair share of funerals too, three of them on two consecutive days. The first in Nürnberg, the next in Esslingen near Stuttgart and the last in Hausen, which is near Mühlhausen, just where the *Autobahn* from Stuttgart to Ulm begins to climb the Schwäbische Alb, almost on my home ground. It was this, the last of these sad events, which was to touch me the most. Even today I still think about it from time to time.

As this was the third funeral I had, to a degree, got used to my part in the routine. We had a steel-helmeted guard of honour and a military band playing *'Ich hatte einen Kameraden'* (I had a comrade). At the appropriate time I would call the guard up to attention, and the traditional rifle salvo would be fired over the open grave. Then it would be time to talk to the next of kin as they, recognising that I was from the same unit, would come to find out more about the death of their son. They were just trying to make some sense of what had happened. A few days or a couple of weeks before he had left home in good health and now they had just laid him out in the ground. Why? How did it happen? The truth was that I didn't know much more than they did, and what I did know I couldn't really tell them; it wouldn't have helped anyway.

At this, the last of the burials, I met the mother of an unfortunate *Unteroffizier*/radio operator who had been part of the Junkers' crew. She was a widow, having already lost her husband in the First War. She was a very stolid person and had braved the awful circumstance of being informed of her son's death well. There had been a bit of a mix-up and the usual procedure had not been initiated. What usually happened was that we would call the nearest *Lufwaffe* base and they would send an officer around to the next of kin to break the news personally. In this case that didn't happen and the first she knew about it was when she received a notice to go to Ditzenbach, a village close by with a railway station, to collect a wooden case. She didn't know what was in it and the only clue was its size and weight and the fact that it had been sent from Eger. She dutifully set off with her small wooden handcart to walk the 6 kilometres to Ditzenbach, not daring to believe that her worst fears could be true. But it all became tragically clear when she had to sign the bill of laden - there in cold hard script was the single word - 'coffin'. She said that it had only been due to the quick intervention of the railway staff that she hadn't fainted on the spot. What a terrible way to find that your only son was now dead. Amazingly this brave little woman still had the strength to push the handcart, now laden with the remains of her son, all the way back to Mülhausen, alone.

It was heartbreaking to listen to her as she told me with such pride how her son had been a crew member and how well he had done, how much he had learned. She had known that flying was dangerous and she had, to a degree, prepared herself for the worst, but to learn of things like this had hurt her so badly. Even in the face of such evidence she still wondered if there might have been a mistake - were we sure it was him? All I could do was to gently insist that there had been no mistake.

Soon it was time for the actual burial and it was only with the help of the pastor that we got to the graveside ready for the ceremony. With her tragic story still fresh in my mind I felt my throat tighten as I gave the orders: *'Hoch legt an!* (raise rifles), *'Feuer! - Laden!* (Fire - load) - *'Feuer! -Laden! - Feuer!'*

Every time the fuselade echoed around the churchyard in the cold winter air the poor widow flinched. With each volley the reality was driven home. As the band played *'Ich hatte einen Kameraden'*, I nearly cried, not for the young man who was being laid to rest in the cold ground, but for the poor woman who had suffered so much and was yet still so strong.

After the burial she didn't want to go back to her little roadside house right away but wanted to talk some more. Back at her home she had laid out a beautiful buffet for the mourners with ample wine and beer. But there were neighbours who were willing to supervise the meal if she didn't want to be there yet. We walked away from the church and she suggested that we make for a small hill a little way off. We walked for about an hour and a half getting some way up the hill before the snow became too deep and we had to turn back. She told me about her philosophies and how she had managed to educate her son after her husband had been killed, how well he had done at school and what a credit he had been to her, all of this dashed out in a few minutes, somewhere far away. But what had hurt her most was the way in which his body had been returned to her, like a broken machine that was no good any more - send it back to the makers - we'll get a new one. This hadn't of course been the intention at all, the whole thing had just been a tragic catalogue of disaster, right from the time the Junkers had lifted off the runway. But this poor woman could only see her end of it all and was bravely trying to make some sense of it. I listened and helped the best I could.

When we returned with our boots soaking wet and chilled to the marrow, a sort of party was in full swing. The military band had loosened their uniforms and played light music for the villagers who rallied around and tried to lighten things as much as they could - one of the benefits of the old type of village life. When the time came for me to leave, the band stayed on and I imagine the party continued well into the night. I said goodbye and this brave woman told me sincerely - and I believe that she meant it - that the funeral had been an honour to her late husband and to herself. She had begun to be able to recognise that the actual death of her son had been a tragic accident and that we had, in the end, honoured him in the best way we could. In particular she was grateful for my 'wise counsel' - the accrued wisdom of my twenty years, something which I felt paled to nothing when compared to her clear philosophy of life and sheer guts in face of over-whelming grief. All of this was to greatly influence my own view of life for a very long time to come.

Events like this clearly showed me that the preparation of a fighting unit was not going to be trouble free. It also caused me to look closely at my own philosophy of life and, to a degree, at that of others. There seemed to be, on the surface at least, two types of officer around. Firstly, those whose main priorities were to their men, to the *Luftwaffe*, to their country and to their own personal codes. And another group who, whilst still supporting the other principles, had one overriding dedication and that was to their own careers and personal advancement. If a situation arose where they had the choice to stand their ground to support one of their men at the possible expense of their personal standing with high command, then the man would have to go to the wall. I decided I would try to stick to the former and I think that whilst it was far from the easiest route, I have never been troubled by a bad conscience. I had determined that I would never seek to become successful if the only road to success was by climbing over people and riding roughshod over common decency. It was not, however, to stand me in very good stead with some people who clearly belonged to the latter group.

But what was success to be? My view of what constituted success was something which was to constantly change and evolve during my life. As a young man, it was to be a pilot and to see the world. Then, as an officer, to serve my country as best I could, to defend the underdog and even to risk my life for this principle, to follow the national leadership in lifting the yoke of the *Versaillier Diktat* from around the neck of our country and to destroy the infamous clauses of this document, article by article. If the French wanted to fight to uphold this wholly unpleasant Treaty, then we would fight them if it came to it. And if the British wanted to side with the French, then we would have to fight them too. When we beat them we would introduce them to the idea of the United States of Europe (something which, of course, came about anyway some forty years later led, ironical-ly, by the French).

All of this, of course, requires courage but of a particular kind, not that which might place one's life at risk in the short-term. I don't think this requires an abundance of courage because it is often achieved with no more complicated motivation than irresponsible recklessness. Courage, in my view, is sustained strength in adversity, either in your private life or in business. It is necessary to show stamina under stress, to follow your ideas and speak out for your principles. To be firm but fair with those who are above you and those for whom you are responsible and when you succeed, without corrupting those values, then you can then look back and know that you have achieved something worthwhile.

This is a philosophy which has been formed after a full and demanding life, but its roots lay back in my early years and was shaped by important events and by people like the poor widow who courageously pushed the body of her only son 6 kilometres on a handcart, never faltering and never losing her dignity.

Notes on Chapter 7

1. *Glühwein* - Literally 'glow-wine'. Warm mulled wine which is infusedwith a mixture of spices, particularly cinnamon

2. The *Schwarm* -   The basic air-fighting unit of the *Luftwaffe*. Four aircraft made up this loose formation in two *'Rotte'*, each of two aircraft. It was a tactic which had been developed in Spain by Werner Mölders and later adopted by the allies as 'Finger Four'.

3. *Vati* - Werner Molders nick-name - 'Father' or 'Daddy'.

4. *Jagerblatt* - The modern-day journal of fighter pilots published in the Federal Republic of Germany.

5. The Legion Condor veterans had accrued substantial back-pay and generous allowances whilst fighting in Spain and, as a result, nearly all of them had flashy cars.

6. *Werkmeister* - *Stabsfeldwebels* (Staff sergeants) who were responsible for technical services within the squadrons.

7. Adolf Galland had a theory that clay-pigeon shooting improved a pilot's shooting ability by sharpening up his perception of deflection. Later, when he was commanding officer of *JG26 'Schlageter'* in Caffiers he had all of his pilots clay-pigeon shooting as a regular training activity.

8. *Schirrmeister* - In charge of all motor transport for the *Jagdgruppen*

It is important for clarity for the reader to understand the arrangement of the German Squadrons as well as the system of numbering to avoid confusion.

The number which appears, for example *JG 52* means *Jagd Geschwader 52* or a Fighter Wing. The *Geschwader* is the air equivalent of an Army Regiment and like a Regiment is divided up into Battalions which, in the *Luftwaffe*, were called *Gruppen* (Groups). Each *Gruppe* would be given a roman numeral as its designation, for example *I/JG 52* was the first *Gruppe* of the *Jagd Geschwader 52*. (Fighter Wing 52) Similarly there would be *II/JG 52* & *III/JG 52*. Each of these *Gruppe* would be individual and quite separate, usually only three but sometimes four *Gruppen* formed a *Geschwader*.

Typically, a *Gruppe* would have three *Staffeln* (Squadrons) and a *Stabs Schwarm* (Staff Flight), making four squadrons to each *Gruppe*. These individual squadrons would be numbered in the Arabic numerals so that they were not confused with the *Gruppen*. Thus *1/JG 52, 2/JG 52, 3/JG 52* and the *Stabs* (Staff) *Schwarm* made up *I/JG 52*. This continued with *4/JG 52, 5/JG 52, 6/JG 52* and the *Stabs Schwarm* making up *II/JG 52*. Clearly then, *9/JG 52* would be the Third Squadron of the Third Group of the Fighter Wing 52.

Stabs Schwarm (Staff Flight): 4 Aircraft comprising:

Ist Rotte

Group Commander with his wingman who would be either the Adjudant or *Nachrichtenoffizier* (Communications Officer) (N.O)

2nd Rotte

Leader Staff Company with his wingman who would be either the Technical Officer (T.O) or Communications Officer (N.O)

The remainder of the squadron would be made up of *3 Schwäme*, each made up of 4 aircraft (2 x Rotte).

CHAPTER 8

1939 - Wireless Transmitters or Aerobatics - Is That The Question?

Under normal circumstances I would have been allowed some time to recover from the attendance to these funerals; after all they had been very harrowing events for me, but there was no time nor thoughts for that.

We had received another movement order, however this time it would be different. The whole Group *1/433* was to be moved from Manching near Ingolstadt to Böblingen which is very close to Stuttgart. This was great news for me! As close to a 'home posting' as I could get, we would only be about 35 km from my parents.

It all looked like returning to civilisation after the comparative isolation of a military base. Although we would operate from Böblingen we, the military, had to share it with Lufthansa and other civilian traffic. Now, also for the first time, there was to be some advantage in being the *Nachrichtenoffizier*. I was to be the advance guard, checking out the communications for the *Jagdgruppe* and making improvements to the telephones where required. I was to be my own boss for a while and close to home, whilst the others had the task of supervising the actual packing and moving of the *Gruppe*. It was now that I found that I had a conflict of interests. I had been invited to attend the communications course at Halle but I was reluctant to leave the unit. The crisis in the Sudetenland had been resolved without armed conflict, but now Hitler was revealing his supplementary demands: he wanted the rest of Böhmen Mähren, which we were calling Czechoslovakia and he also demanded the return of Memel and Danzig from the so-called 'Polish Corridor'. That had been another creation of the Treaty of Versailles, and if there was to be trouble over this, I thought it might be better to be with the unit, rather than taking a course in Halle. However, nothing much seemed to be developing and so I decided to leave for the *Luftnachrichtenschule*.

I left in the Me 109 'Dora', which had been allocated to me and it certainly felt great to be travelling in such a fast aircraft; at last I began to feel that I would actually become a fighter pilot. When I had landed I found things weren't yet completely organised to cope with our aircraft. There were no mechanics to deal with them, nor were there any ground crew who knew how to calibrate and adjust the radio equipment. For any flying to test equipment we had to enlist the help of a nearby fighter group at Merseburg. It took quite a while until we could fly to get some practice. Only six of us had arrived with aircraft and of those only three were radio equipped, another real eye-opener revealing the sad state of radio communictions within fighter groups.

Despite the initial lack of ground-to-air communications, the atmosphere was good. Very early on the commander of the Halle *Luftnachrichtenschule, Oberst* Kühne came into our class to meet us and to ask if one of us gentlemen present who possessed a '109 would be willing to make a special courier flight to *Luftgaukommando* in Munich. Only the three of us with radios fitted to our aircraft still retained them; the base commanders had soon learned about the difficulties with the radio training and had snatched their aircraft back for operational duty. The Me '109, although apparently in plentiful supply, was still in demand at squadron level and squadron leaders would not have an aircraft sitting on the ground at Halle if they could get around it. Three were withdrawn and three stayed.

Of these three I was first to put my hand up, still wanting every opportunity to fly the '109. There then followed a brief debate with *Oberst* Kühne as to which airport I should use at Munich. The closest was Munich-Riem but I had doubts that they would let a military aircraft land because it was a civilian operation and the radio in my aircraft did not match their frequencies. I was told there would be no problem, that permission would be taken care of.

Within minutes I was out of the classroom and heading for my aircraft, taking off at 11:00 hrs. I set the '109 at cruising speed and trimmed out for level flight, navigating by following the Berlin-Munich *Autobahn*. I landed at Riem after just fifty minutes flying and taxied up to park near to the tower. Already waiting at the ramp was a *Luftwaffe Unteroffizier* with staff car and driver. He saluted me smartly and I slipped into the back of the car and we were off to *Luftgaukommando* in Munich. The whole exercise had an air of urgency and importance to it. Everyone in the military was aware of the tension that was building over the Czechoslovakian problems and personal deliveries of sealed material tended to make you feel party to the secrecy and to the important decisions which might be made.

Back at the school in Halle, the Morse section was the province of 'Papa' Gröbsch, who was one of the senior instructors. He personally opened almost every course for *Bordfunker* (radio operator) and gave much of the actual instruction in Morse himself. The pass standards of sending and receiving seemed impossibly high at first, somewhere in the region of 100 characters per minute, but gradually the operators learned and qualified. We, the *NOs* from the fighter groups, also had to learn Morse but our test wasn't a pre-requisite to pass. Nonetheless, I managed to reach 60 characters per minute which allowed me to recognise what was being sent or received without necessarily understanding the full detail of the message. In any event, Morse wasn't being used for either ground-to-air or air-to-air communications in fighters like it was in the bombers, but only for our ground signals under battle conditions, when we might be mobile. Here, before we would be able to set up field telephone links or connect to a proper telephone exchange, our transmissions of information and receipt of orders would be done by Morse Code. One of the two 1.5 kilowatt stations housed in the three heavy trucks was detailed for this task, our tactical nerve-centre.

Twice during the course at Halle I had the opportunity to take a short break away, once to defend *Gefreiter* Huber, and once to check up personally that I wasn't 'missing the boat' as far as the expected battle for Böhmen and Mähren was concerned. In Halle it seemed that everyone was preparing for war and I was sure that the letter I had delivered to Munich had been to do with the Czechoslovakian situation. We, the young officers, were naively keen to become involved, to show our courage, to win our spurs. The older ones who had seen the fighting of the First War were not so keen and warned us that if it did happen we'd soon change our minds and wish we were back at Halle learning to be communications officers.

When I'd left Halle all talk was of a possible war over Czechoslovakia, some serious and informed but mostly just rumours. Nothing grows quite so quickly as rumours in the face of no real hard intelligence, even jokes began to do the rounds. One I remember involved the teller approaching his victim and beginning,

'Now the fighting will soon start in Czechoslovakia.'

'Why?' would be the usual reply.

'Because they've stabbed a General in Eger!!!'

'No! Really!! That must mean war now.'

'Well it might have if it hadn't been so long ago - I was talking about Wallenstein!!!' The trickster was referring to the theatrical play 'Wallenstein' by Schiller which pre-dated the Czechoslovakian problem by many years. When I returned to Manching I caught *Graf von* Pfeil with this story and he fell for it completely but with good humour, swearing me to secrecy about the joke. He then produced it to superb effect in the *Kasino* that evening and then again to High Command in Munich the next day. As a joke it only had a very limited shelf life and it was only a matter of hours before it was coming back to Manching by telephone, although we knew the answer; another example of how quickly exchanges of information could now be made.

The *Gruppe* was still preparing for the move to Böblingen and so, still being based at Manching, we were quite close to the nub of the Czech problem. We were able to gauge the temperature and concluded (rightly) that there would be no fight there. I therefore returned to Halle and continued the course.

In the first part of the course at Halle I had soon began to miss my little DKW car which I had left at Manching. Although the school and the airfield were fairly close to the town, the transport, both public and military, was usually inconvenient, erratic and overcrowded. I had been spoiled by the freedom my little car had given me. Halle, once just a rural town on the Saale River, had now been designated the central training school for communications for the *Luftwaffe*. This meant that personnel were sent from all over Germany to receive their radio instruction and, with Halle the nearest and really the only town for us to socialise, the evening tide of personnel to and from town was quite substantial.

It was obvious that one thing I badly needed there was my car and I was able to get it moved there by a circuitous route. Whilst I was at Böblingen I arranged for a driver to take my car, together with my belongings, from Manching to my parents' home. Not far from there, *Leutnant* Heinz Deuschle was on leave at his parents' home in Bad Cannstatt, a suburb of Stuttgart. Heinz had attended the *Luftkriegsschule* at Dresden and was from another fighter group, but we had met before at Eger and now that we were both at Halle we had become firm friends, frequently socialising together. He had agreed to pick up my little DKW and drive it back to Halle where we might both enjoy a better social life because of it.

Certainly, the appearance of my little DKW car at Halle offered much more freedom to many of my course. Not for the first time, I was the only young officer who had a car and it wasn't unusual to find it burdened down with up to ten tightly packed bodies. How the poor little car took the weight I really don't know, sometimes the springs must have been bent inside out! Going into town was fun, but the return journey together with newly made friends and the effects of a modest imbibing of the local wines and beers was usually quite memorable. There wasn't too much traffic on the roads then and, as I have mentioned before, there wasn't the same high profile on drinking and driving as there is today. So, although we travelled in civilian clothes, we didn't get much trouble from the local police. Only when we pushed our luck a bit and had girlfriends sitting on the roof or the bonnet did they stop us and cheerfully ask us to be a little more restrained. This tolerance was apparent from both the civilian authorities and the senior officers at the school and I have only been able to explain it to myself with the thought that maybe they had some respect for us as being amongst those who had begun to pull Germany from the mire; those who would wield the instruments which would destroy the hated Treaty of Versailles, whose authors had once conspired to cripple Germany forever.

Now that we had all we wanted at Halle, we could enjoy the well planned course and also take full advantage of the lively social life. We had found a cafe where we could dance and meet a good number of the local girls. Later, because we had access to our quarters without actually passing through the gate or the guardhouse, there would often be extended celebrations, well into the night. It soon became clear that the various fighter groups, from which the students were drawn, had very different standards of discipline and demanded considerably differing behaviour from their men. Many were already demonstrating that they were used to heavy and regular drinking, whilst some of the others considered it to be fair play to draw and use their Walther *PPK* pistols quite indiscriminately.

Whenever they took it into their heads they would start shooting, but mostly at night and when they'd had a few drinks. The favourite targets were the electric light standards with their illuminated globes high on the steel poles. I was quite surprised that there was no disciplinary action taken to curb this hooliganism before it had fatal results. At times I felt I had to intervene but was told that it was just 'standard behaviour' in their squadrons. On the whole I just had to let things be, but on one occasion I really hit the ceiling when their tomfoolery came too close to me for comfort. The young officer in the room next door was entertaining a girlfriend when another fellow entered and a nasty situation developed, motivated by jealousy. I was lying on a couch reading and half listening to the hubbub of voices in the next room when there was the sharp crack of two pistol shots followed by a burst of flying fragments in my room as the two 7.65 mm bullets burst through the thin partition wall, very narrowly missing my head. That was the last straw! I jumped up and after grabbing my own pistol I burst into the room and threatened to shoot the stupid fellow if he didn't hand over his pistol. This he did when he realised how close the bullets had come to me. I returned the weapon to him the next day and nothing more was said. All things considered it was fortunate that nobody was seriously hurt or killed and the incident serves to demonstrate how intelligent young men will behave, even if they are part of the military establish-ment and officers, if the rule of discipline is not apparent.

The course itself was well conceived and contained everything which we, as future *Nachrichtenoffiziers*, would want to know. We were also assured that a letter would be circulated to our commanding officers stress-ing the importance of communications and recommending that the subject be given a degree of priority in future planning for equipment and training. That was encouraging but I wondered if even that would make a dent in the entrenched views of people like our 'Spaniards' and, in particular, officers with the outlook of Adolf Galland.

When the end of the course came it was, in many ways, too soon for us. We had had the most fantastic time socially, both in the little cafes in the town and at the *Fliegerhorst Kasino*. Here they had held many festival dance events and never after we left Halle did I have so many opportuni-ties to wear my *Luftwaffe* smoking jacket, complete with silver-striped trousers. It had been designed for the exclusive use of the *Luftwaffe* by Göring and was the envy of the other arms of the *Wehrmacht*. Dressed as we were and now skilled in the social graces we really felt like something special. Even now I still recall the warm heady, happy feeling of those, the last few months of peace in Germany.

Returning to Böblingen I had the same arrangement with Heinz Deuschle. He took the DKW and I flew the Me 109 D back to the Group Headquarters, now at Böblingen. We met at Bad Cannstatt and Heinz intro-duced me to his family and, in particular, to his two sisters, Hilde and Liesel. They were rather beautiful and although friendly to me they thought I was still too young to be of interest to them - they were three and five years older than myself. Nonetheless, the friendship remained and through it I was introduced to the Stephan family who also had two daughters, Gretl and Marianne. Gretl was about the same age as myself and we hit it off right from the start. We began to meet quite frequently and played some tennis, took many memorable walks, swam and danced with all the energy of healthy youth. A favourite place for us to visit was something of a local miracle in Stuttgart, the *Bundesgartenschau* (Garden exhibition) at the Killesberg. It was a national event and the whole site had been fashioned out of what had been a wasteland on a hill near to the town. Every day when it was being built it changed before your eyes and, in what seemed to be no time at all, there were miniature trains, vineyards, a *Landliche Gastatte* (rural guesthouse), a cabaret and all sorts of indoor and outdoor exhibitions. One particular favourite of ours was the indoor/outdoor danc-ing cafe and we had gone there one day to enjoy the 'five o'clock tea danc-ing'. We had just settled ourselves at a table when I noticed that Galland

and Ewald, the Squadron Leaders of 1 & 2 Squadrons were seated close by. They, like me, were dressed in civilian suits and, to be polite, I left Gretl and went over to say hello. They wanted to know who my pretty companion was and for some reason, I still don't know why, I told them that she was my sister, never really believing that they would take me seriously, or be interested anyway.

Der E-ZUG: During the three months training of the E-ZUG, there were sometimes when we could 'get out' together. Here we are visiting in uniform the Stuttgarter Gartenschau (Garden exhibition). Out front Ltn. Ulrich Steinhilper, a guide and the staff sergeant (with his wife) of the Fliegerhorstkompanie.

I returned to the table and told the story to Gretl who thought that it was a bit of a joke too. Soon afterwards I went to the washroom and when I returned I found one of the two officers happily dancing with Gretl! She returned to the table with her face full of laughter and fun, telling me that she had continued the 'sister' story rather than spoil the joke. More invitations to dance came from the other table and I was forced to sit at my table, the victim of my own foolishness. I thought that was where the story would end but soon there was a dance at the Böblingen *Kasino* and I was asked to invite my 'sister' which I did, not knowing really what else to do. Gretl was keen to continue the deception and as far as I could see there would be no harm in it. That evening went off well, but another day Gretl visited me at the airport and, as we sat enjoying the sunshine and some coffee in a little open-air cafe between the hangars and the *Kasino*, it became apparent that some squadron leaders had started their own private air-show ... for the benefit of my 'sister'. Well the time had come to bring the story out in the open and, after so much time, there was no chance that it would be treated like a joke. It just came out as a rather lame prank played on my seniors. It did nothing to improve my relations with Galland, who was still my titular squadron leader, and this was mainly manifest in the singular lack of flying training which was offered to *Leutnant* Uli Steinhilper of the First Squadron. That was bad, but worse was to come.

In a Focke-Wulf 'Stösser', summer 1939 Böblingen near Stuttgart

On April 13th 1939, the Fighter Group *1/433* was officially welcomed to the town of Böblingen. *Graf von* Pfeil led the parade which was a grand affair, with many stirring marches played by a *Luftwaffe* band. Speeches were made, both by *von* Pfeil and by the *NSDAP Kreisleiter*. I really enjoyed leading the *Stabs Kompanie* (Staff Company) in the parade, goosestepping past the dais with sword presented; marching alone something like ten metres in front of 'my' steel-helmeted troops. Above us the *Gruppe* flew in tight formation, drawing cries of appreciation from the crowds. As they landed at Böblingen we made our way out from the town to join them. Once assembled, the whole *Gruppe* took on our new title, *I/JG 52* - the unit I was to fly with for the rest of my time as a pilot.

Now settled at Böblingen we worked in good harmony with Lufthansa, who were still using the grass airfield to serve Stuttgart. At this time Echterdingen, today's Stuttgart airport, was still in the final stages of construction like so much building in Germany at the time. When complete, Lufthansa would move their operation there where they would have concrete runways and more facilities. They were flying Ju 52s and a few Heinkel 70s at the time and it was OK to operate them from grass, but in the spring and autumn, when the field became water-logged, the heavy transports experienced some problems. Here I have to comment that throughout Europe the great renaissance in air transport was taking place which would, in the end, require most airports to have metalled runways and perimeter tracks. This was, of course, accelerated by the advent of war, but at this time the majority of even international airfields had grass runways.

Throughout the move to Böblingen and our steady growth as a unit, the command structure had remained basically the same. Numbers 1 and 2 Squadrons were still led by *Obltns*. Galland and Ewald, but since the death of *Obltn.* Klein in the Junkers 52 crash, the leadership of No. 3 Squadron remained undecided. For a while *Ltn.* Leesman was appointed on a temporary basis but later in April we were introduced to *Obltn.* Kühle, who had served with the Legion Condor. He was to command Squadron No. 3 and was to figure significantly in my later career.

In May nearly all of the pilots, whether NCOs or officers, had been given conversion training from the Me 109 Ds (Doras) to the new and more advanced Me 109 Es (Emils). I say nearly all because I for one had been left out. Either this was because Galland was deliberately ignoring me, or simply because everyone forgot about the *Gruppe Nachrichten Offizier.* I was a little upset about that because I felt that my first job was as a fighter pilot and my second responsibility was for communications. I was working hard to improve the *Nachrichtenzug's* skills and efficiency and I suppose I felt someone should be working as hard with my flying but, for the time-being, that was not to be.

It began to look like I was getting further away from flying and more and more involved in the challenging work of communications. Not only was I expected to whip the *Nachrichtenzug* for *I/JG 52* into shape but I was also seconded to the *Fliegerhorstkompanie* Böblingen. Here I was to work with *Major* (E) Nussbaum (the 'E' designated that he had been recalled from the reserve list) who was a splendid character and a veteran of communications in World War 1. He was a popular officer and managed, through his own good contacts and diplomatic cooperation with the civil airport and Lufthansa, to gain a lot of professional experience and training for his own *Luftnachrichtenkompanie* as well as for my *N-Zug*.

Although I suppose I objected a little to being distanced more from my flying, I could see that *Major* Nussbaum was an officer who had been over-loaded with work and needed some help. He not only had the responsibility for communications for the military side of the airport, but was also supervising the construction of small and self-contained satellite airfields *(Feldflugplatze)* around the area for use in case of war. On top of all this he had to train 60 new reserve operators and only had three months to do it. He certainly needed help and his winning ways and sound man-management made it a pleasant duty to work with him, albeit that my flying suffered again.

It hadn't taken *Hauptmann von* Pfeil long to convince me that I should be the one to help and I was given the task of moulding the reserve personnel into some sort of military shape and teaching them their basic role as reservists. They were a very lively crowd, mostly 10 or 15 years older than me and drawn from the 'professional' groups with a high proportion of lawyers and other academics. Because of this I ran into trouble on subjects like *Festnahme* und *Waffengebrauch* (arrest and use of weapons). There were many searching legal questions as to whether a soldier in uniform - on or off duty - would be required to arrest another soldier, or even a civilian and from where his power of arrest might be derived. There was no doubt that the class enjoyed baiting me and dropping as many 'loaded' questions as possible into the debate. Much of this I'm sure was aimed at testing each other, as professional colleagues, as much as trying to confuse me. I wasn't to be 'wound up' by these vociferous characters and simply side-stepped the issue by joining the class and appointing one of the more active of my audience to take the podium because of his 'obviously extensive knowledge of the nuances of the law'. He soon discovered that it was no easy job to contain and guide such a collection of intellect and talent.

Their intellectual games aside they were a good crew and learned their work well. They may have been lively but they also had a strong sense of responsibility and wanted to play an active part if there ever was to be another war. At the end of their course we had a really good celebration which probably involved a little too much wine and beer. They had made up a poem about me (see overleaf) which was recited with much gusto and suitable appreciation from myself to them. At the end of this party all 60 of them and their training NCOs assembled in military order outside the *Gasthaus* in the middle of Böblingen ready to be marched back to the

Fliegerhorst. On my order they were called to attention and we moved out with just one more order - *'Ein Lied!'* (sing!). There were many loud and merry songs, some a little risqué, others the more traditional marching songs. In any event the volume was directly proportional to their alcoholic consumption ... in other words - loud! We arrived back at the base with only minor casualties at about 2 o'clock in the morning and fell into bed exhausted. Next morning some of the citizens protested to the Mayor who, in turn, passed on the complaint not to Nussbaum but to *Graf von* Pfiel who was the official *Standortaltester* (commanding officer). He called for me but I really got more of a smile than a reprimand.

Leutnant Steinhilper

```
Schlank der Wuchs und elegant:
Das ist unser Leutenant.
Im Benehmen sehr adrett
Fanden wir ihn wirklich nett.
Doch er hat auch seine Mucken,
Die nur schlecht zu unterdrucken.
Spindzustand und Bettenbau
Kontrolliert er sehr genau.
Unterhosen, Hemden & dergleichen
Müssen seinen Argusaugen weichen.
Auch beim Exerzieren
Mussten dicke wir parieren.
Denn er scharf darüber wacht,
Dass jeder seine Griffe richtig macht.
Ist das Tempo dann nicht zackig
Oder gar der Säugling wacklig,
Schon der Ruf ertönt: "Die Spritze runter!
Eine Ehrenrunde, aber etwas munter."
Flaschen war'n wir kurz darauf . . .
Gerne nahmen wir's in Kauf,
Hatten wir's doch bald heraus,
Auf Schikane ging's nicht aus.
Bracht' er uns auch mal in Schwung:
Dieser Leutnant war in Ordnung.
```

A free interpretation of the E-Zug Poem. It is not a literal translation but it is an interpretation of the contents of the German version in which the mood and feeling has been transposed rather than being a word-for-word translation.

LEUTNANT STEINHILPER

Slim of build and elegant,
That is our *Leutnant,*
In manner he is very neat,
We all agree he looks a treat,
But his personal traits he cannot hide.
Even those that are on the negative side.

In locker checks and bedmaking training,
He is most descerning and demanding,
Underwear, shirts and things which tidiness belie,
Must disappear before they catch his eagle-eye.

At drill we must always listen properly,
Because here also he watches closely,
For every hold and proper grip,
Alert to notice the slightest slip,
For if he sees someone like an infant toddling,
Then his voice is soon loudly correcting.

We soon accept this as our fate,
Or else we find we're kept out late,
We know it's not any kind of bullying,
He just brings us all back into the swing,
Thus we have to say at the end of the day,
That this *Leutnant* is really OK.

I was pleased that I wasn't in line for disciplinary action again as, earlier, I had blotted my copy book in no uncertain terms. As I have related, the squadrons were converting from the Me 109 D to the Me 109 E and my training seemed to be non-existant. I rather impetuously decided to take matters into my own hands. At noon, when I knew that all the other officers were at the *Kasino* for lunch, I walked into the hangar for No.1 Squadron where I knew a factory fresh '109 E had just arrived. It had not been assigned and so I told the mechanic who was servicing it to get me a parachute and prepare the aircraft for immediate flight. Unquestioningly he carried out my instructions; discipline in our unit was tight and NCOs would not normally question the orders of an officer. I strapped on my parachute and climbed up onto the port wing of the '109, pausing to ask the mechanic if there was anything new in the handling notes on this '109 E. It was quite different to the old 'Dora' - the Junkers Jumo engine which weighed 440 kg and produced a modest 630 h.p. had been replaced by the DB 601 which was slightly heavier at 600 kg but produced a phenominal 1100 h.p. The mechanic said he thought that the 'Emils' were being land-ed slightly faster. I didn't ask any other questions, what he'd told me had been confirmed by my colleagues; the 'Emil' landed best if flown in at about 10 - 15 kph faster than the 'Dora'.

Somewhat nervously, I stepped into the cockpit and dropped down into the close fitting interior. The aircraft smelled new with a rich mixture of odours; parts still being 'burned off' as the engine began to gain hours and the new parts still being covered with preservative or fresh paint. The mechanic helped to strap me in and I began my pre-flight checks. All was in order. I gave the signal to clear prop and start and the 'Black Man', who was standing on the starboard wing-root, began to wind the heavy eclipse starter. At the right moment I pulled the lever and the starter turned the great DB 601 engine over, roaring into life on the first turn. The whole air-frame shook with the power as I made my running checks prior to take-off. Again all was in order and so I gave the signal to clear chocks and I released the brakes. Taxiing around to line up I opened the throttle and the aircraft leapt forwards, the long engine cowling clearing my view as the tail came up smartly. I was soon in the air.

From the beginning it didn't go too well. Perhaps because I knew I was doing something wrong, perhaps because I was wary of the power of the new aircraft. In any event I was far from relaxed and enjoying myself. The take-off wasn't too different, there was a noticeable surge of power and the aircraft seemed to lift off in a shorter run, but once in the air the handling didn't differ too much. The landing in contrast was a bit of a fight. Cutting back on power for the landing seemed to make the aircraft plunge, losing height much faster than I was used to. Another problem which was to prove crucial in my undoing was a gravel road that crossed the line of the runway. On this day it was approached at an angle and was very slightly raised - not enough to cause a problem under normal conditions but if things weren't going too well...

I had made three circuits, checking myself for the correct height and landing speeds. On the fourth approach I was attempting to find the upper end of the limits for approach speed and was going faster than on the previous approaches. I was pleased, this seemed to be it. The landing was soft and the aircraft handled perfectly. I was almost congratulating myself when I crossed the gravel roadway which caused the aircraft to jump up a little, flying again for a few brief moments. In those split seconds I must have recalled my experience of the new aircraft being heavy and tending to drop at low speed. I decided to give it a short shot of throttle, just to keep the nose up. I might have got away with that on the 'Dora', but not with the 'Emil'.

What happened in those few seconds can be reconstructed by examining the different characteristics of the two types of '109. The 'Dora' had a single blade prop and relatively low-powered engine. The 'Emil' had a much heavier three-bladed prop and nearly twice the power of the 'Dora'. My quick 'shot of throttle' released 1100 hp onto a heavy propeller causing a sharp torque reaction in the aircraft, making the fuselage turn on its own axis in the opposite direction to the propeller. The result was that my left wing dropped and touched the ground. Again there had to be a decision in a split second so I kicked the rudder hard to the right to bring her round straight again and cause the wing to rise a little or at least to take the impact away from the wingtip. That worked OK but I still had lots of forward momentum which threw the aircraft onwards at an angle of about 45° relative. The starboard undercarriage leg hit first and folded under, virtually snapping off, with the port leg being bent outwards at a hideous angle. The big three bladed prop hit the ground and began a creditable job of ploughing the airfield whilst it was twisted and bent backwards like thin tin foil.

As suddenly as the cacophony of noise and tortured metal had begun it was over and I sat in silence, the harness straps biting into my shoulders and chest. The only sound was the odd 'ping' of hot metal cooling. I released my straps and climbed out of the cockpit to survey the damage. At the same time I heard the alarm siren and saw figures tumbling from the buildings to man trucks and begin to rush towards me. It would take a few minutes and so I took the opportunity to look at the damage. It wasn't too bad, the port wingtip was slightly dented, that wouldn't take long. The undercarriage leg had broken at the point where it had been designed to fracture under these circumstances but the propeller would be a write-off. Here was the big question, 'Had I bent the crankshaft of the engine?' If I had, then the damage was serious and would keep the unfortunate '109 out of service for quite a while ... I was already beginning to weigh up what my punishment might be. Like all sanctions it would be commensurate with the damage I had caused.

The emergency trucks arrived quickly, they knew their business and would soon have the wreck back in the hangar. I was offered a lift back to the ramp in front of the tower where I could see that the whole complement of on-duty personnel had gathered at the sound of the 'blood wagon' turning out. I decided to walk, both to clear my head and to gain a little more time to gather my thoughts. My reception committee had already quizzed the mechanic and knew that I had taken the aircraft on my own authority and were waiting for my explanation. I could see *von* Pfeil and Galland and they took me aside to listen to my story. I admitted that I had acted on my own initiative and tried to explain why - how I felt that I had been left out of the training programme and how flying seemed to be becoming very low on the squadron's list of activities for me. *Hauptmann* von Pfeil decided that Galland was my supervising officer and left the disciplinary measures to him. He kept calm, pointing out that through my ill-considered actions I had caused extensive damage to an aircraft that had less than three hours' flying time in its technical log. He said that he would have to consider the matter and let me know in due course. I suspect that one thing he was waiting for was the complete report on the damage in order that 'the punishment might fit the crime.'

Following the accident in a '109 E. At this time it was only 3 hours old.

The other *Leutnants* were sympathetic towards me but we judged the minimum would be 7 days confined to quarters and an entry on my personal dossier. In the event the aircraft was test-flown after just three days and there was no damage to the crankshaft. I'm sure that this influenced the decision and Galland called for me to issue my punishment. He would teach me landing and I would have to do it in our own ancient Heinkel 70 *(Blitz)*.

Further, I would not have the services of the usual air-mechanic and I would have to hand-pump the landing gear up and down for each landing. I was to undertake twenty *Platzrunde* (circuits) in four sessions of five and I would only be allowed to complete the landings if Galland found the direction and approach to be suitable.

Under the circumstances I thought that was a fair decision albeit that Galland was rubbing my face in my complaint about a lack of instruction. It was better than anyone had expected and for me it had two distinct advantages; the accident wouldn't go on my dossier and it would give me the opportunity to learn something more about landing. However, it wasn't entirely as clean cut as it looked. I soon found out that a 'suitable approach' took me very close to a chimney (which was later removed for safety) and very, very low over the roof of the Klemm aircraft factory. A good performance took time, patience and ability but slowly I began to get there.

The landing always had to be made with the wind in the most disadvantageous direction and it was no easy matter to keep the heavy Heinkel on course and at the correct angle of descent. It was hard to believe that this aircraft had once set world speed records, things had come a long way in a few short years. I 'sweated blood' flying that aircraft, both from the physical exertion of pumping the landing gear and also from the concentration required to make the successful landings. In the end I made it and the last of the 20 landings was over.

In a way the whole affair was to bring things to a head and changes were made. It had become apparent that there had been friction between Galland and myself and it seemed practical that I should be moved to No. 3 Squadron. That was alright by me, there has never been any doubt in my mind that Adolf Galland and myself were cut from very different wood. In *3/JG 52* I felt at home straight away, after all my great friend Hinnerk Waller was Technical Officer. *Obltn.* Helmut Kühle had been assigned the command and, even though he too was a 'Spaniard' like Galland and Ewald, he was a much more generous type. Another character, *Obltn.* Horst Tietzen, joined the Squadron on a temporary basis having only just returned from Spain with some seven victories. He was a very likeable man and was one of the few people I met in my military service who had the balance right between being friendly and approachable without compromising his military authority or his role as a leader. When it came to decide which of our two Oberleutnants would leave and which would remain in charge of *3/JG 52*, I have to confess that we were disappointed when Horst left to take command of *6/JG 51*. Helmut Kühle was a good leader and an exemplary officer but he lacked the exceptional quality of Tietzen. We were sad when he left and even some time later, during the 'Battle of Britain', I keenly felt his loss when he was killed on the 18th August.

Obltn. Horst Tietzen only stayed with 3rd Squadron of JG.52 a. short time. He was killed very early during the Battle of Britain. Picture taken during 'Exercise Wengerohr'.

Whilst he was with us I thought that Tietzen was the best consultant *Hauptmann von* Pfeil had and I think we might have made real progress had he stayed, but it was not to be. Kühle was supportive of my work as the *N.O* but Tietzen really worked at it. He was one who could see how valuable good radio communications would be. He was one of the few 'Spaniards' who realised that wing signals and telephone briefings would soon be outpaced if we ever went to war with one of the major European powers.

Although I actually had some help with my work now, there still didn't seem to be enough hours in the day. Only at the weekends were we free to go out and unwind. The Stephan family owned a weekend house on the Rauhe Alb, not far from Hornberg - the 'home' of the free-flight glider. We really had some good times at that little house, everyone including the girls playing soccer or just relaxing in the warm sunshine. Most times we drove there in a convoy of three cars, Mr Stephan's big Mercedes 230 in front, my little DKW in the middle and four pretty girls in a Mercedes Cabriolet bringing up the rear, together with its bold notice *'Endlich Allein?'* (alone at last) which was draped across the boot of the car. They were good days and in many ways I thought I was leading a very satisfying and rewarding life, I felt very privileged on the whole but deep down there was still some rancour.

Weekend House, driving in convoy. The 230 Business-Mercedes on the left, the Cabriolet with the 'Endlich allein?'

*This was after a 'family' soccer match. Picture is taken near
the Weekend House at Hornberg (Rauhe Alb), about 80km
distance from Stuttgart. I am sitting centre and Gretl is on my left.*

It is difficult to express exactly how I felt and it is probably best illustrated by example. At Böblingen we had *Leutnant* Hans Berthel who had been promoted from the ranks, having served as a flying instructor. He had been assigned to Ewald's No 2 Squadron where he was to stay; a few strings had been pulled here. He was exceptionally good at aerobatics and everyone held him in high esteem, even the 'Spaniards'; he was accepted at once and without any apparent reservation. I didn't really envy that, I too admired his skill and dedication to his 'art'. Every morning he would be up in the sky practising over Böblingen before the official day had begun, waking up those who hadn't realised the night was over. The 160 h.p. engine of his Bücker Jungmeister which had been assigned to him for his personal use became our reveille. His dedication was to pay off when he later finished in the top five of the National Aerobatic Championships.

I didn't envy him his success but here to me was the tragic difference. He was a young man who was doing something he loved and which was for his own personal advancement and satisfaction. To this end he had the full support of the Group Commander and the backing and admiration of the veterans. In stark contrast to this was my own position: my efforts had little or nothing to do with my own advancement and I didn't particularly like what I was doing. It had taken me away from flying, it had caused bad feeling between myself and many of the officers and all I was doing was trying my hardest to get an aspect of the Group's combat readiness in some kind of shape. All that my dedication and hard work had ever done was to cost me dearly! It seemed sometimes that things would always be an uphill fight for me. I was never to have any really bad luck, after all I survived the war when so many of my friends and colleagues perished, but I certainly didn't have much handed to me on a plate either.

One thing which did break my way and helped to improve my status was when my father was re-called to service. He had been an officer in the First War with a horse-drawn heavy machine gun unit. He had maintained his love for horses after the war and with the re-armament he was recalled, promoted, and given the chance to work with an artillery unit at Ludwigsburg. Now father and son managed to arrange a deal that would 'further the understanding and co-operation between the Artillery and the Luftwaffe'. In short, he arranged for our officers to have first class riding lessons and we arranged for artillery officers to have flights at Böblingen and some experience as pilots under instruction.

It was an amicable arrangement and we all enjoyed the exchange of roles but it was something which was to be short-lived, to be overtaken by other events. It was obvious from the growing hysteria in the press and the stirring broadcasts by Joseph Göbbels that things were once more coming to a head. Again the storm clouds began to gather and again we began to prepare in earnest for what might be just a few weeks away.

Notes on Chapter 8

1. Black Men (see page 161) - *Luftwaffe* slang for the mechanics because of their one-piece black cotton overalls.

CHAPTER 9

Warming Up and Getting Ready Summer 1939

In the newspapers and on the radio there were constant reports of 'sabre-rattling' going on between Germany and her neighbours. Several incursions into the myriad and pernicious clauses of the *Versaillier Diktat* had been made and each had carried with it the threat of war against Germany. None of these had come to anything, but we had almost become accustomed to living in a state of readiness. Since the Czech 'crisis' things had settled down for a short time and we were able to take stock. The training of my *Nachrichtenzug* was now coming along well. We had most of the equipment we needed and the personnel were now really finding their feet. *Unteroffizier* Krehe, my valuable training NCO and 'jack of all trades', was my right hand man and I recommended his promotion to *Feldwebel,* but even that took time. The *Nachrichtenzug* now began to appreciate that there were some advantages to their work, one of which was to get out on field exercises. Now that we were actually beginning to operate like a professional unit and also starting to use our more powerful equipment, we had to get away from Böblingen because of the interference with the *Lufthansa* radio, our 1.5 kilowatt transmitters on other frequencies blotting them out. So we spent a lot of the summer in the beautiful countryside around Stuttgart and in the *Schwarzwald* (Black Forest) setting up the equipment and carrying out training. That was a lot better than being confined to the base where discipline was high and behaviour very formal.

One of the key operations of the *Nachrichtenzug* was its ability to set up communications at a new location, whilst still maintaining cover at the old base. This is why most of the equipment and, to a lesser extent, the personnel were duplicated. To test this function I would arrange exercises where the mobile unit would move out to another location and set up ready to take communications traffic. One of the first of these exercises took the unit out to the Wolf Hirth glider field at Nabern near Kirchheim-unter-Teck. By noon they called to inform me that all was ready and I flew out in a '109 to test the communications. I couldn't land, the ground personnel had advised that the field was too soft, but I made several low and high passes to test the quality of the transmissions. The range and quality varied tremendously according to the density of the cloud and height, sometimes it would fade off completely. This was something we would have to improve if we were to provide the communications cover that we had promised and which I had so avidly 'sold' to the squadron leaders.

In the afternoon I returned in more sedate transport, the Focke-Wulf Stösser. Being lighter and with a very much lower landing speed I was given permission to make a landing. Apparently my men were very proud when their flying *Leutnant* arrived, proving to the local farmers that they were, in fact, part of a *Luftwaffe* unit. Initially I was pleased with the set-up at Nabern but was a little concerned when it became obvious that the now suitably impressed farmers were being more than generous with a supply of home-made cider for the *Fliegersoldaten*. The drive back, according to *Unteroffizier* Krehe, was something of a wild affair and we were lucky there weren't any serious consequences. Later I cautioned the NCOs that if they wanted to continue the degree of trust and freedom which they presently enjoyed, then they would have to keep a tighter rein on their charges in the field. But with the best will in the world accidents happen when you least expect them.

To gradually develop the capability of the unit it required steadily more complex exercises, leading ultimately to their being able to fulfil their role. For us, the next stage was to set up a full communications unit at a new *Feldflugplatz* and for this *Ubung* we went to a large meadow near the old castle Monrepos - about 5 km from my parents home at Heutingsheim. We were to install everything that would be needed by a *Gruppe* operating in the field. It had been difficult to secure the location but in this case I was able to get my father to pull the appropriate strings.

Such an exercise normally took a whole day, with us leaving early in the morning and sometimes not returning until dawn of the next day. It was quite something for a young *Leutnant* (I was still only 20) to have virtually independent command of a mobile unit like this and I was rather proud of our performance. With all of the vehicles for the mobile unit on the road we looked quite something. There were motor bikes, two KFZ *Kübelwagens*, my BMW staff car and two light and two heavy trucks, my private army. This wasn't the first time we'd set up the full field unit and the troops were getting used to an efficient routine. At about 5 pm we were finished at Monrepos and I was driven back to Böblingen by *Gefreiter* Meier in one of the KFZs. Our regulations were that only squadron leaders and senior ranks could drive themselves, all other officers had to have a driver. This was probably to prevent the younger officers appropriating official vehicles for private use.

By 6 pm. we were nearly back to Böblingen, driving on a good road and in good light when I saw a motorcyclist ahead of us, riding in the middle of our side of the road. We seemed to be closing on him fast and there didn't seem to be any sign from Meier that he'd seen the motorcycle. I glanced at him and saw that his eyes were set in a far away stare ... he hadn't seen the motorbike at all! I shouted and grabbed the handbrake, causing the jeep to swerve . . . but it was too late . . . we hit the back of the bike, catching it between the radiator and the near-side, front wheel. The unfortunate rider had no chance at all, the KFZs were very sturdy vehicles and we slewed into a *KM-Stein* (milestone), crushing him between the stone and front of the unyielding vehicle. The stone was uprooted and the whole sorry mess, rider, bike, *Kübelwagen* and us crashed down the embankment of the road to lodge in a hedge.

As we jumped from the vehicle I shouted at Meier, 'What did you do?' He stared back at me in shock, not knowing what had happened at all. I told him we'd hit a motorbike and at that moment we both saw the man lying by the front of the vehicle. It seemed up to that point Meier had really been completely detached from reality. We reached the rider who had been thrown clear and saw that he'd obviously been severely injured around the hip and the lower abdomen, clearly an emergency case. We were still outside the town so I flagged down a car and we moved the man as carefully as we could into the back of it and then drove as quickly as possible to the Böblingen *Kreiskrankenhaus* (hospital).

The victim of the accident wasn't conscious, but from his papers we could ascertain his address and that, tragically, he was the rather of seven children. The hospital tried hard to save him but despite some huge blood transfusions, he died before I could visit the hospital again. It was another very sad experience for me and another lesson on how apparently unfair life can be. Right away, questions were asked about why such exercises were necessary and why I had chosen to conduct one so close to my parent's home. Nothing was said directly, but the inference was that it had been my fault again. Another triumph for the *Nachrichtenzug!*

When my statement was examined it was decided to take Meier for observation in a mental health clinic. The findings were that he had apparently had a very hard up-bringing and education as a boy and this caused him, upon occasion, to lapse into a semi-unconscious state of reverie, fixating on some aspect of his severe early life. The court accepted this and decided that punishment would not be appropriate, but for safety's sake he should not drive anymore. For my part, I tried to represent my own case to be able to drive myself. I had, in the past, argued that my position wasn't like any other *Leutnants* in the *Gruppe*, I needed freedom of movement but the military mind is slow to yield to changes, particularly when this might become a precedent. It took another accident at Bonn/Hanglar, when I was nearly killed, to get affirmation that I could, in future, look after my own safety.

This picture gives an idea how much the troops liked to practise outside. Unfortunatly on the return from this 'Übung', the accident with the motorbike happened.

The MAST-CAR is well camouflaged, the crew is at ease. On the right is Flieger Treplin, who at Bonn/Hangler, proved his great ingenuity.

In spite of these incidents we were determined to continue our radio testing. The main objective was to improve the co-ordination between the units, to weld them into one cohesive communications service. The mobile group had to work in unison or it didn't work at all; all three of the heavy units depended upon each other for something. The transmitter truck was no use without the radio mast vehicle and neither of those could operate without the generator. Power was always a problem and it would have been of great help if we could have drawn on the mains, but however ingeniously the operators tried they could not achieve a success-ful hook-up with the public circuit. We thought we'd got it right once, but that only resulted in one of the 1.5 kW sets being sent back to the Siemens factory for repair. After that we resorted to the tried and tested, only run-ning on the generator motor.

Here are some of the Nachrichtenzug 1/52.
Treplin is on the far right.

Problems with the evolution of communications were everywhere, it was a continuous process of invention and initiative, and this is where we hit one of the key difficulties again. To sustain the motivation required to overcome adversity, and to stimulate initiative, there has to be the will, or at least a reason, to succeed. At squadron level there was no such initiative and it was always an uphill struggle to get any help. The *Funkwarte* (radio mechanics) had very little experience and looked for guidance to their squadron leaders and from the *Werkmeisters*. Here there was no enthusiasm at all and all too often the problem was left unresolved and with a shrug of the shoulders another radio was shelved until 'they' could fix it.

Typical of these problems was the difficulty in simply fitting a set to an aircraft. The '109s had provision for radio equipment built into them with electrical connections through the main wiring loom and fittings to hold the set in the fuselage, midway between the cockpit and the tail. Right away we had a three-way problem. There was a plug-board to take the electrical connections so that *FuGs* (radios) could be changed easily. The trouble was that the 'Dora' and the 'Emil' had different connections. A radio that might fit one of the 'Doras' would not fit any of the 'Emils' and vice-versa. Some radios wouldn't fit either and some would match the mechanical fixings but none of the plugs on the board. It was too easy for the mechanics just to give up and that was, I suppose, understandable - for even when we had the sets fitted, as I did in No. 3 Squadron, the tuning was a nightmare. The tuning of the crystals had to be so fine and once set could not be changed in the air. Batteries were another complication - whilst we were working we had to hook up spare batteries so as not to drain the aircraft's accumulator, particularly whilst transmitting. These had to be kept charged and carried out to where they were needed then hooked into the aircraft's circuit. It was all very messy and all too easy to leave for more important matters. It was hard work and a constant nightmare for me; I often felt desperate with no help and practically nothing going right. However, on reflection, it was good training for the strain that was to come. One source of relief was gunnery practice and most of us looked forward to that. It was a chance to fly under telling conditions and to release the awesome destructive power of the fighter. A lot of my rage and frustration was worked out on the innocent targets on the range. We used either Schleisheim near Munich or Schwäbisch Hall. The latter was favourite for us because we could reach it easily from Böblingen, but Schleisheim required a landing at Munich before the exercise.

It was at a gunnery exercise where Hinnerk Waller and I once really created a problem for our Squadron Leader, Helmut Kühle, causing him to consider disciplinary action against us. A training shoot was made on targets which were three metres square. To attack these our two fuselage mounted 7.92 mm Rheinmetall Borsig MG 17 machine guns were each loaded with a belt of only 50 rounds (full magazines provided exactly 1000 rounds for each gun in the 'E' and 500 rounds per gun in the 'D' The object of the exercise was to teach selective shooting and to encourage the pilots to fire in short bursts to conserve their ammunition. Five approaches were to be made, ideally firing ten rounds from each gun on each approach. For this we were using the older 'Doras', not only because they were virtually obsolete, but because it was easier for the *Waffenwarte* (armourers) to adjust the machine gun interrupter mechanism for the two-blade prop, rather than the big three-blader on the 'Emil' which was more crucial and still at the training stage for many of them. In the air our experience had shown there was a certain harmonious sympathy between the guns and the rate at which the propeller was turning. At about 1800 rpm the guns fired nicely, but much faster or slower and they were made to stutter by the interrupter unit. We had yet to work out this ideal with the 'Emil'; in many respects it was still a very new aircraft.

The routine was to approach the targets under power at about 200 metres altitude and then reduce the rpm to 1800 ready for firing. The aircraft would settle in a stable glide and we would line up the Revi gunsight, pulling the trigger as the target came to bear. There were strict instructions not to go below 50 metres because some pilots had flown right into the targets or hit the ground after their pass and here was the problem; the lower you flew the better the line you had on the target by reducing the deflection caused by too much altitude. To be sure of a maximum score it was an advantage to be as close to in-line with the target as possible and this might mean gliding down to ground-zero, in contravention of the standing orders. In order to control the enthusiasm of the pilots we would always have an observer near to the targets to report back where necessary.

I wanted to do well with my gunnery; maybe I felt that I had to off-set some of the negativity which seemed to follow me on the ground. In any event I had, in my enthusiasm to excel, flown very low but had achieved a near perfect score. I had rationed my ammunition correctly for the five passes and had recorded 97 hits out of 100. That, I thought, made up for a lot. Kühle wasn't so keen on the result and questioned me closely about my altitude on the approach. I was little indignant and asked him to call *Leutnant* Waller in the observation booth. He did, with nothing unusual being reported by my faithful friend, Hinnerk. However my little triumph didn't last long as a mechanic, who was reloading the magazines, reported that the radiator on my aircraft was leaking. The 'Dora' had the one big radiator centrally located under the 'chin' of the fuselage, whereas the later 'Emil' had two radiators - one under each wing. Kühle came with me to inspect the problem and the reason for the leak was obvious. Inside the cowling and in the fins of the radiator matrix were small pieces of gravel which had been thrown up by the impact of the bullets as I had almost clipped the ground after passing the target. The damage wasn't too bad so I was able to fly back to Böblingen, but later Hinnerk and I were treated to a royal dressing-down by Kühle, who accused us of conspiracy and falsehood. That was a bit hard because it hadn't been premeditated, it had just been that Hinnerk had seen my success and was loath to ruin it for his friend. Unfortunately, Kühle was a stickler for the rules and it wouldn't be the last time I'd be in trouble by virtue of that.

We only attended the ground shoot four times because of the logistical problems of getting to Schleisheim and because the ranges at Schwäbisch

Hall were being used more and more by the bombers. This had an advantage for me which wasn't immediately obvious. My role as *NO* was now being accepted and with my NCOs well trained I was available for other duties. This soon brought me another title, *Flugleitungsoffizier*[1]. Among other duties, I had to liaise with Lufthansa to draw up contingency plans for emergency landings and similar events in the Stuttgart area. But the real advantage of my new position was that I had standing permission for unlimited low flying to locate a possible site for gunnery practice which would be for the exclusive use of *I./JG 52*. At last I had some freedom to fly as I'd always wanted to ever since I had first sat in a '109, and I took advantage of it. I can't say that I flew the aircraft to its limit but I certainly flew it to mine; up the line of the Alb and plunging down past the grey volcanic cliffs into the Neckar Valley; over the tree-lined ridges, clipping their apexes and hurtling low over the small villages on the Alb where I had grown up. For as long as I could justify it, I immersed myself in the sheer joy of flying that machine in the way I had always wanted. It is a memory of my days as a pilot that is still one of the most vivid and treasured.

For my low flying forays there were ample 'Doras' available but the 'Emils' were being kept in strict reserve. Only as many hours as were needed for familiarisation were permitted on the 'Emils' and they were otherwise kept in a state of readiness in case of 'emergencies'. There was constant talk of a military solution to our territorial disputes and more and more the name of Poland was spoken. The media gave increasing coverage of atrocities being committed on German 'immigrants'[2] in Poland and it was hard not to think of war when you saw that your fellow countrymen were being so badly treated.

But before these events were to conspire to overtake us there were two significant manoeuvres to be undertaken. The first was to transfer the whole *Gruppe* to Wengerohr in the Eifel and this, for the *Nachrichtenzug,* would be our first real test. Because of my other duties involved with the move, I couldn't fly in and went with half of my troops in the mobile unit, going ahead and setting up our communications - just as we would in battle. It was exactly what we had prepared for.

We were on site first and the setting up of our transmitter station and hooking into the telephones went like the well practised exercise it was. One thing caused me doubts but that was nothing to do with my unit. The prescribed landing strip was very soft and I tried to make contact with base to advise them to land where we had set up a directional landing 'T' with white linen. However, the message didn't reach the pilots and the first aircraft to arrive didn't have a radio to receive landing instructions. He came in as he'd been briefed before departure and, as predicted, his main wheels sank in, fortunately doing no more damage than standing the aircraft on its nose. Most of the rest had radios and we were able to relay the problem to them and detail a landing where the ground was firmer. It was a small triumph for the *Nachrichtenzug*. Not only had the mobile unit arrived and set up successfully whilst our colleagues maintained the base coms, but we had also, to a large degree, averted more damage and possible fatalities by having clear ground-to-air communications. We were pleased with the result but it would have been foolish to make too much of it within the *Gruppe*.

During the summer most of our air gunnery training took place on the island of Wangerooge in the Fresian Islands. The whole group went for two weeks, but for one of the Adjutants, *Leutnant* Fermer, and for myself, it would only be one week. We had been 'selected' to stay one week each at Böblingen to cope with the routine administration. It was here, as you will remember, that I was able to pull my own personal dossier and discover what poison *Oberleutnant* Schmidt had put in it while I was at *Luftkriegsschule*. Even then I didn't know how much of what this spiteful man had penned was to affect me in the long run. I had the first week at base and then it was my turn to fly out to Wangerooge for my gunnery. The flight from Böblingen would be a treat for me, being a journey of something over 500 km (300 miles); I hadn't done an *Uberland* like that for some time. I was to use the squadron's Me 108 and that was a bonus on a long journey; it was a lot more comfortable than the close confines of a fighter. I was anxious to be off because the weather, which was already bad, seemed to be deteriorating rather than improving. I got permission from the Stuttgart Weather Station but it was a close run thing; I should really have erred on the safe side and waited but I was, as usual, keen to be flying.

As the Met. Men had predicted, I couldn't fly along the Rhine to get out over the North Plains of Germany but I couldn't swallow my pride and turn back either. I wanted to get to Wangerooge and once more my natural impatience forced me into danger. I'd only had eight hours experience of blind flying so I was very foolish to attempt what I did. I flew straight into the weather front and at once was totally dependent on my instruments. At first it was alright but the constant buffeting by the turbulence in the clouds made it a fight to fly the Messerschmitt. Flying in severe turbulence in clear weather is hard enough, even with the horizon and other visual points of reference to help. On instruments alone it becomes a nightmare, a battle between what the swimming instruments tell you is the truth and what your senses tell you is happening. In the end I lost control and the aircraft fell out of the cloud above the middle of the Siebengebirge, the hills which surround Bonn. I had been lucky not to stall, spin or simply fly into a hillside or mountain; so many others had under similar conditions. I had, however, made enough progress through the front to be able to fly on at a reduced altitude and made it to the island. Once there, I told only Hinnerk Waller of my experience and he quietly checked me in.

Wangerooge was a wonderful time for all of us, both pilots and ground crews alike. There weren't any maintenance crews based on the island so we had brought along our own 'Black Men'[1] in the replacement *Tante Ju.*

Wangerooge - Leisure After Gunnery Training Wangerooge was a wonderful time . . . there was swimming and sunbathing . . . This picture shows Hinnerk Waller and myself in the dunes of Wangerooge.

It just couldn't have been a better vacation. There were about two hours flying in the day and then the rest of the time was largely our own. The Frisian Islands were, and still are, popular holiday resorts and we had beautifully sunny weather for our stay. In the daytime there was swimming and sunbathing and in the evening the girls were delighted to see so many young men. Surprisingly, for an isolated culture, the girls were good dancers and pleasantly sophisticated.

Other distractions apart, the flying was the real pleasure for us. For the first time we began to stretch ourselves as dog-fighting was combined with gunnery. The bright sunshine together with low flying made hard, black shadows of our colleagues' aircraft on the sea, presenting fast moving targets. Although we couldn't count the number of strikes we made, this was off-set by the advantage that we could at least see where our aim was and if we were missing to correct it.

The other type of target work was on a drogue which was towed by a Junkers F 13. This was to practise the beam attack and was done at the same altitude as the towing aircraft. Needless to say the job of flying the Junkers wasn't very popular. We were always using live ammunition and a mistake in the angle of deflection could result in the Junkers collecting a burst of fire. It did happen but, I am glad to say, not on our course.

The beam attack was one which would prove to be devastating in aerial combat, though, because of the difficulties of the approach and the very, very limited time 'on target', it was not extensively used. If employed, however, a successful attack would have the attacker flying a parallel course to the target for a few moments and then turning in at right angles and ahead of it. As the target then crossed through the gunsight the trigger would be pressed. The result would be that the target would fly through a hail of fire that would rake it from nose to tail along a line which was generally only lightly armoured. The problems with this mode of attack were obvious because of the difficulty of positioning the attacking aircraft on the correct course and at the right range and relied, to a great extent, on the target 'cooperating' by flying straight and level. On the whole, it was left unused in favour of the traditional attack from astern of the target, which was easier to set up and to control.

With a week of rest and flying we returned to Böblingen refreshed and in the full bloom of health. One thing I wished I'd had there was a cine camera and as I flew back to base in a '109, I resolved to contact Mr Rose at the Zeiss Ikon factory and purchase an 8 mm camera. It is a decision I never regretted and today some of the films that I made still exist. Many, however, were lost as the squadron moved around after 1940. But I did manage to keep some and today they provide a unique view of *3/JG 52* – its machines and more important to me, a living record of so many friends and colleagues who, without my camera, would now be no more than a faint memory.

Although my new role as *Flugleitungsoffizier* had brought me the freedom I had craved to fly when and virtually where I wanted to, it also had an unpleasant side. The Chief Test Pilot for Klemm Werke, the aircraft factory at Böblingen, was Helmuth Kalkstein. He was a very able pilot and a character we had all grown used to seeing about the airfield. On one quite ordinary day, we became aware of the gradually increasing howl of an aircraft diving towards the ground. That in itself wasn't unusual, we were used to it, but this had a strangely oscillating note to it which alerted us to the fact that all was not well - the aircraft was spinning. As people spilled from the building there came a sickening crash and the noise stopped abruptly. A little way from the airfield boundary we could see a column of smoke and dust rising and knew what had happened. The word soon spread that Kalkstein had 'gone in' and as *Flugleitungsoffizier* I was required to attend with the first crews on the tragic scene.

It was confirmed that the pilot had not escaped and there in the shattered wreckage of the Klemm was the body of Kalkstein, horribly smashed and decapitated, an awful sight. That and the crash of my friend Fischer at *Luftkreigsschule* determined me that I would always try to avoid having to see the results of accidents in future. It always brought back too many emotional memories.

Away from such tragedies I, as youngest *Leutnant,* was chosen for yet another 'special assignment'. I was briefed to deliver a huge bouquet of flowers to the *Kommandeuse* (Commander's wife), *Frau Grafin* (Lady) *von* Pfeil. The flowers were selected and purchased by *Leutnant* Fermer and he had also arranged the taxi for me for 11:00 hrs. sharp - a good time for 'official' visits. I duly presented myself in my dress uniform and climbed into the taxi. Fermer gave the address to the driver although he didn't sound too sure of himself.

When I arrived at the address there was no house there at all and I was left to sort out the problem. I telephoned Fermer from a call box and he apologised, telling me that the address was, in fact, Herman Göringstrasse which was situated on the other side of the town. Further, he told me there was no more money for a taxi and so I'd had to walk! So I found myself walking through the town in my parade uniform, white gloves and all, almost dwarfed by the huge bouquet of flowers. To say I felt foolish would be an understatement but I certainly got some very strange looks from the people I passed.

I eventually got to the address at 11:30 and walked up three floors in the neat block of apartments. At the door of the correct number there was a woman, who I took to be the cleaner, on her hands and knees cleaning the floor with a wet cloth. So lost was she in her work that she didn't even hear my approach, I had to reach out and touch her shoulder to get her attention. She looked around a little startled and her eyes darted from the flowers to my uniform and back to the flowers again. Without too much formality I asked if she would be so good as to announce me to *Grafin von* Pfeil und Klein Ellguth. She got up wiping her hands on her apron and looked me full in the face, a little humour in her eyes, 'That's me,' she said, 'Please come in.' She turned out to be a lady of great humour and character and we had an enormous laugh about the whole affair. We had a long talk and began a kind of friendship that was to last for some time into the future. Later, in September, when the war began, she would occasionally send me a letter and a small gift, a book or something similar.

My career at that stage seemed to be a constant and unremitting fluctuation between pain and pleasure; of being almost grounded to being given the virtual freedom of the skies; of seeing Kalkstein killed and the fun of delivering the flowers to *Grafin von* Pfeil. I was half expecting another sad event when it happened, right on cue. It was another funeral, this time for *Oberleutnant* Kraft Eberhardt[3] who had been killed in Spain back in 1936. It had taken that long to be able to recover his body and return it to Germany so that he could have a full military funeral. All the officers of *I/JG 52* were asked to participate along with many of his family, friends and colleagues from other *Gruppen.* It was an unnerving experience, cremating a man who had been dead for nearly three years; it gave a surrealistic atmosphere to the whole proceedings. The family were solemn and grim-faced, but didn't seem to want to talk, or share their grief with others who were present. At the time I didn't quite know what to make of this, whether it was political pressure or possibly direct orders not to communicate, it just didn't feel right at all. On reflection they were just probably upset about having an old wound opened again, after so long a time, so that the Government could stage an elaborate funeral to bury one of Germany's heroic fallen. In any event it was another experience I could well have foregone.

A short while after the funeral we were involved in one of the largest, and one of the last, peacetime manoeuvres the *Luftwaffe* was to stage. It was to be led by *General* Sperrle, who had commanded the Legion Condor from 1936 through 1937, and was focused upon Stuttgart; a huge bomber force composed of He IIIs, Do. 17s, some Ju. 86s and the spectacular Ju. 87 Stukas.

*The funeral of Obltn. Kraft Eberhardt. All the officers of I/JC 52
were asked to participate and many other friends of his and the
family were following the coffin.*

Their targets were Stuttgart and the key industrial sites like the Bosch and Daimler Benz factories. The bombers were in great strength but we were stretched to provide a realistic fighter force. Therefore it was suggested that each individual fighter would represent a squadron; *I/JG 52* being assisted by other fighters from Mannheim and Bad Aibling.

I, in my role as *Nachrichtenoffizier*, was not to fly but to supervise both the communications and the warnings to the civilians. I was still not yet 21 and I was to be responsible for telling 550,000 people when they should scuttle down into their shelters and, at the same time, direct the fighters by radio to attack the bomber force. Yes, at last, we had a situation where instructions had been issued that all available fighters would be fitted with *Funkgerate (FuG* - radio) - and tuned to the same frequency as our 1.5 kW transmitter, which was situated right next to the control tower at Böblingen.

The personnel of the *Nachrichtenzug* felt, as I did, that they were ready for this test and were proud of what we had achieved by hours of practice and many exercises. We had started with nothing and less than no help from our immediate seniors but we had built a competent and confident communications platoon which was as good as any other in the *Luftwaffe*. They were eager to show their mettle and I was confident that what we did would vindicate our hard work and illustrate what effect good communications would have. We had now trained up to the point where the operators could transmit from 40-100 km (25–60 miles), depending on the weather and atmospheric conditions. The forecast for the day of the manoeuvres was good, clear and sunny, the weather would be on our side and we hoped that, by the end of the day, so would some of the squadron leaders.

On the day I made an early start, being driven into Stuttgart in *von* Pfeil's Staff Car to make an inspection and to meet the girls who operated the telephone switchboards for the *Deutsche Reichpost* (Post Office), which was situated below the *Königspalast.* A significant part of this exercise was that it was to put everyone on a war footing and therefore the civilian switchboards were temporarily placed under the control of the *Luftwaffe,* the operators now being part of a nationwide network through which the visual contacts and plots of approaching aircraft would be passed. When I arrived in my uniform, complete with 'Wings', I was applauded by the girls as I walked down the aisles of switchboards and felt a combination of embarrassment and pleasure at the accolade. It had been *Major* Nussbaum's idea that I should visit the exchange and I have to admit that, at first, I had thought it was a bit silly. However, I now saw that it would be a positive aid to motivation and learned what impact the 'personal' touch can have in effective management of people.

My first impressions of the performance of the ground personnel was that things were working outstandingly well. We had some frontline wireless posts reporting direct to my unit with these being backed up by *Luftmeldekompanien (Luftnachrichten* - Observer Corps) reporting by telephone. Altogether there were some 1200 people involved in the reporting network and from their information we were able to plot the track and speed of the incoming bomber force accurately. As a result we were able to scramble our limited fighter forces right on time and to vector them directly onto their targets.

The bombers came in from three directions, Frankfurt, Wurzburg and Nürnberg, and our fighters were able to intercept them between 80-100 km (50-60 miles) from their targets and engage them in dogfights with good success; this time some of the '109s were carrying cameras to record their 'hits'. Only the Ju. 87 Stukas came in very low and were only picked up at the last minute, too late for us to do much at all, but I did try to divert a fighter force by using the radio. I was later told by the Deuschle and Stephan families that the attack on the bridges on the Neckar River by the '87s had been most spectacular. What they had witnessed as a practice would soon be a common sight on what would become the battlefields of Europe

After the exercise the bulk of the aircraft returned to their bases, with just the more senior of the officers-in-command and their crews landing at Böblingen to take part in the debrief. This was to be held in the *Kasino* where a good PA system had been set up by the *Nachrichtenzug*. That, in itself, was no mean feat back in those days; to provide adequate amplification and reliability without feedback or breakdown had involved substantial ingenuity on the part of my men combined with *Major* Nussbaum's own unit. The *Kasino* was full to capacity without a single spare chair to be had and we eagerly awaited the views of *General* Sperrle. He was full of praise for the successful defence of Stuttgart and its industries. The bomber crews, in turn, were praised for their precise timing, assembly according to flight plans and good formation flying to the targets; the fighters, likewise, for their alertness and for picking up the formations early - but nobody seemed to want to say anything about the communications that had been the key to it all. It had been the observers who had been in the right place to make the correct identification and estimate of courses. They had communicated that through our network which had worked virtually faultlessly. We had then been able to scramble the fighters on time and give them solid and accurate vectors for interception. The result had been an almost textbook defence, illustrating how vital good communications would be in the future. But not a word was said.

I just couldn't let this pass, there were too many people who had contributed and deserved recognition; and so with all the courage I could muster I asked a question: 'And what, *General* Sperrle, could you say about the performance of the reporting and directions from the ground?'

He didn't get the chance to answer, Galland stepped forward and took the initiative saying, 'Good Steinhilper, you have reminded me - you were talking too much (I had been told explicitly by *Graf von* Pfeil that I should personally make the radio transmissions). You were just bothering us all of the time. And as I've always told you, it would be best to throw out all of these damned radios! We don't need them. We didn't need them in Spain and without them we could fly higher and faster!'... There was a murmured approval from the audience before the next question was put and that was the end of my attempt at recognition for the people who had done so well, and for the principle of good communications and how well it had been shown to serve us.

I was stunned and humiliated by Galland's attack in the face of what I had seen as an overwhelming vindication of everything we had been trying to do. I just couldn't believe that Galland and so many others were still so blind. As I looked around I could see that nobody was going to pursue the matter any further; it was obvious the subject was closed and in any event the meeting was being brought to a close. Emotion welled up in me, anger, sadness and sheer frustration. I had worked hard to get communications up to the standard that we had. My men and altogether 1200 other people had worked hard to make the exercise a success. Without their help Galland and the other fighter commanders would still have been chasing around the skies hunting for the bombers, which would have undoubtedly reached their targets. Then, not only to let this pass without a word of praise, but to discredit us in front of so many others was not just poor management it was totally indefensible. My morale and that of the *Nachrichtenzug* took a body-blow and there was little I could do about that. It was a time when I despaired for the future. Again I had been taught a lesson and was about to receive another.

As communications officer I had helped set up our teleprinter network and was, by virtue of my position, aware of most of the traffic on this medium. In the middle of July a teleprinter message came from Berlin instructing *Oberleutnant* Galland to assume command of a Henschel HS 123 Squadron which was stationed on the Polish border. I was excited, thinking that without the influential Galland about I would be able to fully develop our communications and hoped for a more enlightened replacement. But I wasn't to be rid of my adversary as easily as that. Galland replied that he didn't like that idea at all, that he had flown more than 300 ground-attack sorties in Spain which had only been recognised by his award of the *Spanienkreuz in Gold mit Schwertern* (the Spanish Cross in gold and with swords) - whereas others with just 7 aerial victories had been awarded the *Spanienkreuz in Gold mit Brillianten* (with Diamonds). He pointed out that this seemed to be an injustice and he didn't want to be party to further injustice and would rather remain a squadron leader in a fighter group. He had done his share and felt someone else should take the role of *Schlachtflieger* (ground attack) this time. I really wondered at the nerve of Galland and was curious about the outcome. That was swift in coming; there was a signal for Galland to report to Berlin, it was signed by Göring himself.

Galland wasn't away long and returned proudly telling of his new decoration, *Spanienkreuz in Gold mit Brillianten.* He explained that under new conditions he was prepared to assume command of the Henschel Squadron. Certainly Galland had judged the situation correctly and had secured for himself what he wanted in return for giving the High Command what they wanted, but it was still a surprise to me that an *Oberleutnant* had such bargaining power. I was reminded of what influence Galland had in the *Luftwaffe* and in what obvious esteem he was held. There would be no doubt that his myopic views on communications would greatly influence the progress of the *Luftwaffe* in this field. At that time I could only speculate as to what the cost of this lack of progress might be; later I would see it graphically demonstrated. *Oberleutnant* Galland left *I/JG 52* in late July 1939, to be replaced by *Oberleutnant* Wilhelm Keidel, another veteran of Spain.

Notes on Chapter 9

1. *Flugleitungsoffizier* (see page 177) - Navigation and liason officer.

2. 'Immigrants' (see page 177) - The ex-patriot Germans in Poland were not, strictly speaking, immigrants. They had been living and working in what had been part of Germany prior to East Prussia being partitioned by the Polish Corridor by the Treaty of Versailles.

3. Oberleutnant Kraft Eberhardt (see page 182) - Killed in action 13th November 1936 in Spain, having scored seven victories.

CHAPTER 10

At the Western Front - Whilst the War is in Poland

In a way it was fortunate that I kept very busy during the months of July and August, or I would probably have got into more trouble. I really resented the way in which our efforts in communications had been swept aside by Galland and how he and his cronies still tried to belittle the importance of good radio communications. No doubt if I had had the time there would have been another minor revolution by me; probably producing something cynical like my earlier treatise about the importance of ensigns jumping out of windows. And, no doubt, that would have had the same consequences as far as my personal dossier went.

Back in June I was very tempted to speak up when the Legion Condor triumphantly returned from Spain. In Berlin they paraded in front of Hitler and in Stuttgart they appeared en-mass with full military bands, to march from the railway station, past grandstands filled with the cream of our *Württenberger* political and military leadership, up the Königstrasse and ending at the Königsbau.

I suppose it would have been OK if the troops that marched were actually from the Legion Condor, but most of our real veterans had opted to stay at home or at the base. The bulk of the returning 'heroes' were just ordinary *Luftwaffe* personnel who'd never been outside Germany. It was all so contrived to exact the last piece of political kudos from the 'victory' in Spain. The whole thing was a sham, a typical Joseph Göbbels Hollywood production. It made me sick.

It was as well that my job as Navigation Officer was keeping me very busy or I would have got myself into real hot water, but I just didn't have the time. A Heinkel *Kadett* had made an emergency landing on the unfinished stretch of *Autobahn* near Marbach. The pilot, a *Hauptmann*, had been increasing his flying hours for his A2 licence when he ran out of fuel. He wasn't seriously hurt but the aircraft had been badly damaged as it hit the embankment of the road. It wasn't airworthy anymore and we had to dismantle it to remove it from the site. On another occasion an Me 108 *Taifun* had also run out of fuel but in this case the pilot had executed a first class landing in a field about 80 km (50 miles) from us. We drove there with fuel and I had the responsibility of deciding whether it could be flown out by the pilot, a grave responsibility for one so young. He managed it but the paperwork which these incidents generated was phenomenal to say the least.

Another occasion again took days of my time: An Me 108 (4 seat Taifun) had run out of fuel, but had been skillfully landed in a field. We had to drive there (about 80km), equipped with gasoline to refuel, inspect the aircraft and I had to take responsibility for permitting it to be taken out by the pilot. Fortunately he managed.

I seemed to get the duties that had very loose job descriptions and because of this I was constantly the recipient of tasks that other people could clearly say were not theirs. As Navigation Officer I had been responsible for the work generated by the emergency landings and now another little 'plum' dropped onto my desk. The *NSFK (Nationalsozialistische Fliegerkorps)* had arranged the 1939 *Küstenflug* (Coastal flight - a civilian flying competition) and it had been arranged for it to pass through Böblingen on the leg from the North Sea. The letter had been addressed to *von* Pfeil and agreement and co-operation had been promised by *Leutnant* Fermer, the Adjutant, and *Leutnant* Geller of the 1st Squadron. That was kind of them but in reality the work fell to me. In all there would be 50 aircraft, both large and small, landing and taking off and I was to be responsible for it all. And naturally if anything went wrong I would be to blame. As it was the whole thing went well, but I was getting more than a little fed up with people saying on the one hand that it was OK for me to be responsible for an event like that or deciding on the spot whether an aircraft was fit to fly – but then taking no notice of the good work that we were doing on communications and dismissing me as the youthful and over-enthusiastic communications officer.

There was a break from this when we went to the University of Freiburg, which had a small department specialising in aeronautical medicine. We were to undergo some high altitude simulations which would give us experience of high altitude flight, whilst helping the staff of the University with their research. During those early days of the War, we were really pushing back the limits of technology. For instance my aircraft, the Bf 109 E was capable of flying up to and just beyond 10,000 metres (33,000 ft). That, by today's standards, is nothing special, but then we felt like we were on the threshold of space, without pressurised cabins. Oxygen equipment in those days was very crude and, for the most part, consisted of a rubber tube which terminated at one end in a mouth piece and at the other in a fitting for the oxygen cylinder and regulator. The mouthpiece was held in place by the teeth - the ori-nasal face mask would not be available to us until March 1940.

On the appointed date we all drove there in our own cars, motoring through the beautiful Schwarz Wald (Black Forest). The former Legion Condor men drove their fancy sports cars, mostly Adler Triumph. I drove alone with Seddy, my dog, for company in my DKW. Hinnerk Waller rode with Kühle. Horst Tietzen, who was still with us then, brought up the rear.

At the university we were put into a barrel-shaped pressure chamber, four at a time. Then the chamber was sealed and the air inside evacuated, as though we were rising in altitude. We were taken up to an equivalent of about 8,000 metres (26,000 ft) - our metabolism and general health being monitored all of the time. For the purposes of these first experiments the air mixture remained constant, at the same proportions as we would experience at ground level. The test was focused on the effects of pressure, the oxygen testing was to come next.

Leutnant Fermer who went on to become Squadron Leader 7/JG52
seen here with his standard poodle.

This was not to train us to be able to resist the problems of oxygen starvation, there is no way of resisting it, but to enable us to recognise the first subtle signs and act before events overtook us. The test was set up in a room where we would sit comfortably, but still wear an oxygen mask through which different mixtures of gases could be fed to us. The masks were of the ori-nasal type that were to be issued to us later on. To help us and the supervising staff to judge our progress at the various 'altitudes' we were given a simple task to perform, writing consecutive numbers on sheets of paper; first progressing numerically upwards and then counting backwards. This, of course, would have been child's play under normal conditions but, as the oxygen content of the breathing mixture was reduced, so the problems became apparently more difficult.

The main point of the test was for us to begin to feel when the insidious effects of oxygen starvation began, so that we could recognise them and take appropriate remedial action. Therefore, during the test, if we felt that we were beginning to lose concentration or to feel light-headed, we were to indicate to the supervising officers and doctor that we should go down by showing the thumbs-down sign. We all performed the tasks to various levels of success but, in all cases, we were taken to the point where we lost consciousness. As this was done the doctor would be constantly monitoring our pulse and as soon as we passed out, the oxygen mixture was enriched and we would struggle back to consciousness.

Our visit to the University of Frieburg. Our cars are lined up -
the ex-Legion Condor men having the better cars. Left to right:
Horst Tietzen's Adler Truimph Junior with special Glaser body.
Horst at the wheel and Hinnerk Waller about to get in. Behind,
Helmut Kühle's Triumph, Kühle about to get in to the driver's seat.
Behind that is my little DKW

It was curious to observe that my colleagues seemed to react to the rarefied mixture in a very similar way to which they reacted to alcohol. We had been together as a unit for some time now and had, from time to time, been present at celebrations in the *Kasino* and a few private parties. Each of us was, therefore, fairly well aware of how the others would react if well imbibed with drink. Like the individual members of any group we each reacted in different ways. Some would become softer and more amiable, everyone their friend or the love of their life. Others, me included in this group, became hostile and aggressive.

So, as the level of oxygen was lowered, effectively climbing higher into the rarefied atmosphere, the tell-tale signs began to emerge. Hinnerk Waller began to laugh and chuckle. Very soon the complexities of the simple mathematics were too much for him and he reverted happily to drawing ever larger circles and spirals on his note-pad. I, however, concentrated fiercely on the sums. I would not be defeated by this simple law of nature. Soon I was breaking pencils in my effort to concentrate and prove that I could overcome this phenomenon. Nevertheless, as the signs began to show I would give the thumbs down and the oxygen level in my mask would be increased, but it wasn't easy. The tell-tale signs were very subtle and I could see afterwards that although I had given the right signs eventually, I had, in the interim, made several errors in the simple mathematical progression. It was easy to see how high flying accidents happened when oxygen failed. Later, when we resumed our normal operational flying, we would not only watch out for ourselves but would always keep an eye on our fellow pilots in their aircraft. Any strange behaviour would be met with an order to take their aircraft down to a safe altitude.

Apart from short breaks like this the work was fairly unremitting. I really found it difficult to find time to see Gretl and even harder to get some flying time in. However, one time when I got the use of a Focke Wulf Stösser, I took an aerial photograph of Mr Stephen's beautiful house and also of the Ski Club's country retreat. The Stephans were impressed with the picture of the Ski Club and turned their copy into a postcard. Maybe, if it hadn't been for the advent of war, I would have been successful with my idea to fly about the world photographing it from the air.

The political situation looked clear to us. There was much discussion in the officers' mess but not too much wisdom. Our sources of information were a little one-sided; we could listen to the political speeches which had never been more than economical with the truth; or we could read the newspapers, but they were really only another organ of the government.

There weren't any independent views to be had, other than our own. The general attitude was that sooner or later the politicians would finish their posturing and then it would be up to soldiers like us to sort out what they'd done.

There seemed to be little doubt that it would end in a military solution. There were some discussions about the return to us of Danzig and possible solutions to the problems of connecting East Prussia with the rest of the Reich, but the fanciful talk of neutral territory autobahns eventually came to nothing. There was no solution to this, the most vexing of the clauses of the Versailles *Diktat*. More and more we were receiving news of how the Poles were treating the Germans in Poland. There were interviews on the radio and, if we got the chance to get out to the cinema, there would be newsreel footage of these atrocities. I don't think there was any question at the time that this was substantially the truth and that we would soon have to go to the assistance of our fellow countrymen.

When I had the opportunity to talk with my parents or with Mr Stephan, Gretl's father, I would take a predictably impatient line: 'Wouldn't it be worth taking the risk of the military option instead of all this 'horse trading' with Italy, England, France and even Bolshevik Russia?' It wasn't only my father who erred on the safe-side, saying that once started, a war is not so easily stopped. He spoke of his own experience of the First War and how difficult it had been to find a reasonable solution to stop the bloodshed. Mr Stephan, who was involved in the construction of the Westwall on the French border, was also very cautious. Because of the closeness of his work with the government he had to be very careful in what he said, but his general opinion was that another war would be lost before we had even begun. All that was missing was the death and destruction in-between.

Athough Gretl's father could say little about what he learned in the closed circles of Berlin, it became obvious that things were coming to a head. More and more frequently he was being called to the capital to report on progress and it was obvious that he was under pressure to complete by a certain date.

This brings us to a point which is worth examining - to see how transport communications have changed. Mr Stephan was at great pains to evaluate which was going to be to the best advantage to him - to take the night sleeper train to Berlin or to take the daytime flight from Stuttgart. On the train he could arrive refreshed by a night's sleep but a flight on a Lufthansa Ju. 52 would be 2½ hours of noise and turbulence, not to mention the anxiety of actually flying. When balancing out the two, Mr Stephan chose to undertake the journey by train, involving two nights away, rather than the five hour return trip by air. Air travel was still something quite extra-ordinary in Germany, as it was everywhere.

On the 23rd August the Hitler/Stalin non-aggression treaty was signed and for a few days it looked like another deal for peace had been struck. But it was confusing and seemed to be a complete reversal of what we had thought was Hitler's policy. At the time the real enemy of Germany was not thought to be France or England or really even the Poles; it was the Bolsheviks. That was very understandable - following the First War the communists had almost run riot in Germany. My own father, when returning from the front, did not get a hero's welcome after years of fighting for his country, but had the badges and insignia torn from his uniform and a beating from a marauding gang of German Bolsheviks. It would become clear what this 'alliance' with Stalin was about when, at Christmas 1939, Hitler visited our *Gruppe*. He would make a speech which spelled out how he saw our new 'allies' and it would also give us an insight into what motivated him, and what kind of man he was.

But for us, the military, it was better that we turned our attention to the tasks in hand. We would have no influence over this political philandering and it was better that we demonstrate strength by our state of readiness - in that way there might still be a chance for peace. And there were sacrifices enough without the necessity of war to produce them. On 15th August there had been an horrific flying accident at the military training area at Neuhammer, near the Polish boarder. I suppose it was a symptom of the times that we didn't hear of this on the radio, or see any newsreel at the cinema, but, gradually, details began to emerge from confidential reports and rumours. *I/StG 76* (The 1st Group of Stuka *Geschwader* 76) took off from Cottbus, near Berlin, for the exercise at Neuhammer. The early weather reports were for cloud from 2000 metres to 900 metres (6500 – 3000 ft) above the ground. If this were the case, the squadrons could assemble above the cloud and dive through with 900 metres being ample for them to identify the target, make any minor corrections, and pull out after releasing.

It was early morning when the Group Commander, *Hauptmann* Sigel, took off, flanked by his Adjudant, *Oberleutnant* Eppen, to the left and Technical Officer *Oberleutnant* Müller to the right. In all he led three squadrons up for the attack, thirty aircraft. The sequence was to be 2 Squadron first, followed by 3 Squadron, then 1 Squadron bringing up the rear. The first three aircraft peeled off into the dive and Sigel anxiously watched the altimeter as the hands wound around, winding off the precious height. At something like 100 metres (320 ft) he burst out of the cloud and had to haul back on everything he had to clear the ground. As it was, he ended up flying down a fire-break in the forest. Eppen crashed into the trees and Müller's plane burst into a ball of fire. Sigel shouted to his wireless operator/gunner to alert the others, but for a few it was too late. The remainder of 2 Squadron either didn't hear the message or were too far committed and one after another they hurtled out of the clouds and into the ground. Most of 3 Squadron managed to correct and clear the area as *Oberleutnant* Dietrich Peltz heard the alarm call and pulled 1 Squadron back up through the cloud without casualties. But in a few tragic moments thirteen crews, twenty-six young airmen, had died in a tragic accident.

The inquiry, chaired by *General* Hugo Sperrle, didn't find anyone culpable and the decimated ranks of the group were soon filled with new pilots and new machines from other squadrons so that the wound would heal quicker. But the lesson had to be learned that the weather, at peace or at war, would always be an unpredictable factor. The funerals were quiet and largely unreported affairs - a stark contrast to the 'Victorious return of the Legion Condor'.

At the beginning of August, together with *Major* Nussbaum, I had been to Echterdingen, the new airport for Stuttgart. It was a very modern complex complete with every new facility and convenience. A tarmac runway had been laid and the whole site had a feeling of being complete, of being purpose built. This was in contrast to Böblingen where so much had been 'bolted on' over the years. It was an architect's nightmare with its different hangars of various ages, barracks, weather station, tower, workshops and decrepit hotel. The representatives of *Luwag,* the airport handling company, were pleasant to us and friendly enough, but they couldn't hide their disappointment at our arrival. They were fearful that at the last minute they wouldn't assume their planned role as the terminal for flights from Stuttgart to Switzerland, Spain, France and the internal flights for Germany. They could see their new facilities being turned over to *I/JG 52* as our base, instead of having their official opening in September. As it was the opening was to be overtaken by other events and they only just managed to maintain a small service to Switzerland and Spain.

I imagine there was great relief when it became known that we were to transfer to Bonn Hangelar to protect the industrial Ruhr. Apparently this had been considered a more vulnerable or more important potential target than the Daimler, Mercedes and Bosch works which were located around Stuttgart.[1]

The first real indications of war had been apparent for a while. Whilst still at Böblingen, around the 25th August - just 9 days before the declaration of war on us - we had initiated the necessary military precautions. The reserve soldiers were mobilised and appeared in great numbers, so many in fact that we had to send some home. We, the regulars, were going about the business for which we had trained so long. All the fighters were loaded up to capacity with live ammunition and then moved out from the hangars to be dispersed around the airfield, squadron by squadron. Now our *Nachrichtenzug* could come into its own and we began to hook up telephone links to the remote dispersals. Our transmitter was rigged up by the tower, the mast rising majestically above it and dominating the transmitting frequencies. The civilian traffic still flew, but it began to look out of place as trenches were dug beside dispersed aircraft and machine guns and light AA guns began to appear. It was all hard work for the squadrons, but a spectacle of great interest to the local population, who would line the fences to see our preparations. It may have been their way of verifying that it was all true - that war might just be a few days away.

Quite out of the blue I was instructed to go as advance officer to Bonn Hangelar. Assisted by my batman, Hans Steeger, we loaded all my belongings into my faithful little DKW and drove off home to Heutingsheim to leave the bulk of my kit there. My radio, movie camera, laundry and spare uniforms all went into the house and my car was garaged in the barn opposite, which belonged to the vicarage. That was soon done and, with a few words from my mother to be careful, I got back into the staff car, which had followed me, and I was on my way back to Böblingen ready for an early start the next day.

Now I thought I was going to war. All I had with me was a very basic travelling kit, very Spartan indeed. First we drove on the *Autobahn* towards Frankfurt which, north of Heidelberg, was new to me. The driver knew it well and even stopped the car to show me the memorial stone which indicated the spot near Langen where Bernd Rosemeyer was killed attempting a land-speed record for cars in January 1938. We drove on through the beautiful countryside which was in the full bloom of summer; it was hard to believe that we were on the threshold of the abyss.

No sooner had we arrived at Bonn Hangelar and made contact with *Ltn.* Geller than I was told that the move was off. A change of orders; for the time-being we would stay at Böblingen. Nobody seemed to know why;

there were rumours - there are always rumours - that the Italians had intervened and so on but the result was the same for me, a long drive back. This time I stopped off at Heutingsheim and picked up some of my stuff; I had learned that I had been a bit too Spartan in my approach. I suppose I felt a little embarrassed too. After the soldier's farewells I was back because someone had changed their mind; a bit of a let-down.

Just a day later the orders were revised and the move was on again. This time I was to move with the complete *Nachrichtenzug* and set up ready for the arrival of the *Gruppe.* So our reconnaissance trip was not a waste of time. We had indentified all the bottlenecks and bad roads and so the trip, though slower because of the heavy vehicles, was really quite smooth. We even stopped off again at the Rosemeyer memorial and some other historic sites.

At Hangelar we were fully occupied from the outset installing the *Gefechtsstand* for the *Gruppe* in a small bus which we had requisitioned. We were so occupied hooking up telephone lines to the public circuit, laying out field telephones for the squadron dispersals and assembling the main transmitters that we didn't realise that general mobilisation had been declared. The *Wehrmacht* was already in Poland before we knew what was happening. The war had started without us. Three days later, on 3rd September, France, Britain, Australia and New Zealand declared that a state of war now existed between them and us. Although this monumental step struck fear into the hearts of many, especially the older generations, I rather welcomed it. I reasoned that it had to come sooner or later, so better make it sooner and the earlier we will be done with it. Either win or die. The ebulliant but naive philosophy of youth. I was not yet twenty-one.

Generally, the attitude was that what the government was doing was right. The Treaty of Versailles had crippled Germany and no country would have continued under its yoke. Once strong enough we had to overturn the clauses and, where necessary, recover what had been ours. The Treaty had been punitive and we had served our sentence. Thousands had starved following the first war and the economy had been left in ruins. We had rebuilt our health and our industry and it was time to throw off the shackles of that Treaty for good. It was time to go to the rescue of the German minority and liberate the *Korridor* and the City of Danzig. It had been obvious that some kind of fight would come with Poland and maybe also with France, but if Britain wanted to get involved then so be it. If they came to our backyard - then they could expect a fight too.

And that really was my only regret. I had never been to England although I had been taught good English in school. But I had, during those impressionable years, been convinced that to be English would be something great. One of my teachers, *Studienrat* (student teacher) Wobbelmann had been a real anglophile, telling us that the most wonderful thing he could conceive would be to have an English passport. Further, he had formed the opinion that they had the best developed secret service, which extended its tentacles all around the world. I had thought I would have liked to visit the English who, if the history books were to be believed, were our cousins in Europe. I would get there one day but not, perhaps, in quite the way I might have planned.

We, of course, felt disappointed to have been left out of the fighting in Poland where one victory had followed another. But we were proud to hear on the radio and to read in the papers what a decisive role the *Luftwaffe* was playing in the successful advances. Acting as accurate and highly mobile artillery, the *Luftwaffe* was working in close liason with the ground forces and would soon be largely responsible for the new tactical evolution later named *Blitzkrieg* (Lightning War). In the air the Polish airforce put up a stubborn fight and were not, as is popularly reported, knocked out on the ground. It was just that their aircraft were both inferior in design and too few to make a sustained impression on the *Luftwaffe*. We were still a long way from all this, but it still fell to us to do the best we could in case things went against us.

I really didn't have too much respect for most of the military and administrative nonsense which had been drummed into us at *Luftkriegsschule,* but every now and then something of use would emerge from my memory. For example, one of the many bright minds in my *Nachrichtenzug, Gefreiter* Treplin, came up with the idea that we should replace the obsolete field telephone network with a more moden 'Tannoy' system, with loudspeakers at the squadron dispersals. Like most innovative ideas it was great, but where would the money come from? Here my memories of the intricacies of military administration came back as I remembered 'In the case of mobilisation and the resulting emergency, there would become available special funds for urgent purchases direct from the public sector.' I got together with the *Gerateverwalter* (equipment clerk) and a *Zahlmeister* (quartermaster) from the *Fliegerhorst* and we discovered there was some 30,000 Marks set aside for exactly this kind of exigency. It was an enormous amount of money, my own little car had only cost 2,000 Marks, and we felt more than satisfied that we had uncovered this little oasis in the supplies desert.

We explained the scheme to *von* Pfeil and his reaction was to be a little amused by our enthusiasm, but why not do it? He said he'd sign the papers, it all looked legal. That was only the first hurdle, the rest of the course would require great initiative and determination from me and the *Nachrichtenzug*. Why was it always so difficult to effect change? I had to convince so many people of the existence of the fund and of the emergency, then acquire the newly introduced purchase orders from innumerable different public offices and last, but by no means least, we had to actually track down the equipment we needed.

At the core of the system would be a powerful amplifier, a massive multi-valved powerhouse which had multiple inlet and outlet sockets. Then we bought literally miles of heavy gauge copper wire because our own telephone wires were too thin and would have offered too much resistance to transmit a powerful signal to the speakers (to get all that we required, we virtually bought up the entire stock of the area). Then there were the speakers and the mounting poles and soon we had enough to start. The clever young *Gefreiter* Treplin had even had the foresight to include a record player in his shopping list which would add the last, really professional touch to what we were doing. It took about a week to complete what we had planned and we really didn't want to commission it until we were satisfied with the results. There were now speakers at all crucial points on the airfield; at each squadron's dispersal, adjacent to the hangars and even one close to our own *Bus-Gefechtsstand* (mobile battle headquarters or ops room) so that we could monitor what alarm we might be spreading. We hadn't raised any enthusiasm for the scheme when we first started but now, when it was operational, it was received with great acclaim. The benefits were more than we had expected and it added greatly to the quality of life of the *Gruppe.* If you wanted to contact someone you could just put a call out for him with a number to respond to, no more endless telephoning around the dispersals and hangars. When, later on, one of the squadrons was scrambled, the others wouldn't have to ring in to see what was happening, they would have heard the message as well. Probably best of all, due to the foresight of Treplin, we could play music all day and even hook in the radio for up-to-date news broadcasts. This really helped, we were told, when the pilots had to sit around in the famous deckchairs and cast-off armchairs, waiting for the scramble. The only problem was that you couldn't appeal to all tastes all of the time and sometimes we had to consider disconnecting the field telephones because of the constant stream of requests for favourite tunes.

In Hangelar at the beginning we were busy installing the
'Gefechtsstand' of the group in a conscripted bus.

Our conditions 'at war' were quite good but not as good as we had enjoyed at Böblingen. There was a canteen which served good, if rather plain, food. We had an officers' mess, as did the NCOs, and sleeping accommodation was in the form of some Nissen huts. Our *Gefechtsstand* was situated in a corner of the field where some cover was provided by birch trees and camouflaged netting. About 300 metres away lay the entrance to the Monastery of St Augustin. The monks were very interested in our activities and were quite open to us in return. It was the first time I had seen the real heart of a monastery and in particular their individual cells. I could see at first hand what a Spartan life was really like. We might have felt deprived in our field conditions but, compared with these hardy monks, we lived in decadent luxury.

We had just about settled down when a new unit appeared, *10/JG26.*.They called themselves *Nachtjager* (Nightfighters) and were equipped with the older '109 Doras. Due to the difficulty of night take-offs and landings they had been allocated the Doras in preference to the Emils because of their comparative stability. The squadron leader, *Oberleutnant* Johannes Steinhoff[2], was apparently a good friend of Kühle's, even though he had not been to Spain.

Our own squadron leaders seemed to talk about Steinhoff with pity, saying that he'd been crazy enough to 'invent' the idea of night flying and then went on to form the first *Nachtjager Staffel*. Our people thought the whole idea was ridiculous and were obviously glad that there was only one squadron operational. The idea that air warfare could, and would in the future, continue after dark was beyond their imagination. It was another example of the short-sightedness of some of the officers. I was interested in what they were doing and saw that good communications could be of value to them at night. So when they flew their night exercises I tried to communicate with them, but on the whole they seemed shy of the radio. I did succeed in exchanging a few sentences with Steinhoff but they didn't seem to want to try it. Maybe they had already heard enough funny remarks about their enterprise without getting involved with another faction which had already been labelled lunatic. I had thought they could have done with all the help they could get, their flying being to us nothing less than a nightmare. Whenever they had to scramble (and at that time they got more than us), or even when they were practising, they had no lights on the aerodrome at all. Nothing to mark the runway but two of their own staff cars with the headlights on. No direction finding equipment and no special radio. It was remarkable that there were not more accidents.

Their goal was to try to get some co-ordination between the huge searchlights which were based with the flak batteries around the Ruhr. I tried to establish if they had any plans to use direction finding radio or any navigational devices and found that there were none. I was interested in this particular idea and could see that it might have great potential for the nightfighters, but I couldn't make any progress. Later, when we left Hangelar, the idea dropped.

For our own interest we tried to develop the idea of direction finding by radio. *Uffz*. Krehe, my resident joker, had made firm contact with the airfield's direction finding *Feldwebel* on his own initiative. They talked a lot and involved more of the *Nachrichtenzug* who had been 'radio hams' (amateur radio enthusiasts) and, after some time, a possible method by which my idea of being able to give bearings for fighters came to light. Initially everybody thought the short wave transmissions would offer no solution, but together we developed the first crude method. By using feedback we could generate an oscillating signal that would produce an audible whistle on which we could take a bearing. This would be sent out from my aircraft and, because the source was known, the ground station could judge my range and bearing relative to them.

I had told *von* Pfeil what we were doing and he approved our continued research. First, I tested the method in good weather, high clouds and good visibility, but having my approach directed from the ground and only verifying my course visually. It was a far from simple method. *Uffz.* Krehe was seated next to the man who was taking the readings on the direction finding equipment (located some 2 km from the *Gefechtsstand* and the main transmitter). Krehe would talk by field telephone to our radio operator in the *Gefechtsstand* who would be in radio contact with me. He would tell me when to press the button in my aircraft so that they could take a bearing and have this fed back to me by the ground-station. I could then set my compass and fly on. Because there were two communication links, the direction finding equipment to ground-station by telephone and the ground-to-air communication by radio, it was a little complicated but nonetheless it worked. By keeping a steady speed on the approach we could easily calculate when I was overhead of the airfield. Our initial trials had been done with me flying at 2000 metres and later, under more realistic conditions, with a heavy cloud layer with a base at about 1000 metres. Just as we felt we were making progress I had the order from *von* Pfeil to stop. Apparently our neighbouring fighter units had been complaining about the whistling on air and our short-wave conversations. He was sorry but that would have to be an end to it. Again, I have to observe that the lack of foresight on the part of the *Luftwaffe* in general was appalling. Very early on we could have saved many crews and aircraft if we had been able to talk them in instead of letting them fly around in fog or cloud until they ran out of fuel. For instance later, over Dunkirk, our whole 1st Squadron became lost with every aircraft being damaged in emergency landings in the fields of Belgium. If we had been able to continue our experiments we would surely have refined our technique by then and have been of valuable assistance then and on numerous other occasions.

On a brighter note, our loudspeaker network at Hangelar was being heralded as a great success. Word of it even got to *General* Martini, whom I had previously met when struggling to establish our *Nachrichtenzug*. We were ordered to leave everything installed at Hangelar when we left and were assured that all *Heimat Jagdfliegerhorsten* (fighter bases on German soil) would have similar systems installed as standard, using ours as a pattern. Further, wherever we were to be moved to next would have a system installed by the base *Luftnachrichten* ready for us. No more emergency purchases and endless trailing around government offices for chits to buy equipment. We couldn't believe it - we had actually made a dent in the otherwise unyielding and entrenched views of High Command!

In fact it was a little too much to hope for. Some systems were built in but all too quickly the emergency mobilisation funds ran out and the work stopped.

Notes on Chapter 10

1. Even today some of my old troop remember the visits to historic sites on the way to Bonn Hangelar. They thought it was unusually thoughtful ... for an officer.

2. Johannes Steinhoff (see pages 202/203). Later to figure strongly in the 'Battle of Helgoland Bight' the first offensive by the British Bomber Command. His squadron shot down three Wellingtons albeit, ironically, in daylight. Post-War *General* Johannes Steinhoff was responsible for solving the so-called 'Starfighter Nightmare'. The new *Luftwaffe* had been equipped with the American Starfighter Fighter. An incredible number of these jets were lost together, in many cases, with their crews (something like sixty). He later went on to become Inspector General for NATO 1971-1974.

CHAPTER 11

First Combat and Letters Home

One of the most valuable parts of my own personal record of the war is a collection of some fifty letters which I wrote to my mother at the time. They are a perfect record of how things were, encapsulating the feelings and events of the time in a way that is not subject to the vagaries of memory or the ravages of time. From here on I will quote from this source hoping that the accurate feelings of those heady days will come across.

4 September 1939

We are stationed here to protect the *Ruhrgebiet* (Industrial Ruhr) and nothing happens. We are afraid that the French and the English will withdraw (before we get a chance to fight). There is little time for writing, I get up at 04:00 hrs and our 'readiness' lasts until 20:00 hrs With Father (by then a Reserve Army Captain) also gone, how do you feel? Can my car stay in the barn? Should the war last much longer will you have it raised to relieve the springs and have the petrol taken out. A parcel with dirty laundry will leave here the day after tomorrow.

9 September 1939

Probably the Feldpost (field post) doesn't work, no answer yet. Every day an aircraft flies Bonn - Böblingen and back, therefore write there (old address). From 05:00 hrs we are sitting around. The weather is beautiful. Again there is dirty laundry. Ju. W 34 takes off at 10 am for Böblingen.

Nothing to be seen of the war, probably Father is closer to events? At the moment there are reports about AA guns firing near to Karlsruhe and Baden-Baden. It looks like the war in Poland will be over in 14 days. 100 Marks herewith - please take them to the Sparkasse (savings bank).

September 14th 1939 On this, my 21st birthday, I had just been wakened for some signatures. Note my dog, Seddy, also awaiting a scramble!

24 September 1939

Nothing new. No contact with the enemy. It seems better at Wiesbaden and Mannheim, they have recorded victories there. Böblingen and Eutingen have one each. Our life is similar to Straubing, with the difference that there is much more for me to do. My job has great responsibility: the *Gefecktsstand* is my duty exclusively. However eight days ago a reserve officer, *Oberleutnant* Forster, arrived and he takes over when all of the *Gruppe* is in the air (including myself). Now I am with the Staff Flight, I have my own aircraft which I had to fetch myself from Erding/Munich. On that trip I stopped at Böblingen twice - the first time because I couldn't reach Munich with the Alb closed in with cloud. Both times I stayed with the Deuschles in Bad Cannstadtt to see Gretl.

We lead a sorry life, waiting is probably worse than war. Hope there will soon be a decision. I didn't feel too much on my birthday (14/9 - my 21st) but considering there is a war that isn't important. On the day after, many packages arrived. Thanks very much for a good letter.

Above, I mention quite casually that I had been unable to reach Munich because of the low cloud of the Schwäbische Alb (south of Stuttart). There was actually much more to this. It was to be one of the most potentially dangerous situations I'd ever experienced. I had set off with an Uffz. from the staff company to collect some new parachutes from the supply depot at Erding and to bring back my own Emil. He had volunteered because he wanted to visit relations near there and I because I wanted the chance to stop at Böblingen.

On the outward leg we had only been cleared to fly our Junkers W 34 as far as Böblingen and to get a fresh weather report there. They told us that the clouds were shrouding the tops of the hills at 800 metres (2600 ft) but that later there might be a 'weather window' which would allow us to fly through, crossing the Danube near Ulm. We were impatient and as the weather men were my old friends from the time when we'd been based at Böblingen, they said that we could try anyway. So we took off and followed the Stuttgart-Munich autobahn as it led up the Alb. The road was only open on one carriageway at that time. It followed a steady slope up towards a narrow pass in the Alb known as the Drackensteiner Hang (Dragonstone Rise/Cliff). This lead up to a rather dramatic pass over the Alb and is fenced in tightly on both sides by steep unyielding rocks, escarpments and forest.

We carried on climbing in the lumbering old W 34, keeping the road on our right and all too soon it became obvious that we were heading for trouble. Up ahead the *Autobahn* just slid quietly up into the ceiling of cloud and we would have to follow. The W 34 was not built for flashy aerobatic turns, so there was no way that we could wheel around in the steadily rising and narrowing confines of the *Drackensteiner Hang*. Coupled with this was the fact that neither myself or the *Uffz.* had flown the W 34 much since training time. I felt that horrible knotting in the stomach as I began to realise that what was ahead was potentially lethal and there was no way it could be avoided. We plunged into the heavy cloud and the Junkers began to be shaken about like a leaf in a gale. We both stared fixedly at the instruments but to no avail. The artificial horizon was being thrown from side to side by the violence of the gyrations and the airspeed dropped back to a very dangerous 120 kph. The throttle was slammed forwards but we dare not drop the nose too much for fear of crashing into the steeply rising ground we knew to be below. Still the instruments made no sense. As suddenly as the indicated airspeed had dropped to 120 kph it now leapt forwards to register 300! Impossible for our plump old lady.

There is nothing quite like the fear that this kind of experience can generate. If you have never flown into conditions like this it can only be related, perhaps, to driving a car, which is only moving two dimensions, into a wall of freezing fog when the car is on ice. The difference is that in a car you gradually slow and hope that you don't hit anything before you stop. In seconds the experience is stabilised again. But in an aircraft that terrifying tension, feeling that a sheer rock wall might be only a few metres in front of your aircraft, or that you might already be diving towards the ground, can last for many minutes and can be completely overwhelming. There is only one certainty - if you panic you are dead!

For a full five minutes we were tossed around in that aircraft, not daring even to look at each other, desperately trying to regain control before we, and our aircraft, became so much scattered wreckage littering the beautiful Alb. Luck must have been with one of us for, after what had seemed like hours of tension, the aircraft exploded from the cloudbase in a high speed and at an impossibly steep turning angle. That was easily corrected now that we were back in visual contact with the ground and we quickly re-trimmed the Junkers for level flight and breathed a hearty sigh of relief. How we escaped I don't know to this day. Every time I drive over the pass now I wonder how we missed the sheer rock cliffs and the tall pines that form the Schwäbische Alb. But we did and found ourselves flying over Kirchheim, a little town very well known to me. Needless to say we flew back to Boblingen to wait for clearer weather. Once more I had impetuously pitted myself against what commonsense dictated, but again I had survived.

We stayed overnight and set out the next day, with the trip going much more to plan. At Erding the *Uffz.* stayed overnight again, whilst I returned with my '109 that evening as far as Boblingen and then flew the Bonn leg the next day. These flights were less eventful than our first attempt to reach Erding.

My own - the first '109, to be assigned to me, Yellow 16.
The yellow numbers indicated the third squadron.

When I look back through my letters home I am amazed that there is no reference to the war with Poland, not even of the more significant events like the bombing of Warsaw, which took place on or near to the 17th September. It couldn't have been because of any military restrictions on what I could write because I seemed to have passed on much information about our operations and location without any fear of censorship. What I do remember is my strong impressions regarding Russia entering into the Polish Campaign as they did on the 17th. I was very sad and, to a degree, angered by the fact that they had just come along to share the booty. The battle itself had been won without their help and now they just rolled in against virtually no opposition to take over half of the country. I had never liked the idea that we should be allied in any way to the Bolsheviks and this had done nothing to change my mind. At our 'Front' there was little to report:

5 October 1939

Still nothing new, . . . we are flying around all day long, sometimes very close to the border, without any contacts. We search the horizon without result. So far there is no victory for our *Gruppe*. However things might change, Hitler will speak tomorrow ... I don't think that England will agree to peace and the war will really get started now. Don't worry about me.

7 October 1939

Now there is a reason to write. You must have heard on the radio ... Our *Gruppe* brought down two French aircraft yesterday. As we sat at the *Gefechtsstand*, listening to the Führer's speech, there were some Fluko-warnings from Trier. As this was outside our area, I didn't order take-off yet. We continued listening. For one moment I thought I'd heard engine noises, but at the same moment a column of motorised vehicles passed, but I still thought I'd heard aero-engines to the south of our field. No reports came in. In spite of that I had two red Very lights fired up. (These were still required by *Luftwaffe* operations instructions in spite of the Tannoy system which we had operating.) And within no time two '109s were in the air. As there were several layers of cloud we could see nothing. Then we got Flak reports from Siegburg and Godesberg. I sent up a few more aircraft. Altogether there were 11 aircraft airborne. Then we saw a Potez 63 and, by radio directions, I guided our aircraft as much as possible. The AA guns were firing at the same time without results but the black residue from their shell bursts showed clearly the progress of the aircraft which was hopping from one cloud layer to another. We had aircraft between each layer and soon one of the French machines was shot at by one of the *Oberfeldwebels* and the crew took to their parachutes. The other was trying to escape at low level but was caught by *Ltn.* Berthel and shot down at 10 metres altitude. It skidded on its belly and the crew were wounded by the machine gun fire and taken prisoner. In 20 minutes it was all over and we fell about each other's necks and jumped for joy. The ice has been broken. You ask why I write so rarely. Father, what shall I report when nothing is happening? When our *Kommandeur* returns, he has been gone for two days, he will be happy when hearing that we now have victories ...

*First Victory - The day after Ltn. Berthel (6/10/39) had achieved the
first victory, a French reconnaissance plane. Many visitors came.
Here Hauptmann v. Pfeil (left) explains how it had been done.
Behind him is an official from the local SA. Central is an
army officer and right a government officer.*

10 October 1939

On the public radio you will now have heard more about our two victories
as there as been much drama about this. I am also sending a newspaper
clipping. I have to laugh about it because the *Kommandeur* was in Berlin
on this day and I had to handle the *Gefechtsstand*. However I feel inside
that part of this success was mine. It was me who gave the orders for take-
off and the directions by the transmitter.

Most important now: I will now fly with the 3rd squadron. The plotting
and all other associated activities I am now turning over to a most reasonable Reserve *Oberleutnant* (Forster) who has now had 14 days instruction
from me. My *Nachrichtenzug* will be kept in trim, in the meantime, by me.
Whether there will be more fighting now nobody knows, but I am burning for action now that I am in a position to be able to pull the trigger
myself.

I don't know anything further. I live well or as much as is possible and tell everybody how proud I am of our family. That is with all four members servicing: Mother teaching at school, Trude working with the telex and both father and son as soldiers. Isn't that great...?

After the first victory of Ltn. Berthel, - all 'dressed up', he got the EK II. From right: 1. Ltn. Steinhilper, 2. Ltn. Spenner, 3. Ltn. Geller, 4. Ltn. Fermer, 5. (rear) Ltn. Höschen, 6. (with the EK II shining) Ltn. Berthel, 7. (little fellow with the moustache) is Squadron Leader Obltn. Ewald (in Spain called 'Pequeno' - the small one). The others are not relevant.

16 October 1939

Only very short today. Soon I shall be on alert. Last night I was duty officer. Last Friday *Ltn* Kirchner (1st Sqn) had a victory. I had taken off as well with my squadron leader, but was too late. I don't like this waiting...

Things didn't change too much in the following two or so weeks. There was a steady exchange of information with my parents but nothing which I see as interesting or illustrative of the time. I note that we kept up the exchange of laundry and that my mother was sorely in need of my military soap ration for this purpose.

9 November 1939

Tonight this attempted assassination of the Führer will play its part and lead to new action. I was duty officer when the wing's duty officer telephoned and just told me 'Assassination attempt on the Führer.' My breath almost stopped. I was happy that it turned out OK. To me it is clear that England is behind this.

(The so-called *Buergerbräukeller Plot.)*

***

As I have mentioned before we had nothing against England and really didn't see our fight with Poland as being much to do with the British. I probably saddled them with the blame for the assassination attempt because, when I was at school, *Studienrat* Wobbelmann had convinced us that the British secret service was the largest and best in the world. Similar to the way, in later years, the Western countries blamed the KGB for everything before the arabs came on the scene.

12 November 1939

We are going to be moved again. Got the laundry at the very last minute. In future please send it to Mr Uli Steinhilper, Lachen bei Neustadt a.d. Hardt 'To be called for.' Please leave off *'Leutnant.'* I suppose my new posting won't be more than about 50 km from Father (He was 'guarding' the Rhine further to the south).

16 November 1939

Now we are close to the front, however the weather is bad. Our barracks were built by the French (after WW I). We have small individual rooms . . . some kind of home . . . however I feel that I have no roots . . . like a Gypsy. Again you write *poste restante,* please leave off the military rank, only Mr Ulrich Steinhilper . . . one never knows what might develop . . . don't tell anybody where I'm stationed. Laundry will follow.[2]

On the 21st November *Hauptmann von* Pfeil had his 32nd birthday. At our improvised *Kasino* we, his officers, gave him a set of small silver cups. Out of these we all had a few schnapps, even *von* Pfeil, who rarely drank.

At the end of his party he decided to fly a surveillance patrol with his *Stabs - Rotte* (staff flight). *Ltn.* Geller was now his adjutant, replacing *Ltn.* Fermer who had been promoted to Squadron Leader of *7/52*, and would fly as *Rottenhund* (wingman in the classic *Rotte)*. It didn't take long at all for them to get airborne because the aircraft were always kept at a high state of readiness[1]. They had not been away long when we monitored some excited shouting on the radio from them, but we couldn't make out what was happening. Then the telephone rang and we heard the stunning news that they had both been shot down.

Later, also by telephone, we learned that they had been surprised by some French Morane fighters and brought down, *Ltn.* Geller had made a belly landing near Edenkoben, about 10 km south of the field, and his air-craft was repairable. But *von* Pfeil had baled out and was badly burned. He was taken to hospital in Heidelberg and was reported to be in a very seri-ous condition.

So there it was. The war had really come to us now and the real impact and its consequences were well and truly driven home. Somewhere some French pilots would be celebrating their victories with champagne, their groundcrews congratulating them, eager to paint small crosses on the air-craft of the victors; much as we had done when we had 'broken the ice'. But for us, Geller was badly shocked and *von* Pfeil was horribly burned. We had lost two aircraft and some of our naivety. 'So this is what the real war is like,' we thought - we had no idea how bad it would become. The next day was to bring no better news for us. During the Polish campaign no problems with altitude and oxygen starvation had been experienced, but already in late 1939 the first reports of problems were coming in. Confidential notes indicated that some bomber and reconnaissance crews had suffered collapse whilst high flying. For the most part this wasn't fatal because there were always other crew members to replace mouthpieces or turn oxygen cylinders on. The affected airmen then usually recovered quickly, with no lasting injury. However, in the single seater fighter you are alone and any such error was almost certain death. This was almost certain-ly the case with *Uffz.* Hellwig. Whilst on patrol over French territory he inexplicably dived straight into the ground from a height of 9000 metres (29,000 ft). He was killed instantly and the cause was recorded as oxygen failure. Our record wasn't looking too good. Two aircraft lost and one dam-aged, one pilot dead and one seriously injured. I was nearly added to that list myself on the 25th November.

The Squadron, led by Helmut Kühle, was on an escort flight with some reconnaissance Heinkel IIIs. We had taken off from Lachen Speyerdorf, which is south of Neustadt an der Weinstrasse and north of Karlsruhe, quite close to the French border. Only 30 km (18 miles) away was the massive 'Maginot Line' which was particularly heavily fortified here. As we were returning I saw a high flying French Breguet aircraft, probably also on reconnaissance, but in the opposite direction. I called up to tell Kühle but for some reason he didn't seem to receive the message. Radio communications were still not too good and we had no contact at all with the aircraft which we escorted. The radio sets were tuned to the operating frequency whilst the aircraft was on the ground and after that there was no altering it until we landed. So, if the tuning was slightly off, your communications were poor for the whole of the flight. Even if the set had been calibrated perfectly, the range was only about 40 km (25 miles).

For whatever reason, Kühle could not understand my transmissions, so I decided to go it alone ... to break away and attack on my own initiative. My *Rottenhund* came with me but, as I pulled into a steeper and steeper climb, he stalled his aircraft and was forced to drop away, leaving me alone. The Frenchman must have been somewhere about 10,000 metres (33,000 ft), almost at the operational ceiling of my aircraft. Nevertheless, I climbed at full power to attempt an interception, turning on the oxygen and putting the mouthpiece in at about 4,500 metres (15,000 ft). I climbed to within range of him and was about to open fire when I stalled and fell away. I soon regained control of the '109 and began to climb once more, juggling with the propeller pitch control to get the best from the turbocharger. Again when I thought I was about to bag my first 'victory', evening the score a bit for the last few days, I stalled and fell away. I had been so close that I had clearly seen the French pilot, he would have had no chance had I had time to fire. For a third time I began the climb towards the interception. This time there would be no mistake. At a shallow climb I came within range of the target, only to find that my guns had frozen in the extreme cold of the high altitude. I was infuriated and begun to actually curse my bad luck and the good fortune of the French pilot. I must have articulated this with some vehemence and dislodged the oxygen mouthpiece and I passed out. My next memory was waking up in the plane with it flying in a slow curve and still losing height. I looked at the altimeter and was astonished to see that I was down to just 3,000 metres (9,800 ft) and still going down. I quickly levelled out and corrected the circular course. Then I had to get some idea of where I was, I didn't recognise the area and the compass was still running wild. So I used the old ways and looked for the sun. It was morning and I knew where it should be to set a course to find the Rhine.

Soon, I found my landmark and began to fly parallel to the great river. I was looking for a large wooded area where I knew I had to make my turn to head for home. I saw it and followed what I thought was my home route, soon seeing an airfield. I duly put the undercarriage down and selected the flaps, slowing down for my approach. Before touching down I took a last look around to make sure that there was no other traffic and suddenly realised that one of the hangars seemed to be in the wrong place, then other buildings didn't look so familiar. My heart seemed to jump into my throat as I realised that I was trying to land at the wrong airfield![3] With reactions faster than I thought possible, I pushed hard on the throttle, retracted the undercarriage and wound the flaps in. I set course east, back to the Rhine, but at an altitude of only 500 metres (1,600 ft). On the way I saw two low-flying monoplanes who made steep turns when they saw me. I judged them to be artillery spotter planes because I could see a member of the crew sitting in an open cockpit right at the nose of the aircraft.

When I arrived back at the Rhine I saw clearly that the bridges had been blown up. I was horrified as I realised that I had tried to land at the French airfield at Haguenau! I had earlier mistaken the forest of Haguenau for the Ordenswald (both are north of Strasbourg and to the left of the Rhine). The two aircraft that I'd seen had been really lucky; in those days the French didn't have many fighters, especially at that low altitude. If I had been more alert they wouldn't have stood much chance of surviving an attack. In any event I was very low on fuel and so I had to conserve what I had to get back to base. Again I followed the silver surface of the Rhine until, this time, I saw the correct forest and made my turn in for home. Just to make sure, I overflew the field and took a good look around. I made the approach circuit and landed feeling a little tired and a bit shaky. When I had taxied the aircraft into its proper place I switched off and pulled my flying helmet off. My hair was matted with sweat. I had been very lucky. The ground crew came over as I stepped out of the cockpit and one of them spotted a bullet hole in the wing. I tried to shrug it off with a flippant remark, but inside I knew I had had two very close escapes that day.

Far from being impressed with my initiative, Helmut Kühle was not at all amused by my report and bawled me out for leaving the squadron. He wasn't about to listen to any excuses about unheard radio messages and so I just took it. This would not be the first time that Kühle and I would not see eye to eye over the question of fighter tactics. During the fighting in Spain with Legion Condor he had developed the code of action. He thought a fighter pilot should not attack unless he was certain of success. In that way, he felt, pilots would grow more experienced without any needless loss. Apart from mentioning part of the story to my parents in a letter I decided to say nothing about the incident to anyone else. I thought that I had acted properly and bravely, indeed if I had succeeded in downing the Frenchman the result would have been considerably different. I didn't take it to heart for too long though, one thing I had learned in my early life was that sometimes you have to just take it, to grin and bear it.

6 December 1939

I report that life is back to normal again. Yesterday I returned by train a little late. I was picked up by my batman. Our doctor, who lives in Böblingen, (Dr Lenz) returned on the same train, a coincidence. On the way to the base we ran short of petrol and that made us late. Otherwise nothing new.

Our *Kommandeur* seems to be improving, his fever is down. They hope that he is 'over the hill'. We have been offered some leave and I have skiing at Riezlern in mind. The flying weather is lousy.

16 December 1939

My leave to be 28th or 29th? I am planning to go to Riezlern with Berthel. I have been Adjutant for ten days. *Kommandeur* is better, he now takes a few steps.

19 December 1939

Yesterday was Christmas for me . . . lights on my advent garland. I unpacked my presents. *Ltn.* Bert Göbel and *Ltn.* Fermer were visiting me. We had some schnapps and Christmas cakes and talked late into the night.
Christmas Eve I shall be duty officer and will think about you all. Do understand that I want to go skiing to keep fit (rather than go home).*
Didn't fly for 14 days because of bad weather... From God?? I have been reading of thirty-four British aircraft being shot down (the so-called 'Battle of the Helgoland Bight'). We will have our chance sometime. However it won't be as easy here, there are too many fighters around.

* I deliberately didn't tell my girlfriend of the time (Gretl), I wanted to be on my own. In any event she was away doing her *Arbeitsdienst* (one year of government service work). The uncle of my batman had an auto-repair garage in Riezlern and we were going to be skiing near there.

Adolf Hitler - At Christmas luncheon making a speech.

Christmas 1939 - Hitler being presented with the model of '109 by Gefreiter Artur Fischer. Today he is a Senator and owner of an international business, employing in total 1500 people. Before the war he did an apprenticeship, as a mechanic. At the end of the war he started from scratch with no money and no property making and selling gasoline lighters.

At this time the squadron was visited by Hitler. He had decided that he should spend his Christmas with his troops at the front. He had arrived in his special train at Neustadt and Landau and went to visit the infantry, who were stationed north of Weissenburg, then he came on to us.

He stayed with us for about two hours, taking lunch from our 'field kitchen' and I had the interesting experience of sitting across the table from this formidable character and listening to his speech. Here I heard something which I didn't care for at all and, on reflection, probably gave a clear indication of how this man thought and what he might do in the future. He said, with reference to the alliance with Russia: 'If it would ensure victory, I would even become ally to Satan himself!' My admiration for Hitler and what he had done for Germany took a dent then and it would not be the last time those words would echo in my mind.

11 January 1940

Today I have returned by train from skiing. Arrived at 09:30 and took-off at 11:30 to accompany reconnaissance Do. 17. Beautiful: seventeen aircraft over France for fifty minutes, almost undisturbed. No enemy fighters but a remarkable display of AA shooting. We might fly again tomorrow.

On the 22nd January I both wrote to my parents and sent them a telegram. I now urgently needed my skiing equipment. Imagine my surprise and joy when having only just returned from leave I found that the squadron was to be sent on a skiing trip to Kleines Walsertal, which was identical to Riezlern. Leave for the squadron was well overdue, mainly because we had been selected for a visit from the *Führer* over the Christmas period. Because of this individual leave had been restricted and, to get everyone away in the shortest time, we were offered this 'state' holiday.

The scheme had a couple of distinct advantages, firstly we were all kept together and were only 300 km (186 miles) from the front if an emergency should occur and, secondly, we would all get some altitude familiarisation. The latter of these two was not, according to Dr Lenz our medical officer, strictly true. He felt that ten days at 1100 - 1400 metres would do little or nothing for our bodies, he thought that three weeks at a height of 2000 metres (6,500 ft) or more might do some good.

At Lachen Speyerdorf we began to prepare. The army unit which was stationed near our airfield issued us with skis and training began. I had organised some motorised *Skijoring,* towing up to six people behind Kühle's staff car. Flat airfields are ideal for that kind of sport. However, this was no real preparation for individual cross-country and downhill work.

In the meantime the war went on. I was pleased with the way that the '109 performed in the very cold conditions, it was proving to be a very reliable aircraft. Between what action there was we would take turns in gunnery and then a little time *Skijoring* on the new snow. The winter of 1939/40 was to be one of the coldest on record.

Recreation at Laachen Speyerdorf Skijoring behind a staff car.
Preparing for the 'Kleine Walsertal'.

27th January 1940

Another chance: we were to pick one of our returning reconnaissance planes at about 7000 metres (23,000 ft) to escort it in. It hadn't arrived when, at about 1000 metres (3,300 ft) above us, we saw an enemy reconnaissance plane which was escorted by fourteen fighters. I thought that we would attack and went ahead with my *Rottenhund*. Kühle still waited for our aircraft to arrive. The enemy fighters didn't see me at all, probably still concentrating on our remaining six aircraft. I followed the reconnaissance aircraft - climbing steeply and losing my *Rottenhund* again. At about 9800 metres (3,200 ft) I was some 10 metres higher than him but I want to attack out of the sun ... He veered over to port and as I tried to follow I slid away, also to port, and lost about 200 metres (650 ft) altitude. Once more I was climbing to start shooting at about 500 metres (1,600 ft) but after 220 rounds I stopped firing because the guns had jammed again; probably because of the extreme cold (outside temperature about - 57° C). He flew on but it must have given him a shock to have been attacked by a German

222

fighter so far inside France, near to the city of Epinal. I got back unmolested however with the positive thought that I must carefully trim and tune my machine in every respect, motor and everything so that I can get more height.

Again the result of my initiative was a telling off from Kühle. He was a real stickler for the rules and even though our reconnaissance aircraft was late and there was a tempting target, he wouldn't attack. I suppose neither of us was totally right. It was part of his job to maintain discipline and follow orders as far as possible and youngsters like me were hungry for action. I had ended up, as had my *Rottenhund,* on my own over hostile territory with enemy fighters about. I suppose it was impetuous but I was keen to prove myself in combat.

Soon after this it was time for our skiing. We were accommodated in the *Darmstadter Hütte* where one small wing had been given over to our use. In our party there were four officers, Dr Lenz and eight NCOs, but there were a further 50 guests at the *Hütte.* It was typical rural accommodation, providing us with meals and rooms but any drinks had to be paid from our own pockets. At this time Riezlern would take about 300 skiers and Mittelberg another 200. There were no ski lifts or services like that, all that was offered was the snow and some advice as to the best routes. I was the only one with any skiing experience and was therefore appointed by Kühle as Instructor. His orders were strict, 'No injuries' and it was clear that I would be held responsible for any accidents, an unenviable position. I didn't mind being the instructor, although it did restrict me somewhat, not being able to take off on any long or difficult trips on my own.

During the day we were skiing from about 09:30 to 12:00 and then, after lunch, from 13:30 to 16:30. After supper we would generally walk from the guesthouse to Riezlern, about 2 km, to have our first drinks of the evening in the Post Hotel. As we became 'regulars' we were allocated a table in a function room where we were free from the curious gaze of the other guests and visitors. We had, for the time being, dispensed with the formality of military rank and instead addressed each other by Christian names. However, some formality was retained with the NCOs addressing the officers as Mr Kühle, Mr Steinhilper, Mr Waller and Mr Spenner.

Skiing in Riezlern - Kleines Walser Tal. This time with the
complete squadron - Official Recreation. From left, Obltn.
Kühle, Feldwebel Rüttger, Feldwebel Schieverhöebelfer
(little fellow), and now from right, Ltn. Waller, Ltn. Spenner,
Feldwebel Voss, Dr. Lenz. The two in the middle are not in the story.

For entertainment, we invented a game of numbers which got faster and more boisterous as the evening wore on. It was a simple task; we would circulate the table, each person calling out the next number in the normal series. But, any number which contained 3 or could be divided by 3 had to be missed by the player shouting 'Hopp'. Each time one of us made a mistake we were awarded a match and at the end of the competition we all had to reckon up our penalties at the rate of about 20 *Pfennings* per match. When 3 went too well we added 7, and so on. It was a happy game and soon drew an audience, drawn by the noise of our revelry. Some of the onlookers were, of course, girls and some of them joined in with the game.

At about 10 o'clock we would move out to the *Stern Bar* (Star Bar) where there was music and dancing, but the drinks were much more expensive. One of the girls who came to watch the game was the young wife of a lawyer from Stuttgart. She was very intelligent and bright and we enjoyed her company. She seemed to take a special liking to Hinnerk Waller. One evening during the game she joined in and sat with myself and Hinnerk, with Helmut Kühle seated on the opposite side of the large round table. On this special occasion Waller and Kühle had a private bet to see who could drink most *Obstler*[4] and still be sharpest at the game. The penalty for a mistake in this case was to drink a glass of the schnapps. Somehow Kühle was cheating and so Hedda Seiffert decided to intervene on Hinnerk's side. She had hidden a bottle of mineral water in her handbag and had a schnapps glass ready at hand. Beside her she kept a long glass for the purpose of keeping the real schnapps. Each time Hinnerk lost and collected a penalty she cleverly swapped the schnapps for mineral water and poured the schnapps into the long glass, refilling the now empty glass with water, ready for the next round. After about twenty glasses, Kühle wasn't showing any effects of drink at all, he was as sober as when he started. At the next penalty Hedda got up, walked around the table and, picking up Kühle's glass, said 'cheers' as she downed the 'schnapps'. She then resumed her place with us, confiding that Kühle was also drinking mineral water! He wasn't the Squadron Leader for nothing!!

The redoubtable Frau Seiffert was not to be outsmarted by Helmut Kühle and later, in the *Stern Bar,* she invited him to the bar for a drink. This, of course, he couldn't refuse and two long drinks were ordered. During the conversation Hedda pulled her swapping trick again. With the consummate skill of a conjurer, she managed to take the long glass filled to brimming with neat schnapps and exchange it for Kühle's long drink. Then she gave the toast *'Ex!'* which means that the drinks go down in one hit. Kühle dutifully emptied his long glass in one and we had to carry him home; poetic justice for his cheating at the game.

At the end of our leave, when everybody had some skill at skiing, I thought we should have one last long trip to finish off in style. I planned for us to go up to the *Hahneköpfle,* which meant a climb to about 1900 metres (6,200 ft). We had already done the *Ifenhütte* before. This had taken us up to 1400 metres (4,600 ft) and I judged that we could make it down the whole run. Kühle cautioned me to be careful and I promised to keep the downward skiing under strict control; he didn't need to remind me of my responsibility for the health and safety of the personnel.

First, we had to ski cross-country for an hour to *Auenhütte,* which was at an elevation of 1200 metres. Then it was off with the skis for the climb up to *Ifenhütte,* about one and a half hours' hard work. There we had lunch and then pushed on to the top, wading through deep snow and zig-zagging upwards for about two hours. The effort was worth it when we finally stood gasping for breath at the *Hahneköpfle.* The air was crisp, cold and clear, and the sun shone down upon us, burning our faces brown. We rested for a while and enjoyed the view before our descent. I was a little shocked to see how exhausted everybody looked, the climb had taken an awful lot out of them.

Skiing - on the way up to the Hahneköpfl at Ifenhütte - halfway up (no lift yet). From left, Fw. Ruttger, unknown, Ltn. Steinhilper.

I cautioned them to take the descent slowly and under control but they were all tired and wanted to get down any way they could and as quickly as possible. Soon they were falling and diving all over the place and discipline was abandoned. I soon reached the *Ifenhütte* and stopped where the route passes down a narrow path in the forest. As I came to rest, Lothar Schieverhöfer passed me at tremendous speed, taking a huge dive forwards and crashing into the snow. Fortunately, it was loose powder snow and it broke his fall well. He just stood up and brushed the snow from his clothing. Smiling, he said, '122'. I skied down to him and asked him what he had said. '122', he repeated. 'What are you counting?' I asked. He replied that the other skiers had taken a bet to see who would fall over the most times on the downward trip; he had just taken fall number 122!

I was relieved to get the whole bunch down without serious injury. Only the next day did the aches and pains of the gruelling day begin to show. Kühle was worst, with some pain in the ankles; he didn't ski on the last day, not wanting to aggravate the condition so near to our return to base. In the evening we had our farewell celebrations. I don't remember too much about that - only that on the way back we marched, as was our habit, and someone suggested that we shouldn't march in step over the small bridge on the route, for fear of breaking it. So we all dutifully fell to our hands and knees and crawled across the bridge. All too soon, the week was over and we returned to the front, happily without losses.

THE DOGS OF WAR

Many of us had adopted pets and in particular dogs whilst in front-line service. This has, over the years, been common practice for many soldiers, and I'm sure that it has something to do with the fact that, as a soldier, you have no real home, as you are constantly on the move. It is very uplifting when returning from a mission to have someone or something that is pleased to see you. Many of the pilots had bought pets, but I never really went out to get one; rather they seemed to seek me out on their own account. The first dog I had was called Seddy, a fox terrier. I was still at Böblingen, in the officers' quarters which I shared with Robert (Bert) Göbel. This consisted of an apartment with two bedrooms and a common lounge situated on the ground floor. One night in May I was awakened by a tremendous snoring which I traced as coming from under my bed. There was a small dog, fast asleep, having made itself comfortable. In the morning I handed the dog over to my batman and asked him to find the owner. At lunchtime he reported back to me that it belonged to an Austrian, *Obltn.* Karl. Apparently the dog had been given back to Karl's batman. Karl himself was away in North Africa.

That evening I again found the dog under my bed, having made its way some distance from Karl's quarters to mine. He'd either got in through the open window or had waited for me to leave the door open for a moment to creep inside and go to sleep again. I didn't mind; I quite liked the little fox-terrier, so I let the two batmen come to the agreement that the dog would stay with me until Karl returned. After two weeks Karl came back and resumed ownership of Seddy but to no avail. The dog still insisted on occupying my flat and just kept turning up. In the end Karl was so disappointed in the dog's conduct and apparent lack of loyalty that he turned him over to me. That is how I acquired Seddy. He was a true delight to own and we enjoyed many hours together.

We soon became an inseparable team, with Seddy coming most places with me in my car, to the delight of my parents and my girlfriend. When we took the trip to the pressure chamber at Freiburg for altitude tests the others had people for company in their fancy cars and I had my loyal friend. He loved to fly with me and frequently took low altitude flights sitting on the shelf behind my head in the '109. Naturally I left him at base when we were on active patrol, but on the transit flights to Hangelar and Laachen Speyerdorf he was right with me. Sometimes it made him airsick and he would end up being sick down my collar, but it didn't matter.

Seddy on the wing of a Me 109 E

If I wasn't around there were always willing hands to look after this affable little dog, either my batman, Hans Steeger, or one of the NCO pilots. *Feldwebel* Sigi Voss had a great affection for Seddy and also took him flying; he would always take the opportunity to look after him if it arose. It was really something to have this loyal little character waiting for me at base when I came back from a flight. It was a sad loss to me when he was run-over by an army truck and killed in Laon.

When, later on in the war, we had set up our headquarters at Coquelles we, the officers, decided that we would stay in tents rather than take billets in neighbouring houses. The tents covered a pit which had been dug into the ground over a metre deep. This was lined with timber slats to prevent the earth from collapsing inwards. Kühle, Hinnerk Waller and myself occupied one tent along with some sticks of furniture, which had been salvaged from bombed and burned houses in and around Calais. Amongst other things the French had been required to hand in any shot-guns or rifles to the German authorities and then, in turn, the guns could be released to us. It was only a loan because the German clerks had meticulously documented from whom the guns had come so that, in time, they could be returned. We could loan them out from the stores, but we had to sign for them and agree to keep them in good order. We used them for a little hunting on the airfield and the surrounding farmland, helping to keep the rabbit and partridge population in order. This had the benefit of giving us some badly needed exercise and also supplementing our diet.

In the corner of our tent stood a gun rack with four good double-barrelled shotguns. One day, on returning to the tent, I found a black and white dog sitting next to it, for all the world as though he was meant to come along on the next hunting trip. He was obviously a mongrel with some spaniel at the front and some collie at the back, finished off with a long and perpetually wagging tail. At first I tried to chase him off but he kept coming back; he really meant to stay with me. There was no question about that because when Kühle and Hinnerk Waller appeared later the dog stayed at my feet, barely acknowledging their presence.

Still missing the friendship of Seddy, we let him stay in the tent overnight and in the morning a French farmer came from some distance away to claim his dog. He had heard that the dog was with us, and it was no problem to let him have his animal back, although the dog seemed less than happy to go. I didn't think too much more about this until two days later; the dog was back, following me everywhere. I think I was a little irritated by this show of affection; maybe I didn't want to get too close to another animal the way I'd been to Seddy. In any event the farmer turned up again, all but accusing me of stealing his animal, and off went the dog. Again a couple of days passed and, sure enough, my friend came back. This time the farmer came, but didn't want his errant hound back anymore, and just asked if I'd be willing to pay for it. I agreed and we struck a bargain and once more I had a four-footed companion.

Terry with me, in front of the entrance to our dug-out tent at Coquelles.
At this time. September 1940, the outside of it is protected by
pressed straw bales.

I asked the farmer what the dog's name was but, what with my heavy accent, the dog didn't seem to want to respond. So I decided upon Terry and he seemed to like it well enough. Certainly as soon as he became settled, he proved to be a very disciplined and well-behaved dog, with one notable exception. He loved to hunt and would worry me by sniffing the guns in the rack and then prodding me with his wet nose until I got up and took one of the guns out. I'd never been a hunter before and it was really due to the ministrations of Terry that I began. At first I wasn't much of a shot and often only winged partridges and pheasants, and we had to search them out in the grass, which Terry thoroughly enjoyed. Then I'd have to dispatch the wounded birds by wringing their necks. I didn't have the stomach for this, and so the game-shooting didn't last long. I just didn't have the soul of a hunter. But when we had been successful we would enjoy outstanding meals at camp. The squadron cook had been drafted from the Stuttgart Marquardt Hotel and could normally provide fine meals, even given the unimaginative supplies. But give him a brace of game-birds and he could work his own special culinary magic. Unfortunately, I just couldn't handle the killing of the birds and so I stuck to rabbits, just to keep Terry happy and provide a variation in our diet.

Our hunting trips didn't go off without incident, and I nearly ended up in a duel with an army *Hauptmann*. Our routine was to hunt in a specific area that was within easy reach of the airfield, in case there was a scramble. If it happened, then a flare would be fired up at the airfield, a car could be sent, and I'd hot-foot it back and jump straight into my plane. We were out in a beetfield when I spotted another hunting party in an adjacent field. If they hadn't been firing the occasional shots I probably wouldn't have noticed them at all, but as soon as Terry heard the shooting he was off like a rocket towards the sound of the guns. He charged straight through the beetfield flushing out all of the game-birds as he went, much to the cha-grin of the Pioneer *Hauptmann* and his party. I ran to catch up with Terry and got close enough to see the *Hauptmann* levelling his gun and firing at my dog, or at least very close to him, and not just once but several shots. I could now see that the rest of his party were just soldiers that their officer was using as beaters and that they were unarmed. I started a shouted exchange with the officer, asking him if he couldn't see that his shots weren't scaring the dog - all he was doing was searching. And the more the fellow fired the more frantically the dog searched for kills. The exchange got quite heated:

'My dog's just searching - can't you see that I'm an officer too?'

'You've got a hunting licence then. And why are you shooting with such an undisciplined dog?'

'Don't you know that it's cruel to hunt birds without a dog?'

It gradually became more and more heated and turned into an exchange of inter-service insults:

'Why aren't you up in your plane fighting the British instead of walk-ing around on the ground shooting birds? You *Schlippssoldaten* are no good anyway! When are you going to clear the way so the real soldiers can get on with the invasion?'

We were really getting close to starting to shoot at each other when I noticed that Terry was bleeding from the hind leg and broke away to seek

out the farmer to locate a vet. It had all been unwarranted and perhaps a
sign of the tensions which existed all-round. Terry wasn't badly hurt. He
had received a few shot pellets in one leg but it didn't teach him any
lessons.

Coquelles 1940. Before take-off, Terry is unleashed by Siegfried Voss,
I talk to him, in vain trying to keep him back from running along
on our take-off. Lothar Schieverhöfer looks doubtfully at the procedure.

Whenever the armourers were aligning and harmonizing the guns on the '109s they fired bursts into some straw bales at the edge of the field. Once more Terry could become a nuisance, running towards the bales at the sound of the first burst and often arriving at the time when the armourers were about to loose-off a second hail of bullets; he had several narrow escapes. He was otherwise a most enjoyable dog. One of his most endearing characteristics was running alongside my aircraft as I took-off and being there as I landed. Always as I touched down and taxied my '109 I could look down and see Terry running along with me. He always knew which aircraft I was in and never made a mistake, even in the early days when nearly thirty aircraft would be landing.

One occasion, which I don't think anyone in No 3 Squadron will forget, was the late afternoon of 30th September when there had been such huge losses and we had stopped over in Boulogne to refuel before making the last leg to base. It was almost dark and all around our field were '109s that had been forced to pancake as the last drops of fuel had been used. Our No 1 and No 2 Squadrons had tried to make it back without refuelling and those that had made it were already in. Amongst our squadrons' ground crews there was little hope that we would be back this time. Kühle (who hadn't flown) and the crews all sat around the dispersal point where my aircraft usually stood and where Terry sat on guard. There seemed little doubt as far as the dog was concerned that at least I was on my way back and they hung onto this as an omen, asking the dog if anyone was coming back. From Boulogne I telephoned Coquelles to let them know we were on our way back and the mood of doom was broken, with the crews coming out ready to welcome us back. Only Terry remained on guard until his sensitive ears picked up the drone of my DB 601 engine many miles out from base.

After 27th October Terry was taken to my mother's home at Heutingsheim, but later the squadron began to miss the dog and asked if he might not be returned to them. Mother agreed and Terry went along with them until later in Russia where any trace of him was lost.

Notes on Chapter 11

1. There were three stages of readiness: Stage 1 with pilots strapped into aircraft for take-off within one minute. This was later changed to a situation where the pilots would sit in deckchairs adjacent to the aircraft, still for one minute take-off. This is the more traditional view of the fighter pilots on both sides of the Channel. Stage 2 would be in the air in about one hour. And Stage 3 where the time would have to be specified, sometimes two or three hours.

2. It is interesting to see the amount of information that Ulrich sent to his parents by ordinary mail. The British Armed Forces had very strict guidelines on what could be put in letters. There would certainly have been no mention of the movements of squadrons and/or personnel. Equally the collection of photographs and movie film is testament to a much more relaxed attitude to such things. My father commented that anyone seen with a camera in an RAF establishment would have been in serious trouble (supposing that you had managed to get any film in the first place!). PJO.

3. It was not uncommon for pilots to become lost on operations and land at the wrong (enemy) airfield (see pages 216/217). Enemy airfields look very much like friendly ones and the borders are not always obvious from the air. On 24th September 1939 the Allies came into possession of their first full airworthy Me. 109 E when one from II/JG 51 landed in error at Stassbourg-Neuhof airfield. This aircraft was lost in a collision on the 28th November. Meanwhile, on the 22nd November another Me. 109 E-3 landed near Woerth Bas-Rhin when the *Oberfeldwebel* pilot became convinced that he was back in Germany. This aircraft was extensively flown by the French and was then sent to England to the RAE at Farnborough. There it was flown against the Hurricane and Spitfire. These were not the only instances.

4. *Obstler* - Fruit schnapps made from apples and pears.

Flugmelde - Reporting - mainly through manned telephone stations.

Fluko-warning - Alert from enemy activity in the area.

Fluko - Flug-Kommando - was issuing reports about enemy aircraft all across Germany.

CHAPTER 12

Now the War Comes to the Western Front

The desire to get one's own aircraft in top shape changed the procedure for the *Werkstattflug* (Test flight following maintenance). Previously this had required the *TO* (Technical Officer – *Ltn*. Kirchner) to fly the aircraft before signing it off. But now, mainly due to his initiative, we introduced a system whereby the 'owner' of the aircraft would also make the *Werkstattflug*. This was more practical particularly when the work had been of a personal nature - trim, polish, radio, oxygen etc. We each had preferences in our aircraft. But even having our aircraft tuned to personal perfection didn't improve the weather.

10 February 1940

Saturday. Duty Officer. Snow is turning into water... partly frozen... airfield unserviceable... everybody is out in town... I'm bored.

16 February 1940

Nothing new... had myself a beautiful leather jacket made... cost 48 *Reichmarks*... quite expensive.

23 February 1940

Some flying, I was *Rottenführer* ... It almost looked like spring for a few days... Seddy (my dog) reported killed by a propeller... (this later proved to be untrue).

4 March 1940

Congratulations to Father on his promotion to full *Hauptmann* in the army... Thanks for many packages from people in Heutingsheim.

8 March 1940

In the newspapers there were reports about air-fighting at the Western Front... Don't worry... we are not involved... However now weather and ground conditions are good...

21 March 1940

The airfield is under water again... when a plane takes off, a fountain of water chases it across the field... We now have long hours... from 05:45 to 19:00 at constant readiness ... Happy Easter.

11 April 1940

So Father is back as a soldier again . . . stationed near Prague? . . . Then he'll be near to Trude (who was in the army, training to be a telex operator). Even though nothing happens around here I can't get away...

These letters record very well the situation and my feelings at the time. There was a war going on and we, particularly the younger pilots, didn't want to be left out. But the weather conspired against us leaving the airfields (on both sides) awash with water and offering little opportunity to fly. In England they were coming towards the end of what they called 'The Phoney War' - and that was how it had felt to us. We called it the *Sitzkrieg* (sitting war). Things were soon to begin to change.

By April, the weather had improved and stabilised and Kühle used the good conditions for intensive training in squadron strength, twelve aircraft. We were to fly in three *Schwärme,* each consisting of two *Rotten.* The groups would be at three staggered heights, each separated vertically by about 200 metres (650 ft). Kühle would lead the lowest *Schwarm, Oberfeldwebel* Grosse, our NCO Condor Veteran, would lead the middle formation, and either myself or Hinnerk Waller would lead the top *Schwarm.* The idea, which had been invented in Spain by Werner Mölders, was that any enemy aircraft which attacked this formation would themselves be attacked. It was simple in theory to operate.

1940 - Laachen Speyerdorf - Special sunglasses by Zeiss.

At Laachen Speyerdorf - About March 1940.
From left: (replacing Hauptmann v. Pfeil) The new Kommandeur
of I/JG 52, Hauptmann von Eschwege, visiting (seated) Major
von Merhart, the wing-commander JG 52 (Geschwaderkommodore),
behind Obltn. Ewald, Ltn. Geller, Obltn. Kühle.

If the lowest *Schwarm* was attacked it would dive and the upper *Schwarm* would be able to follow on the tails of the enemy. If the middle *Schwarm* was attacked it too would dive, but this time in front of the lowest *Schwarm*. The theory was simplicity itself, but in practice it took some time to learn as a squadron. If you consider that within the *Schwarm* the distance horizontally between each of the two aircraft in the two *Rotten* was about 150 metres (450 ft), and the vertical separation was about 200 metres between the *Schwärme* - it can be appreciated that the simple theory led to a complicated structure in the sky.

The only way to improve was to practise with constant drilling and exercises. One of the most difficult positions was leader of the *Schwarm*. When turning right or left or even more difficult turning 180° about, the leader would have to throttle back and wait for his *Rottenhund* to dive under him and come up forwards and to the side as quickly as possible. It was important to execute the turn and to be back in the lead as soon as possible so that the tail of the *Rottenhund* could be kept in clear sight. This was the object of the *Rotte* which enabled the two partners to keep observation on each other's tail and be able to make a steeply banked turn to shoot at anyone who took up an attacking position behind the partner.

Later, in actual dogfights, this was to become a valuable tactic and the Allies soon dropped their inflexible formations based on the 'V' - vics - and formed up in their copy of the *Schwarm*, which was called 'Finger Four'. They also learned, as we did, that however good these tactics were, they did have a weak spot and that was in the turn. As a group began a turn after attacking a target it would be at its most vulnerable, and it soon became the time when we could expect an attack. But this was all some way ahead. In the meantime we continued to practise and to perfect the movements which would strengthen us when the real fighting began.

It was whilst undertaking one of these practice manoeuvres that I had another close brush with danger. I was leading the top *Schwarm* with *Feldwebel* Siegfried Voss as my *Rottenhund*. We were flying between 3,000 and 5,000 metres (9,600 and 16,000 ft) without oxygen (just about the limit). It was a brilliant, clear day with the sun shining and superb visibility. We had been flying directly into the sun and had just executed a complete 180° turn, now flying down-sun when I felt the aircraft shudder a little. I had initially throttled back for the manoeuvre and now that I pushed my throttle forwards I found that it felt loose and there was no response. Immediately I found the rudder pedals loose and unresponsive and the stick way back against my belly and completely slack. I glanced down as I felt cold air blasting upwards and saw a ragged hole in the floor. I tried to ease the throttle back but the engine went to full power as the '109 rolled over into a power dive.

I took a last glance at the instruments - speed 550 kph, height 3,600 metres, engine revs ... off the clock! There was no more time to think now; I would have to get out while I could. Hurry! I pulled the emergency lever and the canopy rumbled away down the fuselage. Get out! Get out! Radio jack-plug out. Release harness and push up - and out! Then the slipstream hit me and, boy oh boy, did it hit me!

At something approaching 600 kph (350 mph) I was tossed around like a piece of rag in a hurricane. I was terrified and there seemed to be no time to remember the instructions about the parachute, to count nicely and calmly twenty-one, twenty-two, twenty-three ... As soon as my right hand found the metal handle tucked away at my left shoulder I pulled for all I was worth.

Nothing happened. I just tumbled end over end in the void. I reached towards my bottom, towards the pack, when suddenly and cruelly I was jerked upright as the canopy deployed and I decelerated at a phenomenal rate, the straps biting into my body. Incredibly both the straps and the 'chute absorbed the strain. I had pulled much, much too soon.

In seconds the explosion of noise and assault on my senses was over and I was in complete peace. There was virtually no sound other than the distant noise of the other aircraft in the squadron and the ripple of the silken canopy as the air passed over and through it. It is freezing cold at this altitude, somewhere about -15°C and although my flying kit protected me against this, it was still a severe contrast to the comfort of my cockpit. From this great height I could clearly see my '109 hit the ground far, far below. There was a brief puff of dust and smoke, then a blue/black column of smoke began to rise into the clear sky as the wreckage burned. It was quite some time before the faint sound of the impact reached me. I checked my watch, it was 15:49. It would take until 16:00 before I reach the ground at a somewhat more sedate pace than my luckless Emil.

As I floated down, the squadron came back and flew around me in steep banking turns. It was a beautiful sight, but more than this, I became aware of a sound which I had never experienced before. Within the confines of my cockpit I'd often seen the squadron airborne in full strength but, blotted out by the noise of my own aircraft and masked by my helmet and phones, I'd never heard it like this. To be suspended there in the air on such a wonderful spring day and have those beautiful aircraft curving around, their powerful engines growling, was something I'll never forget. Kühle came by close, leading the squadron and gave me a cool and friendly wave then returned to base, no doubt wondering as I was what the hell had happened.

When the last of my comrades had left I became aware, once more, of the quietness and peace of my journey downwards. I was close to a small village and I could see children scurrying around like ants and could even catch their voices as they watched me. '

'Look,' they squealed excitedly, 'Look up there. There he is'. I floated on past the village, borne on the prevailing winds and finally came to rest in a vineyard, being caught in the arms of the gardener. He then helped, with almost professional skill, to fold my parachute. The wreckage of my aircraft was close, or at least what could be seen of it, having dug a huge crater as it impacted at phenomenal speed.

Wreckage was scattered around over a fairly confined area with some of it, like the tyres, still burning on the surface. I appreciated just how close I had come to having been part of that hideous mess.

I had just begun to talk with the gardener when, chest heaving with exertion, a Pioneer Corps *Major* came running across the field to take me prisoner. His disappointment was obvious when he saw that I was on his side. Still he was able to give me a lift back to my base which was only 20 km away.

When I reached the airfield I still had no idea what had happened to my aircraft. Certainly it had been badly damaged but had I been hit by a stray flak shell or become the victim of fighters we didn't see? I had no idea. I was just grateful to be in one piece, if a little sore in places. It was then that I learned that my *Rottenhund, Feldwebel* Voss, had also had problems, landing short of the airfield with a badly damaged propeller. He had reported by radio that his prop blades had been shortened by a mid-air collision and that he had to over-rev his engine to get any pull at all.

Voss was advised to make a belly landing but thought that he could get in for a normal wheels down approach to lessen any further damage to the aircraft. But as he lowered the gear the drag increased to the point where the stubby blades of the propeller and the screaming engine could no longer provide enough pull. He had no choice but to put down short of the field and rolled right into the side of a farmhouse, demolishing the outside wall completely. Voss was alright; he was still strapped tightly into his seat and there was no fire. The farmer and his wife were grateful that it had been such a fine day and they'd decided to get out and work in the spring sunshine.

Knowing what I do now it wasn't too hard to reconstruct what had happened. We had been flying into the sun and Voss had had problems in seeing me as we turned. As he dived below me he had come too close and the blades of his propeller had scythed through the belly of my Emil, cutting all the control wires. It was just an accident and we had both been very lucky to survive. In the evening we had the traditional celebration in the *Kasino* and Sigi Voss was similarly entertained in the NCOs' mess. I have no doubt that he had more than enough ribbing about his first 'kill'. When I turned in for the night I could see the livid red weals on my body where the harness of my 'chute had bitten into me. In places they turned blue and yellow where the bruising had been worst. I certainly found a parachute harness uncomfortable to wear for the next few days.

That night I was awakened by an angry call from *Obltn.* Ewald, 'For heaven's sake, Steinhilper,' he shouted into the telephone, *'Sind Sie verrückt?* (Are you mad?) There is a man phoning me every hour on the field telephone in my room and when I answer he just says, "Thank you. All's well, *Leitungsprobe* (line-check)".' Now I realised that the same thing had been happening to me since about 10 o'clock, but I'd been so exhausted by my traumatic day and was fairly well-imbibed so I'd not really risen to full consciousness. But there it had been, every hour *'Leitungsprobe - Danke Herr Leutnant - Alles in ordnung'*.

Ewald was really furious and demanded that I stop the nonsense immediately, slamming the telephone down. I was now fully awake and things began to come together in my mind. I dressed and marched across the courtyard of the barracks to my *Nachrichtenzug* switchboard and there I found the culprit. I was greeted by the grinning cheeks, all four of them - backside and all - of *Gefreiter* Hatz, a well-known comedian in my outfit.

'What the hell are you doing, Hatz?' I enquired, somewhat less than amused to have been dragged out of bed at such a late hour to be met by a *Gefreiter's* hairy backside mooning at me.

'Just obeying orders, *Herr Leutnant,'* he replied holding out a copy of the typed instruction that I'd issued earlier in the day.

I had ordered that all strategic telephones to the squadron leaders, the group commanders and other important staff lines were to be tested hourly. This had arisen because earlier in the day one of the squadron leaders out at the remote *Staffelliegeplatz* (dispersal) had been cut off whilst talking on the telephone. He gave me hell about it and wanted to know how we expected to be able to give emergency scrambles and pass on vital orders if the lines were being disconnected. I, in turn, passed on my fair share of hell to my subordinates and issued the instruction that the lines should be tested on the hour. I couldn't blame Hatz, he was a good-humoured youngster and had seen the opportunity for a relatively harmless prank. I duly modified the instruction and went back to bed. However, in the morning I had a lively reception at breakfast because just about everybody who was on the important list had been rung on the hour up to 1 o'clock. I'd been lucky that *von* Eschwege, the new *Gruppen Kommandeur,* was away.

There was a fair bit of horse-play amongst ourselves at that time and practical jokes were high on the agenda. One would be to bet that you could take off all the buttons from another's uniform jacket and replace them within two minutes. Of course the buttons could be cut off in no time. Then they would be handed over to the luckless victim, with a shrug of the shoulders and the forfeit for the bet. He would have won a couple of bottles of wine but would be left holding a handful of buttons which would have to be laboriously sewn back onto the uniform. Another involved opening bottles of beer in the trouser pockets. The victim would end up with trousers soaked in beer for the dubious benefit of winning a bottle of wine. It's fair to say that all concerned needed to be fairly well-imbibed both to become involved in such pranks and to really appreciate them. Perhaps this kind of behaviour seems a little childish now, but we were young and full of energy and enthusiasm and our circumstances in this phoney war were really disappointing. The real war had not begun to sap that vitality from us yet.

3 May 1940

Boring again. But after a short but nice visit to the Hotel Zeppelin in Stuttgart we hear on returning that yesterday our 2nd Squadron had dogfights - 8 Me 109s against 22 Curtiss Fighters. All our aircraft came back safely but nobody knows if any of the Curtisses were hit, it happened over French territory. Since then... boredom. One enjoyable event, however. As long as Kühle is on leave I will lead the squadron and we are flying to practise. No celebration of 1st May (May Day) two days ago... We were flying at 15:00 with all the NCOs. This afternoon we had a scramble with my *Rotte,* but when we caught the enemy it turned out to be one of ours. Please send my tennis equipment. It looks like I may have the chance to play.

9 May 1940

This evening... like never before, it seems tomorrow things will get started. I am ready. Rarely have I felt more fit both physically or mentally.
At least in the morning we will know... Now I will go to bed because I want to be well-rested and in the peak of condition.

10th MAY 1940 THE WEHRMACHT ATTACKED FRANCE

The 'Phoney War' was Over

On that morning the sky was filled with aircraft of all types, heading towards France and returning, bombers; Stukas and '109s, but we were kept in strategic reserve. We were flying from dawn, but as high-level cover, not participating in any of the ground attacks. The Allies had been surprised, with many of their aircraft knocked out on the ground by the combined strategic bombing and strafing runs. Although active for the first few days of the campaign we had no engagements and simply policed the skies as our colleagues flew their missions, steadily deepening their penetration into France.

By 15th May we moved to a place called Hoppstadten, just slightly North of Laachen. This necessitated the squadrons being split up a little and we had to find private billets and thus, for the time being, did not meet up as a *Gruppe*. The decision as to whether to move the *Nachrichtenzug* as well hung in the balance for days. I had to fly back and forth from Laachen-Speyerdorf so that we were prepared. For a lot of the time during those few days it seemed as though we were cut-off from the rest of the communications network; the orders were far from dear. We soon found out what had caused part of the confusion and lack of positive leadership; our new CO, *von* Eschwege, had been shot down by French fighters whilst on patrol with his *Stabs Schwarm* (Staff Flight). They had got our Technical Officer *Ltn*. Kurt Kirchner at the same time and he was now a POW in France. *Von* Eschwege had been luckier and come down within range of our artillery but it took him three days to get back.

Again it was brought home to me that events depended very much on the luck of the draw. It was a question of being in the right (or wrong) place at the right time. This was what we didn't like. We seemed to be far above the action, always flying high cover, whilst what seemed to be more important events went on below us at the lower altitudes. On one of these high patrols I had another experience which, at the time, was quite frightening. We had just crossed the Luxembourg border, flying at about 8,600 metres (28,000 ft), when the small indicator arms of my propeller pitch control started to move to the 9 o'clock position. The face of the indicator looked just like a clock with one long and one short arm. For take-off, using the finest pitch, the arms would be at 12 o'clock, for cruising speed about 10:30 and for gliding the arms would show 6 o'clock. I had begun to scan the instruments for clues when the aircraft's engine began to shake the airframe and found the unusual reading on the pitch indicator. Now the question was: what to do?

On the throttle lever were the two control buttons for the propeller pitch. They were operated by the thumb on a rocker-type switch - one way to coarsen the pitch and one to flatten it. I decided that because the pitch was already very coarse and becoming more so by the second I'd press the lower switch and try to flatten it out. It at least stopped the problem getting worse, but I was still in bad trouble. I radioed Kühle and told him of the problem and said that I was returning to base. With that I peeled away from the formation and headed to Laachen. We were about 120 km out, but with plenty of height in hand, so I thought I'd make it OK. The angle of descent for the '109 in a gliding configuration is about 12:1. In other words for every one thousand metres of altitude I would be able to make about 12 km across the ground towards home. A rough calculation indicated that I should be OK if I could use a little power from time to time.

Now I started experimenting to see if I could find a solution to the problem but each time I released the pressure on the pitch control switch the hands on the indicator crept closer to 8 then 7 o'clock. This required a very delicate hand on the throttle. Because the coarser pitch was set, any rough handling of the engine's 1100 hp shook the aircraft horribly. I continued to glide back on my course with the engine barely ticking over, still searching for an answer, when a quite radical one occurred to me. If I switched off the main electrical switch it would shut down all auxiliary electrical systems, including the motors which operated the pitch gears. The aircraft's engine would keep running because it was powered independently by two magnetos. That seemed to be the short-term solution. I would lose my radio link with Laachen but it would increase my chances of getting back. I began to juggle with the switches but gradually got the pitch indicator to read closer to 6 o'clock, the setting for *Gleitflug* (gliding) then switched off for a while. When I wanted to transmit I had to hold the pitch switch down with my left thumb as I held the throttle so that I could hold the stick between my knees as I reached over to operate the main electrical switch. Then I could operate the radio using the little finger of my right hand on the control column switch.

I called Laachen and spoke to Förster, telling him that I was returning with a lame duck. He wished me luck and advised a belly-landing. Then for a while there was nothing I could do but hope and keep the aircraft in the most efficient gliding attitude. Every now and then I would try a little throttle but it shook the airframe, much like driving a car down a badly pot-holed road.

Soon I could see that I would make it to base and that lifted my spirits a bit, but it did nothing for the conflict of ideas which churned over in my mind. I had plenty of height, over 2,000 metres (6,000 ft), but I couldn't make up my mind whether to take Förster's advice and belly-land, or to attempt a normal landing with gear down. All landings are made as a glide but one always had the engine available for a short *Schnirpsen* from time to time (short shots of throttle which had, strictly speaking, been cheating when simulating an engine failure in training). The question that faced me was one of damage to the aircraft as opposed to the potential damage to me. With a belly-landing there was little chance of the aircraft somersaulting but there would be severe damage to the radiators, flaps, propeller and probably a bent crankshaft, taking the aircraft out of service for a long time. A normal gear-down negated the possible damage to the aircraft but placed me in grave danger. I had the height and I was close to the field so I made my decision, I would attempt the normal landing.

I called Förster and asked him to clear the circuit. I would come around and approach from the south-east, into the prevailing wind, trimming the aircraft's attitude to give the correct approach speed and finally progressively lowering the flaps to reduce the speed. I lowered the landing gear at a greater height than I would have normally, to allow time for the gliding aircraft to adjust to the drag, then made my final hard-banking turn in. I was almost too high and had to use heavy pressure on the rudder to sideslip and lose height. It is very unnerving to know that you can't go around if things aren't right. But I made it, straightening up in the first third of the field and then putting her down, rolling to a halt before the end of the runway. I tried to taxi, but the propeller wouldn't generate any pull, just shaking the airframe terribly.

Setting the mixture control to fully lean I waited while the big DB 601 engine stopped and then switched off. Releasing my straps, I took a firm hold on the windshield and heaved myself upright and stepped out of the aircraft. I was still a bit shaken by the experience, my mouth was dry and I felt the effects of the adrenaline still in my blood, but I'd made it back and that was what counted. Soon the ground crew was there and I was being congratulated on my return flight which was being heralded as *Ausserordentlich!* (outstanding). I was just happy to be back at base. The fault was later diagnosed as being a defective electrical switch.

15   May 1940

I am doing very well, however, I have not yet managed to get any Frenchies in front of my guns ... but we will continue until we see action too. Sometimes we wish that there should be more time to sleep ... especially now that I have private quarters and a good bed.

16   May 1940

Very short today. Still no contact with the enemy. We do a lot of flying, without success so far. We've looked at Metz, Longwy and Sedan several times. Also escorted bombers, but where the others had dogfights... when we arrive everything seems to be quiet. Still, it will come. We have moved temporarily near to Trier.

17   May 1940

Very short on your Mother's Day. Nothing special to report. We escort bombers to Verdun and the area around there. For me there is still no need to use my guns.

21   May 1940

Today we are told that we will move to Charleville . . . Now everybody is full of hope again...

22   May 1940

Still here. However this afternoon I was on French soil for the first time. Kühle and I were in Sedan to look at the lie of the land. At least we could hear some honest shooting from there (artillery). After our visit we had a look at Sedan from low-level and I can only say how glad we should be that we don't have this war inside our country. We couldn't get to Charleville because of bad weather. This evening I flew again, a weather reconnaissance up to the River Maas. Again I couldn't fly any further because of a low cloud-base. Please send me as many films as you can get for my 8 mm movie camera, black and white or colour.

On 23rd May all three squadrons in the group moved to Charleville. I took my '109 whilst the Nachrichtenzug followed quickly on the ground, putting into practice the carefully rehearsed manoeuvres of the previous summer. So well practised were they that it took less than a day to move and set up our new communications network. This, in my mind, fully vindicated the exercises which had been condemned by the short-sighted. Even more remarkable was the fact that they made the journey in the time, so clogged were the roads with French prisoners. Great masses of them were filing away from the front and in many cases were completely unguarded. We all wondered why they didn't run away or at least do something to hold us up and help their colleagues who were still fighting.

War in France. 23ʳᵈ May 1940
Our ground personnel on their trucks on the move towards
Charleville. Many French prisoners came in the opposite direction.
From Rocroi, there were about 30 km more to the airfield at Charleville.

In what seemed to be no time the switchboards and telephone connections had been hooked up, not only to the squadron dispersals, but also to the civilian network. The radio station was soon in place and began to operate as though we were on a German airfield back home, it all seemed to be so natural, working like a well-oiled machine. The only problem was the supply of fuel for the aircraft. Although the transport Junkers 52s were arriving and off-loading huge stocks of petrol in barrels, it was soon reloaded onto trucks and transported to the front. The tanks could not run on air and the battle was moving forward at an incredible pace. We had initially, therefore, to ration the use of fuel until we could build up our own stockpile. There was plenty of French fuel at Charleville but we were under instructions to leave that alone, suspecting that the French had spiked it with something which would ruin our engines.

With the initial restriction of flying time the crews looked for things to do. One of our 'Black Men' found a French tracked ammunition carrier, like a small tank, and used some of the suspect fuel to get it running. Everyone, including myself, enjoyed some hours of fun tearing around in this machine. Gradually this activity extended beyond the airfield, but it was soon stopped when the tank collided with, and badly damaged, a truck. After two days, when samples of the French fuel stocks had been properly tested and cleared, we were allowed to use them and came back to full flying status.

We now even a French tank on our Squadron strength and
we were living in a nice country-home. The population was gone,
we had our own cows, horses, ducks, rabbits, everything.
Plenty of food therefore.

Another less comical scene was the number of cows that had been abandoned by the French farmers who had scattered in front of our advancing troops. We couldn't understand why they had seen fit to run away. This was a military campaign and they wouldn't have come to any harm. But they had left and the poor animals suffered horribly. All of them had badly distended udders, some of which had already turned black. The days and nights were full of their agonised mooing. Others had already died, their swelling bodies pushing their legs into the air. Our men did what they could, often milking the cows onto the ground, just to give them some relief from the pain. Others that were too far gone were given more permanent relief. To help in our rescue attempt one of the huge Junkers G 38s was flown in with a Milking *Kompanie* from home. The aircraft would fly out with wounded from the front and then return with more *milkers*. It was an impossible task to visit regularly all of the scattered farms but at least they brought some humanity to the terrible scene.

One of the milking Kompanie flown in to save the French cows.

There was a little bombing from the French at night but without much damage, we were more in danger from ourselves. One night I was sleeping close to the *Gefechtsstand* when a whole lot of shooting and shouting started. Some of our guards, already warned that they might be attacked by partisans, had seen some silhouettes inside the farmyard where we were located. They were rather keyed up and didn't ask too many questions before they started shooting. In no time at all there was return fire and it seemed as if there was going to be a real battle. I was just drawing my pistol when someone shouted in German, 'Stop all this nonsense! *Aufhören!'* The shooting stopped as even the partisans apparently understood the command. Then, with the use of flashlights, it was easily established that two patrols had been shooting at each other. It was a good job that we *Schlipssoldaten* were obviously poor shots; for all the rounds that had been fired nobody had been hurt. In the morning nobody wanted to put their name to a report on the 'battle' and it was difficult to explain how so much live ammunition had been fired.

Having arrived at Charleville on 23rd May without any ground support or supplies we took the opportunity to take a look around the town itself. It was an amazing experience for those of us who had never been at war before. There was a beautiful town centre with plenty of shops, and all the trappings of a country town. But it was completely deserted. The shops were well-stocked with all manner of goods, and Kühle, Hinnerk Waller and I were especially impressed by the shoe shops. There were also textiles and household furniture and fur coats and stoles still on show. Nothing had been touched - only the people had gone.

There was little evidence of fighting to be seen. Here and there we could see fresh bullet strikes on the walls and some holes in windows. Some of the shop fronts were broken with glass still lying inside and out of the shops. But on the whole there had obviously been little resistance. On the walls and virtually everywhere we looked there were the newly posted warnings which had been pasted up by the *Feldgendarmerie* (Military Police) giving the stark warning for all:

NICHT PLÜNDERN

PLÜNDERN WIRD MIT DEM TODE BESTRAFT

(No pillaging/plundering - Death penalty for pillaging)

I was very uneasy when Kühle began to examine some ladies' shoes and to compare the quality of the workmanship with our own. I was relieved when one of the army guards who had been left there came over and respectfully pointed out that even though we were officers the rules applied to everyone. He went on to say that two privates had been caught stealing some shoes and furs and had been summarily court-martialled and shot within hours. Kühle hadn't wanted to steal anything, he was just looking, but I was relieved when we returned to the airfield.

The same afternoon we flew our first mission towards Dunkirk and this was followed up by three more missions on the following day. These missions were undertaken in poor weather conditions and very bad visibility. We were still some way away and our flight times, which were recorded in Gunther Büsgen's and Karl Rüttger's *Flugbuchs* (Flight Books) (unfortunately mine was lost later in the war), were between 65 & 75 minutes. That took into account about 15 minutes at the target area of Calais and Dunkirk.

We had been briefed about the quality of the British pilots and their aircraft and expected a hard fight. Indeed, when we first saw the Hurricanes and Spitfires attacking our Stukas it was immediately clear that we were up against very tenacious opposition. Equally clear now was the vulnerability of the Stuka when met by experienced and determined pilots. Inland from Dunkirk and off-shore the RAF was exacting a very high price from our dive bombers.

May 25th 1940 - Behind our billet, preparing for take-off for a mission to Dunkirk. From left to right: Ltn. Steinhilper, Gefr. Bott; standing - Ground crew sergeant sent to pick us up, seated - Fw. Urlings, Schieverhöfer, (hidden) Ziegler, Uffz. Wolf, Sigi Voss, Ofw. Grosse.

The Dunkirk - Calais area was easy to spot as we flew in from our forward base, the whole area being shrouded in smoke and fog. We would approach at about 800 metres and search for the fighters which would be attacking the Stukas and their escorts. We would circle the area but found it hard to engage the British as they pressed home their attacks on the bombers with great determination. Kühle seemed to hold back a lot as well, only giving the order to attack when the odds were very much in our favour. We would argue a lot about these tactics but his opinion was firm, he would only order us in when there was a good chance of success, with as little chance of losses as possible. In that way, he argued, we would gain experience without losing pilots. That was a good and mature policy, but most of us wanted just to get stuck in, to test ourselves and to claim a victory. We had been waiting on the side-lines too long. For the time being we had to be content with strafing freight trains and military convoys; this relieved some of the tension and was of some military value, but it didn't make up for the lack of success in the air. As we wheeled around the dark cloud over Dunkirk, Kühle cautioned us to stay well clear of its sinister billows. If we wanted surprises, he warned, there were plenty scudding around the edges of that forbidding mass.

From the right - Fw. Karl Rüttger, Fw. Lothar Schieverhöfer,
Sigi Voss (smoking), Kurt Wolf, with two trainee pilots.

After each mission we would return intact, but with nothing to celebrate other than that. Our 2nd Squadron had one victory and that led to some good-natured banter in the officers' mess. On the 26th the weather deteriorated, and although we tried to get through there seemed to be no way. In the evening things seemed to be improving, and *Obltn.* Lommel, another veteran of the Legion Condor, led the 1st Squadron out at 18:50. Like the closing of a grey door behind them, the weather closed in. Forecasting, like so many other things which we take for granted today, was still in its infancy and they had not been able to predict the sudden change. On the radio we could hear the traffic between the fighters as they tried desperately to find their way back to base. In the end they had to belly-land, one by one, in Belgium and Holland. If we'd had just a little more encouragement with our direction-finding experiments we might have been able to talk them back.

There was never any official confirmation of incidents like this, it was only speculation and rumour. It might have been different if our own Group Command had been set up but at this time events were moving on at such a pace that it was difficult to consolidate. We got our orders from *JG 53* and these were usually brief and to the point - 'Fly to Dunkirk'.

On 27th May, in an effort to increase efficiency and to be able to reach the battle zone more often, we landed at Cambrai which was about halfway. Here we refuelled and were able to return for a second sortie. It was a day of intense activity against the land targets and the ships that were massing off Dunkirk and Calais. Our bombers pressed home their attacks but were constantly harassed by the RAF who inflicted substantial losses. I understand that it is a complaint of many British and French soldiers who were on the beaches there that the RAF was nowhere to be seen. Believe me, they flew to their limit. By the end of the day II Air Corps alone had lost twenty-three aircraft with sixty-four aircrew missing. At the end of the day we flew back to Charleville.

Just before we left Charleville I was witness to a horrible accident which was nothing to do with the war at all. Between flights I was standing on the grass and my attention was attracted by the sound of an approaching Dornier 17. He was making a normal approach for the airfield, undercarriage down, lined up on finals ready to land. Then I heard the approach of another engine but this time a '109 at full power for take-off and from the opposite direction. There was nothing we could do other than hope that by some miracle they would miss each other but it was not to be. Just as the Dornier's engines were throttled back there came the sickening impact as the aircraft collided and wreckage scattered across the field. The '109 removed the whole cockpit of the Dornier, killing the crew

During the time at Charleville I observed one terrible wartime 'loss',not caused by the enemy, but by accident.

There was nothing I could do, apparently the '109 pilot, taking off in the opposite direction, had neither noticed, nor seen the other plane.

instantly before breaking up and falling to earth. There were no survivors. There was no way I could have avoided being involved, but as we raced forward the *Sankas* (ambulances - the blood wagons) were quicker. I had been unfortunate enough to witness several tragic deaths and their gruesome consequences, certainly enough to allay any morbid curiosity I might have felt. It was a natural reaction to run forwards immediately after the impact to see if there was any way in which the victims could be helped. But as soon as it was established that all had perished I left the scene. Similarly, it was not my habit to photograph such tragedy, but in this case I seem to have made an exception.

28 May 1940

My Dear Ones,

Now we are here at Charlesville for a couple of days. Our Squadron has, so far, not experienced any air-fighting. Only our 2nd Squadron has had combat with Curtisses twice, with one victory. We are, therefore, still doing nothing more than hoping; however, since yesterday I know with some certainty that it is harder to fly missions continously without victories, than it is when some success is seen. Yesterday we made an intermediate landing at Cambrai and from there we flew one sortie to Boulogne, Calais, Dunkirk and outwards over the Channel. One *Gruppe*, which is based closer, now has 70 victories but when listening to them it is clear that this is like rolling the dice, looking for the six. If you can throw it enough times you must throw more sixes. The time will come for us, I'm sure, in the meantime we are doing our duty. At this time, with one foot in Laon, we should fly a couple more missions to the Channel. Up there one *Gruppe* of *Zerstörer* Me. 110s (literally destroyers) just one hour in front of us met with fourteen Hurricanes and then, about two or three hours later, with fifty Hurricanes and Spitfires; but when we arrived there was nothing. We could clearly see the English coast and the Thames Estuary, even a convoy on the Channel, but there was nothing at all in the air but us. Whether that is specially bad luck or not I don't know, but it's damned hard on our pilots. Here we are living in a nice country-home. The French population has gone and we now have cows, horses, ducks, rabbits - everything, even a French tank. Also plenty of food.

With heartfelt greetings,
Your Uz.

p.s. Please send more films for my camera. 6x9 - metal spool.

*Final Goodbye to Charleville on the 29th for Laon. Some people apparently
enjoy a walk, taking their belongings along on a wheelbarrow. On the way from
the 'Villa' to the airfield. From left, an Uffz. of the
weaponry, Fw. Urlings, Fw Schieverhöfer, Fw. Ruttger, Siegfried Voss with
Seddy. Note steel helmets, and gasmasks, (round containers), pistols.
This is also the last picture of Seddy.*

Soon after the accident it was discovered that there was another serviceable airfield a little further to the north at Laon and on the 29th we moved there. It was a beautifully kept little airport with some French aircraft still there and plenty of fuel in the underground dumps. I went in advance of the rest of the squadrons to begin to arrange billets in the small town. Most of the menfolk had gone, either in the army or fleeing to avoid capture by us. Many of the women, however, had stayed behind to protect their homes and belongings. I opted to take quarters in a house with three women, one quite old but two who were younger and quite pretty. However, I was amused to see that they had deliberately dressed in their oldest and most dowdy clothes to appear as unattractive as possible. To further dampen any interest they thought I might have had they also introduced me to the wine cellar. One experiment with an exploding bottle of homemade champagne was enough to convince me that I was courting danger in that cellar and left it alone. Seddy, my faithful little dog, was run over by a truck here; it was a real loss for me.

Understandably, the French lived in fear of us, the invaders, but my experience was that our soldiers were well-behaved. Looting was punishable by summary court-martial and execution and I heard of few instances of personal violation. Certainly our conduct as a unit was good with only one case of real note experienced. Kühle had heard on the grapevine that our *Oberfeldwebel* was looking after himself rather well. That was easy here. The pilots from the 3rd Squadron, for instance, lived together in a large private house at Poury aux Bois. The owners had left in a hurry and most of their belongings were still in the house. It was obvious from the quality of their clothes, china, etc. that they had been very wealthy indeed. We didn't think that we had any right to touch any of these goods and everything stayed in place. However, this didn't apparently apply to the *Oberfeldwebel* in question.

The NCOs and the 'Black Men' had been billeted in houses spread around the village and it was here that the *Oberfeldwebel* decided to begin his own export business. There were still trucks regularly travelling from Laon to Böblingen to exchange technical spares and bring parts up as required. On the whole they had to run back empty, and this is where this Staff Sergeant saw an opening. His wife lived in Böblingen and it was whispered to Kühle that she was taking delivery of loot from Laon. As the next trucks were preparing to leave, Kühle asked me to come along and take a look at the contents of the trucks with him. There, sure enough, was a large box addressed to the NCO's wife in Böblingen. The colour drained from the *Oberfelwebel's* face as Kühle asked him to stay while the box was opened to reveal a fine collection of fur coats and delicate china and glassware. There was no doubt that the *Oberfeldwebel* saw himself looking down the barrels of a firing-squad but Kühle took the matter into his own hands and reduced him to the ranks on the spot. For a long serving NCO that was punishment indeed, but at least he had been spared a court martial and almost certain death.

CHAPTER 13

Intermezzo - June/July 1940
Tasks of Value but with little Reward

On 31st May and 1st June, the weather changed to allow some operations to Dunkirk and the Channel. We were hopeful that we would soon see some action when, right out of the blue, we received a message to withdraw from France to protect the *Leuna Werke* at Merseburg and *Junkers Werke* at Dessau.

To say that we were disappointed didn't come anywhere near expressing adequately how we felt. After days of frustration through bad weather and then sorties which just missed contact with the enemy, we thought we were poised to support the immediate crossing of the Channel. Then came the order to withdraw. It had a devastating effect on the Squadron's morale, but orders are orders. We waited for as long as we could, knowing only too well how the military machine was prone to changes of plan, but this time there was no mistake.

There is little doubt that the withdrawal had been ordered because of our losses. Although not completely written-off, all the aircraft of 1st Squadron were out of commission due to the forced landings a few days earlier. They could be repaired but first they had to be recovered and transported and there was no pool of spare aircraft. On paper we were down to two-thirds operational strength and so we'd been withdrawn to regroup and refit.

It was just bad luck again, sheer frustration for us who wanted to test our mettle. From the edge of the *Blitzkrieg* to the boredom of another

Sitzkrieg. An army train was made available to move the bulk of our support units; the *Nachrichtenzug,* being more urgently needed, would travel by air in our own transports. Our new destination was to be Zerbst near Magdeburg, and I was able to fly that in three stages, stopping over at Frankfurt for the night and arriving at Zerbst on 3rd June. On the way, at Trier, the 2nd Squadron had only just landed when they were scrambled. During the take-off one of the '109s crashed with another, running right into it and somersaulting. *Feldwebel* Munz, one of our veterans from Spain, was very badly hurt and was taken to the *Lazarett* (military hospital) in Trier - another couple of losses without enemy action.

7 June 1940

Yes, now we have been here for two days. Shortly before the great air-battle that has been reported near Paris we were pulled out and are now back in the *Heimat* (Homeland). Our disappointment and frustration knows no bounds. One minute we were at the middle of it all and now we are at peace again. It all happens so quickly - Laon, Sedan, Frankfurt and now Zerbst. We all feel like we are in a dream. However, we do still have hope. Today I received my first mail from you and an abundance of packages. Many thanks. It is fortunate that there is always lots of work to do to keep us busy, otherwise I might get desperate. But if we are to be good soldiers then we must follow orders ...

Zerbst was a quite well-established *Luftwaffe* airfield, with everything newly built. There were hangars with plenty of space, excellent quarters for everyone, as well as a very comfortable *Kasino*. But this wasn't what we longed for. It soon became apparent that this really was a quiet zone, nothing was expected to happen. That would have been fine if we'd really needed a rest, to recover from the rigours of combat and to repair battle damage; but we really felt that we were frauds. We had suffered only at the hands of bad weather and bad luck. We didn't feel much like heroes.

Amongst the first of the packages I opened, I found quite a few of my 8 mm movie films which had been processed. I staged a show in the *Kasino* to everybody's general approval. *Hauptmann* Ewald, who was back as temporary *Gruppe Kommandeur,* suggested that it would be a good idea to start a movie *Kriegstagebuch* (War Diary) to run parallel to the official written one. Having long seen the potential of movie film I agreed and donated my first films to the starter package. I had already shot quite a few reels, both black and white and the very early Agfa colour, and we began to cut and splice these together for the record; I enjoyed the work so it was no hardship. It also had another advantage in the short term.

At that time nobody else had done any filming in the *Gruppe* or really knew anything about it, so it was only natural that Ewald called upon my experience, limited as it was, when the decision was made to purchase a camera for the *Gruppe*. That on its own wasn't going to be an easy task because, at that time, just about everything was rationed to support the war-effort. I called a dealer in Stuttgart and, with the help of the Stephan family, managed to secure what seemed to be a good buy at around 400 *Reichmarks*. It was all that was available and, from the price, I thought it must be a good one. In the meantime I had bought myself a second camera. Each of mine had only cost about half what we were paying for the *Gruppe's* camera. Now I had one that was driven by a spring, and one battery operated unit. With these two I was able to carry on making quite good films, usually with black and white in one and, subject to availability, colour in the other.

Another real advantage for me was that I was to be entrusted with the task of collecting the camera from Stuttgart. This purchase had to be handled with relative confidentiality because there was no official funding for such things. For this secret mission I was given the squadron's Me. 108 *Taifun* four-seater, which we had been using for conversion to the '109. This lovely little aircraft was still in its light civilian livery and gave a certain anonymity to my comings and goings. Another thing I would be able to do on the way would be to fly a mission of mercy to pick up *Feldwebel* Munz from the hospital in Trier, and transfer him to a hospital at Goppingen near Stuttgart. His wife lived near and she would be able to tend to him instead of leaving him in what amounted to a field-hospital, near to the border with Luxembourg.

After a flurry of last minute telephone calls, all looked well. By coincidence Mr and Mrs Stephan had to be in Trier on the 19th June, on business, looking after the building of the West Wall. They said that they'd take Gretl along so we'd have a chance to be together. With my constant moves it had been difficult for us to see each other for a while. They said they'd take care of my accommodation arrangements and it was to be the first time I'd ever stayed in a first-class hotel like this one, the Porta Nigra at Trier. It really was an eye-opener for me, all finished off by a splendid dinner, courtesy of the Stephan family, for their front-line soldier.

In the morning, after farewells over breakfast, I left the opulence of the hotel for the stunning contrast of the hospital where Munz was to be found. It really was a horror. I had no idea in what terrible circumstances I would find him. It was a new and frightening face of war that I'd never seen before. Army casualties were lying everywhere on thin mattresses, lined up in a large hallway of the Trier monastery. Some were badly wounded, obviously in need of attention, others were plainly too far gone for any help from this world. The aspect was of pure misery and utter depression. When they saw me in my *Luftwaffe* officer's uniform they really started to let out some of their pent-up anger and frustration. 'To Hell with you, *Herr Leutnant!* To Hell with the whole bloody lot of you! Now we're wounded and not much use, we're on the scrap-heap. Nobody cares!' It was a shock to me to see how men who had been wounded fighting for their country were being left to die. The medical staff were doing all they could, but there just wasn't enough of them to go around. So many of these brave men would die here unnecessarily. It was sickening.

With the help of one of the nurses, I found Munz way up near to the roof of the building. As soon as he recognised me he started off, almost begging me to find a way of taking him away, 'Please get me out, any way you can. They haven't enough surgeons, not enough time to care. People are dying all the time ...' I asked the nurse if there was anything I could do to help. But, as it happened, I was to have enough problems doing what I had come to do. First I had to see a medical sergeant who asked a whole host of questions, 'What kind of aircraft did I have? Did I know how seriously injured Munz was? Why was he to be flown out? Wouldn't it have been better to transfer him to Göppingen by *SanKa (Sanitatskraftwagen* - ambulance*)'* I lied through my teeth, hoping that if we could get him to the aircraft it would be too late to turn back and we'd have to make the best of what we had. I said that we could take the seats out to accommodate him comfortably. Every question led to another, but gradually I cut my way through the red tape. I knew that if I didn't get him out right away, we'd never do it. As each new question came up I would glance at Munz and read the pleading in his eyes. I was sure that if I failed he would die; he was in such a pathetic state.

We succeeded in overcoming the first hurdle and actually got Munz into an army *SanKa* and drove out to the airstrip at Trier. Fortunately, a nurse came with us. When they first saw the cramped interior of the *Taifun* and realised that we could not, in fact, take any seats out, we nearly lost the day.

But together we convinced them that we could make it and they gave over to us all the pillows and duvets they had and we managed to make up a fairly level airborne *chaise longue*, on which Munz was as comfortable as possible beside me.

It was with a great feeling of relief, tinged with sadness, that I was able to push the throttle forwards and feel the *Taifun* begin to gather speed along the runway at Trier. Munz was going home but behind us we had left all those wounded men for whom we could do nothing. A little of the glory that I youthfully saw in the campaign was left amongst those stinking rows of blood-sodden mattresses. In just about ninety minutes we were touching down at Göppingen and I soon arranged for an army *SanKa* to take Munz on to the hospital. He was unbelievably grateful and happy. Anyone would have thought that I had walked into a burning wreck and carried him out in my arms. He was soon in a good hospital and made a full recovery, returning to the *Gruppe* in December 1940.

I'd found the conditions in the monastery in Trier very depressing; it was the real face and consequence of war. In contrast we had been treated as conquering heroes when we had stopped off overnight at Frankfurt on our way to Zerbst. Everybody wanted to shake us by the hand or to buy us a drink. Most of us felt a bit like frauds. Although we had been on many operational missions and could, at any time, have actually been in great danger, things had not worked out that way. That wasn't our fault, we were still anxious to fight, but inside we knew that we'd not yet really been initiated. A few months later we would have given a lot to have been withdrawn to Zerbst for a rest, but just now most of us just felt a bit foolish.

Once settled at Zerbst we still had to carry on the farce for the benefit of those who wanted to celebrate us. We were well-prepared for that too. Our quartermaster had stocked up well in France from the supply dumps which had been abandoned by the French and British. In our canteen there were ample supplies of chocolate and sweets and every type of drink, from real scotch whisky to the best champagne, cognac and French wines - all things which were no longer available in Germany. Soon the word spread that we could be counted upon to be generous with our gifts and one invitation followed another. Kühle and myself, for instance, went to have our teeth fixed and, of course, took along an appropriate offering (this was actually the first time that I'd been treated by a female dentist). But the real fun was at the open-air swimming pool at Zerbst where we used to go in strength. We used to invade the pool as a virtually complete squadron - pilots, mechanics, staff clerks - everyone who was free, sometimes numbering over 100 people.

The pool was set in what was a small park with plenty of tables and solid benches around the pool itself. The diving boards were great too, the highest being 10 metres high, Olympic standard. We could take along whatever our hearts desired - chocolates, a couple of bottles of champagne or a case of wine. We felt like kings. We weren't mean with our spoils either. Everyone soon learned that we were there to share our good fortune and we soon became firm favourites with the people of Zerbst. The weather was now what you would expect for summer with plenty of sun and clear skies. The combination of the warmth of the sun, the friendly atmosphere and a few drinks loosened us all up, but on one occasion nearly caused me to injure myself.

Feeling full of bonhomie I announced that I was going to attempt a dive from the top board. I purposefully climbed up and stood at the edge, looking down. It seemed a lot further down than it had done from the ground. But with the crowd cheering and egging me on I couldn't do the sensible thing and come down, although I realised that I was taking on too much. Gradually I shuffled my toes up to the edge of the board and with a sustaining thought like, 'If I can fall out of an Me. 109 at 3,000 metres, I can dive off this,' I let my balance tilt forwards and I was off. There was a sudden rushing of air and then a blinding pain as I hit the water with my back too bent. I thought I'd damaged my spine, but it was OK after a while. It had been very foolish. I'd only been off of a board at that height once before at school, and then I'd jumped. Still my effort was well received and an encore called for. I gracefully declined, making my way out of the water with as much dignity as I could manage. That was the signal for the others to have a go and one after another the pilots jumped off of the board, led by Hinnerk Waller. I voiced my opinion to Kühle that things might get out of hand and he agreed, bringing the capers to a stop before anyone was hurt, much to the disappointment of the crowd.

Our festivities were not confined to our base and Zerbst, and we often visited other airfields which were close. On one such occasion we were having a really fine time and had been introduced to many of the people who lived at and around the base, as well as our own colleagues. Amongst these people were two really lovely young women whose husbands were still on ops in France. One of the girls was even showing-off her young baby whose father had not yet seen it. At around dusk the telephone rang. Quite unobtrusively a message was taken which had to be passed on to the two women as a matter of urgency. They were taken to one side by one of the senior officers from the host airfield and told that they had just received information that both of their husbands had been killed in action. Confirmation was sought that the operative word was killed and not missing but sadly there was no mistake. The mood of the whole party changed; just as a sudden thunder storm might ruin a summer day, everything became black. We tried to console the two women but to no real avail. They both just floundered about in welter of despair, almost beating the walls whilst they began to suffer the full gamut of human grief. Needless to say the party soon broke up and we all went our various ways, each reflecting on what we'd seen. More than one of us wondered how grief would take those whom we might leave behind.

However, life had to go on for the living. In the 3rd Squadron we had a new toy, and it was always good to have a diversion. In this case we had been allocated a new Hanomag heavy tractor unit which had to be run in. Without a trailer behind it it was just like a big truck, and both Hinnerk and myself had the appropriate licence (from *Kriegsschule)* to drive it. Kühle gave us permission to use it so we dutifully ran it in by making trips to Magdeburg, where the cafes and restaurants were better. We both cut splendid figures, parking our huge tractor-unit outside a small cafe and dropping in for a drink and a dance.

17 June 1940

Dear Mother,
What I'd really like to do most would be to beat up the dear people of Heutingsheim! (Someone had spread a rumour that I'd been killed in France, and after witnessing the problems at the party, I could well imagine how my mother had felt until I was able to confirm that I was OK) What nonsense! Those two days must have been very bad for you when really we are doing very well ... I feel healthy, just never felt so good. We have plenty of sports, even a tennis court ... I bought a new racket ... however there are no balls or tennis shoes ... they cannot be bought. As it looks like we might be here for a while please send some by express post to the address at the *Fliegerhorst Zerbst.*

Letters and packages from the 6 June all received, everything else is still in transit in France or Germany. I'll get it in the end. The disappointment is slowly passing, after all, as soldiers, there is no other choice but obey and fulfill our duty; which I feel we have done ... To predict what is to be done with us is impossible. In any case, future disappointments could not be worse and so I know I could *take* it. Let's close that chapter now.

Please don't allow yourself to get upset again like last time. Should we really get involved I will be writing immediately ... A few days with no mail is meaningless. Should something happen to me you would be informed immediately by the *Kommandeur*. Everything else is just rumour.

And now, Mother, just rejoice at our victories. Who had dared to believe it could be! An extra greeting to my little sister, Helga.

Herzlichst Dein Uz. p.s. I got the EK II a few days ago.

(EK II - *Eiserne Kreuz* - Iron Cross - Second Class)

Both the content and layout of my letter are very reflective of my true feelings at the time. I have gone into some detail about my disappointment and given some hints as to my feelings about duty; yet as a post-script I mention that I'd been awarded the Iron Cross. That was how I saw things. I wasn't out to get decorations; I was out to prove myself by serving my country and demonstrating my value as a fighter pilot. My own personal evaluation was that I had not, at that time, done anything which I regarded as challenging.

On 28th June we lost *Unteroffizier* Neumann whose aircraft was seen to dive straight into the ground without any obvious cause. Another useless loss with no contact with the enemy.

Once more I had the opportunity to fly the *Taifun* because the camera dealer in Stuttgart had telephoned to let us know that he now had a good projector and screen in stock. It was agreed that these would be added to the *Gruppe's* inventory, and so the officers made a collection for it. Another part of the flight was to collect some of the personal belongings of our senior officers which had, because of our movements, been left at various points around Germany.

I was delighted with my new mission. I loved flying and this would be a real challenge. The furthest point of the trip would be Liegnitz in Silesia (now Legnica, Poland). There I would have to collect a heavy trunk which belonged to *von* Pfeil and take that right across Czechoslovakia to Stuttgart. Then I would unload and make the purchases for the *Gruppe* and collect a few things of my own and for others. My final stop would then be Mannheim where I would collect some luggage and then fly directly back to Zerbst.

I wasn't about to ask if it was an appropriate use of a *Luftwaffe* aircraft, or if it would be more expedient to use the normal freight services; I was looking at a real challenge, flying alone over great distances, with no navigation aids or radio, just a bunch of maps and my compass. It was great. Zerbst to Liegnitz was about 450 km (280 miles), then down to Böblingen was a lovely 630 km (390 miles), with a flight right over historic Prague. On to Mannheim, 100 km (62 miles) and back to Zerbst another 400 km (250 miles). In all about 1,600 km (1,000 miles). The *Taifun* was ideal for a trip like this, so light and easy to fly; cruising at 265 km/h (160 mph) and with a range of about 950 km (590 miles) or about three and a half hour's flying time.

My flight plan was split over two days, covering the Czech leg on the first day and staying overnight in Stuttgart. Quite early on the Friday morning I left Zerbst and arrived at Liegnitz at around 10:00. The staff at the airfield had been advised of my ETA by telephone and everything was ready, working like clockwork. The heavy trunk was strapped down as the aircraft was refuelled. Then came the second leg.

This was a difficult decision; in order to reach Prague I would have to cross the Riesengebirge, and it was the first time I'd flown in this area. All I knew about it was from fairy tales, where it was the home of gnomes and trolls, the *Rübezahl* in such myths. Evil spirits or not, it could easily become the last resting place of unwary airmen. The line of peaks contained some that topped 1600 metres (5,250 ft), and there was always some cloud cover around as well as all the other problems of up-drafts, downdrafts, the so-called *Föhn* wind and mountain waves. The weather station said that I could have a try and see if I could find a clear valley where I could slip through. The forecasts coming out of the newly occupied Czechoslavakia were still not up to our usual standard and that was about all they could advise. If it turned out that the mountains were completely closed I would have to fly around the range, more or less back to Dresden and Leipzig and then try to cross the *Fichtelgebirge* before dropping down to Stuttgart. If this became the case, I would have to take another look at the range and make an intermediate stop for fuel.

I had to notify my flight through the *Fluko* system to *Flugleitung* at Liegnitz, and they approved my route into Czechoslovakia, which was still a very sensitive area. They did, however, recommend that I remained at an altitude of about 500 metres so that the big white letters, WL *(Wehrmacht Luft),* on my *Taifun* would be clearly seen. I hoped that would be OK; I really didn't fancy being shot down by a trigger-happy '109 pilot or our own flak. Before noon the weather improved and I took off and headed for the Riesengebirge in bright sunlight. Instead of the poor conditions which had been previously forecast I had fantastic visibility, a beautiful view of the mountains and valleys; it was a shame I hadn't thought to bring the cameras. Within half an hour I had reached Prague, clearly recognising the Karlsbrücke and the famous Hradschin near the centre. I just couldn't resist playing the tourist and flew a complete circuit of the city, taking in the beautiful sights. It was the only time I was ever to see Prague, but I wasn't to know that at the time. I had no radio contact and I wondered what the people on the ground thought of this nice little blue plane circling over their city, sightseeing in the middle of a war. Having done Prague I set course for the Böhmerwald, and after two hours flying over this beautiful area of Germany I reached the familiar landmarks around Stuttgart and landed at Böblingen.

I really felt rather proud of myself. The flight had been long and over areas which were completely out of my previous experience, but I'd coped. It had been a real coming together of all of my training and experience. I really felt as though there wouldn't be anywhere in the world I couldn't reach now. I was resolute that, as soon as we had won this war, I'd be off in an aircraft just like my little blue *Taifun*, and bring the sights like those I had seen that day right into people's homes; captured through the lenses of my cameras and on movie film. Once the heavy trunk had been unloaded from the *Taifun* and I had arranged for the security of the aircraft I left to make my purchases before the shops closed. At Böblingen most of the personnel had changed around and I couldn't get any transport. I'd have to rely on the buses and trains.

After picking up the equipment from Photo Binder, in Stuttgart's *Königstrasse,* I made my way out to Heutingsheim to stay at my parent's home overnight. I couldn't see Gretl on this trip because she was still away on her labour service, but I did call her father just before take-off. The various packages were loaded into the small luggage compartment of the *Taifun* and I left for Mannheim, about half an hour's flying.

Now I had to change my plans due to a slight misunderstanding. Mannheim had two aerodromes, one at Käfertal and the other at Sandhofen where our Wing HQ had been. The baggage that I was due to collect was at Sandhofen while I was on the other side of Mannheim. There wasn't enough time to arrange a transfer and so I opted to stay another night and finish the trip in the morning. I wasn't going to lose by this either; I was offered a room in one of the best hotels in Mannheim, the Palast, with our *Kommandantur* picking up the bill. I really enjoyed my dinner that night in what for me was a taste of real luxury. Afterwards I went down to the *Holzkistl* (wood-box) Bar in the Hotel for a nightcap. There was good music and dancing, but this was brought to an unceremonious halt when the air-raid sirens started up at about 10 o'clock. If it was a real air-raid I wasn't too surprised; quite close, at Ludwigshafen, was the BASF works which would be a prime target if bombing started.

Far from striking terror into the hearts of everyone it actually turned into a rather happy social event. Because the Holzkistl Bar was built well below ground level, it had been designated as a kind of air-raid shelter and soon filled up as the guests came down. It was a really great atmosphere, nobody seemed to be scared, even though upstairs the heavy guns were hammering away loudly without us knowing if it was all AA fire or if some of the explosions were in fact bombs. The barman did very well that evening, and even when we heard the 'all-clear', just before midnight, many people stayed on even though they were only dressed in their dressing-gowns and pyjamas. This kind of thing demonstrated one of the advantages, few as they are, of wartime. A combination of common purpose, of all being in it together. The necessity to take unusual measures brings people together and offers them a platform on which they can communicate without the hindrance of the usual social strictures. It's a shame that we've never been able to foster the same egalitarian society without a lot of people being killed as a by-product.

My nocturnal socialising caused me to sleep late on Sunday morning, and it was only after a nice lunch at the hotel that I felt up to the last leg of my journey. I caught the bus to Käfertal and, to my surprise, I found that the outstanding bags had arrived and were already loaded into the *Taifun*. However, being a Sunday, there were few staff on duty and I couldn't get any fuel. But in my estimation I still had enough for the leg back to Zerbst and set off, landing there at 17:00 hrs. After such an adventure I suppose I thought there might be someone there to welcome me back, but they were all in town, enjoying a Sunday off.

During our time at Zerbst we did get some special missions to fly as a squadron. Hitler was making his speeches in the *Reichstag* in Berlin and we were based just over 100 km away, close enough to be ordered in for fighter cover. Thus we spent quite a lot of time on patrol over and around Berlin, waiting for the RAF to try to bomb Hitler in the *Reichstag;* not much hope of action there. On 18th July we were transferred to Neuruppin, north of Berlin, where some of us stayed until the 23rd. Then we all assembled as *I/JG 52* again at Bayreuth, down in the south-west, again flying fighter cover for the *Führer* as he attended the Wagner Festival.

Bayreuth was pleasant enough, with its small airport up on the hill, and it was good to be flying, although, for most of the time, at readiness from dawn to dusk. But most days we would have time to go into town and take part in the festival which was being celebrated. This had brought a great collection of interesting guests from all over Germany, many of whom were pleased to invite the victorious *Luftwaffe* pilots for a meal or just for a drink. We felt important, if a little fraudulent.

I was still the *Gruppe's NO* (Communication Officer) and responsible for having the appropriate systems set up. At Zerbst there wasn't too much of a problem, the facilities being fairly modern anyway. All that the *Nachrichtenzug* had been tasked to do was to run out field telephone links to the squadron dispersals. There was no RT so we had to get our 1.5 kW stations set up - one in use and one for back-up. The well-trained crew saw to this with little or no supervision. By now this had become routine and I felt little ambition to improve things or come up with innovative ideas. I still believed that our communications could be greatly improved and that they would be the key to sustained success in the future, but I had no fire in the belly anymore; it had been quenched by repeated frustrations and humiliations in the past. I felt that one can only beat one's head against a brick wall for so long - sooner or later one has to realise that it hurts and stop. Maybe if I'd realised how right my predictions about communications would be and how many air-crew would suffer, I might have tried again.

Experience in the French campaign had shown that we hardly ever needed to use our 1.5 kW transmitters for tactical exchanges in morse. The telephones were always available quickly and it had been an easy matter to connect our switchboards to the French public circuit. Most orders and instructions had been transmitted by use of the telephones. It was really very simple. Staff HQ would call the *Gruppe* or squadron leader or his deputy, or he would call HQ, and the orders were almost always the same: 'Get up there and have a look around. If you see anything that is enemy shoot at it or shoot it down.'

The campaign had gone so well in our favour there had been no need for complex tactical analyses and instructions. Rarely there would be a time when, after we had left, some further information would come in and Förster would try to transmit it to us, but we were most times out of range.

For the most part it was a case of going to have a look and acting on our initiative. So it looked as though my adversary, Adolf Galland, was right after all: 'Take those damned radios out so that we can fly higher and faster.' In the short term and looking at this one campaign it could have been a strong argument; but the battles which followed were not going to be like this one. The enemy was learning by his mistakes and inadequacies and there would be no room for us to be complacent.

Today, as I research the material for this book, it is thoroughly sickening to read how the British developed their direction finding equipment and communications whilst we bathed in the glory of our success. They saw the potential in developing one of the most significant factors in the battle that was to come. It seemed that some people there listened and saw the potential of what could be whilst we, due to the lack of foresight of people like our fighter leaders, would have to be reliant on wing-signals, sign language and vague telephone calls.

There was still some fight left in me so I cast around to see what could be done. Being close to Halle and Köthen (an experimental and research communications station for the *Luftwaffe),* we were at least able to pull a few strings and get the best quality quartz crystals fitted to the radios in our aircraft. I heard rumours about new detection equipment that was being developed called *Würzburg* and *Freya,* but we couldn't find out much more than that. The new crystals greatly improved the range of our sets, but there was nothing much else that could be done.

The French campaign had at least started the debate about the apparent limitations of our equipment and fundamental problems like frequency. How many squadrons should operate on the same frequency? A minimum of three, a *Gruppe,* was set, but was a whole *Geschwader* (Wing) practical? Or even several *Geschwaders* if they were involved in a similar task. The debate ranged about with few, if any, real changes being made from the experience that had been gained. One thing which had proved to be positive was the value of having the two 1.5 kW transmitter units available for each *Gruppe.* This had proved to be invaluable when breakdowns occurred.

In fact the key to the argument about how many aircraft should be on the same frequency lay in how the radio was used, rather than how many people were using it - radio discipline. As soon as a situation began to warm up a bit the transmissions would increase and in moments the frequency would be swamped and all that could be heard was a high-pitched whistling as the receivers became overwhelmed. However hard we tried to maintain some order, as soon as any action began, the radio was swamped. There didn't seem to be much we could do about it.

Equally the radio frequency was common to all on it and sometimes we heard things that might have been better to have missed. For example, on one occasion we were using the same frequency as *JG* 26 and some of our transmissions overlapped. There were probably other units which we couldn't identify, but all we would get was the initial transmission. Something like: 'Attention … three o'clock high …', would be clear - then the radio would become overwhelmed and we could only catch the occasional word. Then everybody would give up and it would become quiet for a while. On this occasion the silence was broken by an anguished cry for help, *'Spitfire hinter mir! Spitfire hinter mir!'* (Spitfire behind me). There was no reply, just the hiss of static on the line for a few seconds before the voice returned, shaking with fear, *'Spitfire immer noch hinter mir. Was soll ich tun? Immer noch hinter mir!'* (Still behind me, what shall I do?) Then came a single clear reply and everyone recognised Galland's voice: *'Aussteigen! Sie Bettnässer!'* (Jump out, you bedwetter). I don't know who the man was or if indeed he came back; we were only pleased that he wasn't one of ours.

Nobody seemed to have learned any lessons from the French campaign and our communications would continue to be fatally flawed. There was no link between the bombers and the fighters. It wasn't just a question of frequency; the bombers used Morse and we used a voice operated system RT (radio telephony). Many instances had occurred where it would have been of great advantage for a fighter leader to have been able to communicate with a bomber group leader, but it couldn't be done. Later I was to make an attempt to get at least one set installed in the aircraft of the bomber wing commander, but without success. In retrospect, I see this gap in the communications link being another of the fundamental reasons why the Battle of Britain was lost.

Another area where this lack of ability to communicate was to have tragic consequences was in air-sea rescue. Again there was no link between the fighters and the seaplanes and motorboats who could rescue our colleagues down in the water. We would see one of our fighters ditch or see our colleague parachuting down and were in a position to help *Seenotflugkommando* (Air-Sea Rescue) to locate the downed flyer. But the best we could do was make direct contact with our own base-station and pass on what details we could. He would then have to telephone the rescue HQ and they would then try to pass on the information via Morse code. Of course each time the information is handled there is a chance for a mistake or for it not be passed on and the more links there are in the chain the more likely it is to break. It would have been so much easier if we could have passed on a position or any other information direct to the rescue plane. I have no doubt that many lives would have been saved if we could have done this. But I had learned to keep quiet about such things and got on with more immediate tasks.

Our filming adventures were beginning to yield good results as we became more practised. When Mr Binder, the photographic dealer in Stuttgart, had developed our films and saw the results he became most enthusiastic and offered us as much film as he could. It is such a pity that so much of it was lost later in the war; it was great stuff. Hardly anyone was using 8 mm film at that time and, had it not been lost, it would have made a fantastic record. Our flights for filming were called Combat Training, and that wasn't wholly untrue, but for the most part we were about getting plenty of air-to-air shots. We would choose the brightest and sunniest days for the best light and colour and then Kühle would take off as my wingman and we'd climb up to about 4,000 metres (13,000 ft). Once trimmed out at altitude I would hold the stick between my knees and film Kühle as he drew up to me in tight formation. But the '109 couldn't be held easily in balanced flight without actively flying it and so my aircraft would always gradually go into a roll and then into a slowly increasing dive. Kühle would follow this through and we would get a beautifully evolving series of shots as we would first see the sun on the upper surfaces of the aircraft and then the pale blue belly. In the background you would have the vivid blue sky as it can only be seen at altitude, contrasting against the clouds and then far below the patchwork quilt of the fields and woods of Germany. You have to bear in mind that it had only been us lucky few that had ever seen anything like this, and to be able to bring something of the beauty of flight down to earth was something special. People are all too familiar today with aerial photography and can even see films of the Earth, shot from the moon, but in those days there were few who had seen the glory of flight.[1]

17 July 1940

If I need something in a hurry I just send a telegram. Thank you very much for reacting with such fantastic speed. We had a film show for the *Gruppe* coming up and I needed the films for that. They certainly went down well. Life is extremely dull... Father may also be disappointed ... but not being an officer by profession, it may be easier for him. In my case, a pilot and a professional officer... believe me... fighting is a real ambition.

It is good to hear that you have enjoyable company... A good change for you... You shouldn't be alone all of the time... Don't be too disappointed if there is little mail from me...

28 July 1940

Now it looks like we will be transferred ... If that should come true it will be Calais - the best place one could imagine. Even though one of our squadrons has already left I'm still not building up my hopes too much... just trying to stay relaxed. We've been disappointed too often. Should it be true then you'll be informed immediately. I enclose the latest pictures from France, each one captioned to detail what it is. Keep your fingers crossed ... this time it will work out. Keep in mind that London might soon be ours ... *Horridoh!* (Roughly 'Tally-Ho')

29 July 1940

Again disappointment. Even though one of our squadrons was already at Calais another Wing, which has a better name, has moved there, taking our place... Really I don't know what to think anymore... Instead of seeing action we will now move close to Krefeld to protect the Ruhr. There we will be effective by just being present.

Best wishes on Father's birthday. Don't know where to write to him. Again we live like gypsies... In general one should try to make the best of things, but in our *Gruppe* so much damned self-control is needed! ...Looking on the bright side at least this move is not as disappointing as when we were moved back from Laon to Zerbst.

Here follows a letter from my mother to my father. It was written on the back of the letter I had sent to her. This both saved paper and forwarded my letter to my father. This chain-letter was finally annotated by my father and sent on to my sister, Trude.

My mother's feelings are well expressed and must be typical of so many mothers who had their children away and, in their eyes, in grave danger.

...Therefore I am using the empty side to write. I am always glad when Uz is *Heimatschutz* (On the home-front); he is such an impetuous dare-devil. Even though I would not begrudge him his desire to see action, I rather prefer, and we can feel more at ease, when he is not at the front. This morning your chocolates have arrived and two days ago two boxes from Trude ...all good provisions. Order's Emma gave me a big bunch of gladiolas, a basket-full of plums and a piece of smoked ham... If she wasn't around it would be more lonesome... My radio doesn't work anymore... waiting for Hesser (electrical shop)... his wife was here this morning... I wonder if it's the fuse? All of my electrical cables are *kaput*...

Last Friday night we had an air-raid alarm... I stayed in bed with Helga, she slept so well, I listened to the aircraft noise. If it had come closer I would have pulled the duvet over my head... Later I was told that searchlights, Very Lights and tracer bullets made a real fireworks display and I regretted not having a look. It lasted about half an hour. We had another alarm on Sunday night. Send the letter on to Trude.

Father to Trude:

How about your transfer? Do you know where? Do you know when? Can you no longer visit me here?   We are going to Konstanz. I will get leave there. 1st August I was in Prague. It was beautiful. Thanks for your birthday greetings.

This compound letter indicates the whereabouts of the whole family Steinhilper in mid-1940 as well as many of their thoughts. However it does not reveal that my mother, as well as her duties as a teacher, had now taken on most of the work of the headmaster.

At Zerbst, Hinnerk and myself were very disgruntled at the prospect of another *Sitzkrieg* in the Ruhr. As a bit of an outlet we hoisted a white bedsheet on the flagpole in front of the barracks as a mark of our surrender. It was well received by the lower ranks but the senior officers didn't seem to appreciate the joke. The flag got tangled around the post and we had to get it down, Hinnerk standing on my shoulders. For this very special occasion we had a photograph taken - the surrender of *I/JG* 52 at Zerbst.

At Zerbst, Hinnerk and myself were so upset about the prospect of again 'protecting the Ruhr' that we used a flag vole to raise some of our bedlinen as a 'white flag'.

Notes on Chapter 13

1. It is only now that I regret that decision. In order to provide the finest record of *I/JG* 52 I used the best of the films and only kept the cuttings. That is all I have left today as my record of the film we shot, about twenty minutes of film which, although good and a unique historic record, was still second-best to the film used for the *Kriegstagebuch*. That, unfortunately, was all lost with the other *Gruppe* records in the retreat from Russia much later in the war.

CHAPTER 14

To The Channel

I had hardly finished my letter home, expressing my bitter disappointment at our 'surrender' at Zerbst, when new orders reached us. We were to return to the Channel and, even better, right into the thick of it - a new airfield at Coquelles, the closest to the British coast. Now we should see what we longed for - some action!

On 30th July, 1st and 2nd Squadrons flew out to Bönninghardt, NW of Krefeld, in preparation, and a selected group of technicians and some of my Nachrichtenzug personnel were crammed into our *'Tante Ju'* and flown down to Coquelles. It was abundantly clear that this was to be a fast move, all indications were that things were hotting up at the Channel.

This time there was no completely organised move of the personnel and their equipment by train; they were just ordered to the new location using their own transport. This all added an exciting air to the proceedings and galvanised everybody into frantic action. The vital ground-to-air communications equipment couldn't be sent by air so I asked the advanced guard if they would give me a call as soon as they were on site and could guide me in with my 'Yellow 16'. Förster went with the vehicles by road but, from past experience, we had learned that we shouldn't send all the vehicles in one convoy, but rather let them all find their own way in small groups or individually via Holland and Belgium into northern France. Both the Poles and the Allies had paid dearly for having too many multi-vehicle convoys as they were extremely vulnerable to air attack. A couple of determined fighter pilots could easily put twenty or thirty vehicles out of commission in seconds. Better to disperse and regroup at the destination.

On 1st August I was just starting to feel a little envious of my fellow pilots, who had left for Bönninghardt, when I got a call from the duty officer to say that he'd had a call from Coquelles to say that they were ready. I tried to call back but that was asking a lot. I had the French telephone network to contend with, which was never too reliable, and to complicate this it was difficult to get connected to the new location. In the end I decided to go without any further contact.

I was pleased that I could act independently and planned my route to Coquelles. I would have to make a stop on the way, but I avoided Bönninghardt in case the squadron leaders there found a job for me. I wanted to get to the Channel and nothing was going to stand in my way. I therefore planned my stopover at Wesel, an airfield very close to the Rhine and easy to locate. Before lunch I set out after asking our *Flugleitung* (air-traffic service) at Zerbst to inform Wesel of my intended arrival in transit to Coquelles. That would ensure that fuel was available for me and, with a bit of luck, I'd be able to call to Coquelles. I avoided any further contact with Bönninghardt; nothing was going to stop me moving *I/JG* 52 to Coquelles.

The flight-plan worked out well, the weather was good and I only had to make one circuit of the area to find Wesel. On landing my aircraft was refuelled like a racing car and I was taken direct to the *Kommandantur* (control centre) to place my call to Coquelles. I was really pleasantly surprised how well-organised the whole thing was. Within moments of my arrival I was talking to one of my men in France, who described the new location. I was to fly to Calais and then follow the coast road until I saw some small woods with buildings at the southern end. This was a monastery and south of that was the landing field. Although it was nothing more than a stubble field, the Ju. 52 had landed there, so why not me? I only hoped that my men had walked the landing strip with a pilot's eye. One deep furrow might not have wrecked our plump old *Tante Ju'*, but it could see me upside-down in a burning fighter.

The only map I could get at the time was a 1:1 million scale and this was really too small a scale for accurate cross-country navigation; more usual is the 1:500,000, twice the scale, and more detailed. Still, I had to make the best of what I had; I wasn't going to hang around waiting for another map. I told them I would depart Wesel at 14:00 hrs and that they should start looking out for me at about 15:00 hrs, I didn't even stop to eat.

Again the flight was textbook - first flying through smokey clouds over the industrial regions of Holland and Belgium, but with the sky clearing the closer I got to the coast. The huge column of smoke which had so characterised our earlier flights to Dunkirk and Calais was now gone, but below me I could see the rows and rows of abandoned vehicles and stores on the beaches. I wondered how any army could lose so much and still be an army. Was there really anyone left in Britain to fight?

The beaches which had not been the focus of the action were clean and clear, looking radiant in the summer sun and giving a feeling more like taking a holiday than moving into a battle-zone. Beautiful as it was I couldn't spend too much time savouring the beauty of the French coast. I had to navigate and, more importantly, keep a weather-eye open for British fighters. The closer I got to the coast the more likely it became that I might run into some intruders. Although there had been little incursion into our airspace since Dunkirk, I was keenly aware that Spitfires could cross the Channel in about ten minutes at full throttle and I was a lone, novice pilot who would be a tempting target. Thus I kept my head down at 500 metres (1,600 ft) and kept my eyes open.

I hadn't been too worried exactly where I met the coast but I soon identified La Panne and, of course, the vast dump that Dunkirk had become was unmistakable. Following the coast virtually due-west I soon passed Gravelines and Calais and knew that I was close to Coquelles. To my right was the Channel, glinting and sparkling as the summer sun was reflected from the rippling waters and clearly there too were the white cliffs of Dover, so close - so very, very close.

Following my instructions I flew down the coast road and soon spotted the woods and the monastery buildings. Closing the throttle a little to lose speed, I pulled 'Yellow 16' into a circular orbit over what should be the field. Below I could now pick out some of our vehicles, most of them already camouflaged and invisible to the casual observer. Then I spotted some of the men in the field and the eruption of smoke from a smoke candle. That both marked the direction and strength of the wind and also the beginning of a landing strip. Nervously I flew around getting lower, checking for power cables and anything that would indicate a hazard in the field.

It all looked clear, but by the time I'd finished my own visual check a second candle was needed. I'd spotted some power lines on the approach route and judged what height I'd need to clear them without approaching too high. Satisfied that things were about as good as they were going to get I throttled back the DB 601 and felt for the pitch control with my thumb, bringing the propeller to fine pitch, watching the hands on the indicator clock come to 12 o'clock and letting the air-speed drop back. Then I selected the flaps and lowered the undercarriage, feeling the reassuring thumps through the airframe as the legs locked down and the two green lights winked at me. Skimming in over the perimeter I rounded the descent out and let the '109 sink onto the field. There was a rumble and she pitched about a bit as we made contact with the rough surface, throwing up a huge cloud of dust and chaff, especially when I re-opened the throttle to manoeuvre. By kicking the rudder left and right and toeing the brakes I could see one of the groundcrew directing me towards the trees and cover. The long nose of the '109 made it impossible to see directly forwards when taxiing and I had to steer a rather erratic course to maintain a clear view. Minutes after landing, my aircraft was under cover and virtually invisible from the sky. Everyone was aware how close we had now moved to the front-line.

From the outset I decided I was going to sleep in a tent, staying close to the centre of things. Our newly arrived personnel had been quick to avail themselves of some of the massive stocks of equipment which had been left by the British and we now had first class bell-tents, much better than our own. These were pitched over a circular hole in the ground, more than a metre deep, and really made for quite a comfortable billet. There were no firm orders or instructions regarding the booty which was everywhere and, in the absence of clear guidance on this kind of requisitioning, the new units quickly stocked up.

Calais and Dunkirk were rather like vast military supermarkets. Virtually anything you wanted could be found in or around the harbours or on the beaches. I have to say, too, that this liberation of the spoils of war was strictly confined to military equipment. As we had seen before, anyone who was caught pillaging from civilian shops or the homes of the French was unlikely to see the end of that day. Transport was in abundance and, for the most part, only the rotor arm had been removed from the distributor to immobilise the engine, but it wasn't usually too hard to find a replacement from a vehicle which had been blown up or bombed.

One of our best finds was floating in the harbour at Calais. We spotted several wooden barrels floating which were well down in the water. When we managed to fish one of them out and un-stop it, we found to our immense joy that it was full with fine French red wine, completely untainted by the sea water. This was a moment for brave and clear thinking. We had a serious situation which demanded immediate and decisive action. I was left with a few of the troops to stand guard while the staff car was sent back at high speed to instruct one of the trucks to attend. This was duly done and with maximum effort we had soon saved many barrels of various sizes from an ignominious and unthinkable fate. We had, as a quid-pro-quo, an almost unending supply of wine for the squadron. Having filled our truck to bursting, we generously then, and only then, told some of the other units of our discovery so they also could be of help in preventing what could have been a tragic loss.

The Port of Calais - August 1940. This was in the very early days when we were still finding things like the wine barrels. The ambulance in the centre-rear was British, probably being used by one of our units. To the left can be seen the twin funnels of a channel ferry.

Back at our new base the barrels were heaved onto stands and tapped. From then on anyone could take a glass of wine when the mood took them, dropping 5 *pfennigs* into a wooden box.

Considering that the supply was to all intents and purposes inexhaustible, everyone exerted disciplined restraint and we had no cases of drunkeness at inappropriate times. Our first real foray into the giant supply dump of Calais and Dunkirk had been spectacularly successful. The next visit found us looking over the vehicles. Our technicians immediately spotted the potential of a triple-axled British Morris weapons carrier which performed beautifully over the rough terrain, much better than anything we had. It was therefore added to the squadron's inventory, as was a long flatbed trailer. Both were to serve the squadron for years, even trekking across the wastelands of Russia and back; something I shouldn't think the manufacturers had ever envisaged for their product, but carrying our highest endorsement. Also to give good service was a large pantechnicon that was laboriously hauled out of the sands of Dunkirk and converted into a mobile tool-truck and parts store. This also was to follow the squadron across many borders and do sterling service. There was no official policy on the stores and equipment and so the individual groups vied with each other to find and remove the most choice items first. Surprisingly, virtually none of it had in anyway been booby-trapped and it was not until later in the year that one of our men was killed when a floating mine exploded while they were retrieving material from the harbour.

Calais September 1940 - Invasion barges which had been brought from the Rhein being made ready. Calais Town Hall tower in the background.

Back at our new base at Coquelles all was activity as we worked to convert the area into a first-rate fighter base. What had lately been corn and potato fields were now our runways and our little tent-village, courtesy of the British Army, was well established. After two days I was still the only officer present and that brought its usual rash of responsibilities. For instance our *'Tante Ju'* had just unloaded her usual load of equipment and personnel and was preparing to leave when the pilot discovered that the starter for the port engine wasn't working. I offered him the services of our 'Black Men' but he felt that with the nose engine and the starboard motor at full power he would get off. I decided to let him give it a try. With two engines at full power the venerable Junkers climbed away from the field and then came a heart-stopping moment as the pilot dropped the nose to gain airspeed, but she picked up and came around. Once straight and level, albeit a bit low, he let the airflow over the propeller of the port engine turn it over and it fired up without any problems. Returning under full power the pilot indulged himself by beating the place up. He then set course for Mannheim without any problems. The Junkers 52-3M was to prove the most versatile and rugged of all of our transport aircraft and its flexibility was clearly demonstrated here, as was the confidence and skill of the pilot.

(Postcard) 4 August 1940

Dear Mother,
Plenty of work here. Have managed everything by myself. So far sleeping in tents, but one barracks being built (Nissen huts). Had a swim in the Atlantic Ocean yesterday.

Hardly had I written this card when the rest of our vehicles began to flock in. Förster, who had now been promoted to substantive *Hauptmann,* had taken a little longer to arrive because he had insisted that his group stay in contact instead of finding their way individually like the others. It was only a matter of hours before our well-trained *Nachrichtenzug* had the main transmitters fired up and a proper switchboard hooked into the French circuit.

From now on we became the Third Squadron again, and there was a real bonding amongst us as we developed and shaped our base out of a farm. This is what we'd so often talked about, living in the field, building our tent-village and setting up our support service whilst still glancing over our shoulders in case the enemy became active. Having made a start on the tented accommodation, Kühle decided that we'd all stay with the squadron instead of being billetted out to the local farms.

Gradually we began to settle in and actually experience our first serious contact with the enemy. Because I had been responsible for the development of the *Nachrichtenzug* Förster seemed happy to retain me on the circulation list for confidential messages, something normally reserved for the senior officers only. Here I began to read the reports on the monitoring of the British radio frequencies, which we could receive as clearly as our own. From very early on we realised they had adopted a system of cover names and special phrases, supposedly to confuse us. But it didn't take much effort to work out who the 'Indians' were and that the sector controls and individual squadrons had names with which we would become familiar like 'Weapon' and 'Dogrose'. Similarly we soon learned that 'Tally-Ho!' meant that an attack was imminent for somebody. More interesting was to listen to the broadcasts live. There would be a series of fairly clear instructions until the attack and then there would be an avalanche of voices, orders, warnings and pleas for help. Then, as suddenly as it had begun, it would stop, to be followed by isolated calls to missing pilots, usually in vain. All this served to key us up even more and I couldn't wait to actually get into some serious aerial combat. The thought both excited and frightened me. What would it really be like? Would we actually get the chance to prove ourselves before the British sued for peace or we invaded?

8 August 1940

Dear Mother,
Your letter arrived yesterday. I was glad because mail is rare here. Thank God I am not alone anymore; one squadron has followed on the 6th. It's good to see the others arriving, but it had been great to be in charge of about 40 men building the tent village and getting things ready. However now that the others have arrived there will be more changes.

Yesterday we pulled a British truck out of a marsh near Dunkirk and also brought back a French car. So far no flying so you may rest easy. That prospect doesn't bother us; now we hope that it will be our turn. I celebrated Father's birthday (2 August) in my thoughts whilst driving to Boulogne.

Here we have arranged ourselves in marvellous comfort. Imagine an orchard with 7 large British bell-tents and two British Nissen huts with everybody sleeping on prima mattresses. In addition we have electricity and a record player. Everything is about ideal. Inside some photographs from Zerbst.

11 August 1940

Dear Helga, (my youngest sister)
A small greeting from your Uz on your birthday.

Dear Mother,

Today I had four missions. Three of us shot down a Bristol Blenheim which was about to attack one of our air-sea rescue planes.

13 August 1940

Dear Mother,
I don't know how the mail here works out, but even if you do receive my letters together it's better than none. The day before yesterday we flew our first missions. Four in one day. First we had to stand guard over an air-sea rescue plane in the middle of the Channel. When almost at the end of our fuel and flying at about 3,500 metres I saw a single aircraft approaching from the west. I reported it and soon recognised it as a Blenheim. The leader of the *Swarm* led us around in a curve which placed us in an attacking position. He began to fire and straightaway pieces began to fly off the Blenheim, then his *Rottenhund* took up the attack as the aircraft began to burn. Even so the rear gunner on the Blenheim continued firing. I followed up the attack until, at about 550 kph, he hit the water. It's horrible to think that four people (at that time I thought that a Blenheim had a crew of four, like our bombers) were still sitting there as it went under.

The whole thing only lasted for about two minutes. When we returned to base the joy was great to behold - our first victory. (Actually it didn't count for me and was given wholly to *Hauptmann* Wiggers of *1/JG51*. I was just flying with them to get some experience. Our rules were that the victory is given to the pilot who makes the most substantial contribution to the attack.) Our first squadron shot down three Spitfires without loss. Yesterday we flew three missions. One was a free-hunt between Dungeness and Beachy Head, the first time over England. In the evening we flew guard to some bomber units that were attacking Lympne.

Everything was black with our aircraft. It was terrific! Within the hour we
will be off again, maybe towards London.

That was how I recorded my first real combat experience. For the first
time I'd seen the form of an enemy aircraft filling the projected circle of
my gunsight and felt the slight vibration as my guns fired and the tracer
raced towards the stricken target. There was the mixed feeling of elation at
having done for the first time what we'd been trained to do, for which we'd
waited so long, tempered by the thought that I might have killed another
human being. In this case it wasn't too difficult to reconcile what we'd
done because the Blenheim had been positioning to attack our Heinkel 59
Seenotdienst rescue plane which was unarmed. Clearly painted white with
the bold red crosses on the wings and fuselage there could be no possible
confusion with any other aircraft. We really began to wonder what kind of
people we were fighting who would attack such helpless targets which,
ironically, were often engaged in rescuing downed British airmen as well
as our own.

This is no better illustrated than in the case of this first combat for me.
We were flying high cover on the He. 59 when we saw the attacking
Blenheim. We shot that down and, unbeknown to us, the crew escaped. A
Heinkel tried to pick up these men (it may have been the one we were orig-
inally protecting) when it was attacked by Spitfires. These Spitfires were,
in turn, attacked by more of our fighters with two of them being shot down.
It was all very confusing and, to us, utterly sickening.

To me and the other German pilots these attacks were viewed as nothing short of murder. Eight-gun fighters and fighter-bombers tore into these
rescue aircraft which were armed with nothing more lethal than a flare-pis-
tol. Even more sickening was when we saw these attacks driven home by
multiple passes over a downed or damaged aircraft ensuring that there were
no survivors.

Apparently the orders for this criminal behaviour had come direct from
Churchill, claiming that the *Seenotdienst* was flying reconnaissance on
convoys. That was, in my opinion, a feeble excuse for justifying the killing
of pilots and crews who might otherwise have survived to fly again. We
didn't need the Heinkel 59s to fly reconnaissance for us. There were ample
'109s for that, some already fitted with cameras for that purpose. Not only
that, from a normal patrol height over the Channel we could see a vast
proportion of it without making any special effort. It is a subject which still

generates much bitterness in Germany particularly when we think about the many, many times when we flew free-hunts over Kent and Hampshire and never ever attacked trains or road vehicles - just targeting our efforts on the airfields and military installations.

17 August 1940

... not much to report. Just five more missions. Three days ago I broke my No.16 at the same time as Bert Göbel damaged his aircraft. At first it looked very bad, but it was repaired quickly. Yesterday I did my *Werkstattflug* (checkout flight) and everything is fine. It is good that I can stick with the same plane - after all, having had some bad luck with her there should be some good luck on the way. The missions we've been flying were not easy, but without any victories. Our second squadron had better luck yesterday. They made an attack on Manston and shot up a gasoline tanker and six Blenheims. I wonder how my '16' will behave on her debut?

The day I damaged my aircraft the weather had started very poorly, and there seemed to be little hope of flying. Therefore Kühle, Hinnerk Waller and I had taken ourselves to Calais for the day. We called into a small cafe, had coffee and ordered a large whisky each. Just as we were served the weather improved and we had to scuttle back to Coquelles. As I crammed my cap back onto my head I decided to down my whisky and also Kühle's and my friend Waller's. Subsequently I was a little tipsy when we got back to base. There was an almost immediate *Gruppe* scramble which meant that all the squadrons took off from their dispersals, over and under each other. Because of this there was no chance to align the aircraft for a take-off into the wind and often, as in this case, we took off with a very brisk cross-wind. I gave 'Yellow 16' full throttle and her tail came up quickly. Soon I was at take-off speed and eased the stick back and she began to come off the field. Just then the cross-wind came at full force and 'Yellow 16' began to side-slip. I tried to correct but the yaw was too much and I began to slide sideways, snapping the undercarriage leg like a carrot. The prop ploughed into the ground, throwing up huge chunks of earth as I slewed to a halt. In seconds the main switches were off and I was out of the aircraft feeling more than a little stupid.

I don't think the accident was totally due to the whisky but it hadn't helped. In conditions of that kind there is no margin for error at all. I suppose I felt guilty about the damage and offered the mechanics a case of champagne if they could fix it quickly. The damage was not too bad in the end. The propeller was replaced and there wasn't any damage to the crank-shaft so it was ready for test in thirty hours. They earned their champagne and my thanks.

19 August 1940

...first to the debut of my '16'. Initially we had been positioned to fly cover for returning bombers. But soon after take-off we were ordered onto a ground-attack on Mansion. At first my heart was hammering in my chest, but when we pushed the noses of our aircraft down for the attack I calmed down. My mates who followed me in confirmed that I was doing well. I aimed at a fuel tanker which was filling a Spitfire, then at two other Spitfires, one after the other. The tanker exploded and everything began to burn around it. My other two Spitfires began to burn on their own.

Only now do I realise what power is given to a pilot with those four guns. In the evening we were once more flying towards London on a free-hunt, but without any results. On the way back we spotted a patrol boat and shot at that until it started burning.

Looking back at yesterday I am satisfied. And now I hope that the weather today will improve. So far it has been too bad to be ordered out.

This letter records the brief details of what was my first serious action. It had been quite exceptional to receive a change of orders from the ground station and in plain language - 'Change of mission - Numerous enemy fighters are landing for refuelling and rearming at Mansion.' Förster had more or less taken it upon himself to order the change of mission based upon the *Nachrichtenzug's* careful monitoring of the British fighter fre-quency. It had become clear that many British fighter units were breaking away from combat to be replenished at Manston. Förster had rightly con-cluded that a ground attack would catch many enemy fighters on the ground.

Setting course across the Channel we had flattened out our *Schwärme* so that we were all at the same height, each *Rottenfuhrer* with his *Rottenhund*. Flying practically due south, we roared over the coast just east of Margate and within seconds were approaching Manston over a small group of buildings. I spotted the tanker refuelling a Spitfire quite close to the boundary of the airfield and moved position to line up. Dropping height to about three or four metres to minimise the height deflection on the shot,

I saw the tanker rapidly filling the red illuminated ring. Increasing the pressure on the trigger and the button I felt all four machine guns begin to fire with a light vibration in the airframe. Grey lines of tracer streaked forwards and focus on the vehicle. I saw the strikes and flashes as the bullets began to hit home and the tanker began to burn. In seconds I had hurtled over it and I turned my attention to two Spitfires, which had been placed out at dispersal, awaiting attention. Again the grey lines streaked out, first tearing up the ground and then concentrating on the aircraft.[1] They both began to burn as the tanker erupted into a ball of fire behind me. Banking left, we hedge-hopped out of Manston and moments later were crossing the Bay of Manston (Pegwell Bay) with its distinctive little river.

Again I was assailed by the conflict of feelings. Firstly I had, at last, done what I had been trained to do and done it well. It was a victory for me and a victory for Germany. I had set thousands of litres of precious fuel on fire and left three Spitfires in ruins. That could save the lives of many of my colleagues. But I had also seen that my attack had cost the life of at least one man and that was, and still is, hard to take.

25 August 1940

…I am well. Yesterday we flew three more missions. One to the northeast of London with nothing but about 150 fighters. It was a terrific merry-go-round. So far bad weather today.

27 August 1940

…The day before yesterday I received my letter, about every eight days we get our mail. When you congratulate me on my victory I'm afraid you're mistaken. (This was the attack on the Blenheim which was credited to *Haupt.* Wiggers). I only participated but it doesn't count for me. That doesn't matter - what is important is that it is one less of them. (I was still very upset about the attack on the air-sea rescue plane). Yesterday better luck and misfortune. We were suddenly scrambled when Kühle wasn't there, therefore I had to lead the squadron. We were to escort some Stukas to Folkstone. When I was leading the squadron we were attacked by about six Spitfires who dived out of the clouds. I was in the lower *Schwarm* with two others (Kühle would normally have made up the fourth in the *Schwarm*) when we heard *Feldwebel* Grosse (flying in the top cover *Schwarm)* calling up that he'd been attacked and taken hits in the engine and was returning to base. *Fw.* Ziegler[1] went down into the sea. We had been attacking barrage balloons without success and hadn't seen anything of this fight and only got some details when we landed. On the other hand the No. 2 Squadron shot down four Spitfires with only one loss.

In the afternoon we had a free-hunt in the area of the Thames Estuary and the No. 2 Squadron was attacked out of the sun by some Hurricanes. In a dramatically short time three of the '109s were diving down trailing smoke. I saw this clearly and when the enemy came diving through I managed to push one to the side to get it away from the Chief's tail, getting a few shots from behind. Then my *Rottenhund* (Karl Rüttger) took it up, firing with cannons. Kühle got another in front of his guns. Then we beat it, satisfied with two more victories. But there is no reason to be glad when some of our people are missing.

Mother, during these last days I am frequently thinking of you at home, how you must be continuously waiting for news and how easy it might happen that I would come to stay over there. Sometimes I wish, and don't get upset at this, that I had nobody who would grieve for me, or who would have to bear the pain of hours and days of waiting for news.

I am writing to you to ask that you never do that. You shouldn't believe that we are wanton or careless in our flying. If we were we wouldn't last long. Here nothing but the call of duty will help survival. One knows that what one does has to be for one's country and I'm glad that I am permitted to do it. Should I get through this war I shall be proud of it.

Later, when thinking over what I had written I began to reduce the number of letters that I wrote to Gretl. I was a serious enough young man to realise that my position was too vulnerable to tie anyone's destiny to mine. I think that this had all been motivated by the loss of *Fw.* Ziegler and witnessing the losses of our 2nd Squadron. The realities of war were really beginning to make themselves felt.[3]

Notes on Chapter 14

1.The arrangement for the firing button on the joy-stick of the Me 109 (see page 292) was that the button which actuated the two machine guns in the nose of the aircraft was on the top of the column and was covered by a metal flap. This metal flap would be flipped forwards on a hinge to hang in front of the column to uncover the top gun button. The cover on this position would then exert pressure on a second, inset, button on the front of the column when pressure was put on it by the forefinger. This fired the guns in the wings which were cannons for the '109 E-3 and E-4 or, in the case of 'Yellow 16', machine guns.

2. *Fw.* Grosse made it back to base. *Fw.* Ziegler was rescued by British boat and became a POW.

3. In retrospect I am amazed that even though my thinking had become a little morbid, I still wrote to a girlfriend for the address of a family in London. Their daughter had married a German and was living in Germany and had just given birth to a son. I was so sure that we would soon be in London that I asked for the address so that I could call round and let the Pearson family know that they had a grandson. This philanthropic idea was to land me in deep trouble later on.

CHAPTER 15

Tactics - The Eternal Debate

During these early days at the Channel coast, as the summer evenings drew out, we began to have debates. After supper, which was usually eaten in and around our tents in complete informality, we would sit about and talk. All of the pilots, NCOs and officers, would gather, and lively discussions would usually ensue. These were generally toned by the events of the day; losses would quieten us down and bring a mood of introspection, whereas success would bring with it a surplus of energy and excitement.

It was here that I would come into head-to-head conflict with Kühle who, to his credit, allowed a free and frank exchange of views without too many restrictions of protocol. I would challenge Kühle on what I saw as our stupid tactics. 'Is it not true,' I would argue, 'that our goal is to eliminate the British fighter force by all means? And to achieve this shouldn't we give freedom of action to each individual pilot to pursue the enemy at every opportunity? To follow them where necessary back to their bases and to destroy them on the ground? Why not,' I would continue, 'leave it to the individual pilots to assess their situation regarding fuel, ammunition and tactical position at the time of contact with the enemy instead of the squadron disengaging and regrouping as a whole after a brief action?'

This, of course, was quite typical of my character. If a job needed doing then why not get on with it and get it done? Hadn't the attack on Manston been a graphic demonstration of what could be done by shaping tactics to suit an evolving situation and letting individuals act in the *Freie Jagd* (free hunt) rather than trying to apply some hard and fast rules to every situation? I was aware that there would be costs involved in such tactics, but then if it shortened the battle there would be a saving in lives and machines. I predicted that if we were to continue as we were the losses would end up being higher because, slowly but surely, we were losing our pilots in a long-drawn-out battle of attrition.

If our leaders were to be believed, what we were doing was a preparation for the invasion of England and therefore that too must add weight to the argument of the Hawks. All that was being achieved with the present tactics was that the personal scores of the leaders of formations were being increased at the expense of those who were protecting them at the rear - the *Katschmarek* (tail-end Charlies). The term *Freie Jagd* was ridiculous in the present circumstances.

Kühle argued back that I was too young and still too inexperienced to understand the full spectrum of our tactical position. He said I should look to my 'old friend' (Galland) as an example of what could be achieved within the prevailing rules. Kühle was well aware of my feelings towards Galland and in particular about his apparent fixation with the trappings of victory (a high personal score and a chest of medals). He had cleverly managed to move from the *Schlachtflieger Gruppe* (ground attack Henschel 123s) after the successful days of the Polish campaign, and get back into fighters - holding several staff positions but always retaining flying status and increasing his personal score. Kühle asked if I'd not noticed the preferential treatment which had been given to the higher scoring Aces when Wing and Group commands had been reshuffled. One of my peers, for instance, Helmut Wick was already commanding a squadron, and other changes put the young Aces in the positions of command. *Major* Mölders took over *JG 51* from *General Major* Osterkamp; Galland (now also a *Major)* took over *JG 26* from *Oberstleutnant* (Lieutenant-Colonel) Handrick; *Hauptmann* Lützow assumed command of *JG 3* from *Oberstleutnant* Vick; *Hauptmann* Trautloft took over *JG 54* from *Major* Mettig and our own *JG 52* came under the command of *Major* Trübenbach releasing *Oberstleutnant von* Merhart.

The picture looked grim. I was thinking we were all fighting to rid the sky of the RAF, and what was really developing was that many individuals were using this battle as a stage upon which they could further their own careers and personal scores, whilst apparently giving little consideration to the overall tactics or the losses of their men who were behind them. There were times when my morale took severe knocks.

At times the debates would become heated, usually assisted by the ready supply of good red wine. Kühle never pulled rank to control a situation but usually successfully employed a diversionary tactic. Unfortunately for my friend, Hinnerk Waller, he was more often than not, the butt of Kühle's attention. Hinnerk came from a farming background and was constantly having his leg pulled about his ability to milk a cow - something which he had been foolish enough to demonstrate with great pride soon after the beginning of the French campaign. Kühle would steer the conversation to a point where he could ask Hinnerk if he shouldn't have stayed milking cows or driving horses in front of a plough, instead of thinking that he could fly a fighter and shoot down Tommies. Mimicking a thick Friesian accent, Kühle would work on Hinnerk, who never really formulated a successful counter-attack. Soon most of us would be helpless with laughter and the uncomfortable moment would pass. At what he shrewdly judged was the right time Helmut Kühle would either wind up the debate for the evening and pack us off to bed or re-establish a dialogue which was less heated.

Hinnerk Waller, seen here prior to his promotion to Oberleutnant.

Hinnerk, to his credit, put up with an awful lot of this good-natured banter, but as the strain of constant combat flying began to take its toll it began to get to him. One evening towards the end of August he reached the point where he'd had enough and ran to our tent. Grabbing his Walther pistol he made off towards the wood nearby with the apparent intention of killing himself. Some of us rose to go after him, but Kühle told us to sit down. He was a shrewd judge of character, and as we all sat waiting for what we thought was the inevitable shot nothing happened.

Later, as we lay in our tent, we discussed the advisability of sending out a search-party, but Kühle dismissed the idea. Hinnerk would be back he said, and we'd talk the whole thing over in the morning. He was right; some hours later Hinnerk quietly returned and got into bed without another word. The next day Kühle and I discussed whether we should have Hinnerk examined by a doctor to assess his mental state but we were spared that decision. Quite by coincidence a message came from Doctor Greiling, who had been treating Hinnerk for stomach complaints, that he should go to the nearby military hospital for x-rays and a general check-up. We decided that if there was anything wrong it would show up on these tests and therefore took no further action. After that, if placed fully fit, we would be able to explain to the other pilots that he had in fact been thoroughly examined and placed fit to fly. Any other strange behaviour would then be written-off to mild eccentricity. After four days he returned to us fully fit to fly. The check-up hadn't revealed anything tangible, but Hinnerk had been recommended to stick to a special diet and to avoid too much alcohol.

What we were seeing, although we didn't realise it at the time, was our first case of *Kanalkrankheit* (Channel Sickness). A combination of chronic stress and acute fatigue. At first there were isolated cases but, as the battle dragged on, there were to be more and more cases of the evil disease. The symptoms were many and various but usually surfaced as stomach cramps and vomiting, loss of appetite and consequently weight and acute irritability. Typically the patient's consumption of alcohol and cigarettes would increase and he would show more and more signs of exhaustion. There was little leave and, unlike the RAF pilots, we were not to be circulated to quiet zones for short periods of rest and refitting. There was nothing our doctors could do either. The principle of battle fatigue had not yet been established and it was felt that as soon as anyone was taken out of the line because he was showing signs of stress, there would be a flood. So the doctors resorted to diagnosing appendicitis. This minor operation ensured that at least a pilot would not be flying for about two or three weeks.

Part and parcel of *Kanalkrankheit* were the symptoms which affected the aircraft. Instruments would fail, motors would run hot or lose oil pressure, just to be remedied by returning to base. Ground crews would spend time chasing a fault through a machine only to find nothing amiss. Following a *Werkstattflug* the aircraft would be pronounced fully mechanically fit for service. A few hours later it would be back with guns that would not fire in the air, but which let loose a hail of bullets on the ground. The ground crews were faithful to their pilots, and to their credit tried to cover for them, but when there was no chance of finding a fault the former had to speak up.

We all felt the strain but when, in the middle of August, the command reshuffle took place, there was damned near a mutiny in our *Gruppe*. Our Commander, *Hauptmann von* Eschwege was called up to *Luftflotte 2* Headquarters and returned with the Iron Cross First Class. It was arranged for the pilots of the three squadrons to be paraded at their separate dispersals whilst *von* Eschwege made a short speech in which he explained that it was with great regret on his part that he'd been relieved of command of *I/JG 52* because of a grumbling appendix. He wished us all 'Good Hunting' and many victories and left for his appendix operation and thereafter on to a relatively safe seat at the fighter training centre at Merseburg.

There was almost uproar amongst the pilots, not only because of his Iron Cross, but also because he was effectively being rested whilst we were still having to remain at the sharp end of things. This wasn't the last time the strings would be pulled for some of the more senior officers and it is significant, I think, that during the Battle of Britain our *Gruppe* never lost any personnel of the rank of Squadron Leader or higher. *Hauptmann* Wolfgang Ewald replaced *von* Eschwege as *Gruppe Kommandeur* and inherited quite a disconsolate brood of fighter pilots.

Outside the realities of the air-war we lived quite well. Our tent city was home now, and we all really enjoyed the outdoor life. We had one of the best cooks for our squadron and he managed to produce attractive meals from the most basic military supplies, sometimes augmented by rabbits or a partridge if I chose to go hunting with Terry. Eggs were always plentiful because there was a standard allowance of eggs and chocolate for each pilot in accordance with the number of missions he flew. To supplement all of this our supply truck was sent weekly to Reims, which had remained untouched during the advance to the coast. It had been declared an Open

City - that is, one which was an island within the occupied zone, still administered by the French but with free access by all; subject to the granting of permission by the Army of Occupation. The French *Franc* had been devalued against the *Reichsmark* and our money had greater purchasing power. Having very soon recovered from the shock of our invasion the French merchants were keen to trade with us, and all supplies at Reims were plentiful.

In Germany we had occasionally drunk our native *Sekt* (champagne) but it was expensive; now we could indulge ourselves with the very best of the French wines and in particular, champagne. We would buy Pommery, Moet and Chandon, Veuve Cliquot and the best of the red wines by the case. Although most of us were still not outwardly showing major signs of nerves, arguments were becoming more frequent, tempers frayed quicker, and the majority found a few glasses of good red wine before bed helped us sleep. The strain of unrelenting front-line flying was beginning to show.

CHAPTER 16

The Going Gets Rough

We had now been in the front line for nearly four weeks and had flown countless sorties over England. *Adlertag* (Eagle Day - the beginning of the all-out assault on RAF airfields) had initially been delayed through bad weather but had now been and gone without decisive effect on the RAF.

Around 26th August we finally got to use a supply of yellow paint which had been held in store and which was supposed to be a great secret. Now we were ordered to have the noses, rudder and wingtips of our aircraft painted up in the distinctive yellow. Naturally rumours flourished, in the face of any concrete intelligence, about the purpose of the painting and the consensus was that this was to be a special marking for the aircraft which would be involved in the invasion. I was so sure of this that I wrote to a dancing partner of mine and asked for the address of her British relatives in London, so that I might call on them to pass on the good news that they were now grandparents.

The paint was brushed on, almost overnight, and the debates about the usefulness of it began. In fact some units refused to comply, arguing that the yellow would render their camouflage useless. But HQ insisted that all aircraft should be painted because there would soon be so many aircraft in the sky that our pilots would need it to be able to distinguish quickly between friend and foe. The enemy soon noticed the difference and our monitoring of the British radio frequencies soon revealed that we had been christened 'Yellow-nosed Bastards'.

Initially we all waited expectantly for the issue of orders that would clearly indicate that the invasion was on. All along the French coast, and in particular in the area of Dunkirk and Boulogne, we had seen masses of barges and large river craft that were being converted into landing-craft. Most impressive were some big flat-bottomed barges at Calais which had been fitted with BMW IV aero engines at the back. With a four-bladed prop these beasts would hurtle across the water at considerable speed and, because they weren't restricted to the use of underwater propellers, they would slide up the flat sandy beaches for some distance, still driven on by the propeller. Quite innovative.

But in spite of all this there was no positive movement, only the inevitable rumours. The only word spreading was that there was to be no invasion and the *Luftwaffe* was to subjugate the British alone. That might have been possible if the RAF fighters had come up to meet us on our now frequent *Freie Jagd* (free-hunts) across southern England. But so reticent was the RAF to engage us, just the fighters, that we had to employ *Lockvogel* (decoy birds) bombers in group and wing strength. That had the desired result and we were then able to take on the attacking British Hurricanes and Spitfires with good success.

Things had just begun to hot up when the weather deteriorated again and we had a few days rest:

29 August 1940

Dear Mother,

Now we have had a rest for one and a half days, and if the weather doesn't improve it'll last longer. During these rest periods we use the cars to get out for excursions. Some days ago we were in Le Touquet, a bathing resort for the Parisiennes at the weekends. There, in spite of our German uniforms, we had a marvellous time, an outstanding *Festessen* (binge). We went there again the day before yesterday. We drove to Brügge yesterday, you see my knowledge of this countryside improves by the day. I hope I wasn't wrong to write to you as I did in my last letter. That was how I felt then but I'm feeling better now. It is our hope that the Army will soon get started so that we will all have a small piece of land on The Island (Britain)[1]. It shouldn't last long, if it does then it's all going to become boring again.

31 August 1940

Dear Mother,

Two days with plenty to do. Yesterday four *Feindflüge* (missions) and three today. One of the missions today was a ground-attack on Detling with two sessions of dog-fighting as well. Our squadron bagged three without loss and the *Gruppe* score was ten. This is the way it should go on with our fighting experience and skill growing. *Horridoh!!* Mother, I believe we'll make it.

Karl Rüttger's flying log shows that he returned with four bullet strikes on his aircraft. Also I notice from the envelope of my letter home, that I had been promoted to *Oberleutnant* - I'd only just been notified of my promotion but unbeknown to me Kühle had marked this part of the envelope to the effect that it (the new rank) had only been applicable for five minutes.

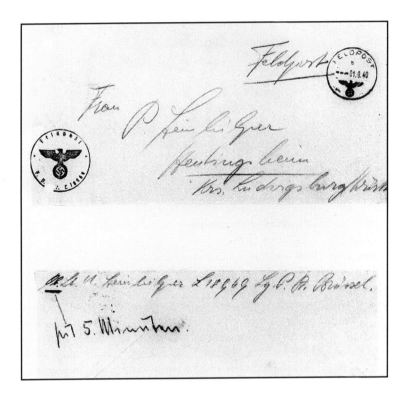

3 September 1940

Dear Mother,

We've been having good weather and have been kept very busy lately. Yesterday there were two more missions with more dog-fighting. On the second mission I was leading the squadron when we were set upon by about eighteen Hurricanes which dived on us out of the sun like the very Devil coming to call. There were only six of us but, with the exception of Waller, whose aircraft took eight hits, I got everyone home unmolested. Our Me 109s are much the better aircraft.

Returning from a mission over England.

6 September 1940

Dear Mother,
The day before yesterday was a rest day but yesterday and today we were fighting again. The Englishman is a tough adversary but he will eat 'humble pie' yet. On the rest day we went to Lille and it was nice to find on my return that I had letters from both you and Father. You ask quite a lot of questions but I ask you not to get upset if I only write briefly today. Suffice it to say that my 'Yellow 16' is a loyal soul and we'll make it through...

I am sure there is one letter missing from the series because I cannot find one which refers to the loss of my close friend Hinnerk Waller. Just before midday on the 6th September we were intercepted by British fighters east of Tonbridge. I was close to Hinnerk when he was attacked but I wasn't in a position to go to his aid. I watched helplessly as bullets ripped holes in the wings and the slipstream peeled the aluminum back like thin springs. Gradually the aircraft rolled away and I saw the canopy come off. Almost shouting all my encouragement to him, I saw him drop from the stricken aircraft and fall away. Still at 9,000 metres (nearly 30,000ft) I saw his parachute deploy and felt some relief, although he hung in the harness like a broken doll. At that height he certainly would have blacked out almost immediately from oxygen starvation. I had only seconds to wish him well in my mind before I had to get out of the area. We were actually back at Coquelles de-briefing before Hinnerk would have landed. Looking at our watches we all agreed on a time and tried to make light of his loss by a brief celebration of his official coming down to earth, about half-an-hour after he had bailed out. I was sure that he was OK but we'd all miss our farmer's son.

Another thing which makes me think there are a few letters missing is that in none of the others do I mention that both I and Hinnerk had been promoted to *Oberleutnant*. There was only Kühle's scribbled remark on the envelope of my earlier letter.

8 September 1940

Dear Mother,

Many thanks for your and Father's letter. His letter impressed me, it shows the true soul of a soldier. It has just dawned upon me what he went through in the First World War, what it means to live for four and a half years not knowing what will happen to one in the next few minutes. But all this thinking is really useless. We have to do our duty and, say more than that is not worth thinking about.

Hurrah! Just now there was a telephone call, *Reichsmarschall* Göring has announced that he gives his highest praise to *JG 52* for yesterday's performance. Yesterday we worked our greatest magic so far over London. During half an hour, more than 500,000 kg of bombs were dropped on London. We were flying fighter escort and, at the moment, I am leading the squadron because the 'Chief' has a stomach upset. Right now we have only four aircraft which are fully airworthy but that's fine. The losses from four bomber wings were only four aircraft but with a further twenty-five fighters and destroyers (Me 110s). But for this the targets in London were erased.

Hopefully the Chief will soon be well again. After all he has more experience.

At this time we were short of fully airworthy aircraft. We had plenty of pilots but there was a dwell in the production and reconditioning of aircraft. This situation would soon be reversed as more aircraft arrived and we lost more pilots. However, for the time being our squadron was flying at one third of its strength.

When re-reading this last letter today I can still clearly see the images of that day; it was an unbelievable sight. In the first wave in the late afternoon there were about 1,000 aircraft assembled in layers, stacked at about 600 metres (2,000 feet) intervals. We were flying high cover as we approached London and there we could already see many oil tanks burning with huge clouds of smoke reaching high into the sky.

The main targets were the docks which were easy to find on the distinctive U-bend of the Thames. Once in a while we would snatch a glance down and see the flashes of bombs as they exploded and the shock waves radiating out with the force of the explosion. But from our height, some 10,000 metres (32,000 ft) these were just pin-pricks of dirty light, more impressive was the oily smoke. There wasn't much time to take anything but the briefest observations. We were in the hottest of combat areas and anyone who was distracted for too long was going to end his day there and then. Everywhere was danger; from the British fighters, from the heavy flak and from loose barrage balloons - one of which was floating around near our altitude and burning in a tumult of colour and smoke.

Now we really came up against the full force of the RAF. If the calculations of our High Command had been correct there should have been minimal fighter opposition to us now. But whilst we saw numerous head-on and flank attacks on the bombers below we were often too busy with our own defence to intervene[2]. There were constant dog-fights with aircraft wheeling and diving, pursuing each other, sometimes with success sometimes not. There were stark black lines diving down, showing the path of a stricken aircraft and parachutes floating in the thin, cold air. There was tragedy, too, as I watched one parachute begin to burn, its helpless charge falling faster and faster. Hard to take, too, were the accidents of identification. I sat helpless with the hard lump of frustration boiling in my chest as I saw below me a '109 latch onto the tail of another of our fighters and then to see them suddenly linked by four straight grey lines as the guns were fired. Quickly the yellow tail of the leading fighter ignited and it rolled out to dive towards the ground. In such tense and charged surroundings such mistakes were inevitable.

Sometimes I wish I had the skill of an artist so that I could have recorded these beautiful but awe-inspiring sights. The pure azure-blue of the sky with the sun dimmed by the sinister smoke penetrating to extreme height; this interwoven and cross-hatched by the contrails of fighters locked in their life and death struggles. In amongst this the burning balloons and the few parachutes in splendid and incongruous isolation. These images are clear and bright in my mind today and it is to my regret that such fantastic scenes will only live as long as the few of us who saw them and survived.

After returning to base we were amused to see *Hauptmann* Förster's intercepts of the British radio. He was still monitoring the frequencies and had picked up many references to an elite 'Yellow-nosed Wing', which seemed to be everywhere at once - very bold in its attacks and very numerous.

We had now got what we youngsters had been waiting for; almost continuous combat sorties. But fairly quickly we began to feel the fatigue and the tiredness that comes with living under constant threat. Time after time the adrenaline would surge into our blood as we flew towards the combat zone. We would feel the relief of returning to base, but would then have to cope with the emotions of having lost friends and colleagues, knowing also that within minutes we would have to do it all again.

It seemed that every time my spirits were at a low ebb something else would come along to plunge me deeper down. Soon after the loss of Hinnerk, for instance, I was just returning to base in our staff-car when I saw a lone '109 make an approach and land. Whilst still rolling the engine stopped and the fighter came to a halt out on the field. I could see from the markings that it wasn't one of ours, and because all our aircraft were down I was able to drive out to it, arriving at the same time as some of our ground crew. They lifted the hood and inside was the lifeless body of an *Oberleutnant,* he must have died the moment he shut the engine down. Taking the body out we laid it out on the ground and found that he had severe wounds to the abdomen; these had caused the young man to bleed to death. Indeed his parachute pack was saturated in blood which ran from it as we moved him. He had done a remarkable job in getting himself and his aircraft home, but it hadn't been quick enough to save his life.

It was a shattering reminder of what waited for all of us, every day we flew. It wasn't often that we actually saw our dead comrades. Initially there was little aggressive action from the British once we were at base. It was rare for us to suffer an attack in the early days, but on one such occasion a light bomber crept in at night and let one bomb go which exploded close to the *Werftzug* (repair shop tent). It only caused a small crater, but when the lists of equipment which had been lost in this explosion began to come through it became more than remarkable how much material had apparently been stacked on the exact spot where the bomb had fallen. Indeed it soon became clear that if it had all perished in the way claimed, the crater itself could not have contained this vast amount of missing equipment. For some time now the quartermaster's bookkeepers had been waiting for such an event to write off everything which had been damaged or lost in our campaigns so far. Certainly the crew of the bomber never knew how successful they'd been.

13 September 1940

Dear Mother,

Many thanks for your congratulations on my promotion. It's really true but still feels a bit strange. Many of the others have got their promotions too.

During the last few days we've had bad weather again. Meanwhile we've installed a stove in our tent. However, with all the rain it's not been too agreeable.

At this time I am planning to be disloyal. Yesterday we received two aircraft which are fitted with the cannons in the wings. I'm taking one, and the 'Chief' is taking the other. Therefore it is with a broken heart that I am abandoning my '16'. It's sad because it was the most loyal aircraft in the squadron, but cannons are cannons. Now another man will get '16', my new machine will be Yellow 2. I hope it will be as good a comrade as '16' has been. Today the new plane is being serviced and tomorrow, on my birthday, I'll take it on a mission for the first time. Let's hope that the weather soon improves so that we can finalise things with the British.

End of August 1940 at Coquelles

From left: Feldw. Siegfried Voss, Feldw. Lothar Schieverhöfer, Ltn. Ulrich Steinhilper (in the background Yellow '16' surrounded by straw bales) Oberfeldwebel Siegfried Grosse, next to him a pilot who never did fly with us, Feldw. Zieger, the first to come down (26-8-40).

I find it curious that I'd become so attached to my aircraft; it was after all only a machine. But pilots are notoriously superstitious and I had done a lot in that aircraft. We'd had our problems, but we'd always got home, and I'd seen my first real combat in '16'. I had spent much time along with my ground crew tuning this aircraft to my personal taste and with that, I suppose, I'd begun to imbue it with some of my personality - certainly I felt that she responded to the odd kind word or the promise of a rest and a full service. But I had to move on and 'Yellow 2' was waiting. However, I do believe that after our last flight I said 'Goodbye' to '16' and gave her unyielding metal skin an affectionate final slap.

Helping to reload the wing guns on 'Yellow 16' at Coquelles.
One of our huts can be seen in the background.

Yellow 2 was a Bf 109 E-4 which meant that she'd been fitted with the new FF-type 20 mm cannons in the wings. This gave her a formidable hitting power and, I hoped, a real edge when I needed it. Yellow 2 wasn't factory fresh but had been used by another pilot and came with three stripes on the tail (three confirmed victories). I was hopeful that this would be a good omen for me and I'd soon be adding my own stripes as we began to gather our strength for what must surely be the death-throws of the RAF over Britain.

17 September 1940

Dear Mother,

Now we've been celebrating my twenty-second birthday for the last two days. Great days. On my birthday I flew two missions, one in my old '16' and then one in my new '2'. It is a much faster aircraft and I don't have to keep over-revving the engine to keep up with the 'Chief' as I did with '16'. However it is not yet as clean and orderly as my '16', but we'll change that in time. In the meantime, Mother, I can feel the anger slowly building inside me that I haven't had a victory yet. I am about the only officer in the *Gruppe* who has not, to date, logged at least one victory. Bert Gobel has three; *Obltn.* Leesmann now has ten and a new *Oberleutnant* with the second squadron has eight. It's just that there seems to be no movement in our squadron. Altogether we now have 55 confirmed victories for the *Gruppe,* but none for me - what a sorry state, but I can't help it. It's almost beginning to look like I'm not meant to succeed here, but I'll stick with it - doing my duty.

But enough of this. There are others who have no victories and have been shot-down. At least I'm in a better position than them. Out of those that are missing we now know that four are prisoners, but we don't know about Waller and Christoph Geller yet. At least I saw Hinnerk's parachute open.

Yesterday we had another large raid over London. Over there we met amazingly strong fighter opposition. I believe that the British are concentrating everything they have left around the capital. It was a wild experience. A pity that the weather wasn't better, if it had been we'd have been in a better position to finish them off. Somehow the army should get into action now.

This morning we wanted to go to London again but there was too much cloud and a high risk of icing, so no chance. Now we hope for good weather; about another eight days would finish things. Let's hope for an improvement.

On the reverse of this letter Mother writes to my father (again saving paper and passing on my letter at the same time):

My Dear,

Your card arrived this evening. You don't seem to be having such nice weather this time. Yesterday and today I have been mending another pair of socks. Would you have time to come and get them on Sunday? Uz's (my) long letter arrived yesterday; I replied by return of post and sent him some colour film. This time I have, once more, to console him and assure him that in spite of everything we are very proud of our young *Oberleutnant.* Should you be able to come please let me know.

22 September 1940

Dear Mother,

During the last few days it was rather quiet here, but not quiet enough for us to have got away from base because we are kept on constant readiness. The only thing I have to do at present is to go hunting, as a result of which several rabbits and partridges have enriched our diet. By the way, at last I have succeeded. Three days ago I shot down a Spitfire in the area of Ashford. Let's hope that this is just the beginning. The British are slowly getting on our nerves at night; because of their persistent activity our AA guns are in virtually continuous use and so we can hardly close our eyes. But there is nothing else we can do about that other than curse. If they'd come in daylight there'd be a reckoning. I am anxious to learn whether, after all we've done, invasion will really get started this year.

I really don't remember much about this first successful action at all. Other incidents are crystal clear but this first victory for me has been erased from my memory. Possibly it was such an emotive experience that my mind had filtered it out. For whatever reason I cannot remember any details at all.

I think that, in view of my previous comments on personal victories and scores, it's worth examining my remarks to my mother concerning my own lack of victories. I didn't see that I should produce an impressive list of victories so that I could compete on an equal footing with some of my peers - rather, I saw our job as being to tackle the RAF and to clear the way for the invasion. My lack of victories just represented to me the tangible evidence that I wasn't doing my part as well as I might; it had nothing to do with my personal ambition.

Also, when reading between the lines, two things seem clear. Firstly, I was becoming very tired through constant action and from not being able to rest at night. Secondly the first doubts were beginning to creep in about the invasion. We were aware that good, stable weather was required and it was obvious that the instability which precedes winter was beginning to come in. I think we all felt at the time that, if the army didn't get their fingers out before long, much of what we had done and suffered might go to waste.

The disturbance at night reminds me of our first personal contact with one of the enemy. At the end of August a lone Spitfire was bold enough to detach itself from a larger formation and make a low-level approach on our field. Unfortunately he was hit and the pilot had to take to his parachute. He turned out to be a sergeant pilot and was taken prisoner and brought to see us. Naturally he was treated like a hero and was offered the best of everything we had to eat and drink and we all had a fine time. One thing I distinctly remember about him was that if any of us made any funny remarks about Churchill - he'd correct us by saying, *'Mister* Churchill if you please!'

Our '109s at Coquelles. Note the squadron badge on the cowling.
The nearest to the picture is 'Yellow 2' having a tyre changed. The
straw bales were for protection against bomb splinters.

Towards the end of September/beginning of October we again had contact with an enemy pilot. At about dawn a light bomber was hit by our flak and tore into the ground just 200 metres from our tents. Naturally we all ran out to see it and found a jumble of wooden formers and other details all wrapped up in the canvas covering. We couldn't identify the type, it was such a wreck. It looked as though all of the crew were dead, but then someone spotted that the pilot was still moving, though trapped in the wreckage. From within the tangle we heard the ominous crackling of fire and soon saw the black smoke begin to curl up as fire took hold. We began to try to pull him from the wreck but it was no use. Then Dr Greiling appeared and told us to use what extinguishers we had to keep the fire away from the trapped man whilst the rescue crew began to cut through the mass of wires and wood. The poor man wasn't even unconscious and knew that the fire was spreading, but he kept calm. I wanted to walk away from the hideous mess; I didn't want to be there if the fire got to him. But then he asked for a cigarette and I was the only one with any to hand. With his arm free he smoked the cigarette and cursed vehemently about his mission.

Soon the pain of his injuries began to overwhelm him and Dr Greiling gave him a large shot of morphine which knocked him out. Through diligent and skilled work our rescue crew got him out and he was whisked off to hospital where, unfortunately, despite the very best medical care he died after about three days. Soon after this another sergeant pilot was brought down near us and he gave me his mother's address so that if we were successful in our invasion, I could pop around and give her the news that he was OK.

The nightly raids had now become so regular that nobody thought to go to the *Splittergraben* (slit trenches). There was no firm instruction about the use of trenches during the bombing raids so we tended to stay in our tents. These, we judged, were just as safe, being dug into the ground by more than a metre, leaving us well below the path of any shrapnel or stray bullets. In any case, it was a damned sight more comfortable. There were, however, some clear-cut rules regarding the guards who now had to patrol the camp.

Because reports were coming in from other units of increased partisan acitivity, we now had a constant standing patrol. This comprised two fully armed guards during the night and one during the day. The two at night had been established because some guards at other units had been found with their throats cut. It was, therefore, the standing order that the two guards at night must remain together at all times and that they were not permitted to use the trenches during raids.

On the whole this worked out fine but for one soldier by the name of Alois. He came from the *Bayrische Wald* (forest area of southern Germany) and was a real bumpkin. He was hugely strong but otherwise something of a simpleton. We didn't know how he'd got into the *Luftwaffe* but he'd managed it somehow. He just loved aircraft and enjoyed being near to them and to us. I don't know that I ever knew his last name; he usually just gave his forename and a broad good-humoured grin whenever he was asked. So we just called him Alois.

On several occasions Kühle and myself had had cause to speak to Alois or his supervising NCO about him diving into a trench as soon as our flak opened up, leaving his partner alone on patrol. This had happened again and it became apparent we would have to initiate some official proceedings. Kühle therefore gave instructions for Alois to attend the Nissen-hut, which was used as an office, and for Reinke, the squadron clerk, to be present to record the interview. There was a distinct possibility that Alois was going to be court-martialled for cowardice with the subsequent formidable sentence.

Alois was ushered in, beaming his usual friendly smile and sat down in front of the desk. He was the complete picture of *bonhomie* ready to do anything we required. Kühle wasn't to be put off and began his questioning. He asked if it was clear to Alois that what he'd done was cowardice. Alois was deeply offended and replied, 'By no means, *Herr Oberleutnant,* I am not a coward. It was just because of my new motorcycle.'

'What motorcycle?' asked Kühle.

'Well,' continued Alois with complete sincerity, 'a long time ago I ordered a new motorcycle and it was delivered just as the war got started. It's brand new. Before leaving for the war I covered it up with hay in the barn,' he confided in a quiet and suitably conspiratorial tone, glancing around to see if we would be overheard and his secret lost. We couldn't wait to see how this related to his jumping into a slit-trench every time the guns fired. We didn't have to wait long. As though the answer were obvious he threw his arms wide and announced, 'When the war is over and I get home I want to enjoy *Motorradl-Fahren* (motor-cycling). If I get killed I won't be able to use my motor-cycle.' Neither of us was able to keep a straight face and, along with Reinke, burst out laughing. The official proceedings were obviously at an end and Kühle dismissed Alois with a helpless wave of the hand. The only equitable solution was to take Alois off night patrols and to give him a greater share of day-work. This worked out well, and it's possible that he did get back to ride his motor-bike in the end, but I don't know for sure.

On 15th September we lost *Ltn.* Hans Berthel from the *Gruppe* Staff Flight due to an accident and not enemy action. In the confusion of a dog-fight over Tonbridge he was rammed by one of our own aircraft and had to bail out. The losses were beginning to build up. The tension was mounting and even the evening discussions failed to help defuse some of the anxiety many of us felt. Perhaps because of this Kühle introduced a traditional card-game called 17-0-4. It was played for money and, although it was an apparently innocuous game, it was still possible to lose half a month's salary in one pot. I would play with my usual competitive fervour, intent on keeping a clear head, even late at night, but many of the others would drink a little too much and fall easy prey. It took different people different ways. *Oberleutnant* Reinbrecht, who was attached to us for a while, was always ready for a game but lost phenomenal amounts of money. I really never lost much or made much from the games, and this despite Kühle's apparent determination to beat me. He'd actually really got to like me and to rely on me as his deputy in the squadron, but at the card table he was determined to beat me. To this end he was constantly trying to get me to over indulge in the freely available drinks or to risk too much on poor hands. I don't know why this was but it almost always backfired on him. At least I knew when I was throwing good money after bad and would stack before I committed too much on a shaky hand.

In the end it was difficult to work out which was more stressful - to lose at cards or to get excited by the continuing debates. Possibly it would have been better just to take a few evenings of complete rest, but after the stress of the day's flying nobody wanted to be alone for too long. The debates nearly always came back to the subject of battle honours and decorations, mostly prompted by the NCOs who felt more aggrieved than the officers. Why was it, they would ask so often, that the decorations are, in the main, only handed out to those with the highest scores? Wasn't it clear that it was those who were flying ahead, and insisting on strong formation discipline around them, who were also running up the highest personal scores - almost exactly matched by the losses from their own formations - losing one *Katschmarek* after another for another white stripe on the tail of their aircraft? And who was it who was suffering the most, they would ask. Of course it was the NCOs who generally flew at the rear or on the flanks[3].

High also on the list of losses as the battle wore on were the replacement pilots. They simply didn't have the experience that we pre-war regulars had acquired. In our *Gruppe* at the beginning of the French Campaign we had thirty-six experienced pilots, none of whom had less than three years flying experience. Now we were getting replacements for the experienced pilots we had lost straight from *Jagdfliegerschule* (fighter school). At that time we still tried our best to take care of these fledglings until they could accrue some experience.

Typical of these youngsters was a young *Gefreiter* who arrived in late September. His flying time was minimal - he had only fired a few shots at a ground target, had never flown on oxygen and still had no idea how to use his radio. We tried to increase their experience before they actually came along on combat missions by taking them up on patrols between missions. Then we would talk on the radio, climb to altitudes in excess of 8,000 metres (25,000 ft) and make them use oxygen. Of special importance was teaching them how to change the pitch of their propeller to get maximum pull from the engine at high altitude. A flat pitch would allow the engine to rev up to its maximum so that the super-charger would deliver the maximum volume of air to the cylinders and produce optimum power; changing to a coarser pitch would have that engine power converted into more pull and consequently speed our rate of climb. It was vital they mastered this technique if they were to keep up in a battle-climb or at high altitude.[4]

'Those who are at the front fire at the Tommy's track, Those at the back catch all the crap! Honour then, people - Your Katschmarek!' Drawing on the wall of a Nissen Hut (unknown fighter squadron at the channel)
'To the unknown Katschmarek'

After about ten hours of 'tuition' we would take them out over the Channel to shoot at shadows on the water or cross to Dungeness and shoot at a black medieval tower which stood there (the old Dungeness

Lighthouse). Finally, when we could not excuse them combat duty any longer, we would have to take them along with us. This became the case with the *Gefreiter* and so I took him as my *Rottenhund* (wingman). We began our climb almost immediately after take-off and he was constantly using the radio to ask us to slow down so that he could keep up. It was obvious that he wasn't manipulating the pitch control with the skill of the more seasoned pilots to produce the same power as our machines. We tried to tell him what to do on the radio but to no avail. Eventually, about half-way across the Channel and at 4,000 metres (13,000 ft) Kühle told him to leave the formation and return to base. He broke away but in his confusion he turned not for home but towards Dover. Kühle realised what was happening and ordered me to give chase and take him home. I rolled out and soon overhauled him, just before we reached the balloon barrage at Dover. I had tried to raise him on the radio but he was in such a state of anxiety that he wouldn't or couldn't respond. Positioning myself in front of him I rocked my wings, using the signal for him to follow me. He dutifully hung onto my tail and we were soon back at Coquelles. This was one of only two missions I missed during the whole of our time in the Battle of Britain.

As a result we decided that we would not take any more replacements on high altitude missions until we could give them more, much more, training. They were supposed to be replacements but in the event they were more of a problem for us than reinforcement for the squadron.

The further we got into the Battle so the bitterness of the NCOs increased towards the victory hunters in our and other groups. The stress was beginning to show in us all. Now also we began to openly discuss the subject of *Kanalkrankheit* (Channel sickness). Kühle told us that some court-martials had been instituted for pilots who had returned too frequently with mechanical faults which could not be found by the ground-crews.

As uncomfortable as they could be we never directly avoided the debates and frequently locked horns with Karl Rüttger, Kurt Wolf, Lothar Schieverhöfer and Sigi Voss. It was a different story with *Oberfeldwebel* Grosse who absented himself if it was obvious a debate was brewing. He had already served with the Legion Condor and already had quite severe stomach problems. He was also one of those who had begun to suffer more than average mechanical returns to base. It seemed you could just wear out like any other machine. After a lot of use and abuse your mind and body began to give minor problems which, if not properly repaired, developed into more serious faults and then to final, total breakdown. The human body is only different from a machine in that it rarely actually needs replacement parts. Given proper rest it will repair itself. And that is where things were going wrong; we just weren't getting a break.

Coquelles 1940
The squadron taking off on what looks to be a routine mission, rather than a
scramble. The '109 on the left seems to be a bit late. In the
distance can be seen the Calais Town Hall tower (extreme right on the horizon)
a real landmark for anyone who worked in the area.

One of the long-range fuel tanks we had at Coquelles. Here Oberfeldwebel
Mohring, our Chief Technician, is carrying it to
demonstrate how light it was. The tanks held 250 litres of fuel
which was a hefty supplement to the planes inboard tank, which
held 400 litres. The securing mechanism (stores pylon)
was the same used for bomb carrying '109s.

Notes Chapter 16

1. 'A Piece of Land on the Island' was something which was talked about a lot by us. We all agreed that we'd give a lot just to have one neutral strip of land where we could land in England if we were in trouble. This is one reason why we were so anxious that the army should get on with the invasion. At least if we were hit we would be able to put down at the coast and not have to brave the Channel with a damaged aircraft.

2. What we didn't realise at the time was that the production of British aircraft was about double the production of ours and that due to the early reluctance of the RAF to engage us in air combat their numbers had not

Spitfire On My Tail

decreased as quickly as the *Reichsmarschall* would have had it.

3. The question of decorations based mathematically on the number of victories was a question which was, and still is, very important to me because I think it had a hugely detrimental effect on the efficiency of the fighter forces. There was no broad tactical plan for units, such as the systematic destruction of specific bases or targets at specific times and locations - concrete goals - just the one consideration: more victories – at almost any cost. Thus it was that many of the higher scoring Aces became *prima donnas* in their time and still retain the airs affected by some film stars. I feel rather bitter about the fact that they never gave the credit due to their ground-crews and to the countless *Katschmareks* by whose sacrifice they rose to prominence.

4. This technique of varying the throttle setting and pitch led to a constant rising and falling of engine speed. One of the observations of people in Britain was that you could tell which aircraft were German and which were British because the German engine noise seemed always to be rising and falling - unlike the British engines which seemed to remain constant. This may explain the phenomenon.

CHAPTER 17

No Let-up

26 September 1940

Dear Mother,

To begin with, the day before yesterday I was lucky again and shot-down two Spitfires near Dover. Otherwise there is little activity, we are kept in continuous readiness but the weather rarely permits flying towards London. Just now I have returned with my Rotte from a reconnaissance flight up the Thames Estuary. Again the weather is no good with the cloud at only 1,700 metres (5,000 ft). Tell me how you feel, are you already in Konstanz? (My father had been moved there as a commander of a mounted company). Or has it been like it has so often with nothing working out? I think that you could also begin to become impatient like us that we don't go to England. In the Berliner (illustrated weekly magazine) of 26 September there are photos of Göring. The place where he was photographed is just 10 kilometres from here, and when returning home we usually whiz across his command post. We have to be patient and wait to see what the near future brings.

Now we were back in the action and on this occasion I was in agreement with Kühle's tactics. I can still see these events as though they were only a few days ago. We were approaching Dover when we saw a whole squadron of Spitfires spread out in line astern with a weaver on either side at the back. They were so well-defined against the blue-green of the sea that we couldn't have missed them. Kühle instructed me to take one of the weavers and he said that he'd take care of the other. When the rest of our squadron saw that this was accomplished they could then pick their own targets. These were good tactics. The weavers were there to protect the rear of the flight and if they could be taken out without raising the alarm there would be a good chance of the rest of the squadron bagging the majority of the enemy aircraft. This is what was so foolish about flying this kind of formation.

We peeled away and I began to position Yellow 2. The red ring of the Revi gun-sight was projected onto the windscreen and I'd already flipped the trigger for the guns over to be ready with both the nose guns and the cannon in the wings. Gradually the Spitfire filled the ring of the sight and I increased the pressure on the triggers. Four lines of tracer hosed out towards the target and I saw strikes, the aircraft spinning away. Rather than chase it I altered course slightly and went for the next in line. Again I saw hits before I broke away. Kühle wasn't so fortunate. His target, whether more alert or pre-warned, dived away and Kühle was unable to get in any decisive shots. However, I claimed my weaver but was told on return to base that the second aircraft had gone down too, this having been witnessed by Kühle and some of the others.

29 September 1940

Dear Mother,

Hearty thanks for your letter and the film. However one thing I have to tell you is that for the time being I cannot think about leave. During the last two days we had plenty to do, but I will send one of the movie cameras to you. Filming is so easy, everybody should try. It's a pity that Herr Roser (I boarded with the family whilst at school) has died. It was strange for me. After I got your last letter I wrote to Frau Roser and gave her my best wishes and so on. Then, almost immediately, I had to follow up with a letter of condolence. Life is sometimes strange like that.

Well, it seems that you don't think it will be over by Christmas. I believe there is still a chance. If not, then all of our missions which have hit the British fighter defences really hard will have been for nothing. If we wait until spring these wounds will have been healed and we will have to start at the beginning again. But if that is the way things have to be then the word duty always gives strength.

Kühle has pains in the ears at this time and cannot fly.[1] The day before yesterday I was leading the squadron three times and we achieved another two victories without losses. We always seem to deal with Spitfires which, when the right man sits in it, is a worthy adversary. On the third mission the *Gruppe* commander and another squadron leader had to turn back because of problems, and I was left to lead the *Gruppe*. Only thirteen aircraft but quite some responsibility. At first we had other *Gruppen* for company, but when we got to London and the dog-fighting started I suddenly found that there were only the five aircraft from our squadron still with me and about thirty to forty Spitfires against us. Had I chosen to turn-tail and run they would certainly have got one or two at the back. Instead I gave the order 'Liga, hinein!' (code word for attack - 'into them'). They were coming at us from all sides and our Me's were tested as never before. I shot at two Spitfires without decisive results and the others gave good accounts too. One NCO (Karl Rüttger) shot a Spitfire to shreds and then there were no more; the rest just taking their *Schwanzchen* (raising their little tails) and disappearing downwards into some clouds. Unfortunately we had a full sixty-minute sortie but only reported one confirmed victory. That was good but I was more proud of the fact that none of us had been hurt and all got home. Hopefully the Londoners were watching this heroic deed by their RAF. Yesterday Kühle tried again in the morning but as soon as we gained height he had to turn back, and in the afternoon I had the squadron again. However this time there was nothing to report, no successes but also no losses.

These two days were, for me, quite satisfying and I believe for the other pilots too. They seem to like it when I lead the squadron and that leads to good co-operation. Let's hope that my lucky star keeps shining.

September 27th was a day I'll never forget; the first time I had to lead a *Gruppe*. I had written the brief details to my mother in the letter but I'd not covered it in much depth. We had taken off at 12:30 (GMT) but over the Channel first one squadron leader and then the *Gruppe* leader had turned back with problems. I was left to lead the small *Gruppe*. Because of the losses there were only thirteen fighters from the three squadrons, but for me that was some responsibility. From our squadron we had four pilots who I had come to know well and myself. I now had three-and-a-half years of flying experience and over one hundred sorties over England under my belt. A real veteran! I had two wingmen; *Feldwebel* Siggi Voss, a quiet unassuming man with four year's experience and a gentle hand with my dogs, and *Feldwebel* Lothar Schieverhofer, a more proud Prussian-type who had a ready wit and a bright sparkle in his eyes, always laughing. They were my *Rotte*. The other *Rottenführer* (leader) was Karl Rüttger, a sturdy Westfalian, always a little reserved but the most experienced pilot. His *Rottenhund* was *Unteroffizier* Kurt Wolf, a sharp-witted youngster whose reactions in conversation were as sharp as those in the air. He always had the answer. But with only three years experience he was the junior of the outfit. It was only with such a crew that I could do what I did that day high over London.

After the squadron leader and then the *Gruppen Führer* (Group Leader) had turned back I had assumed command, and remained on course for our assigned duty. The rest of the small formation was made up of other squadrons from the wing, the rather sad remnants of a once powerful fighting force. We five grouped up in our own *Schwarm*, each of us trusting the others, knowing each other's capabilities. The others grouped up as best they could as we climbed towards the target area.

Suddenly all was action and confusion. From nowhere, thirty to forty Hurricanes and Spitfires were tearing towards us, a wall of aircraft. I took the decision that the best defence was attack and ordered my pilots to hold and attacked, not to break and run. My *Schwarm* stayed with me but the elements of the other squadrons broke away much to the advantage of the British fighters. Then I gave the order, 'Turn and climb . . . turn and climb!' I forced the stick against my leg as I brought Yellow 2 into a hard aileron turn with lots of rudder and then heaved back to get the nose up into the climb. I felt the force of gravity starting to act on my body and knew that unless the force increased I wasn't pulling the nose up enough for the climb. Quickly my arms became heavy and my head began to crush down on my neck as I increased the turn and climb, my whole body being squeezed in the steel seat in the cockpit. We were close to stalling but we had to keep the turn going, impossibly tight, the slats on the leading edges of the wings snapping in and out automatically as the air-flow reached critically low speeds. But still we had to turn harder and climb, the G-force draining the blood from my head and a dark haze beginning to encroach on my peripheral vision - greying out, the precursor to a complete black-out.

It would have been easier to have broken out and made a run for it, but I was sure that our salvation lay in our present position. The British fighters were coming down at high speed and trying to latch onto our tails but they had no chance. Because of their speed there was no way they could have cut inside our upward curving spiral to achieve a good deflection shot. One after another they hurtled past to try and climb for another attack, but we kept our nerve. Every so often I would break in on the radio, 'Stay with me. Stay with me. Turn and climb. Turn and climb. They can't get us if we keep it tight'. Slowly, oh so slowly, we climbed up from about 7,000 metres (22,000 ft), trying to reach our service ceiling before attempting the break-out. Sometimes one of the enemy would cross our sights and we would fire, but it was a very dangerous thing to do. We were so close to stalling that the recoil of the guns made the aircraft wobble badly and brought us closer to dropping out of the sky. None the less Karl Rüttger fired a full burst from his cannons and a Spitfire was literally shredded. That was enough for our attackers and they rolled out and dived into some cloud well below us.

It had been a phenomenally long time to be under such stress. We had climbed about 3,000 metres (10,000 ft) in what had been ten-fifteen minutes. Ordinarily that would only have taken two to three minutes but we had been flying a long upward corkscrew on the limits of stalling all the time. At something like 60° of bank and with the high nose attitude, I was still able to take the odd glimpse at the silvery surface of the Thames far below us, and no more than fifty metres behind and below me was Kurt Wolf desperately hanging onto my tail. It had taken nerve and great discipline on the part of my pilots, but we had succeeded and it was with immense relief that I was able to give the order to roll out at the top of our climb and set course for home. From there on it was literally all down hill, and with a coarse setting on the propeller and full power we could be back over our base in about ten minutes - ready to do it all again.

That mission had taken 70 minutes, and with all the climbing on full power and a flat propeller pitch we had just about used our fuel. In the evening we talked about it. We all felt we'd survived because we were a good team, and I felt that reflected well on me. We felt stronger - we had looked death in the face and come through. It was strange how such experiences could change one's outlook daily and sometimes hourly. Each time you grew a little, but it might also work the other way. One catastrophe and the nerves would begin again; the confidence would ebb away for a while. The other elements of the original small Gruppe which had decided to cut and run had suffered badly. *II/JG 52* had lost seven pilots that day.

It was with our new found confidence that we flew on 30th September, a day which was to see my resolve shattered and restored - within just a few hours. Helmut Kühle was still on sick leave with a severe infection of the eustachian tubes, so I was to lead the squadron again. Many of the young pilots like myself felt that Kühle's cautious approach was too careful to be successful. Fighters, we thought, were instruments of aggression and only really in their element in the 'free hunt'. Kühle preached that we should not attack until we were sure our approach and exit from the target was clear. He always wanted the odds heavily in our favour. In that way, he argued, we pilots would gain experience with minimal losses.

On the 30th I led a flight of four aircraft of our Squadron. *Feldwebel* Sigi Voss was my *Rottenhund* with the second *Rotte* being led by Karl Rüttger with *Unteroffizier* Kurt Wolf as his number two - four of the five pilots who had survived over London three days before. Because of this we were still in confident mood and ready to take on anything, maybe over-confident. As we crossed the Channel we were released from the main formation to undertake a *Freie Jagd*. This couldn't have been better for us as we were in agreement that our tactics had been too timid. We were hungry for the chance to vindicate our theory and a little impetuous because of it. We crossed the Sussex coast at about 09:30 hrs and, having gained plenty of height, we spotted a squadron of Hurricanes climbing below us amongst other formations. They were flying in three 'vic' formations in line astern, very orthodox by our standards. I judged that they must have been somewhat inexperienced and decided to attack. Over the R/T I gave instructions that I would attack the leading formation, Voss the next, Rüttger and Wolf the third. I was conscious there were many other formations of enemy aircraft in the area, but we were hungry for action and thought our height and speed would see us through unmolested.

On my order we dropped into the attack, picking up terrific speed in the dive and dropping below and behind the Hurricanes. From this position we were able to hit from slightly below with complete surprise. I gave the order, *'Nach Angriff in linkskurve sammeln!'* ('After the attack, assemble in left curve!') We were not sure what exactly happened, we think that one of the others pressed the transmission button on his radio at the same time as me, but the actual effect was that the first two words of my instruction were cut off, leaving just the order *'In linkskurve sammeln'* ('Assemble in left curve'). I went on firing for a good few seconds, sweeping right through the 'vic' formation, not realising that the others were breaking-off almost immediately. They were understandably annoyed that they hadn't been able to fully press home their attacks, particularly in the light of our shared feelings about the officers who apparently risked all to raise their own personal scores.[2]

There was little time to debate what had happened there and then because some of the other enemy fighters had seen our attack and turned upon us with great fury. Our small formation was broken up with Voss and myself making it home and Rüttger limping in alone a while later. I was witness to Wolf's fate, seeing him hit by numerous shells from a Spitfire, the aircraft beginning to burn immediately[3].We had paid dearly for our ideals, our only consolation being that we had hit the enemy very hard, myself claiming my fourth victory, albeit with little enthusiasm. The feeling of the time is recorded in a letter to my mother dated 3rd October:

Dear Mother,

You are congratulating me on my first downing. Now I can report that on the 30 September I shot down my fourth Spitfire[4] and on the 2 October I got the EK 1 (Iron Cross 1st Class). Since then it has been quiet and we have had a day of rest. However, if I would have to do it all again, I would not have made this number four - it cost me an excellent pilot. It was stupid of me, as squadron leader, to attack about 40-45 Spitfires with only four aircraft. I came home with only one left, the third found his way home himself and the fourth remained. This almost drove me crazy. But in the evening I had the squadron again with four. This was the hardest mission so far, and when we all got home I was more pleased with myself. We escorted some Ju. 88s to London, flying blind above the clouds. How it came about I cannot explain but they flew past London and only turned when already two thirds of our fuel was used up. Now flying home they took the wrong course, towards the Isle of Wight where the Channel is wide. We could not leave the formation because they were being constantly harried by Spitfires. Therefore: save fuel. That meant flying as slowly as possible and in a straight line, protecting at the same time. And really we succeeded, all the bombers got home safely, and we reached Boulogne with the last drop. There we refuelled and returned home.

The ground-crews had already given up hope but when we arrived back they cheered more than when we'd had victories before. Sorry that Kirchner, who had already been shot down once over France, was hit again, and this time I am afraid that he's not going to return. And now, as much as possible, I will report on those who are missing or confirmed prisoners for the Geiger Family in Heutingsheim. The list in my memory is as follows:

Feldwebel Zieger	3rd Squadron	Prisoner
Unteroffizier Bokel	2nd Squadron	Missing
Feldwebel Bacher	2nd Squadron	Prisoner
Unteroffizier Hartlieb	2nd Squadron	Missing
Obergefreiter Malecki	2nd Squadron	Prisoner
Feldwebel Bischof	1st Squadron	Prisoner
Feldwebel Urlings	1st Squadron	Prisoner
Oberfeldwebel Gerber	2nd Squadron	Missing
Leutnant Geller	Adjutant	Missing
Unteroffizier Kind	1st Squadron	Missing
Oberleutnant Waller	3rd Squadron	Prisoner
Leutnant Berthel	Adjutant	Missing
Unteroffizier Weber	2nd Squadron	Shot through the pelvis. Died after landing.
Unteroffitzier Wolf	3rd Squadron	Missing
Oberleutnant Kirchner	1st Squadron	Missing

When seeing such a long list in one piece it looks awful. But, after a while, some of them will be reported as being prisoners and we are certain that one day soon we will get them back again. Out of our Gruppe in total we can report some seventy downings in aerial combat confirmed, eleven probable and about thirty on the ground. You are writing with the advice

'Uli fly cautiously'. Dear Mother, that's wrong. I am flying the way that I think is my duty. Where should we arrive if we were all flying cautiously?

The package for my birthday arrived safely, and if I didn't say thanks so far please accept my apologies. Of course I was very happy to receive it and we enjoyed the contents greatly.

By the way now, if anybody at home asks about ourselves, of course we are happy and proud of our deeds. Especially if the question comes from the army people. Our task at present and in the long run is not easy to carry out but we are going to fulfil our duty and show that we are soldiers. If the war continues like this I can't imagine how it will go on. Perhaps it will last all through the winter. In this case there are rumours amongst us that we would be withdrawn and sent to one of the other countries on a kind of rest and recovery period. This is certainly wrong as most of the other stories are. I just don't believe them anymore.

At the time of writing this letter I must have been in a very reflective mood. It was uncommon for me to write at such length - some five pages. Reading between the lines now I can see that I must have been very tired. The sense of duty seems strong but there is a certain cynicism about the possibility of rest and recovery. The survivors, who were still flying, were under great stress. Each of us knew by a quick perusal of the casualty list that our time must come soon.

The morning mission had certainly given me cause for reflection. I had let my own impetuosity and that of my young colleagues overcome common-sense. We had attacked with good results which would certainly have been better had we not had the mix-up on the radio; but I'd seen Kurt Wolf shot down for that success. At the time I was sure he'd been killed and his death was lying heavily on my conscience. My managing to get all of our people back in the evening went some way in assuaging my personal feelings of guilt. It had been a mission which went badly wrong for the *Luftwaffe* with huge losses, hardly any of which were actually attributable to enemy action.

It was yet another escort duty, tied to the bombers as their protection. Once more I was to lead, with four aircraft from the squadron. During the morning another machine had been fixed and therefore a pilot was able to replace the missing Kurt Wolf. Our brief was to assemble with squadrons from our and other *Gruppen* to escort Junkers 88s on a mission to London,

330

flying blind, high above the clouds, relying on their navigation. They were using the experimental *Knickebein* radio beams and should have hit the target with great accuracy. I don't know how it happened but we missed London completely, passing it somewhere to the left. It was almost certainly a case that the leading bomber had flown down the beam on course but had missed the crossing beam which warned him that he was almost on target.

The Citation for my Iron Cross First Class

The whole bomber *Gruppe* (about thirty aircraft) flew on, and only turned for home when we had used about two-thirds of our fuel. Even then they didn't take the shortest course, but set off in the direction of the Isle of Wight where the Channel is at its widest. We couldn't leave the bombers because they were being constantly harassed by enemy fighters and so the object became to conserve fuel as much as possible. However, it isn't easy to fly straight and level and give proper protection and so the precious fuel reserves were soon running low.

A crippled '109 that apparently only just made it back to the fields near Coquelles. I am certain this was one of the casualties of the 30th September and that the photograph was taken the next morning.

The fighters held their positions, and as we began to cross the Channel we could see that the bomber force was still intact. Now it became a fight for survival for the fighters. At last we could break away and we all dropped virtually to sea level where the wind resistance is lower. We literally wave-hopped, hoping that our fuel gauges were wrong, and that we would just have enough to get to France. One after another our comrades came on the radio to report that their red fuel warning lights had come on. Below us we could see the grey, uninviting waters of the Channel with waves running very high. We knew that if we tried to land the aircraft in such rough water our chances of survival were slim. So as fuel ran still lower the orders were to try to gain a little height and jump, at least this gave an improved chance of survival, although not much better.

One after another the fighters ploughed into the waves of the Channel or rose in a last desperate search for height before the pilot baled out. Our track across those wild waters became dotted with parachutes, pilots floating in their life jackets, and greasy oil slicks on the cold water showing where another '109 had ended its last dive. Our air-sea rescue people tried their best, but it was so hard to locate the men in the high waves. Most that were located were already dead, victims of exposure or drowning. The next day, I was privileged to see a secret memorandum which reported 19 pilots drowned. In all only two were recovered by the *Seenotflugkommando*.

My group of four survived and had just made it to Boulogne where we refuelled. All along the coast near Boulogne we had seen '109s down in the fields and on the grass, some still standing on their noses. The losses to us had been huge. When we four flew into our base the ground crews went wild with joy, they had written us off with the others and were so pleased that we had made it back.

My feelings of the time were written down after this tragic event in the letter home. The list of the losses from our *Gruppe* in the Battle of Britain is up to 30th September. Of the original thirty-six pilots there were precious few left.[5]

Notes on Chapter 17

1. Any problem with the inner-ear or the eustachian tubes is a real problem for both pilots in unpressurised cockpits and underwater divers for the same reason. Both mediums cause changes of pressure inside the ear and, if the pressure cannot equalise through the eustachian tubes into the throat, then severe earache ensues.

2. Although only one Hurricane was claimed (page 327/328), it seems, from post-war research, that this attack may well have been considerably more successful than originally imagined. It is probable that two Hurricanes were shot down and three were badly damaged. If it had not been for the confusion on the radio the results of this attack would have been dire.

3. It wasn't until I myself became a POW that I discovered, to my immense relief, that Kurt Wolf was alive. He had escaped from his aircraft unharmed to become a prisoner.

4. There existed in the *Luftwaffe* what the RAF christened 'Spitfire Snobbery'. It is now apparent that Hurricanes were the back bone of the RAF during the Battle of Britain and certainly accounted for the majority of the German aircraft shot down or damaged. However *Luftwaffe* pilots insisted that virtually everything they shot down was a Spitfire and almost invariably claimed to have been the victim of a Spitfire.

This is no better illustrated than by an incident involving the late R.R. Stanford-Tuck. Flying a Hurricane he shot down a German fighter which fell close to Tuck's airfield. He promptly landed and jumped into a truck which was speeding out to pick up the German pilot. As they arrived the German was introduced to Tuck and he complimented him on the fighting capabilities of his Spitfire. Tuck explained that he'd been flying a Hurricane but the German insisted that he'd been shot down by a Spitfire.

Similarly Hinnerk Waller was shot down by Hurricanes of 303 (Polish) Squadron including Sergeant Frantisek, the highest scoring allied pilot in the Battle of Britain. I recorded the attacking aircraft as Spitfires.

5. The *Luftwaffe* losses for this day were nothing short of staggering. 'Battle Over Britain', Francis Mason, records 59 losses, some 35 of which were Me '109s. This was mainly due to the error in navigation by the bombing group leader. Rumour had it that he was stripped of rank for his error.

CHAPTER 18

Flying to the Last Man

From the middle of September there was a new procedure whilst our aircraft stood 'at readiness' which showed that supplies were being tightened up on the Channel front. We didn't spot it at the time, but it was probably one of the first signs that High Command was beginning to accept that the battle was over and didn't want to waste any more supplies than absolutely necessary on it.

Normally, when we were in our Stage 1 readiness, the ground crew started the aircraft up every hour to keep the engines warm. This was to keep the engine oil thin and the moving parts ready to go to full power for a scramble. The pilots sat close to the aircraft in deck-chairs, a scene identical to our counterparts, who would be sitting a few miles north across the Channel. It was decided that this constant starting and warming up of engines was a waste of precious fuel and so a technical directive came from the head of *Luftwaffe* Engineering. In future, as soon as the engine had been warmed up for the first time and the oil level had been checked, two litres of aviation grade petrol were to be poured into the engine to mix with the lubricating oil. Any shortfall on the oil level would then be topped up to just above normal. Then the engine was briefly run again to achieve a good mixture of oil and petrol throughout the lubrication circuit.

At first we protested and asked if the HQ engineering section had finally lost its last tenuous grip on reality. Surely an oil/petrol mixture like this would result in vapour accumulating in the sump and under the pistons which would inevitably explode at some time. The theory was that the thinned out mixture would provide efficient lubrication to run from cold to immediate full power, with the petroleum component of the mixture evaporating as the oil temperature rose to normal. It was with very mixed feelings that we tried it at first and then only on training flights, never on a cross-Channel operation. But it soon became apparent that there were no adverse effects and it was accepted as routine. In a matter of weeks I had so completely forgotten about this procedure that I actually seriously took one of my ground crew to task when I saw him pouring gasoline into the oil-filler; he reminded me that it was normal procedure. In those weeks at the end of September and the beginning of October a few days seemed like a life-time.

Another, more welcome, innovation from the middle of September was a scheduled day off, about once a week. Although it was planned at *Luftflotte* HQ we didn't have an advanced list of leave days and would only be officially told on the day. So it became a regular task for *Hauptmann* Förster to telephone around his contacts and ascertain when we were due for our leave. When he was successful (and that was most times) we would get a coded radio message on our way back to base, 'Last sortie today - Lobster tomorrow'.

Our regular haunt was now Lille which was about 100 km from base. This was between an hour and a half and two hours drive for us to relax. In Lille there was the Restaurant Huitriere which had a reputation for good food and, in particular, lobster. Many was the sortie to Huitriere where we met with famous actors, actresses and entertainers who were 'doing their bit' by visiting the troops at the Western Front. Amongst them was the huge and grossly overweight composer, Ludwig Schmidseder, who was quite proud of his corpulent bulk which required the restaurateur to keep a specially enlarged chair handy. We also met Heinz Rühmann[1] who shared our table on several occasions, wearing his *Luftwaffe* uniform and sporting his *Flugzeugführerabzeichen* (wings). As a result of our regular contact with these entertainers a troupe actually did come right to 'The Front' and staged concerts in Calais on 2nd and 26th October.

Lille was a real magnet for troops on leave so there was a great scramble to get away from base as soon as we had landed and to get to the town to enjoy a full evening. Hotel accommodation was never a real problem with others soon making way for us who were, after all, the only ones who were really in the Front Line at that time. The few days we managed to snatch in Lille were some of the most memorable of my time at Coquelles and were always anticipated with great excitement. Indeed, when we received *Hauptmann* Förster's radio message the radio channel would dissolve into chaos worse than when encountering the enemy. Kühle, for instance, would pass a message to his driver to meet us on landing, literally as we jumped down from our aircraft. We didn't want to waste a minute. When it seemed likely that our day was coming up we would fly ops in our undress (walking out) uniforms. The car would be there complete with whatever we had instructed our batmen to pack at the last minute. Again it is interesting to observe objectively how my memory has retained bright scenes from these visits and yet has screened out so many of the horrors of those days.

5 October 1940

Dear Mother,

Having shot another one down yesterday I have to write to you at once today.

Yesterday was more luck than anything else. We just returned home from an escort when a multi-engined aircraft was reported over Calais. Everybody started searching and apparently I saw him first. He had already turned back towards Dover when I pushed Yellow 2 to her limit and soon I had closed on him. Right away he unloaded his bombs into the sea and then waggled his wings in a wing signal. Normally only our bombers did this and it meant: 'Don't shoot - I'm one of yours.' 'Well,' I thought, 'I can see for myself that you're not one of ours so why waggle your wings?' To resolve this I fired a long burst from right to left, the tracer making it apparent to the pilot that the bomber was being fired upon. At this time I realised that in spite of the fact that I'd slowed down he was still slowing, almost gliding. Now it dawned upon me - he planned to ditch without a fight. Therefore, I stayed with him in case he had any other ideas.

Unfortunately my *Rottenflieger* (probably Sigi Voss) hadn't read the situation in the same way and fired once more, but without causing significant damage. The pilot put his Blenheim nicely into the water and we watched as one of the crew immediately appeared on the wing with the yellow dinghy and had inflated as the other two appeared and stepped into it as the aircraft sunk. All of this happened just 10 km from our coast and I called up for the *Seenotflugzeug* (air-sea rescue) to help them. I felt really sorry for those boys, sitting down there waving. In just twenty minutes they were sat in a rescue-boat and were prisoners. One of them is badly wounded and is in hospital somewhere close by. If I get the opportunity I am going to visit him.

Today we had two missions again, but nothing special. At present I am on stand-by with my *Rottenhund* for airfield protection. If another Blenheim came to call it would be a nice reward. Certainly they are easier meat than Spitfires. By the way Bert (Göbel) is sitting next to me and sends his regards.

Soon after this I tried to make an appointment to visit the wounded man but found that he'd died in the meantime. However, it was still possible for me to see the remaining members of the crew but I declined.

14 October 1940

Dear Mother,

Thank you for your letter. I received one from Father on the same day. I changed my mind about the movie camera; who knows whether it might get lost in the *Feldpost*. Therefore I'll keep it for the time-being. I am now quite certain that within the next month nothing much more will happen to us. I should also get some leave and I can do the filming myself. The day before yesterday on our third mission we had three more losses in the *Gruppe*. It was terrible but that is destiny. My wingman was also caught. Myself, I had all four weapons jammed, can you imagine what a wonderful feeling it is when you want to shoot a Spitfire off of the tail of a comrade . . . one presses the buttons and nothing shoots. After that, all alone, I had to get moving and got back with two hits. *Schön!* (nice-wonderful!)

These are black days but on the other hand next time we'll get some of them. This time I donated at least 250 machine-gun rounds and some 50 cannon-shells. As the war is not going to end this year let's hope for some leave.

My reasons for not sending the cine-camera through the *Feldpost* weren't wholly true. Certainly there was some risk but the real reason was that I had been talking to Kühle and Ewald about installing one of the cameras in the aircraft as a gun-camera. I had come up with the idea that I could link a camera to the triggers of the aircraft's weapons so that the camera would roll as I fired. This was not to record my own personal 'victories' but to add an element of the action to our film *Kriegstagebuch*. They had agreed after I had been at great lengths to show that it could be done and had my *Waffenwart* (armourer) confirm it. He said he would mount it inside the canopy in a position that would not obstruct my vision or access to the Revi gun-sight.

The fact that this camera was electrically powered simplified the trigger mechanism; it would be linked in with the wiring which actuated the nose-guns, controlled by the top button on the column. We got the 'go ahead' and the *Waffenwart* began installing the camera in Yellow 2 but this was interrupted by the arrival of a new aircraft for me, Yellow 8; so what fittings had already been made up for Yellow 2 were now removed and re-jigged to fit 8. The main problem was to construct a mounting which held the camera firmly but which absorbed the natural vibration in the airframe. It was a problem we didn't have time to solve as events overtook this innovative idea.

On 12th October, as I'd written to my mother, we had sustained another three losses in the *Gruppe*. I had lost my *Rottenhund* Sigi Voss and what was so galling was that I had been in a position to help but my weapons failed. Frightened and seething with frustration and anger I returned to Coquelles rehearsing the dressing-down I was going to unleash on the *Waffenwart*. When I landed the storm broke and I berated the unfortunate armourer in the roundest terms, telling him that I held him personally responsible for the loss of Sigi Voss who, for all I knew, was dead. I then stormed off to my tent, still utterly miserable. An hour or so later the unfortunate armourer came to the tent and showed me a section of wiring he had removed from behind the head-armour of my aircraft. The wires had been severed by a single machine-gun round that had entered the aircraft from behind. This had rendered the whole weapons system inoperative. I duly apologised to the *Waffenwart* but still felt the loss of another member of the squadron acutely. It was also a disquieting thought to realise how close that bullet had come to my head.

19 October 1940

Dear Father,

From now on I am going to write to your address. First I would like you to understand why I didn't send the movie camera. You know how things get lost in the *Feldpost* and I don't want to take the risk. Anyhow, according to my estimate, we should soon be due for leave. The weather here over the last few days is terrible and we frequently sit around feeling useless. Certainly we shall have to spend the winter getting the level 'up the dam' again. We therefore believe that during the winter period we will be rotated to a place where we can train. All the young pilots we get have so much to learn, we just can't take them along without taking a 50% risk of losing them on their first mission. In our *Gruppe* there are only twelve left from the old crew. We frequently fly missions with only eight or nine aircraft mustered from the whole *Gruppe*, a small force but still full of fight. If we are to rebuild then a certain critical nucleus is required as a core and for this our *Gruppe* shouldn't get any smaller.[2]

The British have, in part, a new engine in their Spitfires and our Me can hardly keep up with it. We have also made improvements and have also some new engines, but there is no more talk of absolute superiority. The other day we tangled with these newer Spitfires and had three losses against one success. I got into deep trouble myself and my *Rottenhund* (Sigi Voss)[3] was shot down. I ended up against two Spitfires with all weapons jammed. There was no alternative but to get the hell out of it. When I got back I found three hits, fortunately none of them in any vital spots. First I was quite shocked, this being the first mission in my new 8, but now I feel quite at home.[4]

You now have Mother visiting. I fear that after a while she may become bored because the service won't allow much private time for you. I myself would like to come and visit. Perhaps it will come true, who knows what is planned and what is not. I only hope.

We were now beginning to feel the effects of being constantly mauled by the RAF. Instead of the promised reduction in fighter opposition over England, we were meeting ever more spirited attacks by the Spitfires and Hurricanes: whereas we, still in the front line, were slowly but inexorably bleeding to death.

I was not untypical of the pilots in our *Gruppe* and I had recorded over one-hundred-and-fifty missions over the Channel. On one day alone I flew on seven sorties. Typically a day would run:

Take-off	07:00, return	08:00. Refuel and reload.
Take-off	08:40, return	09:40. Refuel and reload.
Take-off	10:20, return	11:20. Refuel and reload.
Take-off	12:00, return	13:00. Refuel and reload.
Take-off	13:40, return	14:40. Refuel and reload.
Take-off	15:20, return	16:20. Refuel and reload.
Take-off	17:00, return	18:00. Refuel and reload.

Running with the practised efficiency of the *Deutsche Reichsbahn* (German State Railways) and just like passengers waiting for their scheduled service, the Spitfires would be on station waiting for the next wave. It was stupid to fly a schedule like this; it just handed us to the enemy on a plate. As we approached, the British would be climbing to their patrol height, by now well above our service ceiling, and then after waiting for us to turn, they'd come scything down through us, hacking off the *Katschmareks* and the lame ducks. Then they would continue down to refuel and re-arm and be up ready for the next wave which would obligingly come along in twenty minutes and again the slaughter would begin.

It was developing into a war of attrition, an airborne version of the dreadful trench warfare of 1917/18. Sooner or later one side had to run out of aircraft and young men to fly them. Given that we spent 60% of our flying time over hostile territory and that London was invariably the target, necessitating maximum range penetrations, the odds were well and truly stacked against us. Time was now against us and time was running out.

In the early morning of 27th October I gradually awoke and forced myself to sit up in my camp bed. The tent smelled musty and the damp cold of October began to sap the comfortable warmth from my body. With some effort I pulled the coarse blankets back and shambled over to the makeshift washstand and tried to freshen up. As I shaved I examined my hollow cheeks and sunken eyes. When would my time come?

Shivering a little from cold and fatigue I pulled my uniform trousers on over my thick flannel pyjama trousers, the warmest underwear I had.

Kühle was already up and about, the blankets on his bed turned back to air. Next to that was an empty space where Hinnerk Waller had slept,

Now came the churning in the stomach as the acid bile began to flood in, the sickening feeling in the throat and the sudden, uncontrollable, shudders as images of air-battles and near-misses momentarily flicker in consciousness; Hinnerk Waller falling from his stricken aircraft; Spitfires firing countless rounds in Sigi Voss's aircraft as I impotently jabbed at my gun-buttons; Messerschmitts ploughing into the turbulent green Channel; a dead *Oberleutnant* in the blood-soaked cockpit of his Me 109 ... How much more could we take? It was strange how these doubts and fears only came before the take-off.

After driving out to the dispersal with Karl Rüttger and Lothar Schieverhofer I waited for the orders to take-off, to get into the air when most of the nauseating emotions would creep back into the sub-conscious for a while. Waiting, waiting. Then it was time to start. Erwin, my mechanic, was standing on the port wing of Yellow 2, helping me with my harness and straps, saying that I might be lucky now I was back in my old aircraft. Then I was reaching for the starter lever as I felt the gentle rocking of the aircraft as Erwin began to wind up the eclipse starter before it could be engaged, turning over the big DB 601 engine. I pulled for the start and she roared into life immediately and I set the throttle lightly forwards so that I could complete my after start-up checks. All eight remaining Me's were running now at their different dispersals and we began to taxi out for take-off, the pathetic remnants of a whole fighter *Gruppe*.

Glancing around me I pushed the throttle to full-power and felt the aircraft accelerate, the tail coming up almost immediately. Bumping over the rough field we bounced a little and I felt her become light as we lifted clear of the earth. Retracting the gear, I waited just a few moments whilst the airspeed increased, then eased back with the stick and we were climbing away nicely. The churning in the stomach had stopped now; everything was under control. Check the positions of the other aircraft. Begin to tighten up into a formation for the climb. Be back for breakfast in about an hour...

The Last Letter

Oberleutnant Kühle, L O7141, Lg. P.A. Brüssel,
To:
Herrn Wilhelm Steinhilper,
Heutingsheim
b.Stuttgart.

Dear Herr Steinhilper,

As Deputy Group Commander I have to inform you that your son, Ulrich Steinhilper, did not return from a sortie against England on 27 October. There is hope that he is a Prisoner of War because I was in radio contact with him shortly before his emergency landing. At this moment his loss is irreplaceable for the *Gruppe*. As squadron leader I fought many air-battles with your son and I estimate his capabilities as an officer and a fighter-pilot as exceptional. Not forgetting his own individual carefree vigour which brought him very close to me.
We all hope with you that soon there will be information about him being in English custody.

I greet you and Frau Steinhilper Heil Hitler,
Helmut Kühle.

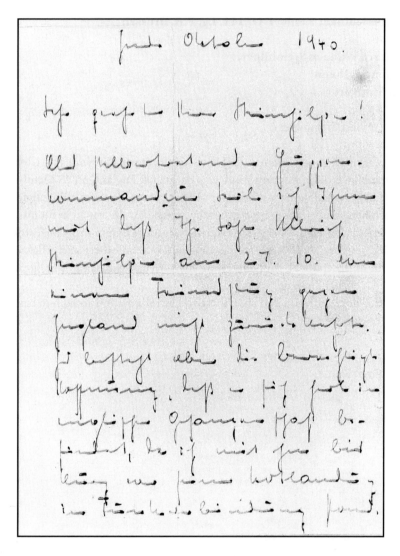

Oberleutnant Kühle's letter informing Ulrich's parents that he was missing in action.

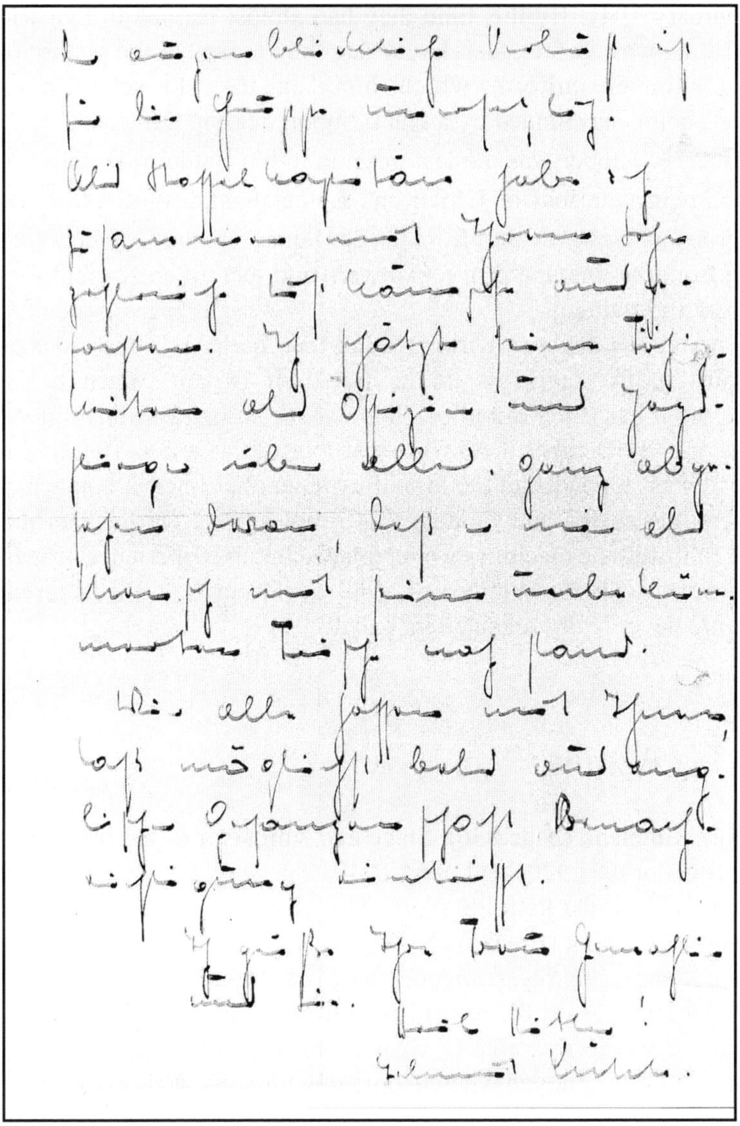

News of Ulrich being a prisoner was not forthcoming and is difficult to conjure up his parents distress, not knowing if he was alive or dead until 5th February 1941. By this time they had almost learned to live with the idea that he was, in fact, lost. Every day they looked at the picture of him in his summer uniform which hung in the old school-house in Heutingsheim, surrounded by a black ribbon, fearing the worst.

The 27th October was the last mission in the Battle of Britain for *I/JG 52*. Following the loss of Ulrich and Lothar Schieverhofer from the 3rd Squadron and *Gefreiter* Bott from the 2nd Squadron, the *Gruppe* were withdrawn from the line and sent to Antwerp and then on to Krefeld for refitting, rest and training.

There is no doubt in Ulrich's mind that the RAF broke the back and the spirit of the *Luftwaffe* in the Battle of Britain. When the *Gruppe* started out it had thirty-six pilots, none of whom had less than three years experience. By October there were just four of those left. The invasion of England was stopped, and the loss of experienced crews in bombers, dive-bombers, destroyers and fighters was irreplaceable. During the build up which followed the machines were replaced but the experience of the pilots who were lost in the summer of 1940 could not be manufactured. The *Luftwaffe* never really regained its balance.

Notes on Chapter 18

1. Heinz Rühmann (page 336). Stage and film actor of the time. He made many films in the 1930s and early 1940s e.g. *Die Drei von der Tankstelle* (The Three from the Petrol Station), The Man who was Sherlock Holmes, Quax der Bruchpilot (Breaking or Wrecking Pilot - in which he did most of his own flying), *Die Feuerzangenbowle* (The Burnt Punch). He was a qualified pilot and was on the reserve list although he probably never flew in combat. Hence he was able to wear a *Luftwaffe* uniform and Wings. He used to get quite annoyed when people saw him and wouldn't take his uniform seriously or offer him the respect he thought it required. So many people had seen him in comedy roles that they really only wanted him to make them laugh.

2. This shockingly depleted remnant of the original thirty-six (page 340) included *Oberfeldwebel* Grosse who was suffering badly with *Kanalkrankheit* and the *Gruppe Kommandeur Hauptmann* Ewald who had, in the meantime, been certified sick by Dr Greiling. In the squadron the survivors at that time, immediately following the loss of Sigi Voss from the squadron, were Ulrich Steinhilper, *Oberleutnant* Kühle (who was suffering for a lot of the time with ear and stomach problems), Karl Rüttger and Lothar Schieverhofer.

On the same day as they lost Sigi Voss from the squadron, *1/JG 52* lost Oberleutnant Günter Büsgen and *2/JG 52* lost *Oberleutnant* Sauer.

3. Feldwebel Siegfried Voss. In 1987/88 a person appeared calling himself Sigi Voss and claiming to have been the same Voss whose aircraft crashed near Ashford, Kent. He further claimed that he had changed places with a German agent whom he met by accident near to the place where his aircraft had crashed. He stated that this agent, code-named 'Bodo', didn't want to return to Germany and that they decided to exchange identities. The agent was supposed to have been captured and Voss claimed to have walked cross-country to Hythe where, upon giving the appropriate light signal, he was picked up by a U-Boat. He then claimed to have been promoted and posted to the Russian Front. Ulrich, when he heard the story was delighted with the thought that Sigi Voss was still alive and rang him at his home in Hamburg. After a while he became suspicious of the individual, especially when he didn't recall that they had been involved in mid-air collision in 1938. Further diligent work by Ulrich Steinhilper finally exposed this individual as a complete imposter whose motives were never clear.

In the meantime the real Sigi Voss was dying of an acute illness and the untimely appearance of this person from Hamburg caused a great deal of distress to the family who were preparing to lose him. He died in 1988. PJO.

4. (Page 340) This was the time of the arrival of the Merlin XII engine fitted with the two-stage supercharger and the Mk.II Spitfire, the first of these being issued to 61 Squadron on the 22nd August 1940. By the end of October, 195 of them entered service and not only gave improved rate of climb and speed but also an improved service ceiling. The Me 109 E-4 was being fitted with the DB 601E engine which improved the power by 100

hp over the N engine. This gave an improved performance but was not keeping up with the Mk II Spitfire, the engine of which had an improved output from 1030 hp to 1150 hp, increasing the speed and giving a huge advantage in service ceiling: the Me 109 E-4 was capable of reaching 10,000 metres (32,800 ft) with the Mk I Spitfire at a comparable 10,3363 metres (34,000 ft), but the new Mk IIs soared up to 11,340 metres (37,200 ft). This gave a tactical advantage of 1,340 metres or 4,300 ft to the Spitfires.

EPILOGUE - Phoenix

Late in the afternoon and into the evening of 27th October 1940 the wet drizzle blew in the wind across the marshland at Sarre, in Kent. It was cold and only the very curious braved the weather to look at the blackened patch of grass and the hole where Yellow 2 had finished her last dive.

Large pieces of wreckage like the wings and tail section lay on the wet grass surrounded by mangled pieces of aluminium and scattered rounds of 20 mm ammunition. Small boys made their way over the marsh to look at the scene and try to 'snaz' a piece of the 'Jerry' plane. An Army guard was mounted until the RAF Maintenance Unit trudged wearily across the sodden ground to survey the crash site. The opinion was that the main bulk of the aircraft was too far into the ground to warrant any attempt to recover it and so only the surface wreckage was cleared away. Slowly the blackened hole became filled and soon the coarse marsh grass grew over the blackened patch. Yellow 2 slept peacefully for forty years.

In 1980 the dedicated work of a five-year search by members of the Kent Battle of Britain Museum Recovery Group was rewarded. The deep-seeking echoes of a powerful metal detector began to excite the aluminium molecules of Yellow 2. The peace of forty years obscurity was over. In a final effort to locate the aircraft, Mike Llewellyn and the Battle of Britain Museum team had enlisted the help of the Rochester-based Territorial Army Bomb Disposal (now Explosive Ordnance Disposal), under the leadership of Captain, now Major, Spencer-Henry. Equipped with metal detectors of various shapes, sizes and power, the team began the last leg of the search for the aircraft.

For five years they had patiently searched the area, knocking on hundreds of doors and always asking the same question, 'Could you tell me if you lived in this area in 1940? Do you remember an aircraft coming down near here?' Gradually the search area was narrowed down to one large field by Sarre Penn and the last sweep was made. After so long the contact was made and a digger brought in. On 26th October 1980, forty years all but a day from the actual day of the crash, Yellow 2 was to see daylight again.

The recovery of Yellow 2 - first contact. The fuselage is uncovered
showing the open radio hatch and control cables. The whole aircraft
is in Kent Battle of Britain Museum, Hawkinge.

As was the practice, the location of the aircraft was carefully marked out and then a hole sunk beside it. After a few metres the dig was carefully extended sideways towards the location of the wreck. As the thick clay was scraped away a long section of fuselage was exposed, even the open radio hatch could be made out. The damage seemed minimal. Mike Llewellyn was overjoyed, it looked like the first time they were going to recover a near-complete fuselage. The hole was excavated further down and more and more was exposed. Then, disappointment, the huge weight and momentum of the Daimler Benz 601 engine had torn free from the airframe and continued deeper into the clay, tearing the aircraft open as it went. From the cockpit area forward was just a tangled mass of wreckage. The engine lay two or three metres further down.

Eventually, the great motor which all those years before had seized up and forced Ulrich to bail out was lifted from the clay and loaded onto a lorry ready for its last journey. Along with it went most of the rear fuselage, the cockpit area, many panels and fittings and a thousand rounds of unfired ammunition for each of the 7.92 mm MG 17 machine guns which had been mounted in the nose of Yellow 2. All of this had to be cleaned and preserved, ready for the museum and now the aircraft is on show at the Kent Battle of Britain Museum at Hawkinge. It is an impressive sight and probably the most complete example of a Bf 109 E to be recovered from a land crash site.

For Ulrich, left injured on the wet marshes of Kent, waiting for inevitable capture, a new and sometimes terrifying episode in his life was about to begin. One that would lead him through the rigours of Interrogation Camp and overseas to Canada and the challenges of escape. But that, as they say, is another story.

APPENDIX

Hauptmann von Pfeil *und* Klein Ellguth (Later Lieutenant Colonel)

Grafin von Pfeil survived her husband and now still lives in Germany. I recently visited her and found out what became of her husband. It was nearly two painful years before he could return to duty and even then there had not been much that the best surgeons could do with his badly burned face. They were not able to replace his eyelids and from then on he was never able to close his eyes.

He returned to service later in the war and might have expected some help from his former *Oberleutnant*, Adolf Galland, but apparently he was badly disappointed. He went on to get a job as a Staff Officer in France at the time of the invasion. He was ambushed and seriously wounded by French Resistance Fighters whilst travelling in a car and died in hospital in Verdun. *Grafin von* Pfeil showed great courage whilst bringing up three children in the ruins of post-war Germany with little or no income.

She had retained the impression that her husband had been hit whilst he was protecting Geller and had stayed too long in his aircraft because of the shame of being shot down. He had tried to fly the burning aircraft back to base.

She still remembered the day I took the flowers to her and caught her cleaning the floor.

Leutnant Herbert Fermer (Later *Oberleutnant* Squadron Leader *7/JG* 52) Killed during the Battle of Britain on 24th July 1940. Fermer was shot down over Margate and crashed into the sea. This was probably as a result of an engagement with the Spitfires of 54 Squadron from Rochford.

Leutnant Christoph Geller. Geller came down in the Channel on 30th August 1940, probably because of engine failure and, unfortunately, drowned before he was picked up.

Oberleutnant Helmut Kühle (Later *Major* - Adjutant - Wing Commander *JG* 52). Helmut Kühle flew throughout the war until the time of 'The Battle of the Bulge' when he was shot down and killed. It is understood that near to this time he had been demoted to the ranks because his squadron wasn't recording enough victories. Knowing him as I did I doubt that this was really the case. I imagine that, as he was always a cautious man with great respect for the lives of his charges, he probably refused to fly in impossible circumstances. Things were getting desperate then and missions were often mounted against overwhelming odds. I wouldn't find it too hard to believe that under such circumstances he would refuse to waste life unnecessarily.

Feldwebel Schieverhöfer. Lothar Schieverhofer survived the war as a POW in Canada, having been shot down on the same day as me. After the war he became a bush-pilot in Africa. He was still living in Africa in the early nineteen-nineties and was working in a photographic laboratory. However, such was his insatiable love of adventure that at the age of seventy-five he went out into the African Bush prospecting for gold.

Leutnant Hinnerk Waller. Albert-Hinrich (Hinnerk) Waller rejoined the post-war *Luftwaffe* and went on to become *Oberstleutnant* (Lieutenant Colonel) and *Kommandeur JG 71* 'Richthofen'. He was a lifelong friend. He died on 28th September 1987.

Oberleutnant Tietzen. Horst Jacob Tietzen became squadron leader of *5/JG 51* and was shot down on 18th August off Whitstable in Kent, probably by Pilot Officer Zenker of 501 Squadron who was later killed on 24th August 1940. Tietzen's body was one of those that was recovered with a single bullet wound in the head. Alone in the sea and close to drowning many pilots took what the High Command saw as the 'easy way out'. Because of this all side-arms were banned in early September 1940.

Karl Rüttger. Survived the war and is at present in good health.

INDEX

OTHER BOOKS BY THE SAME AUTHORS

'TEN MINUTES TO BUFFALO'

The Story of Germany's Great Escaper
Ulrich Steinhilper & Peter Osborne
Non-Fiction Illustrated

ISBN (10) 1-872836-01-1
ISBN (13)978-1-872836-01-0

Hardback only, 431 pages, 45 black & white
illustrations. Price: £14.95

'Ten Minutes to Buffalo' is long-awaited sequel to Ulrich Steinhilper's highly successful first book, 'Spitfire On My Tail'. Unlike the first book, which tells the story of how a young German came to fly in Hitler's *Luftwaffe* and to fight in the Battle of Britain, 'Ten Minutes to Buffalo' is a catalogue of courage and determination on the ground. In this way it is set to repeat the successful formula by providing a rare chance to witness how things were for 'The Other Side,' this time behind the barbed wire and in Ulrich Steinhilper's case - all too often outside the wire! It relates a story of remarkable courage and perseverance in the most appalling conditions, braving arctic weather and appalling hardship with one thought in mind - to get home.

From his first camp in England away to the vastness of Canada, he and a select few of his fellow officers were to become known as *Die Ausbrecherkönige von Kanada* (the breakout kings from Canada) and Ulrich was to shine among them. His escapes were innovative and even audacious and it was only bad luck that seemed to keep him from a completely successful 'homerun'.

Very little has ever been written about the conditions of German officers as prisoners of the Allies and practically nothing of their ingenuity and perseverance in planning and executing escape plans so similar to their counterparts in German hands. This remarkable book is entirely written from original hand-written sheets which date from 1942 and which give it a great immediacy and accuracy.

'FULL CIRCLE'

The Long Way Home From Canada
Ulrich Steinhilper & Peter Osborne
Non-Fiction Illustrated
ISBN (10) 1-872836-02-X
ISBN (13) 978-1-872836-02-7

Hardback only, 408 pages, 74 black & white
pictures and illustrations. Price: £17.95

'Full Circle' is the last of three books which record Ulrich Steinhilper's remarkable experiences in the Second World War. From being a front line fighter pilot in the Battle of Britain he becomes a Prisoner of War, but for Ulrich the war is far from over.

In 'Ten Minutes To Buffalo', the story of the first three escapes is told and in 'Full Circle' the story is continued as Ulrich and Hinnerk Waller find themselves back in custody. But that is far from the end of Ulrich's career as an escaper. Nor is it the end of the detailed and fascinating description of life as a POW. Locking up large numbers of bright young men led to the most ingenious schemes to manufacture their own radios, make their own tools and later, on their *Ehrenwort* (word of honour), to rebuild and run a farm.

Ulrich describes in graphic detail his last attempt to get back to Germany, admitting it was the worst mistake he ever made in his life. From documents, hand-written at the time, and from numerous letters and post-cards home he accurately reconstructs what it was like to be a prisoner of the Allies and the hardships that brought at the end.

'Full Circle' completes Ulrich Steinhilper's odyssey and, with, it what is now being described as one of the most important contributions to the broader history of the Second World War to cmerge in recent times.

BY ULRICH STEINHILPER

'DON'T TALK – DO IT'

Ulrich Steinhilper

Non-Fiction Illustrated
ISBN (10) 1 872836 75 5
ISBN (13) 978 1 872836 75 1

Hardback only, 272 pages, 40 black & white
pictures and illustrations. Price: 16.95

Word Processing is a term which most people understand today, but fifty years ago there was only one voice using it, a young typewriter salesman who was working for IBM Germany. Ulrich Steinhilper had the idea to use *Textverarbeitung* (Word Processing), a new concept, so that office products could be marketed in the same way that Data Processing equipment was sold by IBM. It was not as we might recognise it today; it was more a holistic approach to the diverse skills which are needed to improve office efficiency and to bring streamlined factory production line techniques to the office. Fortunately he submitted his thoughts as a Staff Suggestion and was duly paid 25 German Marks for his trouble, but he had registered it and had proof of it. When others tried to claim that it was they who had first conceived the name 'Word Processing' Ulrich fought for recognition and, finally, IBM committed it to paper and sent him on a trip around the world in recognition of his work.

Over and above being the story of the evolution of Word Processing, 'Don't Talk - Do It!' is a fascinating record of the development of post-war business. It is also an intriguing illustration of how one man made his contribution in the true pioneering spirit, helping Germany rise from the ruins of World War II to one of the world's most successful industrial nations.

THE ROLL OF HONOUR SERIES

Independent Books are please to announce their new series 'Roll of Honour'. This will comprise reprints of many of their own classic titles as well as other titles that have fallen out of print and deserve to be available. In spring 2009 they expect to reprint 'Spitfire On My Tail', 'Test Pilots' and 'Target – Dresden' and in the autumn, 'Born Leader' and two other titles.

REPRINTED FOR POPULAR DEMAND

TARGET DRESDEN
Alan Cooper

Non-Fiction Illustrated
ISBN (10): 1-872836-60-7
ISBN (13): 978-1-872836-60-7

Paperback: 256 pages, 43 b&w photographs and illustrations Price: £10.95

On the night of 13-14th February 1945, 796 Lancasters and 9 Mosquitoes of RAF Bomber Command, dropped 1,478 tons of high explosive and 1,182 tons of incendiaries on the city of Dresden. A firestorm developed, which led to large areas of the city being burned out. At the time of the attack, Dresden was crowded with refugees fleeing the advancing Soviet Army resulting in between 40,000 and 50,000 casualties. On the morning of the 14th a second attack was carried out by the United States Army Air Force followed by two further US attacks.

Target Dresden chronicles the development of bombing from the earliest days through the tactical and strategic bombing of WWII and gives the story behind these controversial raids.

TEST PILOTS
Wolfgang Späte

Non-Fiction Illustrated
ISBN (10) 1-872836-80-1
ISBN (13) 978-1-872836-80-5
Paperback: 304 pages 102 b&w photographs
and illustrations. Price: £10.95

This is an exciting new book relating the firsthand experiences of predominantly German Test Pilots. Including over one hundred photographs and illustrations, the majority of which have never been seen before, it is full of refreshingly new material.

The collection of anecdotal accounts covers such varied flying tests as those of the Natter, a manned, rocket-launched interceptor designed to release a salvo of missiles at Flying Fortress formations; and the DFS 228, arguably the forerunner of the Lockheed U2, with a service ceiling calculated at eighty thousand feet and a range of nearly a thousand miles. There are also vivid descriptions of the first trials of the ejector seat; towing aircraft on a one metre long rigid tow; the beginnings of air-to-air refuelling, and even the plans for a bomber which would tow its own fighter escort across the Atlantic to engage the USAF over their home ground. Test Pilots is essential reading for all aviation enthusiasts and historians.

Foreword by Captain Eric 'Winkle' Brown
C.O. Enemy Aircraft Flight, RAE Farnborough (1945–47)
Author of 'Wings On My Sleeve

'Although Wolfgang Späte never became an established test pilot himself, he has opened the door into some fascinating scenarios which caught his imagination. The reader should eagerly share these.'

Captain Eric Brown, CBE, DSC, AFC, RN

OTHER CURRENT TITLES BY INDEPENDENT BOOKS

BLUE SKIES AND DARK NIGHTS
Bill Randle
Non-Fiction Illustrated
ISBN (10): 1-872836-40-2
ISBN (13): 978-1-872836-40-9

Hardback only, 352 pages, iillustrated with over
90 black & white photographs. Price: £19.95

'Blue Skies and Dark Nights' is the autobiography of Group Captain Bill Randle. From his initial flight training in the United States on the fledgling Arnold scheme, to the bombing of Germany, through a remarkable evasion and successful 'home run', to MI9 and the formation of post-war Escape and Evasion policy with the Americans, to learning to fly helicopters with the US Marines, then on to taking part in search and rescue missions in Korea; this is a honest and straightforward account of a unusual career in the RAF and beyond.

Those with an interest in the RAF and world affairs will find Bill Randle's story fascinating as he describes what it was like to be at the centre of many world events. It also clearly illustrates the frustrations implicit in a service life, as well as the great humour and tragedy which go with the acceptance of the responsibilities of rank.

'Blue Skies and Dark Nights' is an important record of service in the RAF during World War Two and in the 'Cold War' period that followed, together with the great changes in Africa and the declaration of UDI by the erstwhile RAF fighter pilot Ian Smith.

Retiring in 1971, Bill went on to work at the fast growing RAF Museum at Hendon and has gone on to raise a little under six million pounds for Service charities. Now turning his hand to writing, his autobiography is his third book and is both an important story and a delight to read.

SHARK SQUADRON PILOT
Bert Horden

Non-Fiction Illustrated
ISBN (10): 1-872836-45-3
ISBN (13): 978-1-872836-45-4

Hardback only, 193 pages, over 80 black & white illustrations from the war in the Western Desert and Mediterranean theatre, many previously unpublished. Price: £16.95

'Shark Squadron Pilot' graphically illustrates the realities of the air war in the Western Desert. Bert Horden joined No. 112 'Shark' Squadron early in 1942 and was soon initiated into the ground attack role of the 'Kittys'. With their garish shark's mouths painted on their aircraft, No. 112 Squadron wreaked havoc on the German Afrika Corps as the war in the Western Desert rose to its climax. Inflicting terrible damage with machine gun fire on soft-skinned targets, like convoys of trucks, and causing significant damage with their under-slung bombs on the hard-skinned Panzers, the aircraft of '112 Squadron soon became well known to Rommel's troops.

Using his diary and flying log book to preserve the accuracy and immediacy of the events, Bert Horden has written a superb account of desert flying. In places extremely graphic and well illustrated throughout with over eighty previously unpublished photographs from the author's collection, 'Shark Squadron Pilot' will be an important contribution to the recorded history of the Second World War.

All orders:

Crecy Publishing Ltd

1a Ringway Trading Estate, Shadowmoss Road, Manchester, M22 5LH

enquiries@crecy.co.uk - Tel: (UK) 01614990024

The Most Dangerous Enemy

Stephen Bungay

Paperback ISBN (10): 1-85410-801-8
Published by Aurum
25 Bedford Avenue
London
WC1B 3AT

£9.99

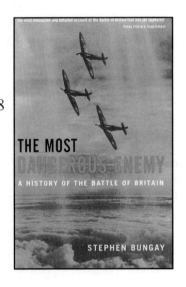

As authors, Ulrich and I were privileged when Stephen agreed to write a foreword for this reprint of 'Spitfire On My Tail'. When he was preparing the material for his own work he asked if he could quote at length from our book and we were pleased to have agreed for what he produced is a masterwork on the great air battle.

Stephen is a scholar and academic, having been educated at Oxford and at Tübingen, in Germany. Understanding a lot about the character of both the German and British peoples, nobody was better placed to write about this clash of the two predominant air forces of the time. 'The Most Dangerous Enemy' is a detailed dissection of the many and various elements which came together in the summer of 1940 to produce the first and only campaign to be decided by air power. The simple fact was that if the air defence of the United Kingdom failed, the German invasion would, at some time, have followed.

Where 'Spitfire On My Tail' is very much Ulrich's personal account of Germany from the end of the First World War to the end of the Battle of Britain, and a chronicle of how one young German's destiny was shaped by great forces, Stephen Bungay's work is a detailed analysis of the bigger picture. That is not to say he has not skilfully woven in material on the personalities who were key to the success or failure of the attack or defence. For instance, the bombastic Herman Göring, the First War fighter pilot, whose understanding of modern war in the air was clouded by Wagnerian myth and visions of Teutonic knights doing battle in the air for the Aryan race. This contrasted against the professional soldiers, Air Chief Marshal Sir Hugh Dowding and his loyal acolyte Air Vice Marshal Keith Park; both men trained in the broad vision of tactics and both with a deep instinctive appreciation of where the aircraft would fit into modern warfare. That is not to say that the British defence was flawless; in the background there was, for example, the squabbling about the tactic of the 'Big Wing' and the bickering about its merits or otherwise between Park and Air Vice Marshal Trafford Leigh-Mallory; together with the oft-forgotten initial problems of aircraft production, the supply of trained pilots and the politics - always the politics!

During the years of research which led to the publication of 'Most Dangerous Enemy', the author must have had many doubters express the view that there was nothing new to be written about the Battle of Britain and, to an extent, that may have been true. Where Stephen Bungay has triumphed is in bringing so much of this material together in a single volume which will be the standard work on the subject for future generations. Why? Because it not only brings together the whole story from all perspectives, but achieves it in an eminently readable style. Taking nothing away from the facts and anecdotal information, the material is presented in a very accessible format, sometimes with a touch of humour or pathos, which does not diminish the content in any way. Many authors have taken their subject so seriously as to produce works which are almost impenetrable and are, inevitably, laid aside. For the future, we must leave a legacy in the form of a body of work which future students and emerging historians will be encouraged to read without the pain of hours of drudgery. In this way we might hold their interest and stimulate their understanding of our history and their heritage; for it is said that those who do not understand and revere history are doomed to repeat it.

'The Most Dangerous Enemy' is the pre-eminent work on the most crucial turning point in the twentieth century and should become a set book for all GCSE studies in the UK as well as recommended reading for history graduates.
